Celluloid Sermons

Celluloid Sermons

The Emergence of the Christian
Film Industry, 1930–1986

Terry Lindvall and Andrew Quicke

NEW YORK UNIVERSITY PRESS
New York and London

NEW YORK UNIVERSITY PRESS
New York and London
www.nyupress.org

References to Internet websites (URLs) were accurate at the time of writing.
Neither the author nor New York University Press is responsible for URLs
that may have expired or changed since the manuscript was prepared.

Library of Congress Cataloging-in-Publication Data

Lindvall, Terry.
Celluloid sermons : the emergence of the Christian film industry, 1930–1986 /
Terry Lindvall and Andrew Quicke.
p. cm.
Includes bibliographical references (p.   ) and index.
ISBN 978-0-8147-5324-8 (cl : alk. paper) — ISBN 978-0-8147-5325-5 (ebook)
1. Christian films—United States—History and criticism. 2. Motion picture industry—
United States—History—20th century. 3. Motion pictures—Religious aspects—
Christianity. 4. Motion pictures in Christian education. 5. Christianity in motion pictures.
I. Quicke, Andrew. II.
Title.
PN1995.9.C49L56   2011
791.43'682773—dc23   2011018456

New York University Press books are printed on acid-free paper,
and their binding materials are chosen for strength and durability.
We strive to use environmentally responsible suppliers and materials
to the greatest extent possible in publishing our books.

Manufactured in the United States of America

10 9 8 7 6 5 4 3 2 1

Dedicated to Lisa and Tim Robertson,
for their bountiful generosity and artistic vision
in supporting the cinema arts. Deus Gloria.

In Memoriam Ken Curtis (1939–2011)

Contents

Preface

> If Shakespeare could see sermons in stones, we of today ought
> to be able to see sermons in pictures.
>
> —Thomas Opie[1]

The hostility and antipathy that some groups expressed toward Hollywood in the 1930s seethed through the pages of the evangelist Robert Sumner's *Hollywood Cesspool*.[2] The book catalogued a legion of immoral deeds on the screen and within the Hollywood community, citing divorces, adulteries, murders, and other crimes against humanity and God.[3] In recognition of his critique of the American entertainment business, Sumner received an honorary doctorate from Bob Jones University in Greenville, South Carolina, a fundamentalist Christian university. That Christian fundamentalism would castigate the Hollywood industry, even during the days of collective studio censorship, is no surprise. What might be unexpected is that the same fundamentalist institution that lauded Sumner's critique of the entertainment industry would build a significant film program of its own and make credible films for its own audiences. Respectable dramatic features would roll out of the university under the oblique, even self-effacing, imprimatur of Unusual Films.

The unexpected development of an underground movement of religious pictures offers an odd revelation, a mixing of oil and water, of God and Mammon. In 1939, the film historian Margaret Thorp stumbled on peculiar cooperative ventures of churches and theaters, finding drive-ins near Los Angeles that offered their exhibition facilities to all churches for Sunday services during any part of the day. She discovered movie theater managers in Wilkes-Barre, Pennsylvania, who promoted a "go to church on Easter Sunday campaign," and in Elroy, Wisconsin, film exhibitors who arranged a special screening of the 1938 Norman Taurog film *Boys Town* for all the local clergy. For Thorp, however, the acme of cooperation occurred in Thomasville, Georgia. When a Gypsy Smith revival tent hit the town, the local exhibitor recommended the revival meetings over his own shows, declaring that Mr.

Smith "has more to offer you than we have. If you want to see a picture, there will be one here for you, but there will be more for you at the tent. If you can't come to both, go to the revival." The evangelist spoke well of the theater from the pulpit, and the exhibitor got more good press out of the strategic recommendation. As the manager wrote, "It undid the lifetime work of some fire-eating local preachers who had for years been advising their followers that the road to Hell was bordered by picture houses. It got us fifty new patrons, several of them zealots who had never seen a motion picture before."[4]

While the suspicion and resistance of some Protestant groups to moving pictures did persist into the 1930s, a host of denominational and para-church organizations began to imagine how they might "baptize" the technology and use it for the Kingdom of God. In 1935, the Lutheran lawyer and journalist Milton Anderson's *The Modern Goliath* compiled a statistical survey of "talking pictures," with Hollywood being indirectly cast as the Philistine giant. On the question of content analysis—on what was seen and heard on the screen—Anderson noted that 80 percent of the pictures were wet (i.e., portrayed drinking favorably), while 90 percent exhibited smoking.[5] Anderson recommended a program of action for the Davids of the world (namely, Christians) to counteract the detrimental behaviors promoted by Hollywood. His practical advice aimed first at bolstering the field of nontheatrical films, supporting those movies of character education shown outside normal theaters of exhibition in places like churches and Sunday schools, and second at guiding church organizations to logistically coordinate movie programs. Most important, he argued, there are sound reasons for believing that churches need movies (he listed seventeen of them). He confidently claimed that congregations would welcome *Old Truths in New Garments*, echoing the observation of Dr. Franz Kordac, archbishop of Prague, that "if St. Paul were alive at this hour he would use talking pictures to spread the gospel of Jesus Christ."[6] Anderson's final attempt to prime the pump involved fund-raising for the production of his own five-reel roadshow picture, *Ruth and Naomi*, and a Hollywood Bowl drama, *David*. His clarion call focused on making talking pictures the servant of the church, rather than allowing the celluloid "Goliath" to make slaves of God's people.

Christians of all denominational stripes and theological persuasions would respond to his call to make celluloid sermons for various audiences. The concept of celluloid sermons is grounded in the historical Protestant roots of an evangelistic rhetoric of conversion. It refers to the corpus of film work generated by religious groups that seek to evangelize, preach, teach, provoke, or convert, rarely to just entertain. The historian Harry Stout has revealed the potent effect of early American sermons as a "public act of cultural formation, not just religious expression."[7] The people and organizations that made these religious films sought to convert their spectators, to draw them into their spheres of influence in both ecumenical and sectarian ways.

In this work, we continue an investigation into the history of the Christian film industry, building on previous work on the silent era and previewing the period at the end of the 1980s, in which the apotheosis of religious filmmaking would culminate in Mel Gibson's phenomenally successful and controversial 2004 film *The Passion of the Christ* and a subsequent sprouting of independent religious filmmaking. Our emphasis here is confined primarily to Protestant groups, although we find much to note and celebrate in the appreciation of Roman Catholic film artists. In particular, we honor the creative work of the Franciscans and their visual parables such as *The Stray* (1971), a charming retelling of the parable of the lost lamb in the wild, set in the context of a group of first graders going to the San Diego Zoo with their bus driver/shepherd, who warns them not to stray.

We begin this book by tracing the advent of the production of sound movies for the church, however limited, in the early 1930s. Due to budget constraints and other pressing needs and priorities for churches during the Depression, little work was achieved in the media arts. The early 1940s saw the blossoming of the Christian film industry in the works of pioneers like Rev. James Friedrich, Carlos Baptista, and Irwin Moon. Paralleling their work were the productions of Protestant denominations, followed by the building of a studio system of Christian organizations.[8]

Our purposes in this volume are threefold. First, we are documenting the history of this alternative film movement, a widespread, disconnected, but overlapping association of religious filmmaking concerns that ran concurrently, but largely invisibly, alongside the mainstream Hollywood film industries. Even taking into account the media historian Quentin Schultze's learned study *Christianity and the Mass Media in America*, we have found that no other research has done the preparatory work of providing a reference guide to the particular set of institutions, individuals, studios, denominations, and films that make up a Christian film industry.[9] While much more scholarship has addressed religious publishing and television broadcasting, very little has explored filmmaking advanced for religious purposes.

Second, we explore how media consciousness contributed to or detracted from the work of Christian communities. Church historians have largely ignored the cultural impact of film in their research and analysis. While theologians like Paul Tillich have reflected on the place of culture in their theological construction, and many have explored the intersection and dialogue among international and Hollywood films and theology, very few, if any, have specifically identified the role that Protestant films have played in constructing culture. Yet the media technologies employed by religious communities have exerted an influence on the shape and meaning of those communities. Protestant films may be a small determinative factor in the web of meanings within a denomination, but they contribute to the cultural identity of that community. In particular, they are the repositories of unique memories. Celluloid sermons are remembered more frequently than verbal sermons. More people can recall a World Wide Pictures film like *The Hiding Place* more readily and vividly than any Southern Baptist discourse. The imprinting of dramatic visual images on the memory persists, inducing different patterns of perception and augmenting nonrational religious consciousness. We examine here whether the church's commitment to filmmaking accelerated its missions of evangelism, religious education, and social justice, or if it detoured the church into areas in which it had no expertise or prospects of success.

Certain cinematic practices of the Christian film industry are derived from theological concerns and rhetorical forms of the Bible. The adaptation from verbal text to visual media raises the question of whether the transposition from one medium to another alters the message. In particular, the models of evangelical sermons, including telling Bible stories and moral lessons, shaped the narrative structures of Christian films, often making the films into existential proof texts of the need for conversion. The Christian cinema's relationship to these religious traditions, rhetorical styles, and denominational motives was more formational than its relations to Hollywood modes of production. While certain individuals may have put faith in technology as a means of effective religious communication, the results were firmly anchored in Protestant modes of discourse, namely, sermons that taught morality or preached the need for individual transformation. Significantly, as most denominations embraced visual technology, their films tended to emphasize ecumenical concerns rather than sectarian ones, marking a movement toward cultural modernization and assimilation. Their films found common ground in showing people how to behave, rather than in telling them what to believe. Films thus became both a symptom of and a contributing factor to the secularization of liberal denominations in the 1950s and 1960s.

Finally, we found this topic irresistibly intriguing and personally salient. Both of us have produced "Christian films" and so have some stake in this history, and in keeping the memories of these pioneers alive and fresh so that ensuing generations can appreciate their foundational contributions. In this book, we document their trailblazing work, both as individuals and within Christian studios, and as precursors to the religious filmmaking of the 21st century, from Mel Gibson to Tyler Perry.

This book traces the trajectory of the production, distribution, and exhibition of Christian films from the early days of "talking pictures" around 1930 through the late 1980s, a time when videotape began to replace 16mm film and the church film market appeared to be doomed. While our study is marked, whether for weal or woe, by overlapping chronologies, it seeks to establish a general historical overview from the 1930s through the 1980s. To ensure that the overall trajectories are clear, we have included an appendix that provides a time line of key events and films in the history of Christian cinema.

Chapter 1, "God Talks," sets the stage for Christians becoming involved in filmmaking, from the 1934 Roman Catholic boycott of the movies and the development of the Breen Production Code through changing Protestant attitudes toward the brazen "celluloid serpent" of film during the Depression years. It also seeks to define the primary religious genres that emerged. The appearance of three exceptionally visionary pioneer filmmakers during the 1940s—Friedrich, Baptista, and Moon—forms the hub of chapter 2, "Evangelical Film Auteurs."

Two chapters explore the work conducted by mainline Protestant denominations. Chapter 3, "Methodist and Ecumenical Films," surveys the efforts of the Methodists and the inclusive Protestant Film Commission, while chapter 4, "Reformed and Dissenting Images," delves into the cinematic output of Lutherans, Presbyterians, and Baptists.

Chapter 5, "The Studio Era of Christian Films," investigates the evolution of various mini-studios (Family Films, Gospel Films, and Ken Anderson Films) that sought to coordinate and vertically integrate the Christian film industry. The growth into global cinema markets marks chapter 6, "The Master Filmmakers," in which we chart the impact of Billy Graham's World Wide Pictures and Ken Curtis's Gateway Films.

Mark IV Pictures' venture into apocalyptic works with *A Thief in the Night* is taken up in chapter 7, "Mark IV and the Apocalyptic Film," a harbinger of the evangelistic outreach of later end-times movies, notably the *Left Behind* series. Chapter 8, "Global Film Evangelism," investigates two international "missionary films," particularly the phenomenal success of *The Jesus Film* in 1979.

Finally, the conclusion, "A Modest Renaissance before the End," plots the role of the Christian Film Distributors Association and the flowering of young, educated filmmakers who breathed creativity into Christian filmmaking in the early 1980s, before the sprawling industry imploded and slipped into the backrooms of Christian bookstores. Yet their films established a model for the new millennium and developed an audience for the blockbusters of Walden Media, Tyler Perry, and a legion of other filmmakers. We confess that, like many of our subjects, we are pioneers in exploring this fertile field, and regrettably we have neglected or overlooked significant and valuable contributions. But we hope that our work is an impetus for further critical research in this area.

In looking back at the outset of this journey in the 1930s, one realizes that the church and Hollywood did not fully understand each other. One of Hal Roach's "Our Gang" shorts titled *The Little Sinner* portrays, however unintentionally, this prevailing ignorance of one group regarding the other. When the Little Rascals characteristically decide to skip school one day, they run off into the woods for adventure. What they come across befuddles them: an African American baptismal ritual. They find the Pentecostal revival meeting so unusual, so frightening, so beyond their typical experience, that they flee back to school immediately. Out of this mutual confusion and suspicion would emerge a full-fledged cottage industry of nontheatrical Christian films.

This book excavates the lost histories of nontheatrical religious films, made outside the corporate Hollywood industry specifically for Christian churches. Our goal is to map the highways and byways, the broad and narrow paths that Christian individuals and groups chose to follow in adapting movies for religious purposes. This volume chronicles some of the dominant movements, people, and films that counteracted the secular Hollywood industry product. It charts the ongoing involvement of Protestants in the production, distribution, and exhibition of films from the onset of sound motion pictures up through "box-office Christianity," a contemporary trend in which Christian films have crossed over into mainline distribution and exhibition. In their early involvement with films, churches aimed at functioning as a significant countercultural influence in translating their messages into moral and religious tales that would edify the faithful in the vernacular of the day. Celluloid sermons would not only alter liturgies, but also change the ways in which congregations saw the truth and themselves.

Special thanks go to so many people who made this work possible: Ken Curtis, Bill Curtis, Rolf Forsberg, Mark Fackler, Jim Friedrich, Michael Korpi, Chris Simmons, Bill Romanowski, Mel White, Mark Tuttle, J. R. Whitby, Billy Zeoli, Doris Anderson, and scores of graduate students whose names appear in the endnotes, particularly Brian Hess, Paul Stevens, and Harold Buchholz. Special thanks go to the Virginia Wesleyan College librarians Patty Clark and Nichelle Mack, and Regent University, which provided

Andrew Quicke with two sabbaticals, enabling him to cross the country and interview retired Christian filmmakers. Thanks also go to the Regent University archivist Donald Ganz, who has expertly looked after the Regent University Religious Films Archives (RURFA) for more than a decade and opened the secrets of the vaults for our whims. Our deepest gratitude and respect go to our editorial muse, Jennifer Hammer, who both humbled us by her keen critical insights on our egregious literary faults and encouraged us with astute corrections and guidance. Rarely have two old men had such a Beatrice to lead them out of their own scripted purgatory into something more paradisiacal and readable. So, too, we thank Gabrielle Begue for keeping us on task, Despina Papazoglou Gimbel for managing the copyediting and production, and Nicholas Taylor for his amazingly rigorous editing in getting this unwieldy manuscript into shape. We also thank the scrupulous reviewers who critiqued an earlier draft with sharp insight, helping us to move toward some coherence and significance.

Our families also deserve more praise and gratitude than we can give them. Karen Lindvall kept her husband focused, disciplined, and happy, steering him from playing too many electronic chess games and reminding him of the delight at the end of the tunnel of writing. So, too, Chris and Caroline humored their father, blessing him with love and laughter and not asking for money, realizing quickly that in the writing of academic books there is not much profit. Juliet Quicke continually edited and inspired her loving husband.

Abbreviations

ALC	American Lutheran Church
BFC	Better Films Council
BGEA	Billy Graham Evangelistic Association
BR	*Biblical Recorder*
CA	*Christian Advocate*
CC	*Christian Century*
CFDA	Christian Film Distributors Association
CH	*Christian Herald*
CT	*Christianity Today*
ES	*Educational Screen*
FCC	Federal Council of Churches
IJRE	*International Journal of Religious Education*
LCMS	Lutheran Church—Missouri Synod
MBI	Moody Bible Institute
MIS	Moody Institute of Science
MM	*Moody Monthly*
MPH	Methodist Publishing House
NCC	National Council of Churches
PCUSA	Presbyterian Church USA
PFC	Protestant Film Commission
PMPC	Protestant Motion Picture Council
RFA	Religious Film Association
RFC	Radio Film Commission
RMPF	Religious Motion Picture Foundation
RURFA	Regent University Religious Film Archives
SBC	Southern Baptist Commission
TRAFCO	Television, Radio, and Film Commission of the Methodist Church
TRAV	Television, Radio, and Audio-Visuals (Presbyterian)
WWP	World Wide Pictures

God Talks

One late spring day in May 1934, the Roman Catholic cardinal of Philadelphia, Dennis Dougherty, ordered his diocesan flock to "stay away from all [movie theaters]." He framed this exhortation not as pastoral counsel, but as a "positive command, binding all in conscience under pain of sin."[1] The same year, a forceful Roman Catholic layman, Joseph Breen, commandeered the reins of the Production Code Administration board, believing, like many frustrated church people, that the movie morality czar Will Hays had compromised the mission of guarding the public from Hollywood excess.[2]

When Hollywood looked at religious concerns, they were likewise frequently nonplussed. On one hot July morning in 1934, as Hollywood moguls grabbed bagels on their way to work, they glanced at their own trade paper bible, the *Hollywood Reporter*, and may have been startled to read the headline "Taking It on the Jaw." The surprised executives read that it "seemed that every living soul (if you are going to believe the newsprints) was lined up against the industry, and the Churches of all denominations have created a new sin—THE SIN OF GOING TO THE MOVIES."[3]

Christian fundamentalists and Roman Catholics, and even many mainline churches, believed that lax enforcement of movie morals had allowed film content to degenerate. Such accusations were extended into a general condemnation of all movies as sinful. Frustrated grumbling from clergy and laity toward Hollywood during the early 1930s percolated into a vocal, even vociferous protest. The campaign for decency in the moving pictures pitted religious people of all stripes against the devil's minions who shot out filth and violence at twenty-four frames a second. It was, in a strange, unforeseen way, a truly ecumenical movement, uniting Protestants and Roman Catholics in a joint crusade.[4]

The religious boycott of movie theaters in Philadelphia spurred Hollywood to recognize that it knew little about this giant block of ticket buyers.[5] Acknowledging the powerful lobby of the Roman Catholic Church, with its

Legion of Decency driving a protest against Italian gangsters in *Scarface*, the suggestive naughty bits of Mae West and Betty Boop, and film exports that exemplified the "morals of the barnyard," Hollywood moguls conceded that they needed the support of religious audiences to insure the industry's profitability, especially during the Depression.[6] Deals were made and the Roman Catholic influence substantially shaped the golden age of Hollywood filmmaking. Acquiescing to religious pressures, Hollywood essentially decided to avoid religious topics in its films throughout the 1930s, and only tiptoed back in the mid-1940s with inspirational priests played by the likes of Patrick O'Brien and Bing Crosby. As film the historian Francis Couvares adroitly pointed out, a grassroots Kulturkampf took place on Main Street America.[7]

Just before the Production Code secured its teeth to guard against "immorality" in Hollywood, numerous testimonies were broadcast against the kinds of films being exhibited, suggesting the kind of public struggle over cultural authority. One Methodist layman, A. H. Beardsley, attended the movies in the early thirties and found himself confused by what he viewed as Hollywood's religious worldviews. On the one hand, he found much to laud about the 1929 feature film *Evangeline*, with its portrait of a kindly, courageous priest. He judged an accompanying short comedy less favorably. Its amusing plot centered on an urban rescue mission, where samplers like "Remember, Jack, your mother is praying for you tonight" decorated the walls. Beardsley interpreted the scene as mocking religion, as when a "bad boy" passed around a large bottle of "lemonade" laced with glue to all the parishioners, so that everyone in the whole mission got their lips stuck together as they attempted to sing a hymn. In the accompanying newsreel, a Catholic priest was called to bless hunters and hounds before a fox hunt (at which the writer wondered, "Who blessed the fox?"). The Methodist who visited the moving picture that day found that religion had been positively portrayed in a heartfelt drama, satirized by the ridiculous scene of a puckered-lip congregation, and finally thrown to the dogs. He left the theater feeling fully betrayed.[8]

The critical discourse of conservative religious spectators during this era marks a cultural divide on the nature and purpose of movies. With such a chasm opening between Hollywood and Christian traditions, it is not surprising to see the emergence of an alternative film movement, an independent cottage industry of religious filmmakers making movies for their own constituencies. For some Protestant and Roman Catholic leaders, policing a commercial industry was not as promising as growing one's own media products for teaching, worship, and missions. The British journalist G. K. Chesterton had once recommended such a self-reliant strategy when he visited the United States in the 1920s. The problem with movies, he wryly observed, is not that they go to places like Middle America, but that they don't come from places like Middle America.[9]

Moving pictures became an evangelistic complement for many churches, supplementing traditional forms of communication. Among the various denominations, films became extensions of their sermons. For Protestant fundamentalists and conservatives, the films preached repentance and conversion. For the more liberal groups, films sought to promote social justice and to bring a global consciousness to American congregations. As institutions whose primary missions were not to make movies, however, denominations would be supplanted by individuals and studios that sought only to produce movies. The emergence of a marginal troupe of film artists, outside the realm of traditional film history, suggests a subterranean industry and culture that reflected what the evangelist Jerry Falwell once labeled the "silent majority." Ironically, this separatist movement by Christians paralleled the Yiddish film movement of the silent era, with many involved in the making of those films assimilating into the larger film culture. Christian involvement in the industry would culminate in creative artists, directors, and producers like Scott Derrickson, Tom Schatz, Ken Wales, and Ralph Winter contributing their talents directly to Hollywood. However, early experimentation of religious filmmaking would open the church up to new forms of communication, particularly in modes of reception. Religious moving images would function in conjunction with the preaching of the Word, as congregations might find parables not only in stone and glass, but also in digitized images. Churches adapted to a visual culture and found ways to show the Gospel instead of just telling about it.

The Silent Backdrop

In his earlier *Sanctuary Cinema*, Terry Lindvall ferreted out the origins of the Protestant film during the era of silent American cinema. That work culled forth unexpected details regarding the church's involvement in exhibiting, making, and distributing films. Yet it all seemed to come to naught, with barely an image enduring into the Depression era. The advent of expensive mainstream "talkies" and the popularity of radio supplanted religiously oriented filmmaking in the 1930s, as churches did not possess the discretionary funds with which to make films. But that earlier blossoming of religious filmmaking was but the preface to the various future film enterprises to be addressed here.

To put the 1930s and beyond in context, it is worth looking back over the first quarter century of nontheatrical religious films, those films exhibited outside the normal channels of theaters in church basements, schoolrooms, and religious halls. The historian Arthur Edwin Krows divided the development of sponsored nontheatrical films into seven stages that corresponded with national American progress in an ongoing series published in *Educational Screen*.[10] His first division covered the preliminary stages of World War I, when many educators and clergy differentiated between entertainment films and sponsored, nontheatrical moving pictures. During this era, the producer George Klein had tried, albeit unsuccessfully, to pioneer efforts in organizing the nontheatrical field for churches and schools. He tried to salvage old theatrical films, particularly travelogues and Passion plays, and offer them to churches for educational and mission use. During the second phase, wartime, films were intentionally produced for cantonments and for military companies overseas in order to inculcate moral and religious values in the soldiers. Third, immediately after the war, overseas projection equipment used by the military was returned, with much of it put on public sale and bought up by nonprofit institutions, especially schools and churches. The distributor Warren Foster tried valiantly to adapt noncommercial films into the civilian economy through his Community Motion Picture Bureau, but he fell far short of his goals. One organization that did stake out a modest foothold, the YMCA, inaugurated a Motion Picture Bureau under its tireless leader, George J. Zehrung. It slowly began to flourish, and in time it provided the vigorous impetus that would give rise to a viable nontheatrical movement. While many churches and schools supported the vision, they committed only trivial amounts of funding to sustain it. Nevertheless, a prominent trend began with small independent producers such as James Shields contributing significant product for distribution and exhibition (such as *The Stream of Life*, 1919).

Krows's fourth era traced the momentous development of a visual educational movement, principally with the 1919 founding of the Society for Visual Education in Chicago, underwritten in large part by the public utilities magnate Harley Clarke. Through its official trade journal, *Educational Screen*, the organization was able to propagate an infectious vision to attract progressive educators and clergy to incorporate film into their work. Simultaneously, Eastman Kodak, the primary supplier of film and cameras, offered the Presbyterian Church two thousand projectors so that they might learn to exhibit their own films. In 1919, the Methodists held their centenary in Columbus, Ohio, and converted hundreds of ministers into "visual exhibitionists," placing an emphasis on each of them becoming missionaries for using film in their own communities. For Krows, the fifth stage occurred when specialized users decided they were more competent and knowledgeable about their own needs than outsiders and could thus produce their own visual materials. Within this development were included the debut of the Christian Herald Film Bureau, the University Film Foundation of Harvard, Eastman Teaching Films, and, under the auspices of the Harmon Foundation, Yale University's pedestrian *Chronicles of America* book and film series. The sixth and penultimate step for Krows involved the discovery of the need for specialized exhibition sites and a national system of distribution, particularly among churches of different denominations. Simultaneously, many intriguing and independent undertakings of groups that sought to capitalize and exploit a nontheatrical market proved quite speculative and quixotic (e.g., Pictorial Clubs and the American Motion Pictures Corporation headed by Paul Smith, now reposed in the "pathetic graveyard of worthy but premature endeavors" of those who risked capital and came up bankrupt). Finally, when talking pictures became commercially practical, Krows celebrated a revolution of cooperation in the production of educational talking pictures for schools and churches. Krows's chronological account suggests a trajectory in which the church slowly came to the realization that it could make its own movies to instruct, evangelize, and even entertain its congregants. The optimistic prophecies of the historian writing in the mid-1930s would form the backdrop for the filmmakers emerging in the 1940s.[11]

Along with Krows, Mary Beattie Brady, director of the Harmon Foundation, envisioned the 1930s as a new era for the church to invest in sound moving pictures. The Harmon Foundation had been set up by a wealthy real estate tycoon in the late 1920s to investigate how religious groups could use the burgeoning film medium. Since denominations had largely retreated from motion picture production on grounds of the cost of sound, the Harmon Foundation was the one organization that championed the use of film in Protestant circles. For Brady, the usefulness of film to the religious field had become axiomatic, although from its early entry as a novelty to its strategic use by Protestants to get people to Sunday evening services, it had proved a dismal and disheartening failure due to inadequate equipment and lack of suitable products. Yet, as a by-product of the Legion of Decency movement of the early 1930s in which the Breen Code policed film content, Brady saw more visionary and creative approaches in the religious appropriation of film. Denominational visual education boards, the use of the moving picture in missions, academic courses, journal columns, and a focus on religious education through visual means evinced a persuasive case for optimism.[12]

The New Era of Religious Emotion

Various attempts at religious film production, distribution, and exhibition by churches in the silent era had been erratic and serendipitous. Filmmakers from the Protestant tradition usually exhibited an overt emphasis on the Word, demanding that images and music serve the verbal narrative in clear, definite, and propositional ways, by emphasizing doctrinal instruction over entertainment. Religious filmmakers often favored direct and moralizing address rather than such indirect communication as parables. Didacticism underlay and defined most Protestant silent films. Dogma prevailed over drama.

Back in 1927, the *Christian Statesman* reported that the Harmon Foundation had conducted an interesting experiment in the making of religious motion pictures and distributing them to churches. It pointed out that while the commercial side of the film industry had experienced an astounding growth, there existed a notorious neglect in creating worshipful pictures that could become part of the regular, formal service. Thus this attempt was commendable, in that the Harmon "pictures have been designed, through their direct and simple treatment of biblical themes, to enhance for the church the richness and dramatic qualities of worship. That they may not conflict with the continuity of the service, they are short and nontheatrical, appealing to the emotions much in the manner of the beautiful anthem or stirring hymn."[13] The key here was the cinematic appeal to the emotions.

Despite dogmatic concerns among conservatives, the evolving influence of the liberal ideas of the 19th-century German theologian Friedrich Schleiermacher began to inform what many saw as the emotional bases of religious education.[14] For Schleiermacher and his German romantic disciples, religious experience, or our consciousness of an absolute dependence on God, underlay the reality of religion. God's immanent presence was communicated through and in religious feelings, and the moving pictures were prime vehicles for evoking such spiritual experiences. Schleiermacher's means for achieving spiritual knowledge was not through objective content or traditional doctrines, but via human feelings, imagination, and intuition. Movies could manipulate such emotional states and conjure up pathos, passion, and artificial euphoria. The Swiss neo-orthodox theologian Karl Barth once summed up Schleiermacher's theology as speaking about humankind in a loud voice. Sound movies could now amplify that voice into mythic encounters; one could penetrate through the material aspects of film to awaken "cultural despisers" to a sense of holy and divine things. In the finite and temporal medium of film, one could contemplate the infinite and eternal. Schleiermacher advised his fellow travelers to "transport yourselves into the interior of a pious soul and seek to understand its inspiration." For the feeling theologian, the "sight of a great and sublime work of art" can accomplish the miracle of lifting the soul above the finite.[15] As the historian Anne Morey has pointed out, film and religion shared a goal of producing a rapt or elevated state.[16]

The *Congregationalist* editor George Reid Andrews opined about the relation of old revivals and modern motion pictures, pointing to the common excitement of the soul:

> I could but think in that connection of the way in which the old prayer meetings, revivals, camp meetings and sermons had served just that purpose for the mass of humanity in affording them temporary release from the corroding cares of the day and giving them a prospect of the streets of god and the gates of pearl.
>
> In a way the motion picture does just this. The beauty and romance of the silver screen help the toilers of farm and factory, of kitchen and office to forget the humdrum of life for a period and come back renewed for the task before them. Any picture which does this is, to my way of thinking, religious.[17]

Key to propagating this notion of the experiential religious potential of film was the educator H. Paul Janes, whose pamphlet for the Religious Motion Picture Foundation (RMPF) recommended *How to Stimulate Greater Activity in Your Church through Motion Pictures*.[18] Silent pictures accompanied by hymn singing and organ playing had enhanced the sensory experiences of worship, but now the sound picture seemingly would bring in the finest music of the world's great cathedrals and choirs, which would *elevate* the spiritual experiences of all congregations. While it would also afford an opportunity to listen to sermons and personal messages from church authorities, Janes's emphasis was on the values of an emotional pietism that could be experienced through sound pictures.

Discussing the purpose of the RMPF, its executive director R. F. H. Johnson explained that the "business of the Church, and of the motion pictures designed for its use, is to help us *experience that true spiritual emotion which gives meaning to life* and arouses us to action and service." The RMPF believed that churches were not yet weaving the medium into the warp and woof of the church fabric. When it did utilize moving pictures with a modern 16mm projector and a good screen, however, the church could assure itself a praiseworthy exhibition that would move congregations and enable them to develop character.[19] The roots of character development, according to Janes, were "in the feelings"[20] and the potential to arouse those emotions was viewed clearly as within the power of the movies.[21] Alert *modern* ministers were advised to "capitalize emotional responses" from their congregations through the effective power of moving images.[22] In contrast to the Marxist cultural theorist Walter Benjamin's notion of the reduced impact or aura of mechanically reproduced art, liberal religious leaders believed that an authentic piety could be elicited by watching movies. Where Benjamin would argue that the mechanical reproduction of film would emancipate spectators from the aura of religious ritual and could recommend revolutionary politics, religious leaders believed they could harness the power of filmmaking for religious ends—for proselytizing, for deploying entertainment strategies to bolster church attendance, or even for supplying faith as a commodity that could be transferred via celluloid.[23]

In the early 1920s, movies had allegedly performed other spectacular miracles, including making men sober by closing down saloons, making girls more beautiful by offering models of mimesis, and making the mute speak, as the *Los Angeles Times* reported in a story about a deaf little girl, Lillian Ostereizer, who was aroused to speak for the first time as she watched a silent film.[24] Enormous faith was put in the modern technology of the moving picture. It offered a miracle for communicating with the masses. The director D. W. Griffith believed it had even been prophesied in the Bible as the universal language that would usher in the Kingdom of God. For many clergy, however, films remained in the old era of Babylon, even Hollywood Babylon, a place of exile and corruption.

Changing Protestant Attitudes toward the Movies

The Roman Catholic Church had been instrumental in the implementation of the Production Code that Hollywood studios reluctantly accepted in 1934. With threats of national censorship, the film industry negotiated their "capitulation" to Breen and his colleagues, making a show of cleaning up their own stalls. But many conservative Protestants resisted engagement with Hollywood, sulking in their tents and complaining about the industry's immoral depravity; only later would Protestant leaders discover that they could use Hollywood studio products to convey religious sentiments, or at least spark dialogue regarding latent spiritual issues in films. This followed their strident criticism of the industry and, in particular, Production Code Commissioner Will Hays. Hays had, in fact, once asserted that "schools should stick to educational subjects, the church to religious films, and that amusement films be restricted to theaters."[25] For conservatives, it had been easier to retreat from the secular world of theaters and curse the cinematic darkness than to spend time and money on lighting one candle, or making one movie. With increased public scrutiny of Hollywood product, various clergy discovered the latent, or at least potential, religious and moral parables of box office hits. Thus theologically moderate magazines like the *Christian Herald* puffed the most promising films with positive reviews, featuring photographic spreads and full-page advertisements. The professional images of the Hollywood Babylonians outshone those of any homegrown, amateur product.

Hollywood images were more captivating. For example, in her letter to the editor, a Mrs. Morrow, concerned about the vulgar movie magazines her daughter had collected, decided to check out the movies rather than reject them in toto: "I suddenly was realizing that Hollywood was the single greatest influence in the world on people's thinking and I simply had been trying to ignore the fact." Thus she marveled at *The Courtship of Miles Standish* and *The King of Kings*, and commended other movies as wholesome and highly educational entertainments.[26] This practice of finding pearls of value in Hollywood movies would persist until after the World War II, as Christian periodicals would boost good Hollywood product at local theaters more than they would address the issue of films in churches.[27]

Belatedly recognizing the magnitude of the social impact of movies on the young, the Better Films Council, working through the Federal Council of Churches (FCC), continued to suggest suitable films. The time had come, announced the Better Films Council in 1933, that Protestant churches "exert their educational influences for better films."[28] They hoped that this goal could be achieved by the Federal Committee on Motion Pictures organizing and coordinating local church boards on the community level. What this meant primarily, however, was that groups would study motion pictures as an art of expression, supervise children, collaborate with local theater managers on current pictures and programs, and organize fan clubs. Near the end of its recommendations for action was the "Study of the Use of Motion Pictures for Religious Purposes, and *If* Found Practicable, Assistance to the Pastor and the Church Board in Equipping the Church for Showing Pictures, and the Education of the Church in Their Proper Use."[29] The council basically surrendered the art of making one's own movies in favor of the more passive task of exhibiting pictures made by others. It also advertised, in a blatantly self-serving fashion, its own national religious monthly film review column in its *Federal Council Bulletin*.

Columbia University Dean Howard LeSourd suggested extracting "vivid scenes of pedagogical worth" from Hollywood motion pictures to use in religious education. LeSourd wondered if motion picture companies would allow him to collect scenes from films like *The Passing of the Third Floor Back* (1935) so that schools and churches could "take excerpts from the best photoplays and teach appreciation of pictures and solve our problem of production, all the while building character and developing visual teaching." The episodes, he hoped, would inculcate character, in his words "plucking berries from the garden of Hollywood fit for kings."[30]

Most religious use of feature films thus stressed the promotion of good character and social issues rather than the teaching of religious doctrine. The Committee on Social Values in Motion Pictures (with LeSourd as chair) applied educational theories to teach people how to meet life situations by showing them stories, leading to a national Character Education Program. At a 1936 National Youth Conference, for example, scenes from 1932's *The Sign of the Cross* and other features were shown, followed by discussion groups about Christian persecution and martyrdom, peace, and racial prejudice. The leader would show clips and then ask, "What's wrong with this picture?"[31]

What emerged among many mainline Protestant churches was a grudging engagement with film culture to teach and refine moral discrimination through such blockbuster films. The educator Paul Vieth scheduled a series of twenty single-reel cuttings from commercial pictures, which he called *The Secrets of Success*.[32] He planned it as a project that reinterpreted success in terms of social values, with each edited section leading naturally into discussions of morality.[33] The experimental series was made possible by the Motion Picture Producers and Distributors Association, headed up by the ubiquitous Professor LeSourd, now of Boston University.[34] But the number of people engaged in using film media for religious education remained very limited, and few conservatives would have called it "religious" education at all.

Building an Audience

At the annual convention of the National Board of Review in 1934, Dr. Worth Tippy, the executive director of the Department of the Church and Social Service of the Federal Council of Churches, addressed the board on the gratifying increase of the appreciation of the motion picture in churches.

Is This the Church of Tomorrow?

A drawing in the October 1949 issue of *The Christian Herald* inquired about the role of technology in the future church, questioning whether it would speed or hinder the Kingdom work. Courtesy of the Library of Congress.

While the early 1930s was mired in Roman Catholic and Protestant protests against the evils of commercial cinema, Tippy noted the positive work of both Bishop John J. Cantwell of the International Federation of Catholic Alumnae, who had been reviewing and broadcasting since 1924, and of the Protestant churches that had used films in their services and parish houses for many years.[35] For Tippy, such ecumenical coordination augured an auspicious future for church–motion picture relations.

In the wake of the moral codification of Joseph Breen's Production Code, which set moral guidelines for all Hollywood movies, the Committee on Motion Pictures of the Federal Council of Churches of Christ in America—comprising church boards, the National Council of Federated Church Women, and other interchurch agencies—issued a brochure on "better films." In their Better Films Council (BFC) manual, Cantwell called for churches to become fundamentally constructive toward visual media rather than unfriendly and iconoclastic. Tippy scripted a litany of directives to promote the motion picture as an art of religious expression: through consultation, research, collaboration with local theater managers, the study of social control, and coordination with production companies. All this preparation would assist the minister and the church board in practical ways of equipping the church for showing pictures. The BFC sought cooperative ventures of Protestant, Catholic, and Jewish groups to organize film clubs in churches. They invited these groups to explore how they could control acceptable movie content and to study local theater ordinances, proposals for censorship, and federal legislation of the new motion picture code as it might affect the public welfare and quality of pictures. The FCC's committee on motion pictures published a sixteen-page pamphlet titled *Source Material on Motion Pictures for Pastors*, distributed to all denominations, partially to secure its allegiance to the Legion of Decency and to promote the use of the third Sunday in October as an occasion for discussing the movies as a potential positive resource for society and religion.[36]

But the vision to incorporate a system of exhibition into religious settings faced several problems. First, there remained restrictions against inflammable films in the churches. Other practical challenges pressed in on church leaders, such as the need for insurance, the industry's transition to sound, the establishment of standard film width (35 or 16mm), the unlikelihood of finding suitable films every week as appropriate content, and the religious leaders' own ignorance regarding the effective use of film for religious purposes. (Some ministers, for example, would use films to substitute for sermons or as advertising to attract new audiences.) The transition to sound movies aggravated economic and logistical problems in church exhibition up until about 1936. The supplier of 16mm equipment, Bell and Howell, did not think churches were ready for proper projection of sound pictures. Others complained that there were not sufficient products to exhibit. The RMPF thought otherwise and developed a catalog with listings for over thirty distributors of religious films, including the Bell and Howell Company, Eastman Kodak, the Catholic Film Guild, the Lutheran Film Division, and the Methodist Episcopal Church. The catalog encompassed old films from the Harmon Foundation and newer ones from various denominations. In *Church Management*, the church educator Dorothy Fritsch Bortz agreed, pointing to a remarkably full list of sources for religious films in the mid-thirties.[37]

Significantly, the RMPF coordinated the interdenominational growth of a Christian League of Nations, formed in 1932 around the World Sunday School Convention. Their most pressing concern focused on the use of films in teaching children. This organization would also coordinate the distribution of religious films for decades to come, as we will see, from early visual documents on authentic mission work to the more progressive works coming out of a refurbished Harmon Foundation, such as *The Negro and Art* and *Negro Artists at Work*.[38] The genres of movies, from mere biblical reproductions to topics of social and political concern, would expand the definition of Christian film-making and open up doors for more creative and provocative films.

Defining the Religious Genres

In the early 1930s, the Protestant establishment felt hoodwinked by the sham promise of a sanctified Hollywood. By 1934, the premiere liberal religious periodical, the *Christian Century*, had surrendered any iota of hope for a moral film industry under the leadership of Czar Hays. They called on Americans to "engage in a critical assessment of Christ and culture," and to reject the status quo.[39] On the horizon they saw, through a glass darkly, some positive Roman Catholic action in the militant words and deeds of Joseph Breen and others under the banner of the Legion of Decency, but they remained suspicious of the commercially driven enterprise of moviemaking.[40]

One educator saw an alternative. Having been accused of attempting to camouflage a relationship between Hays and his own Committee on the Use of Motion Pictures for Religious Education, Chairman LeSourd, now professor of religious education at Duke University, declared that he was not connected to the Motion Picture Producers and Distributors Association in any way.[41] He averred that his committee had nothing to do with entertainment pictures, but rather was concerned with conducting nationwide surveys of the ways and means to use motion pictures in churches and schools.[42] While few believed his protestations of innocence, he did draw attention to the emergent movement of nontheatrical religious motion pictures. The hope of the churches was not in Hollywood; it was within their own missions.

In a series of five articles in *Christian Century* in 1930, Professor Fred Eastman of Chicago Theological Seminary depicted movies under the reign of Hays as a "menace to the mental and moral life of America."[43] Eastman delineated how the motion picture code under the National Recovery Administration intersected with the public interest at three points: stopping immoral pictures, preventing block booking, and promoting the renting of pictures to schools and churches. Of immediate concern was the first category, with Eastman pointing to how producers had bamboozled the public for four years, primarily because of a "metropolitan influence." But central to East-man's argument was his castigation of the Hollywood monopoly for making it almost impossible for small, independent producers in schools and churches to make and secure films relating to their own needs. He suggested that studios should reorganize their production and distribution apparatus, even converting some of their facilities into specialized production centers for nontheatrical films. Hollywood, he argued, must contribute to becoming *community builders*.[44] While criticizing Hollywood's waywardness, *Parents' Magazine* printed Eastman's plea for the church to reclaim opportunities missed by the movies.[45] According to Eastman and Robert Hopkins Jr., what was needed was a program of nontheatrical films for character building. The most auspicious site for viewing these films was in the churches, whether in their auditoriums or their parish halls.

In his own study on film, Rev. R. Hellbeck concluded that the Protestant film had been created and enabled by the work of the Harmon Foundation, whose productions had become the basis of cinema activities in Protestant circles. As part of the progressive vision, he announced that Protestants no longer needed to consider film to be "The Cannon That Shoots Twenty-Four Times a Minute." The superannuated notion of film as the devil's work was, according to Hellbeck, inherently misleading and mischievous, in that it assumed that the moving picture was an instrument of evil taking us to hell and back in a basket of filth and pornography. Essentially, Hellbeck claimed, the medium exists as a neutral instrument.[46] What Saint Augustine had declared regarding rhetoric was true of film: film was a neutral art that could be used for God's glory. The oral art of persuasion could now be enhanced by a technological art of communication, the moving picture.

While in the late 1920s the Harmon Foundation had invested heavily in nonsectarian religious production for churches and schools, the economic pressures of the Depression squeezed them out of competition. The beginnings had been auspicious, and one important legacy endured. Harmon's vision to produce wholesome religious motion pictures encompassed and defined five categories: biblical, missionary, historical/biographical, pedagogical, and inspirational films,[47] all of which were intended to fulfill the foundation's motto to "support, not supplant, the sermon."[48] These general categories remained stable throughout Christian filmmaking for the next fifty years under five larger umbrellas identified by the Harmon Foundation as "Bible Stories and Bible Lands," "The World and Its Peoples," "Religion Historically Treated," "Church Activities" or "The Church in Action," and various subgenres of "Dramatic Films," also known as "Religion and Life."

Categories and Genres
Biblical Films

Within these five categories of Christian films produced in the 1930s by both denominational departments and independents, the biblical film remained the staple and possessed the longest history. Bible stories had remained popular since the director Henry Vincent's *Passion Play of Oberammergau* in 1898. Replacing it and Sidney Olcott's groundbreaking *From the Manger to the Cross* (1912) was Cecil B. DeMille's classic *King of Kings* (1927), which enjoyed worldwide distribution, financed by the New York philanthropist Jeremiah Milbank's Cinema Corporation of America. The blockbuster film illustrated familiar Bible stories, incorporated numerous hymns in its presentation, and washed away audience fears of the new medium. Its impact proved monumental; in fact, many viewers testified that they saw the face of H. B. Warner (DeMille's actor playing Jesus) whenever they prayed.[49] It would be followed by notable works such as the Episcopal minister James Friedrich's *Living Christ* series (1951–57) and Campus Crusade's "most seen movie in the world" version of *The Jesus Film* (1979). The apotheosis of this category would be Mel Gibson's bloody and violent *The Passion of the Christ* (2004), a remarkable cinematic achievement, based in part on the visions of an obscure 19th-century Roman Catholic nun, Sister Emmerich.

This category established itself as the most frequently exhibited type of religious film in the 1930s, dominated by the Harmon Foundation's own 1930/31 series on the life of Christ, *I Am the Way*, incorporating reedited portions of DeMille's *King of Kings*.[50] In fact, the critic Gretta Palmer identified *The King of Kings* as Hollywood's most far-reaching success, noting that thousands of 16mm versions (in Chinese, Turkish, Arabic, Hebrew, and Hindustani) were distributed to missionaries around the globe: "In our Southern mountains, the Paulist Fathers have shown *King of Kings* to audiences who have seen no other picture. Three missionaries in India still replace their old prints every three years."[51] Palmer cited Alexander Wolcott's classic review that "it is my guess that *The King of Kings* will girdle the globe and that the multitude will still be flocking to see it in 1947," and concluded that he was right.[52]

Artistically it did not matter that DeMille's theology was a bit fuzzy, a sort of nebulous liberal Protestant humanism. In defending his use of the story for a universal audience, DeMille explained that it did not matter "whether one believes that Jesus was a divine being who descended into humanity or a human being who rose to divinity, it is not after all tremendously important in view of the fact that His ideals apply to us all."[53] *The King of Kings*, like a

Shroud of Hollywood, allowed viewers to project whatever theological significance they wished onto the silent images.

Nevertheless, some missionary bodies believed that the exhibition of *The King of Kings* internationally was needed to counteract the deleterious effects of Hollywood's other corrupting movies. Rev. Charles Gilkey, pastor of Hyde Park Baptist Church in Chicago, told attendees at the scholarly Fourth National Motion Picture Conference meeting in February 1926 that on his recent visit to the Orient, he had "learned that the motion pictures . . . were misrepresenting American ideals, thus prejudicing foreign people against our country."[54] Based on questionnaires to several hundred students in India, however, one study argued that Hollywood's films had a relatively small influence on Hindus who lived in villages, away from larger urban centers.[55]

One of the grandest works to come out of the foundation was a scenario on the life of Christ from indigenous Indian filmmakers. *For God So Loved*, a seventy-minute Kodachrome film, was based on *Love Divine*, a sort of Passion play performed regularly in a natural amphitheater. Native Indian Christians made and performed the film under the auspices of Rev. Ralph Korteling and Rev. Harold Heckman of the National Christian Council of India. It was edited and prepared for distribution by the Harmon Foundation, with sound commentary and Eastern music provided by Wasantha Singh and his Indian orchestra. "Devout men, women and children in homely garb" acted in this community project, a folk presentation by village people against a background featuring the hillsides of Pasumalai, South India. Two miracles were highlighted, namely, the exorcism of the demon-possessed man in Gadarene and the bringing of sight to the blind. Despite imperfections of camera techniques and costuming, *For God So Loved* boasts a simple and authentic story that was "true to the spirit of Jesus though not bound to the letter of the New Testament." In various prologues, native Indians announced that Jesus too often seemed wholly European, so "it is only natural that we Indian people think of Him as one of ourselves." Even in its raw and primitive form, the film elicited fervent religious responses and provided fresh and genuine perspectives on the Gospel story from a non-Western culture. An epilogue shows Jesus appearing to a farmer, a carpenter, a housewife, and a nurse, saying "Lo, I am with you always—even to the end of the world." The film concludes with a universal appeal from the Scriptures, declaring, "For God so loved the world, *all* the world, without distinction of time, or race or station that He gave His son that all might be one in Him."

Other biblical films went global as well.[56] These films would be followed by the remarkable *Daya Sagar* (*Oceans of Mercy*), a graphically powerful all-Indian production of the Jesus story distributed by the producer John Gilman in 1979. But that is a later story.

Missionary Films

Under this generic rubric were gathered missionary films from Africa, China, Japan, Latin America, and Native American Indian tribes, which had a twofold purpose. First, they sought to explain the cultures and needs of designated mission fields. Second, they were made to use in mission work, both at home and overseas. Most of the films addressed the salient concerns of medical missions, Christian education, and evangelistic work of international missionaries. An early series on *The Spirit of Christ at Work in India* (1931) and a three-reel study of *The Moslem World* (1931) sought to understand other religious cultures in light of the Christian faith. The latter covered "From Lands of the Camel" through "Out of the Desert," probing the roots of Islamic thought, a history of Muhammad, and the rapid rise of Islam. In its concluding reel, "Christianity Faces Islam," it presciently addressed crucial challenges in Muslim missionary work.[57] In the *China Our Neighbor* series, the Harmon Foundation produced a script by Sue Chien titled *Mr. Chang Takes a Chance* (1932). The film, still silent, introduced a drama about a desperately ill, prominent Chinese citizen, a Mr. Chang, who visits a missionary hospital, is cured, and shows his gratitude by endowing it with generous funding. As part of a travelogue series, *What a Missionary Does in Africa* traced the life of a missionary in the Belgian Congo who followed Stanley's expedition by riverboat, planted a mission, and won the confidence and friendship of its people.[58]

Most mainline denominations participated in some significant way in making use of films related to missionary work. Rev. Andrew Burgess, Lutheran missionary to Madagascar, produced "fine quality" movies of native life and island scenes, taking his pictures with Bell and Howell equipment. His colleague Dr. Benjamin Gregory declared that their mission to gain converts was enhanced by using such modern methods of evangelism.[59] For Christian Reform ministers, "the movies that picture life on our Indian mission field, or the work in China, are good enough to be shown in any of our churches."[60] Methodist churches in particular were attracted to mission films. Their Board of Foreign Missions filmed a low-caste village in India, which was used in a work titled *Touching Untouchables*. This film vividly and realistically portrayed the social change among the lower strata of the Hindu social system through Christian teaching on the value of human nature.[61]

While James Joy, editor of the *Christian Advocate*, the official organ of the Methodist Episcopal Church, lambasted Hollywood for establishing a seminary of vice, a school of crime with "foul-picturing writing," he also believed that "the cinema is a true school" with appealing methods for nascent minds.[62] Home missions would showcase summer camp work for city children, urban mission activity in Chicago and Philadelphia, and activity in more rural areas in northern California, among the logging camps in Washington, and in the occupied territories of Hawaii and Puerto Rico. *The Open Door* captured a survey of the Methodist Episcopal movement while the denomination's vanguard work in race relations was showcased in its far-sighted *Investment in Negro Youth* galvanizing a growing social concern. In conjunction with their films, the Methodists published *Methodist Educational News*, which served as a screen magazine. In addition, one of their preeminent schools, Drew Theological Seminary, actually produced a promotional film advertising its own mission. The Board of Foreign Missions of the Methodist Episcopal Church, in consultation with the RMPF, engaged Rev. W. S. Reinoehl (a scenario writer of the Amateur Cinema League and a missionary) to dramatize mission work in Singapore.[63] Methodist churches lauded their *Land of Cherry Blossoms and Snow* (1936) as the finest missionary and scenic picture ever made, showcasing the exotic beauty of Hirosaki, Japan, and the success of their boys' school there. Rev. Floyd Shacklock had borrowed a camera and found it more effective in disseminating his vision than the usual missionary sermons.[64]

The Northern Baptist Convention, through their Board of Missionary Cooperation, captured exotic footage of their international mission work. In *Burma* they showed buffalo, elephants, and the jungle villages where they had instituted medical missions; in *China*, they presented newly constructed schools and hospitals; *Philippines* boasted a snake charmer; lepers and holy men represented *India*; Buddhist temples symbolized *Japan*; and in three reels of *Africa*, cameras crossed the equator and gazed on Victoria Falls via railroad, with stops to examine the Baptist dispensary along with opportunities to view baptisms and schoolchildren singing. The films on Asia were worked around the hundredth anniversary of Baptist mission work in India, under the leadership of Harry Myers, secretary of the Department of Stereopticon Lectures, Moving Pictures, and Exhibits of the Northern Baptist Convention, who on special assignment in Burma and Madras documented mission work for the annual convention in 1936.[65] H. E. Goodman, president of the Women's American Baptist Foreign Mission Society, juxtaposed travel and scenic shots of Japan, China, Burma, and India with their Baptist mission work.[66]

Mission films proliferated. In their effort to educate, films taken by missionaries "penetrating strange lands" provided documentary teaching, such as Father Dufays's *From Dakor to Goa*, which displayed aspects of French Africa.[67] The Presbyterian Church (USA) (PCUSA) empowered its Board of National Missions and Board of Foreign Missions to produce such films as *Among the Navajos*, *A Friendly Hand* (about a Christian Neighborhood House's influence on Russian boy), and such standard travelogue mission films *Behind the Scenes in Chinatown* and *Beneath the Arctic Circle*. Verna Lotz of the Board of Foreign Mission's Visualization Bureau released and recommended *China Today*, with its curiously titled segments on *Babes in Chinaland* and *Siam: Land of the White Elephant*.[68] The Board of Foreign Missions further illustrated its work in world missions in Syria, Asia, and the Near East under the guidance of Dr. James Detwiler, secretary of the board.[69] It paid particular attention to making and using films for promotional work, including the multi-reeled *On Wings under the Southern Cross*, capturing a birds' eye view of Latin America ministries, and *Skylines*, displaying its mission work in New York City.[70] Having received more than two thousand projectors from Eastman Kodak, Presbyterians actively promoted the use of 16mm films throughout their denomination.

Research findings on motion pictures in the 1930s demonstrated that Hollywood movies—in contrast to church-made films—handicapped missionary work, especially in the Orient, where viewers could not distinguish between true and false portrayals of American life.[71] The *Christian Advocate* attacked Hollywood for its tendency to corrupt overseas missions, where "eighty per cent of the films shown in China come from Hollywood," with complaints that our celluloid American garbage was being dumped on their shores.[72] The slick professionalism of the Hollywood product overshadowed the simple visual documents of missionary films.

Church Activities: Historical and Biographical Films

The third and fourth categories of genre involved "Church Activities," principally a group of historical and biographical films stretching back to early actualities, mere visual documents of events and people, but which have since become fascinating historical records. For example, the "unexpectedly festive but dated" General Convention of the Protestant Episcopal Church in America gathering at Atlantic City in 1934 was preserved as an ecclesiastical yearbook on film. Silent film had previously captured the former Chicago

White Stockings baseball player turned evangelist Billy Sunday in several of his dramatic poses. The flamboyant Aimee Semple McPherson of the five-thousand-seat Foursquare Angelus Temple in Los Angeles spoke directly to film audiences, boasting of her church's pioneering work as the first to own a radio station, announced that "with the talking movie picture comes the great privilege of getting out the message to the ends of the earth."[73] In 1929, she agreed to appear in a "talker [talking picture] presenting her life story" through her own Angelus Productions.[74]

In a promotional strategy to persuade clergy to sign on for his "Protestant demonstration talkie," Swedish Evangelical Church member Milton Anderson asked a mysterious character, the self-promoted filmmaker Colonel Erpi, to help him make "the first talking picture church service." They developed the film by incorporating a male quartet, a celebrated soloist dressed in "appropriate costume" interpreting one of David's Psalms, a YMCA secretary giving a business talk, and two ministers concluding the presentation, one with short sermon and the other uttering a benediction. But when one quartet member would not wait for the filming, the song became a trio. Anderson featured Rev. F. W. Sockman of Christ Madison Avenue Methodist Episcopal Church in rendering this first talking picture church service. Finally, Anderson dubbed in organ music to give the film an aura of reverent atmosphere. Hollywood industry personnel told Anderson his production was not big or spectacular enough, as though Jesus needed forty disciples rather than twelve. So Anderson added members of a Los Angeles dramatic school to enact a parable, used some stock footage of the Holy Land (including snow on mountains), drafted a female choir of three dozen members, and secured the actor Alec B. Francis to read Scripture. Shown in the Hollywood Bowl as *Old Truths in New Garments*, the film expanded to several reels, which made it an extremely long church service.[75]

The omnipresence of such recorded church services was illustrated in a *New Yorker* cartoon of July 20, 1929. Bruce Bairnsfather showed a couple sitting in a mainline denominational church (possibly the historic Riverside Church) watching a film of a projected minister in a pulpit, and one says to the other, "I hear we've got Fosdick next week, in full color."

Rev. Harry Emerson Fosdick, a famous liberal Baptist preacher renowned for his radio addresses, had been showcased on the cover of *Time* magazine in October 6, 1930.[76] The cartoon suggested an emerging trend among several modern churches to project their ministers onto movie screens. Television would soon open the floodgates for a legion of egocentric preachers to appear.

"I hear we've got Fosdick next week, in full color."

The *New Yorker* cartoonist Bruce Bairnsfather presciently sketched the future of moving pictures in the church on July 20, 1929, suggesting that the Modernist Baptist preacher Rev. Harry Emerson Fosdick of Riverside Church would soon be preaching through color films. Courtesy of the *New Yorker.*

Recording church activities on film ranged from the neophyte to the more sophisticated productions. Rev. Father Yunker of Springfield, Illinois, pioneered amateur 16mm moviemaking for church work, as he took one of the first Bell and Howell cameras to a Lithuanian parish in Europe and staged pageants depicting epochs in Lithuanian history. Upon his return, he exhibited the various parish scenes on a screen in the parish house.[77] On the other end of the spectrum, David O'Malley produced impressive historical surveys of the Roman Catholic Church in *Through the Centuries* (1934) and

The Shepherd of the Seven Hills (1934). Distributed by Faith Pictures, these works combined newsreels, pans of the Sistine Chapel interiors, and classic artworks accompanied by a lecture contrasting the ruins of a pagan Rome with the glories of the Vatican. The progress of the church through history, often shown in animated drawings, was designed primarily for Catholic audiences.[78] The *Educational Screen* columnist Edwin Buehrer praised the comprehensive cinematic vision of the Roman Catholic churches, noting that they had long known about the importance of visual religious education, and adding it was time the Protestant churches caught up.[79]

The Harmon Foundation aided the Episcopal Church in 1934 in producing *The New World*.[80] The church exhibited the film, which depicted the history of the Episcopal Church in the United States, at their general convention at Atlantic City, demonstrating that one denomination had the wherewithal to undertake such an enterprise.[81] The idea that one could visually record religious history sparked a reviewer's challenge. Extolling the virtues of *The Story of Louis Pasteur* (1936), the editorial inquired that if Pasteur could be made "picturized," why not Wesley or Luther or Knox? The article continued, "There should be money enough in the stewardship of Methodists to produce a picture that would compare in power and beauty with Pasteur, where Jews and Catholics as well as Methodists and Presbyterians stand in queue."[82] So, too, the zeal to produce a feature version of *The Pilgrim's Progress* on the 250th anniversary of John Bunyan's death sparked the idea of a

> moving tale full of unexpected turns, that lends itself to the kaleidoscopic art of the screen. The characters are simple and vital, the stereotypes who can always be depended upon to be "dopey" or "sneezy" or "bashful," the kind of folk whom the director can be sure will always be true to type. The Valley of Humiliation and Vanity Fair would lend themselves to the talents of the master minds of stage setting. And the popular appeal is unquestioned. Best of all, *The Pilgrim's Progress* has a happy ending, to be [assured of becoming] a box office success.[83]

Dramatic Films

Finally, "life situation" pictures taught about Christian living, focusing on personal, social, and even economic issues (e.g., the Harmon Foundation's *Our Children's Money*, ca. 1931). Films even provided guidance on the proper ethnic etiquette for missionaries in approaching a tribal chief or in building one's own lean-to shelter in the jungle.

More dramatic films covered a host of styles and formats, ranging from the historical and missionary pictures (e.g., the India picture *Padre Sahib*, ca. 1949) to the evangelistic, allegorical, and apocalyptic.[84] The narrative of these films emphasized story rather than instruction, often by illustrating various anecdotes and parables. *The Story of Bamba* (ca. 1939) adapted a missionary's testimony about an African boy who assists the fetish doctor of his tribe in the rites of administrating the poison cup. When Bamba becomes ill, he is healed not by the witch doctor but by a Christian medical doctor. Both he and the witch doctor become Christians as Western medicine and Christian faith are shown to be demonstrably superior to the old ways. In the first decades of the talking picture, churches mostly avoided narrative films in favor of biblical and didactic works. This genre would dominate after World War II, however, with the transmission of numerous subgenres in melodrama and apocalyptic films. Nonetheless, a few religious dramatic films were produced that reflected the progressive concerns of liberal denominations, such as the Yale Divinity School's *If a Boy Needs a Friend* (1939), which promoted tolerance toward other races and religions.

Summary

In 1947, recognizing the existence of a growing trend of religious filmmaking, Michela Robins published "Films for the Church" in *Hollywood Quarterly*.[85] Robins discovered a wellspring of religious production, finding a heterogeneous output for the approximately fifteen thousand churches exhibiting films. An industry periodical, *Film World*, even launched a new quarterly publication, *Church Films*, to exploit the burgeoning interest. While Robins saw great possibilities for the emergent church picture, she wondered whether the films would be insipid "missionary conscience-tweakers" and regurgitated Bible stories, or whether they would expand into vital dramatic films dealing with pressing social and moral issues from Christian perspectives.

These categories or basic genres of filmmaking as delineated by the Harmon Foundation would endure through the emergence of the Christian film industry, with instructional and dramatic films predominating by 1985. Yet at its outset, religious leaders recognized the visceral impact of film and envisioned the medium as a means to develop character, primarily through moving the emotions. If film could be used for ill, it could also inculcate virtue and promote religious devotion. Satan's tool could be converted for godly uses. Such viewpoints of Protestants revealed changing attitudes in the

1930s toward moving pictures, with more denominations actively investigating how they might appropriate the media for religious purposes. Films functioned as sermons. Certain denominations, like the more conservative Southern Baptists, primarily concerned about evangelism, would focus on preaching the Word through their films. Others, like their more liberal counterpart, the Northern Baptists, would stress missionary work around the world. As we will see, all these categories—biblical, missionary, historical/biographical, pedagogical, and inspirational films—were to be practiced by the various denominations.

But as denominations sought out how to articulate their distinctive messages on celluloid, three unique filmmakers would set standards for biblical, evangelistic, and instructional films for the church market in the 1940s. The pioneering ventures of Rev. James Friedrich, Carlos Baptista, and Dr. Irwin Moon would lay clear paths for future Christian filmmakers.

Evangelical Film Auteurs

At the outset of the 1940s, a trinity of undaunted filmmakers would spark the eruption of the Christian film industry, fulfilling what they saw as their roles in the Great Commission, the call to go, teach, and make disciples of all men and women. James Friedrich, Carlos Baptista, and Irwin Moon would each, in their own peculiar way, adapt the marvels of filmmaking to tell biblical stories, call for personal responses, and reveal the wonders of God's creation. Their celluloid sermons would, respectively, hark back to rhetorical modes of Gospel stories, evangelistic appeals for repentance, and Psalm-like reflections on the glory of God's creation.

The Vision of Rev. James K. Friedrich

A 1937 senior thesis at Virginia Theological Seminary launched a vision of Christian filmmaking from one of the most enduring and engaging personalities in the industry. Despite the problems of the Depression years, James (Jim) Kempe Friedrich had been a successful young businessman working for his father, a wholesale grocer in Red Wing, Minnesota, and was recognized for natural talents of creativity, persistence, and persuasive sales techniques. But while attending the University of Minnesota, two changes interrupted his career: a new Episcopal rector, Rev. Earle Jewell, introduced him to the Christian life, and the movie bug bit him. For a brief time he took to the road hawking cameras for Bell and Howell, and he then tried, unsuccessfully, to work as an extra in Hollywood. In 1933, he enrolled at the Episcopal Virginia Theological Seminary in Alexandria, Virginia.[1]

Friedrich recalled the Sunday school days of his youth where "flip" charts, glass slides, stereopticon projectors, and chalk-drawn maps on blackboards had been used to tell biblical stories. In his percolating imagination, he dreamed of translating the stories of Daniel, Samson, David and Goliath, and Jesus onto the silver screen.[2] He acknowledged that his "strange idea" certainly was not one that promised much profit. In his seminary studies, Friedrich concentrated on the life of Saint Paul when he "suddenly realized what possibilities for a motion picture lay hidden in that dramatic character."[3] He was convinced that film heralded "the most potent thing that man has yet created for getting ideas across."[4] Finding dramatic raw material in the book of Acts, he wrote his senior thesis on the adventures and journeys of Paul in the format of a screenplay. He confessed that they weren't very good scripts, but "his professors didn't know anything about scriptwriting either," so he passed.[5] When Friedrich finished his seminary training in 1938, now Rev. James K. Friedrich, he traveled to denomination boards and national conferences seeking religious education leaders with whom to share his vision for showing the Gospel message on 16mm film.[6] For Friedrich, his calling was clear: "What they see impresses people more than what they merely hear. . . . There are hundreds of thousands of little feet toddling over the thresholds of the theatres of America. . . . Too many of our boys and girls are growing up with no knowledge of the Bible. If I can rouse in them an interest to read the Bible, then, thank God, I shall have done something worthwhile."[7]

The challenge of churches embracing films was complicated by three pressing problems: First, there were few suitable films to be shown. Second, very few churches possessed sound 16mm film projectors for exhibition. Finally, widespread opposition to Hollywood simmered among numerous conservative Christian leaders. Yet several religious periodicals, notably the *Christian Advocate*, discerned a change of cultural climate in the late 1930s, especially in the cheerful and original talent of this newly graduated seminarian. Friedrich shared that "we can reach the largest number of people through motion pictures. It is the easiest and most influential medium today. There is a psychological effect, too, because when a person is absorbed in a story and sitting in a dark theater where he can let his emotions go without being observed, he is more deeply stirred than ordinarily."[8]

Many religious leaders came to agree that film exhibition would benefit their ministries, but they also believed that it was not a feasible route to pursue as few churches possessed the necessary equipment. Friedrich recognized that virtually every city in the country had a movie theater and projector and so modified his plan to make a biblical feature film rather than a short film on Jesus's parable of the *Good Samaritan*. But studio heads politely passed on his proposal, acknowledging that while DeMille's *King of Kings* had been a box office success, it was only a novelty.

Stemming from the question "How can I make the Holy Scriptures a living experience for others?" Friedrich decided to spend an inheritance of $100,000 by investing it in a nonprofit motion picture company through

Rev. James Friedrich responded to a religious calling to produce moving pictures for churches, incorporating Cathedral Films to revive the telling of Bible stories. Courtesy of James L. Friedrich.

which he might unify Christendom by means of the visual medium.[9] He even persuaded the assistant rector of All Saints Episcopal in Beverly Hills to risk $200,000 in his inaugural film.[10] He wanted to make a movie "unbesmirched by the gaudy opulence that churchmen found so distasteful" in DeMille's biblical spectaculars.[11]

Friedrich's first project as an independent producer was titled *The Great Commandment* (1939). According to Friedrich, "The idea of the time was to put the Bible on film to show in secular theaters since there was no existing church market."[12] The film tells the story of a Jewish Zealot who shows mercy to a Roman soldier after hearing Jesus preach. Directed by Irving Pichel, the story follows two brothers, Joel and Zadok. Joel loves Tamar, who happens to be betrothed to his younger, more impulsive brother, Zadok, the angry Zealot. The melodramatic plot revolves around Zadok seeking the overthrow of Rome, Joel seeking the Jewish Messiah, and a Roman centurion whose sword will pierce the side of a crucified Jesus.[13]

Finding expert talent was another challenge, but Friedrich wandered around studios making friends with numerous filmmakers, becoming known as a "priest without a parish," although he served as an assistant at Saint Stephens Episcopal Church.[14] One of his meanderings led him to a "jovial, jug-shaped" entrepreneurial character known as Jed Buell, a small-time producer of "all-Negro films" and other offbeat projects like the all-midget production of *The Terror of Tiny Town* (1938), and titular head of Dixie National Pictures on Sunset Boulevard.[15] Friedrich, the "cinema-struck Episcopal minister," became Buell's biggest investor.[16] Friedrich's loitering and networking on various studio lots enabled him and Buell to assemble skilled artisans from within and without the Hollywood community and to form a new production company, Church-Craft Pictures, exclusively dedicated to the creation of religious films. The organization included "Ralph Jester, who had worked with Cecil B. DeMille, Paramount Studios, and . . . Charles Breasted, born in Egypt, who knew the background of the Bible and [how to secure] properties and equipment from the Holy Land for the biblical films."[17]

Friedrich recruited an impressive creative team headed by his director Pichel (later to direct his own religious feature, *Martin Luther*, in 1953), with the American poet and author Dana Burnett as his writer, and John Coyle as producer (later to direct Friedrich's series on the *Life of St. Paul*, the *Living Christ*, and *Day of Triumph*). Auspiciously, Friedrich shared the same location in Culver City as the independent producer David O. Selznick, where shooting for *Gone with the Wind* had commenced. Friedrich's wife, Elaine, remembered, "There we were: the smallest and newest company in

California sharing a lot with one of the greatest pictures of that or any other year. I'm sure that Vivien Leigh, Olivia de Havilland, Clark Gable, and Leslie Howard were not even aware of us, but we—still getting used to life in Hollywood—enjoyed them wandering around in their nineteenth century wardrobes. And when we compared the Cathedral budget with their costs for one week, or even for one day, we had to laugh."[18]

Thus, during eighteen days at the Selznick International Pictures, ironically on sets remaining from *The Garden of Allah* (1936), Friedrich gave birth to his feature-length version of the Good Samaritan. Other locations stretched from the boulder-laden Santa Susana Hills to the "Sea of Galilee" shot off the picturesque sweep of ocean beach near Malibu. The "Motion Picture Commentator" of the *Christian Herald*, Howard Rushmore, reviewed the film as good propaganda, implying that it encapsulated the Gospel story of forgiveness quite effectively.[19]

Perhaps the biggest and most delightful surprise to the Friedrich team was that the film proved an instant, though perhaps qualified, success. When it opened in Joplin, Missouri, and Emporia, Kansas, for test preview showings, audiences loved it. In addition, the press was enthusiastic. The industry paper *Variety* reported, "Tense drama . . . high production standards . . . moving romance . . . excellent script . . . artistry in both direction and performances." *Film Daily* thought that Friedrich's feature had a "splendid cast" and an "excellent script," while the *Los Angeles Times* wrote, "Christ speaks to us as though it were today. . . . This is a story of a man who meets Jesus and chooses to follow him. It is set at the time of a Jewish revolt against the Romans in 30 A.D., and as the people follow Jesus around the countryside, they hear his teachings."[20]

Its favorable audience and press reception convinced Twentieth Century-Fox, formerly skeptical of the film's prospects, to buy it outright—not, however, for a general release, but for a rewrite on a top-quality scale with studio talent. Fox production head Darryl Zanuck optioned it for $170,000. Originally, Fox had decided to remake the entire picture as a big-budget spectacle. As war clouds loomed, however, a screening scheduled for the White House was canceled, and finally the project was put on a shelf. The theme was out of step with the times. Who would be taught to love your enemy when he may soon have to learn to kill him? As Pearl Harbor did not encourage such charity, the film was not released in theaters across the country. The critic Margaret Frakes reviewed *The Great Commandment*, quoting the studio's regret about the pacifist movie, writing, "Its message is just as wonderful and true as ever, but I can see how right now it would seem to American audiences like nothing so much as a plea for appeasement of the Nazis."[21] Even though disappointed with this turn of events, Friedrich fervently believed that God had led him in this endeavor. Some twenty years later he was able to repurchase *The Great Commandment*, an impractical but sentimental investment.

The buyout from Fox not only returned Friedrich's initial investment, but it turned a handsome profit as well. Friedrich's official restructuring of his original company, Church-Craft Pictures (1940), into the nonprofit distribution corporation, Cathedral Films (1948–64), occurred with this influx of capital. He shot short incidents in the life of Christ, filmed in fifteen-minute reels. His first release, *The Good Samaritan*, a shorter version of the feature-length *The Great Commandment*, was shot on location at a ranch near Hollywood that looked amazingly like the "Palestine countryside."[22] Other two-reel films followed: *A Certain Nobleman* (1940) and *The Child of Bethlehem* (1940). Each was directed by Edwin Maxwell and Coyle "from reverent scripts" in about a week for about $12,000 apiece. Friedrich's published aim was to educate, not merely to entertain.

Discussing the purpose of his nonprofit company to make authentic, non-denominational religious films, Friedrich argued that

> it is so important that we reach the "man in the street" with the simple way of life that Jesus talked and lived. Few people these days stop to consider the values with which Christ was really concerned, for, in His way of looking at life, He placed new values on certain things that we seldom consider of any importance at all. Yet anyone who has caught a glimpse of what Jesus really meant has found that a man can be born again; and the world he lives in, though its surroundings be the same, is changed completely because he looks at everything so differently. It is through the eye that I believe this transformation may be done quicker; other methods used by the Church have failed to accomplish the task.[23]

Stylistically, Cathedral Films utilized numerous classic cinematic techniques, including fades, wipes, dissolves, and, in what would become a signature mark of the studio, voice-over narration (supplied by the Hollywood voice actor Michael Rye from the 1950s through the 1970s). With this cadre of technically proficient and entertaining films, Cathedral was primed to invade the church market. But one problem remained: there was no church market. Friedrich believed his films would swell interest among Christian leaders, encouraging them to buy projectors for their churches. Explaining how Cathedral found a foothold among churches, Friedrich's director of marketing, Candice Hunt, remembered that "the army had a lot of surplus projectors that they made available to churches and schools for practically nothing, because they had used them for training of the armed forces. Friedrich was the motivator in getting churches to pick up these projectors; in fact, he gave them away. He gave them away so that the churches would have projectors, and having projectors they would start looking at his films."[24]

Serendipitously, as the war ended, Friedrich had found an opportunity to exploit the deployment of military equipment. He aggressively created his own market for films, noting that "we've moved the box office to the church" with a ready-made audience of sixty million.[25] At first, he loaded film cans in his car and set off across the country, displaying them to conventions, seminaries, and ministerial associations—virtually to anyone who would watch. He ran them for Sunday school classes and then quizzed the children. He saw himself as a storyteller, called to "tell God's story and to tell our own story and discover that our own story is part of God's story."[26] In an interview with the evangelical periodical *Christianity Today*, Friedrich explained that "my use of audio-visuals in teaching unfolded for me a vast new world of possibilities for presenting Bible truth in a way that actually makes teaching a pleasure. Out of the experience came a conviction that Christian education had to face realistically the fact that the modern church exists in a visually dominated culture The Church School teacher or leader who is not aware of this is severely limited in planning for and carrying out an effective program of Christian education."[27]

Friedrich's catalog expanded with the *March of Truth Bible Teaching Films* series, including *Daniel in the Lions' Den*, *Abraham's Faith*, and *Raising of Lazarus* (ca. 1940s), each accompanied by thorough Bible study guides.[28] Cathedral even produced a free eighteen-minute instructional documentary on how to use these films in the church, which afforded a glimpse into Friedrich's philosophy of Christian filmmaking. He articulated four general goals: to edify and educate the church; to enhance interest in civic affairs; to promote mission work around the world; and to evangelize. His first priority was to teach church congregations, many of whom he believed lacked a basic knowledge of Bible narratives.

The first twenty years of Cathedral's output consisted mainly of the dramatization of the stories of major and minor biblical characters: *Cain and Abel*, *Cornelius*, and *Zaccheus* (ca. 1940s), culminating in *Queen Esther* (1948), their longest biblical portrait at fifty minutes. Coyle directed many Cathedral works, including *Amos, Shepherd of Tekoa* (1947), a fictional account of the Hebrew prophet Amos's summons to "let justice roll down like waters, and righteousness like an ever-flowing stream" (5:24 NIV). Coyle's general format was to enjoin the historical record with contemporary significance, as in Amos's castigation of a wealthy courtier, an indirect but clear indictment of contemporary injustice and moral decay. With ubiquitous voice-overs, Coyle imitated DeMille's juxtaposition of modern and Bible stories, structuring his *Cain and Abel* by starting with a modern man reading a newspaper, followed by a flashback to the original tale of fratricide. Breaking the narrative illusion, the reader argues with the film's narrator over the origins of hatred and strife. Then, through a flashback with oil-on-glass effects, the film portrays how human conflict began in the first book of the Bible. Dramatic liberties with Scripture did occur, as in the *Calling of Matthew* (1947), which showed the ruthlessness of an unconverted tax collector in order to convey the truth that no man can serve two masters. Similarly, creative license was taken in *Journey into Faith* (1943), a fictional drama of the blacklisted shepherd Cleopas (who had sold sheep to the Pharisees) on the road to Emmaus.

Cathedral's crowning glory began in 1945 with the preproduction of a twelve-part series of short episodes on the *Life of St. Paul* (1949–52), immediately followed by a color series on the *Living Christ* (1951–57). Coyle (allegedly a carpenter on Buster Keaton's *The General*) had joined the team from the independent Poverty Row studio Republic Pictures, and he immediately set up each episode like a thrilling Republic serial, with chapter episodes packed with rousing adventures and suspenseful cliff-hangers, transforming the missionary adventures of the apostle Paul into something akin to *The Perils of Pauline* or the space adventures of Flash Gordon.

All twelve episodes about Saint Paul were filmed in black-and-white and ranged from twenty to thirty minutes each, and the production quality was widely praised as excellent.[29] Friedrich made it a point to use "secular" talent and crews. He believed that if you wanted a good film, then you would have to use good actors regardless of religious affiliation. He defended this practice to those who argued for using only Christian crews by comparing it to the making of a new church sanctuary: if you want a solid and aesthetically pleasing church building, then you get a good architect; and if you wanted it to stand, then get good builders to build it. Despite this attitude, Friedrich would always begin each shooting day with a prayer, and he would always wear his clerical collar to the sets.[30]

The *Life of St. Paul* series began with *Stephen, First Christian Martyr*, followed by *The Conversion*, and subsequent episodes of Paul's missionary journeys, ending with *Voyage to Rome*, showcasing a breathtaking shipwreck at Malta.[31] Seeking to secure biblical consistency, each film was grounded in the

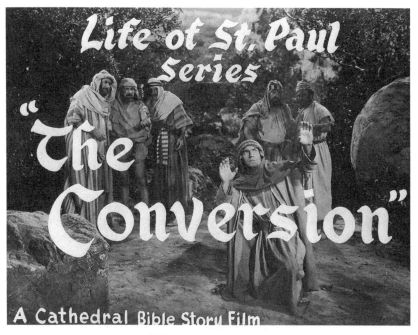

Rev. Friedrich's cliff-hanging, black-and-white serial of the *Life of St. Paul* created dramatic and adventurous episodes from the book of Acts. Courtesy of James L. Friedrich.

historical account of the apostle's life. The films were replete with thrilling moments, showing Paul barely escaping with his life in Antioch and provoking pagan riots in Ephesus.

Like many Hollywood films of the period, the introductions to the *Life of St. Paul* episodes set up the backstory exposition and accelerated the plot. Titles and animated maps helped to orient the viewer and bridge gaps in continuity. Superimposed graphics (opening with a shield of an open Bible and a sword emblazoned with the words *Spiritus Galdius*) and voice-overs evoked an authoritative rendering of the story, a documentary sense of being on the scene. The introduction of Paul occurs in *Stephen, First Christian Martyr*, in which, during the stoning of Stephen, the camera tilts up from the cloaks of the killers tossed at the feet of a man to the face of that man, Saul (Paul's name before his conversion). Stephen's last words haunt the persecutor: "Lord, lay not this sin up against them," and the scene cuts to Stephen's dead hand, which had traced a cross in the sand before he died. The music surges as a melodramatic title reads "The End."

Recognized by *Newsweek* magazine as the "General Pooh-Bah" of Cathedral Films, Friedrich designed his instructional films with detailed study guides, outlining the synopsis of each film and providing supporting biblical references and modestly provocative questions. In a pamphlet for discussion on *The Conversion*, for example, Friedrich's fourfold aims included, first, introducing the dynamic character and personality of Saul of Tarsus. Second, he sought to show the power of "forgiveness of sins." Third, he hoped to dramatize the hardships and persecution suffered by the early followers of Christ. And, finally, he aimed to show that a perceived enemy of God may be transformed into a "chosen vessel." His discussion questions asked the viewers to "describe the conversion of Saul on the road to Damascus and suggest what YOU consider the underlying lessons in this wonderful scene."[32]

Friedrich creatively enhanced minor characters in the biblical narrative (and added extra-biblical characters) as dramatic filler. One meets both Gamaliel, the wise Pharisee of the Sanhedrin, and fictional characters known as Jonathan and Deborah. The purpose of inserting additional characters was to engage the viewer in adjunct dramas in a grander, more compelling narrative. After the series was completed, film editors at Cathedral combined footage of each episode and released an eighty-minute feature called *Magnificent Adventure* (1952). When they completed the project, they realized that they had just "filmed" the book of Acts. Friedrich tinkered with his own techniques for capturing a "spiritual look." To preserve the illusion of a biblical story, none of his actors got screen credit. Lighting remained unobtrusive and subdued. Jesus as an adult appears frequently at a distance, with his back to the camera, or through his voice alone.

In 1948, the *Christian Herald* showcased Cathedral Films, going behind the scenes to investigate the problems and purposes of a Christian enterprise devoted to supplying churches with three to five films a year. The singular purpose for the company was set as serving "the Christian church with the finest films on Bible stories and modern religious themes."[33] Cathedral was poised to produce films for both particular denominations (e.g., the Protestant Episcopal Church and the Disciples of Christ, and the United Lutheran Church in America) and general release.[34]

The stewardship secretary for the United Lutherans, Clarence Stoughton, complimented Friedrich's work on their shared project, *And Now I See*, attesting to both the spiritual devotion of the filmmaker and the professionalism of the final product. For the National Council of the Protestant Episcopal Church, Cathedral Films produced *Thy Will Be Done* (1945) about the need for medical and spiritual missionaries in China following World War II.

In the film, a doctor "preaches" to American congregations about the Lord's call to care and donate medicine to the Chinese people. Such cooperative ventures suggested that the organization's dreams of developing a year-round production schedule were viable.[35]

Friedrich saw himself as a steward of this particular mode of communication: the "motion-picture camera, like the printing press, is a gift from God. We can use it for God's purpose." He compared film to the disciple Peter's boat, from which Jesus could speak. But films were not released until being first tested for "audience reaction." While he established Cathedral Films studio on 100 North Hollywood Way, his laboratory was his Sunday school class at Saint Michael's and All Angels' Episcopal Church, in Sherman Oaks, California. Children from all sections of the San Fernando Valley came to his "motion picture Sunday school." On the Sunday before the showing, he told the children what story they would see, seeking to point out the "real values" of the film beforehand. Afterward he would give a "film quiz" to see what they had learned. He borrowed a technique from the CBS radio show *Professor Quiz*, putting a microphone on the end of a long pole to interview children, and he called on children to answer questions. To help them recall scenes, he projected still photos of the motion picture on the screen. "We keep score, of course," said Friedrich, "as the boys and girls compete to answer the most questions." For example, with *Queen Esther*, he posed the question "What was the difference between the sacrifice Esther was willing to make for her people and the sacrifice that Christ made for us on the Cross?"[36]

Cathedral Films also produced and distributed instructional pictures like *How to Teach with Films* (1948).[37] Friedrich followed this offering with an enhanced version, *New Doorways for Learning* (1953), in which he explained the most effective and rewarding uses for church school instruction. He proposed a five-point program through which churches could incorporate film resources: study the programs of other successful church programs, provide an audiovisual budget, appoint an AV coordinator, conduct leadership training, and train a group of operators, preferably young people who could master technology more quickly and infectiously draw in other young people. He hoped the result would be a well-educated church body. The film shows young adults watching the Cathedral productions of *No Greater Power* and a *Life of St. Paul* episode. The commentator explains that "more advanced classes will take equally keen interest in films that are not only dramatically effective, but biblically correct." Friedrich's secondary goals aimed at sparking children's interest in civic affairs, revitalizing missionary programs ("bringing the most remote portions of the world to your screen"), and augmenting evangelism through media. Friedrich punctuated this last point with a scene of someone carrying a film can of his Lutheran-sponsored drama *Salt of the Earth* (n.d.). His training film ends with a promotional summary that announced, "Studies and surveys have proved that present-day audiovisual aids can open the door to understanding more easily, thoroughly, and effectively than ever before. . . . Modern equipment, moderately priced, is of excellent quality. The picture you have been watching, the sound you have been hearing, is a direct example. We at Cathedral Films hope that they will become a daily and continuing asset to your church program . . . educational, instructive, inspirational." The *Audio-Visual Resource Guide*, put out by the National Council of Churches, recommended *New Doorways to Learning* as a motivation for church leaders and teachers to understand the basics of "audiovisual principles as well as four basic uses for these tools."[38]

The *Living Christ* copied its predecessor with twelve episodes that roughly followed the Gospel accounts. Produced between 1951 and 1957, the series was considered Friedrich's outstanding achievement. The actor cast in the role of Christ was Nelson Leigh, an accomplished artist who regularly played this role in the summer productions of *The Pilgrimage Play* in Hollywood.[39] With its highest recommendation, the *Audio-Visual Resource Guide* praised the films in lavish terms: "These are the best materials on the life of Christ available today. The imagination, sensitivity, and creativity of the producer and director are evident in each film. Some viewers will contend that extra-biblical material has been inserted in places, yet this has only strengthened the dramatic and cinematic quality without diluting the message of the Gospel accounts."

Friedrich had to deal with controversial aspects of the Gospels, such as the turning of water into wine, which caused certain teetotaling denominations to stumble. He responded by visualizing such miracles with a sense of ambiguity and, one might say, mystery. Miracles, however, were recorded with a literal sense of realism, eschewing special effects for "just the facts." In contrast to other cinematic biblical recreations, Jesus and his disciples came across as "flesh and blood persons, not wooden actors delivering their lines. . . . Likewise, the characterizations of John the Baptist and Pontius Pilate probe beneath the surfaces and seek out conviction in the former, conflict in the latter."[40]

The first film of the series, *Holy Night* (1951–57), again directed by Coyle, curiously begins with a brief history of the Assyrians, the fall of Sidon, a voice-over of Isaiah's putative prophesies of Jesus's birth, and a debate among precocious shepherds about local politics and the coming Messiah. Oddly, the announcement of the impending birth to the Virgin Mary's betrothed husband, Joseph, comes not by an angel, as recorded in the Gospel of Matthew, but from his soon-to-be mother-in-law. The filmmakers' view of a relational Christianity (as opposed to a more doctrinal faith) is veiled in the second film, *Men of the Wilderness* (ca. 1951). At one point, a group of men loiter near a well and speak about Jesus: "I don't understand it. I can't explain it, even to myself, the way I feel about Him. I feel at home with men like ourselves, but not with the scribes and teachers, men with great knowledge. Yet this Nazarene reads the Torah as easily as any scribe, speaks with the assurance of a priest. He knows more than any man I've ever met. Still, I like Him. Yes, I like Him."[41]

Day of Triumph (1954) was perhaps Cathedral's apotheosis of sincere filmmaking, unfolding the life of Christ in the larger 35mm format, with Eastman Kodak color, a feature given a wide theatrical release rather than just exhibited in churches like his shorts. Directed by both Coyle and Pichel, *Day* focuses entirely on the political events surrounding Jesus's ministry, beginning three days after the crucifixion and describing the Zealots and their desire to have a king. The excellent character actor Lee J. Cobb plays Zadok, the leading Zealot, who conspires with Judas to provoke a revolt against Rome when Jesus is arrested. The well-known film and television actors Joanne Dru and Mike Connors play Mary Magdalene and the disciple Andrew. The film dramatized Matthew's life of Christ, condensing and heightening the narrative. It garnered praise from *Newsweek*, the *Los Angeles Times*, and other periodicals for its impressive story, outstanding cast, expert direction and cinematography, and "rich inspirational values." Like the Italian neorealist director Pier Paolo Pasolini's *The Gospel according to St. Matthew* (1964), the film focused on the politics of the holy narrative, with incidents invented and manipulated for dramatic effect. Comparing it to other Hollywood biblical extravaganzas, *Newsweek* commended it as "a model of simplicity and good taste." *Film Daily* prophesied that it should "enjoy vast popularity throughout the world." The *Los Angeles Times* extolled it as a "forcefully told story, rich in inspirational values, with scenes of moving power."[42]

Despite such positive reviews, Friedrich's pet project did not fare well financially. The predictions of vast popularity were undercut by industry politics.[43] Ken Dymmel, who worked with Friedrich during this time, remembered how they ran into trouble with the unions three years after the film's initial release:

Wanting to four-wall the exhibitions [rent out entire theaters] during Palm Sunday in 1957, the projectionists' union refused to show the film. Friedrich felt that certain members of the secular Jewish community were resisting his showing, trying to prohibit "what the Bible said." Friedrich tried to get it resolved, but could not overcome the lock on the theater chains. Even independent theaters would not give him the opportunity to project his film. Old Testament material was not problematic. Yet it was a Jewish comptroller who worked the system to get United Bank to loan money to Friedrich, and contacted churches that rented 35mm to support the effort.[44]

Friedrich believed that secular Jews had stonewalled him due to what they perceived as an anti-Semitic portrayal of Judas. According to some critics, Judas looked "more Jewish than the other disciples," and, as the "villain," they feared his portrayal would perpetuate anti-Semitic stereotypes. While arguing that all the characters in the story were Jewish, Friedrich tried, vainly, to secure the good graces of exhibitors. But theater chains had become independent from the oligopoly of studio trusts, due to a 1948 antitrust Supreme Court decision in the *United States v. Paramount Pictures*, which called for studios to divest themselves of their theaters. The newly independent chains feared a backlash and froze out the film before it had played on even 20 percent of screens. Without venues for exhibition, the film failed to recoup its investment.

Despite this failure, the film did inspire future Hollywood productions. Appropriately, as the film ends with the risen Jesus appearing to his disciples in the upper room, a title announces, "AND THIS WAS THE BEGINNING." It was indeed only the beginning, for not long after came Hollywood's biblical spectaculars: Frank Borzage's *The Big Fisherman* (1959), Nicholas Ray's Kennedyesque *King of Kings* (1961), and George Stevens's interminable biblical extravagance, *The Greatest Story Ever Told* (1965).

Friedrich and Coyle persevered in other ways. Two notable Cathedral films were produced in the early 1950s: the aforementioned *Queen Esther* and, in 1953, the somewhat stodgy *I Beheld His Glory* (with George Macready—who would soon play in Stanley Kubrick's *Paths of Glory* and on the *Twilight Zone* and *Get Smart!*). Friedrich's reputation for quality Christian filmmaking, along with Coyle's talents with special effects and directing, opened doors for numerous joint ventures with religious denominations.

The Christian Reformed Church commissioned Coyle to direct *The Test* (1952), in which a pastor helps a councilman vote against a pro-gambling ordinance. The politician is persuaded to do right after the pastor shows him movie clips of a past Cathedral production, *No Greater Power*, about the life of the miniature moneyman, the tax collector Zaccheus. The visual parable reaffirms the importance of gleaning ethical principles from biblical stories, especially for public servants tempted by money. More strategically, the film within a film advertises Cathedral's library of films and demonstrates the evangelistic power of film as communicating the Gospel message.

For All People (1946), made for the United Christian Missionary Society of the Disciples of Christ, dramatically narrates a story about a young minister who reopens a church/community center in a racially mixed neighborhood in Los Angeles, and how he uses children's nurseries, parents' clubs, and other programs to reach people and share the Gospel. It dealt forthrightly with prejudice and integration among the body of Christ. The National Council of the Protestant Episcopal Church employed Coyle to direct *Go Forth* (1946), a story of how a young doctor, rescued by a Christian native during World War II, decides to return to become a medical missionary in the Philippines.

The challenge of missionary work was also one of Friedrich's driving concerns. *And Now I See* (1947) told the story of George Miller, a crusty old man who did not see the need to sponsor missions. He is transformed by a furloughed medical missionary, who heals his daughter and persuades his son to consider going to a Lutheran college.[45] The director Jan Sadlo's *Indian American* (1955) places a missionary pastor in the Southwest in a thought-provoking story about corruption (Christians vs. unscrupulous capitalists) and racism against Native Americans. In a remarkable move for a denomination that forbade all movies, the Assemblies of God Foreign Missions worked with Cathedral to produce a documentary about the struggle for survival among the poor in *Children of the World* (1967).[46] What was striking about all these Cathedral films was that they creatively combined a concern for evangelical missions and social justice.

In the Footsteps of the Witch Doctor (1950) tells of an African medical missionary, Mboola, living in the former Belgian Congo, who challenges the native witch doctor. As a propaganda film for medical missions in Africa, it embellished a true-life story of Mboola, whose mother took him to a Christian mission doctor against the wishes of the witch doctor. The film was produced "not only as a tribute to the courageous missionaries who have gone forth to meet the spiritual and physical needs of the people of deepest Africa, but also as a challenge to those who would heed the call to follow their example." Beautifully photographed by Sven Nykvist, the film employs a documentary style to depict the work of an African medical missionary.[47]

Cathedral also utilized the talents of Walter Brennan, one of the premier character actors, to narrate the lighthearted and provocative *Don't Blame Me* (1962). Scripted with a *Twilight Zone*–style of unexpected consequences, the moral tale warns about judging others, as a self-appointed expert and critic, "John Smith," is himself judged in a dream by a black associate, a police officer, and his own son. He ultimately stands before God and realizes his own flaws. Smith wakes up but sees clues that perhaps it was not a dream after all.

In a 1961 article in *Christianity Today*, Friedrich reflected on his calling, emphasizing that he aimed at making the teaching of Scriptures "a pleasure." What was important for contemporary communicators was the realization that the "modern church exists in a visually dominated culture," a fact that should guide evangelism and church education.[48]

Friedrich was both personable and undaunted in achieving his vision. When he once sought to fix his own air conditioning, he lost a finger but remained undeterred in his resolution to get things done the way he thought they should be. He was successful in establishing a Christian cinema of quality, one that provided engaging drama with a personal, professional touch.[49] As the critic Don Eddy observed in 1946, a whole "new crop of independent producers is following in his footsteps and a small fury of Biblical picture-making is sweeping the film capital."[50] In the later decades, Cathedral Films would become more of a distributor of religious films than a producer, contracting for groups like the United Lutheran Church in America and even Brigham Young University. But the most lasting impact of Friedrich's work remains his development of a church market, of supplying the necessary cinematic apparatus for churches to exhibit all sorts of films—not only his own, but also those of other traditions.

The Miracle of Carlos Baptista

While James Friedrich was formulating a vision of Christian films during his seminary years, what has been repeatedly, but incorrectly, called the first 16mm Christian film ever produced had its origins in a Chicago restaurant. Carlos Octavia Baptista was born a Roman Catholic in San Cristóbal, Venezuela, the son of a Venezuelan ambassador. He immigrated to the United States in 1915 and worked for the Kimball Piano Company, selling pianos to South America by direct mail. In this entrepreneurial position, it took him three months to sell his first piano. Baptista recalled, "It is a strange feeling to find yourself alone and friendless in a big city."[51] As Baptista sat alone in a restaurant one afternoon, a stranger approached him and gave him a copy of the Gospel of John to read. Moved by the message, he wandered into the Buena Memorial Presbyterian Church of Chicago, where he dedicated his life to that Gospel call.

Shortly thereafter, Baptista became associated with a Chicago manufacturing firm, becoming its export distributor of movie projection equipment to foreign countries, chiefly to Latin America. Since it was virtually impossible to sell projectors without Spanish films available, he decided to process sound films into Spanish with the help of several friends in a small film lab.[52] According to Baptista, "If I had only known at the beginning what operating a film laboratory really involves, I never would have gone into such a business. But the Lord kept that knowledge from me. . . . When building the laboratory there was no thought in my mind of making gospel films the important work. The main purpose was to process Spanish films in order to sell 16mm sound projectors."[53]

As Baptista struggled through the ordeal of learning the technical and creative challenges of filmmaking, he received a revelation as the Sunday school superintendent of the Winnetka Bible Church in the fall of 1939: "It became my habit to give an object lesson to the children during the opening exercises. One of these was called *Story of a Fountain Pen*, paralleling a Christian life to a fountain pen. The object lesson was so well received in Sunday school that it occurred to me to put it on film. One of the boys at the office volunteered to take the pictures. So the film was begun and after much hard work, it was completed."[54]

The Story of a Fountain Pen (1939) remains a basic, even simplistic, account of a lost pen that must be redeemed from a pawn shop. The master comes in and purchases the pen's freedom from commercial slavery, and a sonorous voice-over intones the final, obvious message: "We are bought with a price, and can be used to write the truth of God's love on others' hearts, if we let our Master use us." In some conservative Christian circles in the Midwest, the novelty of having such a "sound" film with a Gospel message created a great deal of interest. Neither amateur cinematography nor inept editing mattered to Baptista; the key objective was visual evangelism. Traveling from church to church showing the Gospel message, Baptista had, in effect, revived the tradition of the traveling revivalists of the Second Great Awakening like Francis Asbury. He promoted his "C. O. Baptista Gospel Sound Films" as an "astonishingly effective medium to increase church and Sunday school attendance, and to bring new vision, enthusiasm, and Spiritual uplift, and [to bring] souls to a saving knowledge of the Lord Jesus Christ."[55]

Baptista was forced to deal with the same problems that faced Friedrich as many church leaders remained suspicious of Hollywood's art form. Secular film distributors were also convinced that no one would be interested in watching films that contained too much religion. Despite such obstacles, Baptista adamantly believed that the visual Gospel, like the words of God, would "not come back void." Letters poured into Baptista's office documenting the salvific effects of his simple parable, serving as examples of the one statistic that mattered—the numerous conversions being recorded. Thus a simple object lesson about a fountain pen laid the foundation for Baptista's first production and distribution company, the Scriptures Visualized Institute (SVI), founded in 1942. Wilford Miller, the cameraman for numerous Baptista films, remembered, "Nothing in those early years was professional. We would film our productions in a manufacturing plant, but because of the war, we could only have the silence necessary to film at night. Thus we would shoot from 9:00 p.m. until about 2:00 a.m. All of our equipment was crude and we had to use old flood lamps for lighting."[56]

Baptista's first Gospel musical, *The Singing Heart* (1940), was produced in the house of his first employees, who soon discovered that it "was too difficult to make films in their home," especially when one's wife was not amenable to celluloid cluttering the living room. The film preached a rudimentary illustrated sermon, full of evangelical jargon: "We see two hearts made of cardboard, one black and one white. Guess which one does not have Christ?" In case one missed the point, the omniscient narrator spells out the message in unmistakable terms: "The black heart represents those among us who have never let the Lord Jesus Christ come into their hearts to be their Savior, although he has been knocking, knocking. They have refused to open their heart's door." Later in the film, a red heart, "washed in Jesus' blood," transforms the black heart to white, then asks, "How about it, are your hearts black or white?"

In 1943, SVI produced its first dramatic Christian film, *The Man Who Forgot God*. Directed by a seminary student from Moody Bible Institute in Chicago, Leslie Flynn, this thirty-minute film revolved around a successful businessman opting to follow a path of riches instead of a calling to be a missionary. Baptista represents the backsliding tendency of the businessman by showing him reading a newspaper, rather than the Bible, when he returns home from work. When his daughter becomes ill, the lesson seems to be one of judgment for the father's hardness of heart. She dies and the man who forgot God repents. Unfortunately for the film's aesthetic, not only are basic rules of film grammar ignored (eye lines not matching, uneven cuts, etc.), but a young teenager plays a grown man (with his voice dubbed by an elderly Maxwell Kerr, one of Baptista's employees).[57] In addition to this dramatic foray, SVI claimed to inaugurate the nation's first "talking head" sermon series by filming many of the country's leading preachers, including Dr. Harry Ironside, Dr. William Riley, and Dr. Oswald J. Smith. Likewise, numerous musicians appeared, including a young hymn-singing artist by the name of George Beverly Shea, who soon became the evangelist Billy Graham's song leader and soloist.[58]

In 1944, Baptista and Kerr designed a portable projector that weighed only twenty-five pounds, sixty pounds lighter than the normal 16mm apparatus. Baptista called it the Miracle projector, not because of its weight, but because he guaranteed that the projector would continue to work flawlessly *until* the return of the Lord.[59] The Baptista Company's promotional brochure explained the Miracle projector's origins in pious jargon:

> In 1945 God gave us the vision to make our own sound projectors for the use of the furtherance of the Gospel. This was during the war, when the projector companies stopped supplying us with machines for use in winning souls for Christ. . . . In June, 1950, just before the start of the Korean War, the Lord gave our engineers the idea and design for a still better Miracle. We named it Model 2. . . . The 500 Miracles already in use have proven to be our best advertising.[60]

Advertisements for the projector in the trade journals were exuberant: "*Yesterday they said it couldn't be done, Today, It's a Miracle!*"[61] The promise of technical functioning until the Second Coming was a brazen piece of advertising; however, one original Miracle projector kept in the Special Collection archives of Regent University is still working, and there are those who suspect that some in Pat Robertson's educational compound are watching it closely for a sign of the end of the age.

As war shortages disappeared, projector companies like Bell and Howell and Victor brought out new, lightweight machines that far outsold the Miracle projector, which, despite its advertising, consistently encountered technical breakdowns. The costs of developing the Model 2 and Tel-N-See projectors (a synchronized filmstrip projector developed by Kerr to be used in religious education) were too expensive for a small company to absorb, and Baptista gradually sank into debt. While sympathetic Christian pastors initially lent him considerable sums from their pensions, Baptista was never able to return anything. He received numerous desperate letters from many who had loaned him money. He sold the rights for the Tel-N-See slide projector to a business consortium in 1961, but that sale paid only part of his debts. Eventually his house was forfeited to his debtors.

Baptista strongly believed that everyone who worked on any aspect of his films must be "born-again." Thus, in contrast to Friedrich, he purposely used fewer professional actors and crew members. Only Christian believers could participate in his films. Even so, SVI made inroads in an unexpected genre, the specialized arena of animation. Following the model of animator Ub Iwerks's multi-plane camera for Disney (technology that allowed the development of 3-D images), Baptista's devout staff designed and produced a three-level animation camera that took six months to build and four years to perfect. His film *Thankful Dandelion* (1946) provided one of the first examples of religious animation, though part of the film was shot in black-and-white, seemingly due to budgetary restrictions. Again, the evangelistic message is blunt, unmistakable, and somewhat comic as the dandelion discusses free will with a passing rabbit. "Do you know, little bunny, that boys and girls can refuse what God has for them; can you imagine a dandelion refusing the sun or the rain?" The rabbit can only shake his head. At the end, the thankful dandelion turns directly to the viewers and asks the boys and girls "Won't you say yes to Jesus? He will take all your sin away, and make you the happiest boy or girl in the world." Primitive animation marked much of Baptista's work, with good portion of it aiming to be interactive. In *Happy Times for Boys and Girls* (1944), a narrator instructs children in memorizing Romans 6:23 and then provides them with riddles and drawing lessons. The devout but unsophisticated presentation of Gospel messages is repeated in *A New Heart for Donna* (1951), another short film for children about a young girl leading her friend to Christ by means of a "wordless book," a 1950s evangelistic tool used in many conservative churches. A "wordless book" contained colored pages with no commentary, from black pages to show a person's sinfulness, through the red blood pages of Jesus's sacrifice, to a heart made whiter than snow, to the gold streets of heaven. It was used in evangelism to show and tell about the plan of salvation. Baptista's animation work culminated in the hour-long color feature *Pilgrim's Progress* (1950), which retold John Bunyan's allegory of the spiritual journey.

Baptista never really trusted pictures, as he was convinced of the supremacy and efficacy of the word; thus his films are dominated by voice-overs and preaching. In his corpus of more than one hundred produced films, from animated sermons and children's films to missionary films and sing-alongs, instructional commentary pounded home his messages. For example, *The*

Prodigal Son (1944) relies, unlike Friedrich's dramatic version, entirely on commentary, with no dialogue for the film's twenty-two minutes. The parable is set in modern times, where, instead of feeding pigs, the errant son winds up cleaning spittoons. The film shows the consequences of the boy's waywardness, and then we hear the interpretation of what happened from the narrator. The moral point is accentuated with a sledgehammer. So, too, the obvious lesson arrived at in one very unusual film, *Airmail from God* (1952), which portrayed how bits and leaflets of Scripture could be dropped on unsuspecting poor villages by plane, a concept of Gospel bombing that would be later satirized by Shorty Yeaworth's brilliant *The Gospel Blimp* (1967). Neighbors are mass evangelized by the bombardment of religious tracts from an airship.

Showing his entrepreneurial spirit, Baptista instituted a unique way to break through church opposition to his films. In his catalogs, he offered a free preview service for pastors and church leaders. He would send any of his Gospel films for a free trial use (save a small postage fee). He also started an extensive installment plan for film purchases. In the 1950s, he unwisely offered films for churches to rent, with repayment taking the form of the church offering plate, which did not always cover even shipping and production costs. At one point Baptista conceded that he was "still having a hard time convincing churches that our gospel films honor Jesus Christ. Sold them projectors below cost, and sent many films for free preview by church boards. Practically everyone likes the films. Very little income, and many problems." Looking to the future, Baptista was filled with hope and vision: "Just visualize the inevitable! Low priced, efficient sound projectors in every church, Sunday school, Bible camp, mission, yes, even Christian homes, and a constant stream of gospel films, in the people's own language, going mostly by plane to every locality of the world!"[62] Significantly, Baptista envisioned a home market as much as a church market, proposing that families maintain a library of wholesome Gospel films, long before the advent of VCRs and DVD players.

Baptista's vision was remarkably different from that of Friedrich, for whom professional quality was a significant part of worshipping God through one's talents. For Baptista, quality was of tertiary importance, after the paramount value of evangelism and a secondary concern of financial profit. Mostly Baptista was interested in a strong evangelistic message to the virtual exclusion of other concerns. The church film distributor Harvey Marks summarized, "Baptista was dedicated to presenting that message. That was number one." Baptista's straightforward and unsophisticated evangelistic messages represented little more than sermons on celluloid. The filmmaker Ken Anderson, Baptista's cinematic heir, announced at the start of his films, "Ken Anderson Films, where the message is always first."

Both Baptista and Friedrich felt the call to witness through film; both made their first films in 1939, and both formed production companies in 1942. Both men also expanded from film production to slide production in the 1950s. Frequently they would distribute each other's films. Both men passed within a year of each other, though Baptista died brokenhearted and deeply impoverished, with his equipment and assets sold to pay off his debts; while Friedrich left a prosperous company to his son, and Cathedral continued until the church film market dried up in the mid-1980s.[63] But it was another filmmaker, Dr. Irwin Moon, who would leave a more enduring mark on American culture.

Sermons from Science

The 18th-century Puritan evangelist Jonathan Edwards held that through "God, we love beauty and our joy in beauty is worship." Both earthly delight and spiritual regeneration could be received in enjoying the "Glorious Excellences and Beauty of God." The religious task (and gift) of discerning "divine things" by the beauty of their moral excellence offered a knowledge of God as education as well as revelation. Here was a "great awakening" through the senses that saw the mysteries and glories of God as both Creator and Redeemer.[64]

The grand auteur of creation or nature films, before Disney showcased the wonders of nature in his wildlife classics (e.g., *The Living Desert*, 1953) or PBS's *Nova* series explored the elegant universe, was a modest but creative scientist, Dr. Irwin Moon. At a pastorate Montecito Park Union Church in Los Angeles in the years 1931 to 1937, Moon experimented with illustrated sermons, incorporating electronic, photographic, stroboscopic, and sonic devices to demonstrate the kinship of the Christian faith and true science. For him, God's two books, the Bible and the book of nature, reinforced and complemented each other. His naturalist photography informed with a theological agenda overwhelmed audiences in the breathtaking color and slow-motion techniques of his raw documentary material, showing the marvelous handiwork of God throughout the universe. Moon felt that he had received a biblical mandate from *Isaiah* 41:20 ASV: "That they may see, and know, and consider, and understand together, that the hand of Jehovah hath done this, and the Holy One of Israel hath created it." The place of sight was paramount. Just as Friedrich had a dream while he was in seminary to film Saint Paul,

Dr. Irwin Moon of the Moody Science Institute fascinated audiences with his demonstration of the sounds made by the fish family. Appropriately, the symbolic Ichythus announced God's miraculous creation in Moon's 1948 film *Voice of the Deep*. Courtesy of Moody Publishers.

Moon dreamed of communicating the creative truths of God by illustrating them through science and nature.

Moon did not begin as a filmmaker, but instead embraced an earlier American tradition, that of the traveling showman. In 1937, he resigned his church appointment to travel from congregation to congregation like a sanctified Houdini performing scientific demonstrations (and "gadget evangelism") that powerfully illustrated God's creations.[65] During his pastoral ministry he developed innovative ways to communicate biblical principles to church youth. Rapt audiences were entertained while learning of the laws of gravity or electricity, even marveling at subjects like chemistry and physics, which they had previously ignored in school. During one particular presentation at the Church of the Open Door in Los Angeles, the president of the Moody Bible Institute (MBI), Dr. Will Houghton, was spectacularly impressed with Moon's program and invited him to become part of the institute. Moon joined an extension department of the MBI that supported his research in science, and with the underwriting support of several local business leaders he built an auditorium in San Francisco for the 1939 Golden Gate International Exposition, providing a public arena to showcase his *Sermons from Science* demonstrations. Like the contemporary comic television educator Bill Nye the Science Guy, his experiments unveiled a variety of scientific processes; according to one account, using "polarized light, demonstrations with helium and liquid air, fluorescent minerals, ultraviolet rays and the million volt transformer Moon used to spray electricity from his fingertips to the heavens."[66] For nine months Moon gave eight performances a day, seven days a week, of his "laboratory of faith" to overflow crowds, preaching that the biblical God of creation and redemption was revealed in nature.

A young seminary student at Evangelical Theological Seminary named Harvey Marks (later to be one of the founding fathers of the Christian film libraries) approached Moon about the possibility "of putting this material on film so even the smallest churches around the nation could benefit from it." Moon responded, "It would be nice, but I'm just too busy to take time to do it." Moon also recoiled at the typical dramatic Christian films, calling them "religious horse operas."[67] But after World War II had ended, Moon approached Will Houghton with the idea for a science laboratory with a filmmaking studio. The American Scientific Affiliation, an organization committed to scientific research and Christian faith, helped to underwrite the Moody Institute of Science (MIS; now known as Discovery Media). MIS, founded by Moon in 1945, sought to present live demonstrations (e.g., Moon conducting one million volts of electricity through his body) and film presentations of the *Sermons from Science* (now known as *Wonders of Science*). The latter would become known aptly as a "canned missionary" movement.[68]

MIS purchased an old Masonic temple building in West Los Angeles and Moon opportunistically latched on to a vast surplus of scientific equipment no longer needed by the military.[69] Appropriately, the military would become a prime audience for Moon's science evangelism productions. The office of the Chief of Chaplains even designated the Moon films as core teaching materials for its character guidance programs. Training via motion pictures had begun by 1944, when the Moody Bible Institute of Chicago's motion picture section visually trained missionary students in various trades, from manual arts and cooking to phonetics and anatomy.[70]

MIS announced its mission as communicating the "first century gospel with twentieth century illustrations."[71] *The God of Creation* (1946) became its first production, utilizing color and time-lapse photography to reveal God's "hidden miracles" within the natural order. A telescope explored space; a microscope peered into the world of tiny creatures like paramecia; and a caterpillar metamorphosed into a butterfly. Moon's commitment to capturing such marvels was matched by his eccentric methods. On one Christmas Eve, he lay on a cold floor all night, "focusing his camera on a caterpillar, but it presented the first known color film of the metamorphosis of the swallowtail butterfly."[72] Moon would address his film audience with such simple questions as "How large is our sun?" Using charts and limited animation, spectators would be taken on a journey beyond the stars, discovering the immense size of the Milky Way and recognizing it as just one galaxy among many. Moon's aim was to inculcate an overwhelming impression of human finitude and insignificance in the face of a truly awesome cosmos, in which stars as are countless as grains of sand.

A time compressor allowed one to observe the life of a poppy as it grows, blossoms, closes, withers, and dies. Like Godfrey Reggio's surreal independent film *Koyaanisqatsi* (1982), *The God of Creation* looked to underlying spiritual realities, seeking to find transcending patterns behind things growing in nature. More than a celebration of beauty, Moon explored and exposed the mysteries of vitality and potency in such processes as photosynthesis or the life history of a caterpillar. He was an evangelistic Rachel Carson or Annie Dillard in a lab coat, magnifying God's design and purposes. The historian James Gilbert praised the film for how it "ingeniously blended Hollywood production values and an appeal to American know-how, with biblical literalism, a fusion that claimed the prestige of science for evangelical Protestantism."[73] A reporter from a Southern California newspaper noted that "about 150,000 people all over the United States in high schools, universities, army camps, churches and religious groups see these moving pictures every month. One picture in particular called *God of Creation* has been seen by two million persons."[74] Moon explained to the reporter that "science is certainly well taught at high schools and universities, but there is real danger in the subtle emphasis on materialistic application and interpretation of scientific discoveries. Our job is to teach that the hand of the Creator is in all things of life. We're doing a picture now on undersea sound. Now that doesn't seem to have a thing to do with religion."[75]

In another example of his wide-ranging interest, Moon dealt with the ethical and spiritual issues raised by the atomic bomb in *God of the Atom* (1947). The film stressed a popular science approach with dramatic footage of the explosion at Bikini Atoll, animated explanations, and the physicist Larry Johnston sharing his testimony that "man cannot control himself. He needs help. He needs the kind of help which, in my experience, only God can give."[76]

In his fascinating study of the battle between religion and science for the soul of American culture, Gilbert investigated strategies employed by MIS for "churching American soldiers," fulfilling a vision planted by the populist Democratic presidential contender William Jennings Bryan after the 1925 Scopes trial.[77] Bryan had prophetically envisioned a contest of ideas between the modernism of Darwin and the natural/supernatural correspondences of the biblical tradition. And the arena of this intellectual contest, he suggested to the Visual Instruction Association, was to be on film. For Bryan, "the motion picture is the greatest educational institution that man has known and it won't be long before every school in the country will use the motion picture because there isn't anything good that can not be taught by film."[78]

In addition to its mission to instill religious ideas into educational establishments, MIS found an opportunity to invade the military establishment. Patriotism, science, and an evangelical Christian faith were insinuated into the training of Air Force recruits. Allegedly, they saw the films "before they [were] given complete uniforms."[79] In 1948, Air Force Major General Sanford K. Moats wrote to Moon's right-hand man, Dr. George Speake, praising the "unorthodox preaching" of his films.[80] Speake continued the traveling demonstrations that led him to many World's Fairs and Olympic Games, and hundreds of U.S. military installations, schools, and conventions for the next thirty years, while Moon continued his work in the film laboratory. In 1953, MIS began its educational division, which would ultimately distribute forty thousand film prints of sixty-two different films in virtually every school system in the country.[81] Foreign-language versions of Moon's films invaded the Third World and Iron Curtain countries, becoming one of the most significant missionary voices and propaganda vehicles of the Cold War era. In one anecdote, a certain Russian named Sergei acquired some MIS films and was showing them to private groups. When officials investigated, he buried them in the woods. Escaping to the West, Sergei eventually trained at Moody Bible Institute and returned to lead evangelism in an old gulag camp. By 1968, MIS films were available in thirty languages in more than one hundred countries.[82]

Unlike any previous Christian media propagation, the science films produced by MIS infiltrated non-Christian institutions and nations, even being circulated in the Soviet Union and other communist-bloc countries (as demonstrated by Sergei's story). Films such as *Professors and the Prophets* (1971) and *To the Unknown God* (1976) received the respect of mathematicians and archaeologists. The overt international mission of MIS was "to tell the gospel story in a unique fashion, capturing the attention of those who otherwise wouldn't listen."[83] Yet the mission of MIS was practiced incognito. Building on what the psalmist proclaimed (19:1–6) and Saint Paul preached (Romans 1:20), MIS portrayed the natural world as the workshop and playground of

God, revealing the glory and mystery of a Divine Creator. Moon communicated his religious worldview in a unique and compelling fashion: "The Gospel/Science film is the best tool we have to penetrate non-Christian institutions. . . . No other type of ministry . . . draws the unsaved together for a hearing of the gospel."[84]

The wonders of science were presented as the visible evidence of creation. Like Disney's Oscar-winning film *Nature's Half Acre* (1951), which showed life in a meadow over the course of a year, MIS's *Dust or Destiny* (1949) offered spectators an opportunity to watch fish lay eggs on land, spiders kill their prey, and bats navigate through darkness, but now within the grand teleological purpose of God's grand design. A professor of zoology at the University of Southern California, Tilden Roberts, served as the biological consultant for both Disney and Moon, overseeing the impressive time-lapse photography that would open a flower's petals.[85]

The marriage of science and biblical revelation was witnessed, and celebrated, by evangelicals and fundamentalists who had withdrawn from a modernist culture.[86] In a 1947 *Moody Monthly* article, for example, the scientist F. Alton Everest promoted the use of science (and the technology of film) for evangelism.[87] Harking back to the early inductive scientific methods of the philosopher Francis Bacon and the apologist William Paley, Everest argued that God intended us to observe and investigate nature so that we might see its divine designs and adore the Creator. The institute situated the human as the center of God's creation and destiny, between the giant universe revealed by the telescope and the miniature world magnified by the microscope.

Sixteen different MIS films were showcased at the 1962 Seattle World's Fair, being exhibited 1,548 times to more than a quarter of a million people. The *Sermons from Science* pavilion enjoyed 92 percent occupancy over the 184 days of the fair. Demographic data showed that more than twice as many men and boys responded to the films' evangelistic message compared to women and girls.[88] Among high-school-age attendants, the ratio was seven boys to one girl. Visitors had to wait in line for a couple of hours, and more than a thousand confessed Christ at the show. And at the 1964 New York World's Fair, *Sermons from Science*—attracting audiences of more than six hundred thousand (and close to nine hundred thousand the next year)— continued to be "one of the greatest vehicles for getting the gospel to the unreachables of our generation that has been afforded to evangelical Christianity today, first intellectually, second culturally, thirdly geographically." Reportedly, more than 20 percent of those attending went on to talk in the counseling room, a place set aside to further inquire about science and faith. In contrast to such intellectually engaging films, Moon still dismissed other dramatic evangelical films as "religious horse operas."[89]

In all, eighteen *Sermons from Science* films would be made over the next three decades, ranging from Cine Award–winning *City of the Bees* (1957) to the *Red River of Life* (1957), which explored the study of heart valves and blood pressure (winning Moon the Eastman Kodak Gold Medal Award). For *City of the Bees*, Moon had purchased a beehive from Sears, Roebuck, mounted it on the roof of the building, and observed the activity as they ascended and descended through a skylight. Dealing with the filming of the bees presented numerous hazards, including the fact that proper lighting meant that the honeycomb wax might melt and bees would "fry on the spot" (MIS finally synchronized strobe lights with the camera shutter to avoid such problems).[90]

With a film like *Energy in a Twilight World* (1980), Moon's work paralleled other documentary series to popularize science, such as the producer Michael Ambrosino's *Nova* (1974) and the astronomer Carl Sagan's *Cosmos* (1980). The significant difference was that MIS explored the marvels of the universe from a distinctly Christian vantage point. It sought to instill credibility through the popularized image of a scientist in a white lab coat, surrounded by professional scientific gadgetry. Through Moon's films, spectators could hear fish communicate (*Voice of the Deep*, 1948), with unexpected noises reverberating in the "silent" deep.[91] The Kodak tribute (awarded from the Society of Motion Picture and Television Engineers) praised Moon's significant contribution to science education as uniquely providing "a moral and spiritual frame of reference built into each production."[92]

When the Christian film libraries began to materialize in the late 1940s and early 1950s as the primary means of film distribution to religious institutions, the *Sermons from Science* films not only gave them a base of operations for the evangelistic youth ministries and churches, but also broadened the market to other nonsectarian groups.[93] The success of Moon and Everest was noted in the sheer quantity of exhibitions, conversions, and distinguished members of their audience, including a favorably impressed visitor named Albert Einstein at a showing at Princeton University in 1947.[94] They also brought much needed exposure for and boosted a newly formed Christian film industry. Along with its science films, the MIS produced children's stories with "Mr. Fixit," who wore a striped apron and used flannel boards to explain various phenomena. Film libraries found themselves with a core group of continual church film buyers.

However, public school distribution efforts ran into problems with some administrators and teachers. The films smacked of sectarian propaganda, sparking fear of the intermingling of religion and public education. This reaction caused Moody policy to note:

> This has caused some school personnel to be skeptical of dealing with any organization that could be considered in the slightest to be religious in nature. For this reason, the schools that are contacted should be made to realize that they are dealing with the Moody Institute of Science. This sounds severe, but there is some good in it too. If these schools were open to the Brethren of the First Baptist Church, would not the Mormons and Christian Scientists have equal right to mold our children's minds? We must be careful not to criticize a ruling which protects us in this way.[95]

As a result of these difficulties, Moody removed overtly religious messages from five of its *Sermons from Science* films in June 1954, and by the end of the year ten films had been toned down for public school use. Soon all Moody films were produced in two versions, one for educational use with no Christian message, and one for general release with the Christian message.

The church film producers could not have flourished without a strong network of Christian film distributors, and Moody was known for being very supportive of its dealers. When private organizations wanted to buy prints, they were politely reminded that Moody would only work through established dealers or the armed services. Their policy was clear: "Normally we do not sell our prints to anyone because of our commitment to 84 film distributors throughout the nation that rent our product. The only exception we have ever made has been to organizations that assure us that they will not be used under any circumstance that would conflict with our dealer operation. That is, if showings were conducted exclusively for a well-defined use that we approve, and not be loaned out to churches, schools or other public showings that might conflict with our rental dealers."[96]

In 1970, MIS launched "Operation Mobile Missionary," consisting of a thirty-one-foot streamline trailer for showing films globally in locales with no exhibition facilities. The trailer was complete with towing vehicle, public address system, cassette tape recording faculties, automatic filmstrip projector, rear screen projection facilities, and a complete set of the *Sermons from Science* films in the appropriate foreign language. The MIS *World Report* gushed, "Long before he is able to teach in his new language, the missionary can present his own messages recorded on cassettes by a national. He can listen at his convenience to tapes which would train him in the pure language rather than local corruptions. He can record his attempts at speaking the new language. He can present films and filmstrips which communicate God's love and the need for salvation."[97]

By 1986, a total of thirty-nine educational films had won twenty-seven national and international awards, plus the Eastman Kodak Gold Medal Award was presented to Irwin Moon for "the advancement of the educational process through the many unique uses of the art of the motion picture."[98] Moon retired in 1972, but he left behind a strong organization that continued to flourish for a season. A 1984 balance sheet showed that investments and assets totaled $1.4 million, with a net worth of $2.3 million, while expenditures that year totaled just over $1 million. Gifts and revenues were approximately equal in building a budget. But as the church film market began to implode in the late 1980s, Moody, overwhelmed by competition from videocassettes, suffered severe cutbacks. The institute began to release *Sermons from Science* on videocassette, which reduced its profitable 16mm market but significantly increased its exposure and ministry.

In a culture dominated by evolutionary thinking since the notorious 1927 Scopes trial, conservative religious groups had retreated into social fortresses and thrown stones out at Darwinians and modernists. God and science seemed for many to be on opposite, even adversarial, sides. As a forerunner of the intelligent design movement, Moon argued that God and science were shown to be on the same side; science was the tool whereby the mysteries of God's created universe could be revealed. Moon's science ministry was a restatement of earlier American theological convictions that God was revealed through His universe. His desire to use the wonders of science as a tool for evangelism was carefully conceived and creatively developed over the thirty years he worked with *Sermons from Science*. In reflecting on his work, he noted that

> the principle of tying the spiritual and the physical so closely together almost ensures that people, if they can remember the one, will remember the other. People are fascinated by science and religion. Even though they don't know too much about either, they love to learn and gain new insight into these things. Because the *Sermons from Science* principle is really so different from what most people are accustomed to, they find themselves in a whole new avenue to thought, and they are astonished; they're thrilled, they're excited, both the Christian and the unsaved.

Dr. Billy Graham summed up Moon's career by noting, "Only heaven will reveal the effect of his unique ministry through science."[99]

Summary

Gene Getz's *Audio-Visual Media in Christian Education* (1972) from the Moody Press claimed to be the first evangelical press publication on audio-visual media for the church. Getz had compiled a survey on the uses of such media in select La Crosse, Wisconsin, churches and found it to be widespread and effective. He articulated an apologetic for film use based on the Hebrew proverb "The hearing ear and the seeing eye, the LORD has made them both."[100] Historically Getz pointed to the contributions of John Amos Comenius, who in 1592 promoted learning through sensory experience, and visual aids as foundational for good teaching. "The sense of hearing should always be conjoined with that of sight," argued Getz; just as teachers use pictorial representation on the classroom walls to impress instructions on the pupil's mind, so we should use missionary films, evangelistic films, Christian life films, and documentary science films.[101]

The celluloid sermons materializing from these three pioneers—Friedrich, Baptista, and Moon—marked the way for other individual Christian filmmakers and denominations to follow. While their forays into filmmaking reveal contrasting strategies of communication with their intended audiences—the re-creation of biblical stories, the construction of direct propaganda, and the creation of indirect appeals through the marvels of the natural world—they each guided spectators to the same theme of God's presence in the world. Each emerged as an auteur, an idiosyncratic author whose primary visions of Christian communication shone through his distinctive works. Their primary success was to awaken churches and religious groups to the efficacy of using film for various purposes. They shared a sense of ecumenical, albeit evangelical, focus, making films that could be used in any church community and might also even unite diverse churches in a shared visual tradition. Of the three, however, it was Friedrich's Cathedral Films that branched out to make denominational films as well, moving into specialized markets and expanding the existing models and markets of Christian filmmaking.

-- 3 ----

Methodist and Ecumenical Films

According to 19th-century satirist Ambrose Bierce, the Scriptures were the "sacred books of our holy religion, as distinguished from the false and profane writings on which all other faiths are based." Even as Christians shared a common tradition, differences among denominations shaped the celluloid sermons of each. While some denominational films were designed to show a common ecumenical faith, many others emphasized a particular Christian sect's saints, doctrines, or practices as distinct from others. For example, Lutherans would feature their founder, Martin Luther, and Southern Baptists would stress certain fundamentals of their faith, such as the importance of adult baptism. Of course, some films would unintentionally fulfill Bierce's sectarian definition, as, in one instance, a Methodist reviewer would quibble that in a Lutheran film the minister was unacceptably called a "pastor."[1]

Like the German theologian Ernst Troeltsch's labeling of Christian churches as "sociological types," Protestant denominations in the mid-20th century fell into three general categories: the classical Protestant churches of the Reformation, such as Lutheran, Calvinist Reformed, and Anglican offshoots; the Pietistic or Evangelical traditions emphasizing the experiences of faith, such as Methodists; and a cluster of independent or "dissenting" churches, such as Baptists.[2] These groups, while not monolithic in any sense, would typically express their unique traditions through their films. Celluloid sermons frequently matched pulpit discourse.

Key to the distinctions among churches was the modernist/fundamentalist divide of the early 20th century, frequently associated in the public mind with the culminating incident of the notorious 1925 "Scopes Monkey Trial" on the issue of evolution education in Dayton, Tennessee. The controversy discredited many conservatives, who were caricatured by the satirist H. L. Mencken as the "booboisie," and led to a retreat from cultural engagement for many fundamentalist Protestants.[3] Yet in the 1940s, such conservatives would also emerge to market doctrine through media.

56 |

Despite theological and political differences among the denominations, they all explored the opportunities to use film to propagate their faith traditions. Each denomination sought to provide its flock with "equipment for living" through the medium of the cinema. In his analysis of the importance of film in everyday life, communication scholar Stephen Young found that films contributed to viewers' sense of identity and influenced their "general disposition to act in a particular manner in a given set of circumstances."[4] In seeking to educe certain moral and religious habits and postures from their congregants, church bodies experimented with the process of filmmaking. As early as 1932, the educator H. Paul Janes had recommended that churches "*use [their] denominational education boards*" in exploiting film for serving the missions of the churches.[5]

The next two chapters provide an overview of Protestant denominational films, beginning with Methodists and the Protestant Film Commission, and traversing through Lutherans, Episcopalians, Baptists, and other traditions. After sporadic and spotty ventures during the 1930s and 1940s, denominations boosted their involvement in filmmaking following the success of filmmakers like Episcopal James Friedrich. Friedrich and his ilk blazed trails like knights, cutting through thickets of reluctance and suspicion and challenging churches of all denominations to follow. In efforts to engage culture, various denominations found film to be the strategic medium through which to communicate their visions.

Methodist Enthusiasm

The 1924 edition of *The Doctrines and Discipline of the Methodist Episcopal Church* issued a "solemn note of warning and entreaty, particularly against attendance upon immoral, questionable, and misleading theatrical or motion picture performances." Such an attitude toward needless self-indulgence was rooted in the 1825 Methodist condemnation of the theater as a "charmer of the fancy, a stealer of the affections, a stifler of convictions, a seducer and leader to the ruin in hell."[6] But this edition of the book of discipline was, in part, a reaction to Hollywood scandals of the early 1920s; for when Methodists had held their 1919 centenary in Columbus, Ohio, they had become enthusiastic supporters of film for religious purposes. They erected the world's largest outdoor screen (149' x 136') and exhibited more than eight hundred films for Methodist clergy and laity, many of whom would return to their parishes and incorporate media ministries. Methodists would enthusiastically apply modern methods of film communication to reach their communities.[7] The Methodist centenary committee produced a six-reel photo-play, *The World at Columbus*, under the leadership of Rev. Chester Marshall as a means to perpetuate memories of the gathering, including close-up cameos of well-known Christians (e.g. William Jennings Bryan, Sergeant Alvin York) and images of Methodist employment bureaus, vocational train-ing centers, and welfare societies. With regard to overseas missions, the film featured various customs and scenes, demonstrating by way of contrast the "superiority of Christianity and the offerings of the Christian religion over heathen faiths."[8] Following this national celebration of film as a means of evangelism, eighty-six Methodist Episcopal missionaries set sail for posts in Africa, China, India, and other foreign fields, equipped with moving picture films.[9]

After such an auspicious reaction to film, Methodists delayed film pro-duction for more than a decade, due mainly to economic constraints during the Great Depression. However, amateur Methodist filmmakers dabbled in producing films of regional interest, such as Rev. W. Stockton of Newport Beach, California, who in 1931 shot films of local celebrities, boys with their dogs, and community singing. He drew in curious neighbors to his church, recognizing that "recreation is the end of almost every man, woman and child in the place."[10]

Methodist talkies were all the rage by 1932. Chester Marshall headed up the newly incorporated John Wesley Picture Foundation, with C. F. Reisner as vice president and James Shields (a successful scriptwriter for silent char-acter-building films) as secretary. Few film organizations could find such notable denominational leaders involved in film concerns. Marshall and Reisner had served at the forefront of the sanctuary cinema movement of the silent era, promoting films in Methodist churches. After shepherding his silent film *The Stream of Life* (1920) through production to successful exhibi-tion, Shields scripted a scenario for a sound film on *The Life of John Wesley*, integrating the hymns of Charles Wesley. He pitched this package to a poten-tial investor, Colonel Erpi, for underwriting.[11]

In an editorial in 1934, the *Christian Advocate* lamented that too many American Methodists spent their time agitating against indecent films, curs-ing the darkness, but not helping to promote better ones. The unlit candle in their minds was the dramatic story of John Wesley, still awaiting a pro-ducer and financial backing. In contrast, Methodists in England underwrote a strong organization for filmmaking; they also sponsored a cinema van, a complete moving picture outfit parked in the commons and at the curbs, where "crowds of 100–200 gather to gaze at the religious photoplay and listen to the preacher's amplified address."[12] The Federal Council of Churches, with its Department of Social Services headed by Dr. Worth Tippy, author of *How to Select and Judge a Motion Picture*, set up a Committee on Motion Pictures and Film Service Bureau to assist local churches with visual education. The announcement called for a constructive spirit of relations between church and cinema, not one marked by attitudes "fundamentally unfriendly and iconoclastic": "The motion picture is the people's theater and the public desire must be kept in mind."[13]

Dr. Benjamin Gregory from England introduced two reels of an "evangelistic" talking motion picture titled *Mastery*, produced by the Religious Film Society of London. In contrast to other talkies, which offered noted speakers, musicians, or church services, this dramatic film provided a picturesquely human and amusing story. Rev. William Lax, missionary to the poor, illustrates his theme on finding one's master. His sermon takes him to the sidewalk before a London tavern, through whose door a drunken wretch is forcibly ejected, only to be welcomed by Lax and taught to exchange Master Barleycorn for Master Jesus. The film reignited Shields's vision to produce Wesley's life amid the old-world background of the Epworth rectory of Wesley's childhood in order to celebrate the beginnings of Methodism.[14]

The moral story of a drunk being rescued by Methodist preaching convinced reluctant Methodists to admit there was potential good in films. The Methodist Episcopal Board of Foreign Missions also distributed *In the Shadow of Independence Hall*, shown at their 1936 General Methodist Conference. Showing historical landmarks such as the Betsy Ross house and Old Christ Church, the film traces social and economic changes over many years, showing how the Methodist Fifth Street Mission Center tried to meet the needs of immigrants now settled in this formerly aristocratic center.[15] For Methodists, evidence that religious films could reform drunks and teach history stirred corporate action for coordinating a larger denominational program for the use of such media.

It took a decade, but in September 1946, the Methodist Publishing House (MPH) established eight depositories, which were film libraries designated as visual aid departments, for filing, correspondence, shipping, and repairs.[16] The *Christian Advocate* had begun publishing the "Movies for the Family" column in November 4, 1948, seeking to support good pictures, testing to see if the films met standards of the true, the good, and the beautiful, and offering a reliable guide for readers, informed by reviews from the Protestant Film Council.[17] The magazine warned that just as film could lure thousands into "evil habits," it could "just as easily turn more thousands against immorality and crime, if it will portray sin in its sordidness." Viewing film as an instrument of teaching and evangelism, Methodists aimed at harnessing the medium to transmit Christ's example of brotherly love and service. The Methodist Church believed its mission was to proclaim its message to those outside the church, especially through "its *own* channels of preaching and witness, print, and film."[18]

By the mid-forties, the Methodist student magazine *Motive* devoted significant space to exploring religious themes in Hollywood. The witty style of the influential film critic Margaret Frakes kept her reviews vivid and engaging. In analyzing "Religion on the Screen," she lamented that not only were themes in religious pictures excessively "sentimental" and "maudlin," but that representations of preachers on the screen were usually "poor specimens, ineffective, unadmirable, and pedantic. Their most frequent appearance, of course, is as vague, coatless old men dragged out of bed into stuffy parlors to perform wedding ceremonies."[19] What stood out was Frakes's vision of a Methodist production company that would make 16mm films to be shown in churches and schools, applying biblical truths to modern situations.[20] Significantly, filmmaking was subsumed by the publishing industry. Dissemination of all communication materials could be housed under one agency. In August 1946, the MPH announced "New Film Libraries . . . Coast to Coast."[21] Some of its eight depositories across the nation offered viewing facilities so that ministers could preview the films (the viewing theater in Kansas City was particularly lavish).[22] Profits from the sale of projectors and screens benefited the Board of Missions and the Board of Education.[23]

By 1948, the official organ of the Methodist church, the *Christian Advocate*, was publishing short film reviews.[24] Within ten years, Dr. William Jones (from Southern Methodist University) and James Wall (editor of *Christian Century*) would introduce a church movement that sought to understand film qua film, ushering in an era of church/screen dialogue for mainline Protestants.[25] Most important and far-reaching was their summons to promote dialogue, probing the media's theological implications for the church.[26] Many conservative Methodists, however, still suspected that the boulevard from Hollywood ran nearer "Babylon than Sinai."[27]

In 1949, the Methodist Education Committee of Christian Cinema produced *Two Thousand Years Ago*, a series of five films recreating life in Palestine during the time of Jesus, touching on issues of home, school, work, traveling, and the synagogue.[28] In one film, *The Home*, the director of the audiovisual department of the Methodist Board of Education, Howard Tower, sought to reconstruct the biblical context of Palestinian homes. Dorland Dryer, whom *Time* magazine celebrated as a "muscular, ash-blond" sparkplug and "cineminister," premiered his film *The Templed Hills* at the Wilshire Methodist Church in Los Angeles, declaring that "the visual image is here to stay." But his film was simply a forty-minute church service, with prayers, a psalm, and a sermon, which *Time* dismissingly called a "canned service."[29]

In order to stimulate the development of audiovisual production, a commission was authorized in 1948, which eventually became the independent Methodist Radio and Film Commission (RFC) in 1952, for the purpose of disseminating religious messages through media via the MPH. The RFC produced several dramatic films to provoke discussion about social issues. One of the first 16mm RFC films, *Crossroads* (1950), deals with the theme of recruiting young men for the ministry. A high school boy wrestles with the death of his best friend and a call to Methodist service. His father, a farmer, is at first reluctant to have his son leave the farm, but at last he consents.[30] Written by the Methodist author Richard Belcher, and under supervision of three Methodist ministers (Howard Tower, Harry Spencer, and Rev. N. F. Forsyth), the film was produced by an independent group called the Apex Film Corporation.[31] Copies could be rented from the nearest branch of the MPH, or purchased for $200 from Nashville. The reviewer Walter Vernon was happy to give the film a qualified acceptable recommendation. He believed the film would be ideal for youth groups in local churches and subdistrict meetings, and in helping adults to better understand the tasks and motivations of ministers.

Some Methodists viewed *The Dislocated* (1952) as the most significant moving picture of the quadrennium, the four-year period between Methodist conferences. The Brady family is forced to move into a flats housing project located in a muddy field among other modern houses. As relationships deteriorate due to the pressures of work and school, the family appears in crisis. Voice-over narration represents the minister of the church trying to reach the Brady family, with the film offering an open ending for congregations to discuss what to do to help such needy families.[32] *Make Way for Youth* (1947) dealt with gang warfare in Madison, Wisconsin, where conflicts between two gangs on opposite sides of railroad tracks lead to the death of one young man. In the aftermath, the grieving father and Methodist agencies try to fix their community. Most fascinating, however, was the daring 1955 film *The Sound of a Stone*, produced by the Centron Corporation for the Board of Social and Economic Relations of the Methodist Church in the wake of the McCarthy hearings. It tackled the accusations of being a communist thrown against Mr. Henry Jordan, a devout churchman and high school English teacher, because he assigned a controversial book to his class.

Methodists cooperated with other denominations through the Protestant Film Commission (PFC), an ecumenical organization designed to bridge the media work of various groups.[33] Paul Heard, the commission's executive secretary, promised that it would produce a wide variety of films with help from the major studios.[34] He aimed to produce films of high technical and artistic quality for distribution to churches on 16mm film; these films would use the same techniques of propaganda and attitude formation that had been developed by the armed services during the war: "Some of these films will promote the many phases of the churches' special program. Other specialized films will be developed for use in the curriculum of Christian education. Still other films will show the application of Christian principles to pressing problems in many areas of life."[35]

Heard believed that films could contribute to many areas of church life, such as supporting Christian families, particularly from a "Protestant point of view": "We desperately need today a series of films on the elementary principles of psychology. . . . [But] it is more than a matter of psychology. It is a problem of spiritual honesty and character development." Heard was confident that film could meet many different needs, and that could even promote democracy and peace:

> In the field of social ethics the Commission has an unusual opportunity for the production of films to influence behavior. The right solution must be made to appear more attractive and dramatic and exciting than the "wrong" one, and "goodness" thus dramatized and sold on its own merits. The field of democracy and citizenship offers another most important area of the production of Protestant Films. . . . The worth of the human personality is a basic idea to both Christianity and democracy. World peace, as a subject in which the churches are vitally interested, is another area for films.[36]

On the issue of race, the MPH requisitioned three innovative films. The United Productions of America animators Robert Cannon and John Hubley based their short animated film *The Brotherhood of Man* (1945) on Oscar Peschel's 1876 pamphlet *The Races of Mankind*. The cartoon was lauded as a very effective resource for its emphasis on race relations.[37] Another ten-minute animated film, Philip Stapp's *Boundary Lines* (1946), preached about the dangers involved in marking off lines of separation among various national and religious groups.[38] The most ambitious of the trio was *The Color of a Man* (1954), Robert Carl Cohen's twenty-minute thesis film at UCLA showing "the poor home environment of Negro sharecroppers, contrasted with those who have a chance to attend Methodist schools. It summoned Methodists to help the Negro achieve greater freedom." While highly recommended, some reviewers feared it might provoke racial antagonisms. At a time when white and blacks were still attending different schools and churches, and when the long march of the civil rights campaigns had yet to begin, Methodists boldly entered the fray with such forward-thinking films.[39]

Behind decisive Methodist leadership, the PFC was nothing if not courageous in its choice of subject matter. In 1949, they introduced their longest and most popular film, an hour-long movie titled *Prejudice*, directed by Edward Cahn, about a Christian discovering his anti-Semitic roots and seeking to put his Christian faith into action against intolerance. It examined prejudice with good intentions in dealing with what to do when a Jew comes knocking at the door. The reviewer N. F. Forsyth wrote that "the film makes clear the fact that prejudices affect us all. Whether the person involved is a Jew, Negro, Swede or person of any other national background, he both displays and is in turn the object of prejudice." Stressing that religion can aid in overcoming prejudice, Forsyth conceded, "While audiences will find it interesting enough, it will not be a pleasant picture to see."[40] The *New York Daily News* announced that *Prejudice* would be a milestone as the first film produced under "exclusively religious auspices to receive commercial distribution," and that it would premier in one hundred cities simultaneously in order to combat ugly and debasing forms of racial and religious intolerance.[41]

While less interesting, Methodists also entered the field of documentary filmmaking. *We've a Story to Tell* (1949) covered various aspects of Christian service, from the calling of teaching to the tasks of financing, building, and repairing poorer churches, training missionaries, equipping schools, and ministering to nonchurch communities, all activities carried on through the Methodist World Service.[42]

As few preview copies for religious films were offered to churches, the role of Christian film reviewers for the religious newspapers was particularly influential. Few were more important than the *Christian Advocate*'s Walter Vernon, who tried to group his reviews around various subjects, such as world peace, international missionary outreach, or missions to the American Indians. Vernon believed that although *El Navajo* (1949), a general documentary film produced by the Santa Fe Railroad about Navajo life, made no reference to mission work, it provided useful background material for those working with Native Americans. Regarding *From across the Border* (1949), a Methodist film about a Mexican boy from a poor Roman Catholic family who attends a Methodist church, goes to seminary, and returns to minister among his own people, Vernon commented, "It is a believable story that builds brotherhood without preaching."[43] Less believable, *The Wrong Way Out* (1949) aimed at attracting a youth audience with a fast-moving, cautionary sermon about a boy and girl who elope, rob an office, and shoot the manager. The boy is killed in a car wreck while being pursued by the police. Vernon thought this film would spark vigorous discussion.[44]

Methodists were fairly broad-minded about the films they reviewed, usually accepting films made by Presbyterians and Lutherans. But they were wary of the new evangelical films being produced by independent studios. The first Ken Anderson film reviewed by the Methodists was one of his least polished productions, *That Boy Joe* (aka *Between Two Worlds*) (1949). Vernon gave it one of his most unfavorable reviews: "A high-school boy whose parents take no interest in his outside activities drifts into beer drinking and joins a friend in stealing from a warehouse. Taken before the juvenile judge, he is lectured and the parents are lectured, and the boy's problem is straightened out. Diagnosis of that problem seems too simple. The solution is too easy. Modern counseling techniques are ignored."[45] *Unto Thyself Be True* (1949), another juvenile delinquency film, incurred the same criticism: "The film has a definite weakness in showing an over-moralistic minister giving religious counseling that violates the rules of good counseling."[46]

Many religious films from Hollywood, in fact, were more acceptable to Methodists in the 1940s and 1950s than were fundamentalist films. Since the early 1940s, an onslaught of religiously oriented war films had caught on with Methodist churches, so much so that *Variety* announced a "Wave of Religious Movies Is Due."[47] Explicitly religious films appeared from major Hollywood studios, such as *Sergeant York* (1941), *Mrs. Miniver* (1942), and *Pastor Hall* (1940), the latter a remarkable British film inspired by Pastor Martin Niemöller, who defied the Nazi Party in the late 1930s in Altdorf, Germany, and was sent to the Dachau concentration camp.[48] The film portrayed Pastor Hall preaching resistance during the arrival of storm troopers to their village (marching in after a flock of sheep). The *Herald* critic Howard Rushmore criticized Hollywood for not releasing this "tremendously inspirational" picture earlier: *Pastor Hall* "was allowed to gather dust while Hitler moved history."[49]

The use of such feature Hollywood films in churches triggered a topsyturvy debate on Hollywood between the Methodist journalist Daniel Poling and the renowned "positive-thinking" Protestant preacher Norman Vincent

Peale; the journalist wrote an indictment against the industry and the clergy-man wrote a tribute. Peale pointed to the fact that "as to religion, that area of Los Angeles known as Hollywood has perhaps more crowded churches of all faiths and sects and a greater number of Christian youth than has any other city of its size on the North American continent."[50]

Both agreed, however, on the immense value of one film in particular. Universal Methodist enthusiasm greeted the Warner Bros. adaptation of Hartzell Spence's *One Foot in Heaven* (1941), which starred the Oscar-winning actor Frederic March as the Methodist minister. Reflecting the conflicted wartime spirit, the film inspired many, including Peale. Peale argued that such motion pictures can be constructive: "I believe God gave us the motion picture, just as He gave us the airplane, the radio and every great invention. The fact that man may sometimes use such things for unworthy purposes does not invalidate their divine origins."[51] The film was promoted as a Shakespearean play, holding "the mirror up to nature." Rushmore praised it repeatedly as a "milestone in the history of motion picture" and "good propaganda."[52] Prime Minister Winston Churchill even called for *One Foot in Heaven* to be taken "back to England" for its moral inspiration.[53]

Collaboration between the secular and sacred realms occurred frequently. In March 1950, the *Christian Advocate* reported that "official representatives of the Methodist Church cooperated with producer William Wright in the production of MGM's *Stars in My Crown*. This marks the first time such a relationship has occurred in the filming of any major Hollywood movie." The *Christian Advocate* film reviewer Harry Spencer explained that MGM had sent the shooting script to Methodists in the PFC. In effect, MGM acknowledged that "this film is about a Methodist minister and we want it to appeal to members of the Protestant churches. Will it?" The PFC went over the script and made a few suggestions, which were accepted without question, and during the shooting of the picture a Methodist official worked as technical consultant with the producer on the lot in Hollywood.[54] It was soon followed by the Twentieth Century-Fox movie *I'd Climb the Highest Mountain* (1951), based on the book *A Circuit Rider's Wife* by Corra Harris about her experiences in 1887 with her husband, Lundy Harris, who became a professor of Greek at Emory University.[55]

The Methodist theme of duty to the underprivileged dominated *Again . . . Pioneers!* (1950), William Beaudine's feature about a wealthy middle-class family and a poor immigrant family. The father of the complacent, affluent family begins to "believe that, with Christ's help, he and his fellow church members can find a Christian solution to America's problems," particularly their own local "shantytown." Budgeted at $80,000, the PFC tried to demonstrate that charity in missions begins at home.⁵⁶

In an overview of six other films produced by the MPH in 1950, an announcement appeared in the *Christian Advocate* that blared, "Christianity in Action Today; Dramatic Stories from Hollywood." As an indication of their core values, Methodists promoted films like 1950's *What Happened to Jo Jo?* (with Disney star Russ Tamblyn), about a frivolous seventeen-year-old girl waking up to her own town's problems. When a troubled fourteen-year-old boy hurls a rock though a church window and then rejects all attempts to help him, Jo Jo inadvertently enters his life. She comes to discover conflicts and resentments in her own neighborhood, an indifference of "good citizens" toward less-fortunate citizens, and city officials who ignore campaign promises. Vernon noted that the Wesleyan mandate for social concerns is revived when "the church youth group, by working through a group already trying to improve conditions in a neglected section, enlarges their own attitudes and concepts of Christian service."⁵⁷ Directed for the PFC by Cahn, who would later direct films less associated with the Wesleyan tradition (e.g., *Voodoo Woman*, *Girls in Prison*, and *It! The Terror from Beyond Space*), the film sought to connect good works with evangelical faith.⁵⁸

In December 1950, the MPH announced the creation of Coronet Films, to "enrich every phase of your church program. Teach social studies, teacher training, guidance, health and safety . . . the easy, effective way. Small children enjoy seeing desirable behavior acted on the screen . . . and somehow movie lessons make more impression on them than any number of adult lectures."⁵⁹ For example, one Coronet film, *Birthday Party* (1950), was suited for junior-age girls; it centers on an eleven-year-old, Janie, who persuades her mother to let her have a special birthday party. She glibly talks about it in front of Evelyn, who was not invited. Ultimately, Janie learns the meaning of the Golden Rule.⁶⁰ The films noticeably drifted away from biblical subjects and evangelistic sermons into character-guidance parables. This move reflected changes within the Methodist hierarchy itself, as social justice and action became dominant concerns.

The Emergence of TRAFCO

The 1950s proved a high point in Methodist film distribution. As we have seen, the General Conference of the Methodist Church sought to stimulate development of audiovisual production by creating the Radio and Film Commission in 1952, and the Cokesbury company handled its media distribution needs.⁶¹ In 1956, however, the RFC changed its name to TRAFCO

(Television, Radio, and Film Commission of the Methodist Church) in recognition of the rising influence of television. The main Nashville office of TRAFCO linked the outdoor experiences of early camp meetings with religious instruction and inspiration.[62]

Mindful of their ecumenical obligations, TRAFCO coordinated activities with the Broadcasting and Film Commission of the National Council of Churches.[63] The executive staff of the Methodist Radio and Film Commission included the pioneer communicator Rev. Harry Spencer, the primary reviewer for "church showings" films in the *Christian Advocate*.[64] Spencer then assumed leadership in 1956 of TRAFCO, which grew from two employees to more than forty by 1973, ushering in an era of many of the Methodists' most popular films, including *John Wesley* (1954) and *Hello Up There* (1950s). Spencer also helped bridge ecumenical communications ventures, becoming chair of the cumbersome-sounding RAVEMCCO (Radio, Audio-Visual Education and Mass Communications Committee) and the Broadcasting and Film Division of the National Council of Churches (NCC). In 1968, Spencer served as the president of the First Assembly of the World Association of Christian Communication in Nairobi, Kenya.

TRAFCO released thirty-four films and filmstrips, and reported that the MPH held eight hundred films, renting and shipping about sixty-five thousand prints a year. Each Methodist preacher averaged showing three films a year, with most of them being produced by Family Films, Cathedral, Coronet, PFC, the International Film Bureau, and even the Lutheran Church–Missouri Synod (LCMS).[65] Their most active rental to churches was *The Pilgrimage Play* (1950), a 16mm color recording of the Hollywood Pilgrimage play performed during the summer at the Hollywood Bowl. Although it rented at fifty dollars per showing, which was much more expensive than most other films, it remained TRAFCO's most popular and profitable item.[66]

According to Heard, the films were not designed for commercial release, but for complementing church school teaching. One Methodist leader wrote that "the communication arts for which the RFC is responsible is the modern frontier equivalent of Wesleyan street preaching."[67] The MPH aggressively promoted their films, reminding churches, "Don't let your summer church programs lag . . . use film to create interest, stimulate attendance, and keep up interest." Recommended films were ranked in terms of popularity; the top film (aside from *The Pilgrimage Play*) was director Beaudine's *A Wonderful Life* (1950), an adaptation of Frank Capra's earlier film. The life of a Christian family man, Henry Wood (Oscar winner James Dunn, from *A Tree Grows in Brooklyn*), is seen in retrospect through flashbacks, as his pastor and daughter remember him for his charity and love of God and neighbor. Inspired by a real-life story in Sedalia, Missouri, the faithful church deacon selflessly serves his community and dies, leaving a spiritual vacuum.[68]

In 1951, the Methodist Church sought sponsors for two select films, one titled *The Family Next Door* and the second, long overdue, on John Wesley.[69] The first attempted to undergird efforts at establishing Christian homes. The first movie planned, financed, and produced by the Methodist RFC, *The Family Next Door* (1951) was directed by William Thiele (after he had directed *Tarzan* and before *The Lone Ranger*) and supervised by three ministers, Spencer Tower, Wilbur Blume, and Polly Mudge Holmes. Delegates to the National Conference on Family Life were shown *The Family Next Door*, and this was "the first time all agencies of the church combined forces to produce film to use in connection with their church-wide programs."[70] Gently revealing three minor conflicts in the Howard family—the wife's ambition for her husband, the daughter's selfishness over a kitten, and their son's friendship with a boy from "across the tracks"—all is resolved, suggesting, as the film preaches, that "religion makes a difference." One father, a banker, who brings his daughter to a party at the Howard house, comments that kids seem to enjoy themselves more there than at his house. The film implies that genuinely Christian homes have more fun than nominally Christian ones. Its premier showing at the National Conference on Family Life would set a model of 1950s home life that would soon be imitated by television sitcoms, sans religion.[71]

Fred Eastman, who had scripted *The Family Next Door*, now worked on the proposed film on Wesley. By 1952, the RFC proposed a budget of around $125,000 (with the MPH contributing $226.20).[72] American theatrical executives predicted the film would cost at least $600,000 in Hollywood. Finally, in 1954, the Methodist British mogul J. Arthur Rank shot the seventy-minute feature *John Wesley* for the remarkably low cost of $154,000.[73] In an attempt to garner artistic reviews, *John Wesley* premiered at the Museum of Modern Art in New York City on April 25, 1954, followed by special showings across the country at five hundred churches that had each contributed $500 or more to the production cost.[74]

Some debate occurred in the pages of the *Christian Advocate* about the exorbitant costs of other RFC productions. One critic adamantly demanded that these productions at least carry a distinctively Methodist point of view and communicate "the way that we as Methodists believe." But whereas the Lutherans had spent nearly $3 million on the production of their television series *This Is the Life* (1952), the total budget of the commission was only about one-tenth of that sum.[75]

The MPH waxed eloquently in advertising its production *Easter* (1954): "The meaning of Easter comes to life in motion pictures. . . . The vivid portrayal of beauty, pathos, and majestic triumph . . . a fuller and richer meaning of the Lenten season. Give your congregation their opportunity to really understand Easter, an opportunity they will remember for ever." Its emphasis on the core doctrine of faith paralleled a concern for telling the Gospel story itself, such as in the more controversial *I Beheld His Glory*, a full-color story of the Roman centurion Cornelius. This film was banned by NBC television due to objections about the characterization of the Jews. NBC spokesman Davidson Taylor conceded that the quality of the film also "left a great deal to be desired."[76]

Another notorious film erupted into public tumult during the 1964 World's Fair in New York. Serving on the Methodist Board of Missions, William Fore, the director of visual education (and the executive director of the Communication Commission of the NCC), worked with the Protestant Council of New York and the maverick filmmaker Rolf Forsberg to record one of the most controversial and spellbinding "church" films, the Fellini-inspired *Parable* (1964).[77] The producer Fred Niles had hired Forsberg to develop a script based on the theme of "Jesus, the Light of the World" for the Protestant/Orthodox Pavilion. Forsberg fused various inspired sources to create an allegory of Christ's sufferings, including the French religious painter Georges Rouault's sad-eyed faces of Christ and clowns, Fellini's *La Strada* (1954), and the work of the classic French mime Jean-Louis Barrault (e.g., *Les enfants du paradis*, 1945), all blended to reflect a startling whiteness, a "blank, a motion picture screen of a face."

Reaction was immediate. One fund-raiser resigned in protest, objecting that "no one is going to make a clown out of my Jesus." Others tried to alter the proposed title of *Parable*, with the Episcopal Bishop Wetmore suggesting *Redeemer and Redeeming*, and another merely complaining that *Parable* "rhymed with terrible." But Forsberg was undeterred; the film would represent the "Circus *as* the World."[78]

With his friend Tom Rook as codirector, Forsberg employed professional actors and SAG and IATSE union members. Renting an old, elaborate Ringling theater, and rehearsing the improvising actors in pantomime without a script, they managed to create a mesmerizing allegory of Christ's suffering. The messianic figure was portrayed as a chalk-white, skull-capped clown, who took on the suffering, degradation, and rejection of an outcast woman and a black man and then was "crucified" in the circus tent by the establishment.[79] *Parable* owed more to the symbolic cinema of the Swedish film-

The director Rolf Forsberg's *Parable* amazed audiences at the New York World's Fair in 1964, where it premiered at the Protestant/Orthodox Pavilion. Courtesy of Rolf Forsberg.

makers Alf Sjoberg and Ingmar Bergman, with a diabolic manipulator, Marionette Magnus, controlling the mundane world of a circus. That is, however, until a Pierrot-type clown takes up the burdens of the oppressed workers (women and minorities) and sideshow freaks, eventually allowing himself to be hanged and killed on the "strings" of Magnus, the great puppeteer.[80]

Much like Kierkegaard's parable of the king and the swine maid, or the film *Godspell* (1973), the narrative included no explicit resurrection, opting to emphasize the death and sacrifice of the Redeemer. Nevertheless, the film garnered more rentals than most other films for the next five years. Part of its appeal was its controversy, with *Christianity Today* challenging this liberal experiment as "Christ in greasepaint."[81] The commissioner of the World's Fair, Robert Moses, sought to have the film withdrawn, and one disgruntled minister threatened that if *Parable* were shown at the pavilion, "he would riddle the motion picture screen full of holes with his shotgun."[82] At a press screening with *Newsweek*, *Time*, the *New York Times*, and other key periodicals, the film "worked," eliciting vigorous engagement, even from critics.[83] Most remarkably, the dreamscape setting of the film enables the "offense and scandal of the gospel" to engage the viewer indirectly. Rather than interpret the film themselves, many reviewers asked, "Who is the clown at the end of the film?" "That," Forsberg responded, "you must answer for yourself."[84] The film went on to receive accolades from the Cannes, Edinburgh, and the Venice film festivals, and according to Mel White, it even "inspired Stephen Schwartz and John-Michael Tebelak to write *Godspell*."[85]

In a marketing research query, the *Christian Herald* sought to see how much of the cinematic revolution had filtered down to churches. Asking directors of three film libraries (Sacred Film Library of Pennsylvania, Audio Visual Library of Union Theological Seminary, and the Films Department of Augsburg Publishing House in Minneapolis), the researchers found *Parable* equally popular with liberal and conservative churches.[86]

Despite bungling church bureaucracies, greedy film producers, and the tyrannical mediocrity of corporate interlopers, the film was produced. The Chicago Swede Forsberg acknowledged that it was "only with the Lord's help (literally) did that film come out from 'under a bushel.'"[87] Forsberg's genius expanded the typical format of the Christian film, producing films like *Stalked* (1968), *Peace Child* (1972), *The Jesus Roast* (ca. 1980) (a "celebrity roast," with each disciple at the Last Supper speaking his mind and demon-

Rolf Forsberg stretched the template of Christian films with offbeat and clever films like *The Jesus Roast*. Courtesy of Rolf Forsberg.

strating that the Gospel story contains significant humor), and the disturbing and environmentally prophetic *Ark* (1970), with both greedy, destructive humans and rats as villains. Forsberg's films could premiere at art film houses as easily as in church basements.

Such provocative films sparked clergy like Lawrence Larson, pastor of Parkman Street Methodist Church in Dorchester, Massachusetts, to look at "the church as producer." Larson pointed to the intellectual and metaphysical dimension of the new film age, filled with "gray despair, apocalyptic spectacle, and somber religious depth," all of which seemingly appealed to youth.[88] Larson predicted that church sponsorship of films for pertinent subjects would increase, but lamented that having viewed religious films entered in New York City's American Film Festival, he was appalled at such dull and crude entries. He complained that religious filmmakers needed to understand cinematic language, which he argued should be primarily composed of visual images. He critiqued the saturation of excessive voice-over narration, which emphasized telling over showing. He also criticized the overtaxing length of the films, such as those attempting to show "all" the church work being down in Asia or Africa. Larson argued that religious filmmakers needed to develop sensitivity to film dramaturgy and learn to communicate the subtleties of inner spirituality through visual media. As Heard preached, "A Christian film should be an exciting experience as well as a revelation of a God who is continually engaged in the work of reconciliation in the world."[89]

The complaints continued into 1967, when the pastor of First Methodist in Fitchburg, Massachusetts, wrote a severely critical article for the *Christian Advocate* titled "Church Films Need Reforming," which described a typical Methodist film evening: "The audience is seated; the lights are off; the projector switch is clicked; a series of still cinematic images comes to life on the luminous rectangle called the screen. Expectation keeps this youthful audience involved for ten minutes, but then a sense of fakery and a lack of reality produce a rippling series of guffaws. These teenagers, children of the 'image-age,' find a stark discrepancy between their lives and the movie images portrayed."[90]

Idealistic church audiences had expected church productions to rival those of Hollywood. When films like 1966's *For Better, for Worse* on teenage marriage appeared, its truly tacky disco scene reminded congregations not only of the limited resources for film production, but also the artistic constraints on scriptwriting and acting as well. In contrast, when the Hollywood feature *A Man for All Seasons* was released the following year, Rev. James Wall, editor of the *Christian Advocate*, wrote, "It has been some time since a motion picture with an explicitly religious theme achieved the kind of cinematic height this new generation of church film critics demand." Both the National Catholic Office of Motion Pictures and the BFC gave it their top awards for 1966. In stark contrast, Hollywood's most obvious pitch for the church audience that year, John Huston's *The Bible*, suffered the same fate as the previous year's *The Greatest Story Ever Told*—it was ignored.[91]

Methodists found that less was expected of documentary films, a genre that could instruct rather than entertain. *We Mean to Stay* (1967), a twenty-one-minute film distributed by Cokesbury and the MPH, chronicled the NCC's Delta Ministry, a controversial church program that had been making significant achievements. The title suggests the theme that some "Negroes did not want to flee to northern ghettoes," preferring to remain in the South despite a changing economy requiring fewer unskilled laborers. The denomination's Delta Ministry attempted to prepare them for new vocational opportunities. Cokesbury's distribution of *Japan* (ca. 1967) offered a second non-triumphalist missionary film. The *Christian Advocate* wrote that the film had been prepared for the 1967–68 mission study program and turned out to be "a surprisingly effective film. Churches accustomed to the more success-oriented mission film will be startled to discover a work that concerns itself with the cultural ethos in which Christianity has to witness but makes little direct reference to actual mission work." Eschewing an upbeat conclusion, the film's ambiguous ending provoked opportunities for engaged discussions. In *The Unbelievers* (ca. 1967), a Korean student searches for faith on an American college campus, reflecting the times. Wall, now senior contributing editor of *Christian Century* magazine, wrote that "attractive performers are betrayed by a formula script and conventional dialogue. The film does open with a campus riot and ends with the kind of openness not usually found in religious films. Technically better than most films of this type, but well below secular standards."[92]

In 1968, the year the Methodist Church merged with the Evangelical United Brethren to become the United Methodist Church, leaders took risks with a selection of short films, warning that "not every film handled by distributors is recommended for church use. We propose to discuss only those that have merit for general or specialized church use. Some films will be effective for congregational viewing, others for youth groups, and still others for college groups. In any area of church programming the best guide is mature judgment and sensitivity to audience needs." Aleksander Ford's *The Eighth Day* (1957) provided a montage of newsreel shots depicting 20th-century man busily destroying himself. The Polish director Tad Makarczynski's provocative antiwar film *The Magician* (1951) showed a violin-playing magician who entices a group of young children on a beach into shooting dolls in an amusement park booth. They find this acceptable only after the dolls are identified as "the enemy." *It's about This Carpenter* (1963), an experimental live-performance film made by the NYU film student Lewis Teague (who went on to direct the horror/thriller film *Cujo* in 1983), follows a man who has made a cross, carries it through the streets of New York, and deposits it on a church altar. Along the way, various persons react differently to his presence. Wall wrote that "this film may appeal to those who liked the overt symbolism of *Parable*. Others, like this reviewer, find it rather pointless. If Teague wants to suggest the cross is still an embarrassment, he would do better to depict what it is the cross originally symbolized, rather than suggesting that the symbol itself is the embarrassment."[93] However, Teague's work contributed to the creative output of those wishing to provoke spectators to think and engage with their films.

These choices seem very different from those available a decade earlier, as films evolved from being fairly static missionary films into modern, ambiguous parables. Films were less concerned with tradition, Scripture, and doctrine. They tended to emphasize existential moral choices, provoking discussions more on authenticity of living than on orthodoxy of doctrine. Moreover, the choice of Hollywood films honored by both Protestants and Catholics in the late 1960s differed radically from those of previous generations. In contrast to films like *One Foot in Heaven*, the Protestant Better Films Council and the National Catholic Office of Motion Pictures jointly commemorated politically challenging films like *In the Heat of the Night* (1967) and *The Battle of Algiers* (1966).[94] The *Christian Advocate* reviewer explained that, "instinctively, the BFC reached out to honor those film visions which spoke to issues traditionally in the church's domain. This represents a considerable advance beyond the views of an earlier church generation that a 'religious' film has to make explicit noises about morality, God, and/or the Church. It also indicates that an increasing number of church members are willing and are even quite eager to receive the secular film for its implicit vision."

In the late 1960s, religious groups celebrated Hollywood's daring output. When the Catholics gave awards to *Bonnie and Clyde* (1967), one writer commented that the decision to honor the blood-ridden evocation of the violent 1930s gave the Catholic Office the kind of backlash that the Protestant BFC had received over *The Pawnbroker* in 1964 and *Who's Afraid of Virginia Woolf?* in 1966.[95] What became evident was a growing cultural divide between liberal members of the church hierarchy and the more conservative people in the pews. Methodist leaders were spending more time looking at Hollywood films than producing their own. This posture suggested a subtle abjuration of producing films in favor of the more passive role of critiquing Hollywood's output as pagan parables or the prophetic words of Balaam's ass. Ironically, a denomination that drifted into liberalism in its social and moral concerns also served as the seedbed for a fundamentalist backlash. A Methodist minister from Tupelo, Mississippi, Rev. Don Wildmon, grew his own grassroot organization, the National Federation for Decency, to combat pornography and what he saw as an anti-Christian bias in Hollywood.

As it sought to coordinate a systematic relationship among various media and develop a comprehensive approach, the 1972 General Conference of the United Methodist Church established United Methodist Communications (UMC). In November 1979, the UMC made a report to their General Conference looking back over thirty-three years and recommended the best paths for the future. Significantly, it preferred television over film, as it was more pervasive and influential.[96] From its long-standing commitment to communication in the 18th century, with the Methodist pastor John Dickens's shoestring venture into publishing tracts and books (founding the Methodist Book Concern in 1789 with $600 of his own money),[97] the Methodist enthusiasm for using all available media led them to pioneer religious periodicals such as the *Christian Advocate* and expand into the equally venturesome experiments of using magic lantern slides, filmstrips, and motion pictures.[98] But the era of movie production was now seen as declining.

Rather than producing films, Methodists now assumed the mantle of critical analyses of film, both negative and positive. Writers and scholars like William Miller, Dr. William Jones, Rev. James Wall, Kenneth Winston (editor of the United Methodist Church monthly for high school students, *Face to Face*), and even the critic Bosley Crowther established provocative Methodist templates for critiquing Hollywood rather than contributing to the production of Methodist media.[99] Jones, for example, had proposed in the early 1960s that local churches could hold a three-hour study on the problems of the family by watching the "secular" motion picture *The Dark at the Top of the Stairs* (1960), while a seminary class could be assigned to watch *The Hustler* (1961) and write a paper on its treatment of sin, death, and resurrection.[100] A special issue of the *Christian Advocate* dealt specifically with film, including Malcolm Boyd's discussion of mature, "adults-only" films, and a review of Ingmar Bergman's 1961–63 religious trilogy (*Through a Glass Darkly, Winter Light, The Silence*), which probed the absence and silence of

God in a modern world. The Saint Clement's Film Association out of New York helped to schedule these secular films for local parishes and developed comprehensive discussion guides for each. Howard Tower, representative to the entertainment industry for the Methodist Television, Radio, and Film Commission, examined how to build bridges between a global film industry and intelligent church leaders. By 1964, most critics assumed that churches had failed in making their own movies.[101] Rev. William Dalglish, speaking for the UMC General Board of Education, indicted the denominations that ignored media. In particular, he pointed to the church's neglect of potentially worthwhile resources that instructed one in Christian formation (e.g., many provocative, short, Academy Award–winning animations such as Norman McLaren's *Neighbors* [1952], Gene Deitch's *Munro* [1961], and John Hubley's *The Hat* [1963]).[102]

The UMC did document its history with one of its own animated films, producing Greg Killmaster's *Clayride: A Gallop through Methodist History* (ca. 1970), a lively and quite amusing narrative of the Methodist Church done in clay animation. The fast-paced cartoon starts by saying "Well, back when the country was very young, John Wesley said, 'There's a job to be done,'" and takes off from there, condensing two hundred years of American Methodist history into four and a half minutes.

In a remarkable attempt to research its own denominational traffic, in 1972 TRAFCO surveyed how churches were using films. They found that the greatest setback to usage was the lack of trained or confident leaders who could project the films. TRAFCO realized that it needed to assert more oversight to better equip both the local ministers and the denomination. Education was necessary at both the local and national levels. Perhaps it is not as ironic as it might seem that the filmmaker, and former Methodist, George Lucas would come out of the University of Southern California film school. USC, originally owned by the Methodist Church, saw its cinema program initiated by postwar Methodists such as Herb Farmer and Wilber "Bill" Blume, who had joint involvement with TRAFCO. The California bishop Donald Tippet, the USC jurisdictional representative Howard LeSourd from Boston University, and the RFC had been invited to locate their headquarters at USC in the Department of Cinema.[103] The head of the department, Dr. Lester Beck, encouraged his student Glenn McMurray to bring together his Methodist heritage and his passion for film and take a "part-time" job as executive secretary of TRAFCO, experimenting with a venture to integrate religion, morality, and entertainment. One of McMurray's first undertakings in his concern for Christian relevance was to capitalize on the popular appeal of Bishop Gerald Kennedy for fifteen-minute visual sermons, such as "Good News" (1955) and a series of sequels called "Coffee with Kennedy" (ca. 1960).[104] Exploiting the USC film library facilities, McMurray, like any enterprising young film student, found ways to distribute these films. He coordinated controversial debates on the "just war" in the Bovard Auditorium at USC, drafting the pacifists Dr. Henry Hitt Crane and Bishop Garfield Oxnam, all of which culminated in a film titled *Which Way to Peace?* (ca. 1960).[105] Thus one can find Wesleyan roots in the nation's premiere film school.

USC's Cinema Department also hosted the International Workshop on Audio-Visual Communication in 1957, overseen by the communication researcher George Gerbner and Rev. John Harrell. Cathedral Films sponsored the workshop on religious films with a grant to establish a graduate course for students, seminarians of diverse denominations, and specialized church workers.[106] The Cathedral Studio producer Friedrich argued that expanding such workshops would speedily help to "disintegrate" the "walls of resistance" among churches.[107]

Various steps of expansion occurred through various mergers, as TRAFCO became the Joint Committee on Communications in 1972 and United Methodist Communications in 1976. That year, the Nashville-based UMC studio produced more than twenty 16mm color motion pictures from about eight to thirty minutes in length.[108] The distributor Diane Cristina identified these works as typically focusing on Methodist programs (*One Great Hour of Sharing*, 1969) and on ecumenical productions promoting marriage enrichment and parenting.[109]

The historian Bill Agee found that the UMC "provided a film distribution network for the churches until 1982 when the Methodists combined with six other groups: the Christian Church, the Lutheran Church in America, Maryknoll Missioners, the National Council of Churches, the Presbyterian Church (USA), the United Church of Christ, to form EcuFilm."[110] Established on January 1, 1982, through the merger of the library of the UMC with the film services of other denominations, EcuFilm invited all NCC members to join, united through a new, toll-free number.[111] EcuFilm's catalog provided options for more moderate to liberal religious markets. Classics like Cathedral's *Living Christ* series (1951–57), the works of J. Arthur Rank, TRAFCO's 1956 version of *John Wesley*, and VHS copies of the Lutheran Church in America's 1960s television series *Davey and Goliath* were juxtaposed with more didactic but provocative works or propaganda, such as *Why We're in the World Council of Churches* (1968) from the Disciples of Christ and the

Faces on Faith series (ca. 1970s) from UMC Productions. In *Questions of Faith* (ca. 1970s), twenty-six contemporary thinkers, like Harvey Cox, Martin Marty, Madeleine L'Engle, and Desmond Tutu, reflected on questions like "Who Is Jesus?" and "What Happens after Death?"

Methodists appropriated whatever means of communication they could to spread the Gospel message and to minister to diverse classes of people, just as their founder, John Wesley, adapted the evangelist George Whitefield's outdoor preaching style to develop his circuit-riding ministry to rural, unchurched areas. Brother Charles Wesley's hymns enabled preachers to smuggle theology into the hearts and minds of lustily singing congregations. So, in the 20th century, an innovative Methodist denomination methodically planned and executed a strategy of missions through film, working with Protestants of all stripes to present cinematic stories of salvation, justice, and hope. Methodists, in fact, formed the backbone of the most ecumenical cooperation among Protestants in the use of film, the Protestant Film Commission.

Emergence of the Protestant Film Commission

In 1937, an essay for the *Christian Herald* titled "Berries for the King's Plate" commended the work of aforementioned Dean Howard LeSourd of Columbia University, whom the Methodist marketer William Stidger called "evangelism's first modern media star."[112] LeSourd envisioned developing moral character through visual teaching. Such "character-building" episodes were built on a "study of the screen," from which spectators could, to repeat his famous phrase, "pluck berries from the garden fit for kings." For example, in *The Passing of the Third Floor Back* (1935), a stranger visits a woman named Vivian and persuades her not to leave for an assignation to sell her body and soul. When she asks, "You . . . are . . . the Christ?," he responds, "I am a fellow lodger." Questions would follow asking not who is Christ, but also what would viewers do if confronted with such a choice. LeSourd found character development more important than religious doctrine.[113]

The issue of how Protestants related to films continued into the war years. The *Christian Herald* columnist R. G. Stott asserted, "No, I am not ashamed to be seen coming out of a motion-picture house. . . . An official in the motion-picture industry told me once that the movies were never intended to preach sermons or build character. But they can! And they should!" While some may believe in "art for art's sake," Stott pointed out that "all of the *truly great* films both 'preach' and 'build character'!" Like LeSourd, Stott's emphasis on character development rather than church dogma promoted a form of American civil religion. He believed that a church/Hollywood joint venture could be mutually beneficial, if both cooperated in building a market for moral entertainment products: "Producers cannot and will not please thoughtful, church-centered Americans unless these religious-minded people *support the product!*"[114]

Stott's call for reciprocity paralleled a militant tendency in mainstream American Christianity, with its concern for the moral life of the nation, and particularly of the movie diet of children. The *Christian Herald* trumpeted, "America is movie-conscious. Eighty million Americans pay to see a movie at least once a week. What they get for their money is sometimes good, and sometimes bad; there is inspiration and comfort on the screen, and there is destructive dynamite! The younger generation goes more regularly to the movie than to the church. . . . Character is shaped in the seats before the screen; idols and ideals and models of behavior are created, hair-do's and actions are imitated. Whether we like it or not, the movie is here to stay; it is as potent an educational force as church or school."[115] As the liveliest issue next to temperance, concern for children led to the formation of the Motion Picture Council of Protestant Women in 1945, sponsored by the *Herald*. Twenty-seven women, mostly wives of leading American churchmen, were to attend previews of motion pictures five days a week, "studying them, analyzing them, and telling you in this magazine, month by month, just what they think of them. They will speak frankly."[116]

Their militant Protestant voice spoke out on the movie question, countering those who protested, "It's no use; you might as well try to reform the Devil; this movie business has been his from the start!" The honorary chair, Mrs. Daniel Poling, articulated their twofold charge: first, they would "supply readers of judgments on movies that would be fair and impartial, serving as guides for those who had no way of knowing the suitability of a film they or their children wished to see, and second, they would influence the industry, by the weight of broad Protestant opinion, to supplant the bad with the good."[117]

Two years after the Protestant Motion Picture Council (PMPC) had been formed under the auspices of the *Herald* to provide Hollywood film reviews, the publication asked what fruit had been born from churches appealing to Hollywood producers.[118] As arbiters of Protestant taste who frequently investigated the relations of Hollywood and American Protestantism, the *Herald* concluded that the results were sadly disappointing on the subjects of "Religion and the Church," with spiritual fundamentals escaping most screenwriters and producers. Specifically, they complained that more respectful treatment had been given to Roman Catholic priests than to Protestant ministers, and that "On Film Morals," the bold treatment of sex had given rise to "quite a galaxy of predatory females and philandering males."[119]

Documenting the case study of one congregation's adventures with visual aids ("Starting from scratch and learning the hard way!"), the *Herald* writer William Hockman set forth a blueprint for churches to build "dream" programs with this "new-fangled stuff."[120] He would enlist boys to clean the gates of the 16mm projectors, with others learning to splice film. Inspired by the current best-selling novel *Mr. Blandings Builds His Dream House* (1946), Hockman showed how one man got a "yen" to create a Visual Education Committee and start showing films. Not unexpectedly, Hockman's dream included purchasing books like his own *Visual Aids in the Church* (ca. 1948) as well as subscribing to magazines such as *Religious Education, Church International Journal*, and *Educational Screen*. Most important, Hockman set forth logistical directions for budgets and facilities.[121]

RCA advertised their special "Sound Systems for Churches" in numerous religious periodicals, and Bell and Howell followed suit with their cheap, lightweight 16mm equipment and powerful amplifier.[122] Blueprints for small church auditoriums, with proper installation of projector, speaker, and screens, and advice on ventilation, acoustics, and safe electrical facilities, were supplied by the various producers of film apparatuses.[123] Planning a vital church program now required audiovisual aids. As one church film promoter, Harry Strauss, confessed, "We may as well admit it: when the motion picture was invented, the children of darkness were smarter (as well as wealthier) than the children of light," but churches had been "woefully obsolete and sinfully neglectful" in failing to utilize this potent instrument for teaching and inspiring congregations.[124]

But borrowing Hollywood product was not enough for many Christian organizations and mission boards. In a scathing attack on Hollywood films, the Baptist pastor Herbert Miles published *Movies and Morals*, in which he castigated the *Herald* for leading young Christians into temptation.[125] The only solution he could see was for Christians to plant the seed of filmmaking in churches: "First the blade, then the stalk, then the ear." Although Christianity's use of the "movie invention" was still in its infancy, he envisioned a bright future, as numerous denominations, including Lutherans, Southern Baptists, the Evangelical and Reformed Church, Methodists, and Presbyterians, had joined to form a new organization to "bring about production of films for use in the churches"—namely, the Religious Film Association (RFA).[126] Financing would come, he believed, through denominational channels.

Rather than remain mere consumers of another's product, several visionaries proposed that denominations join in producing their own culture. Leadership came in 1945 from the Protestant Film Commission, which coordinated the labors of nineteen religious denominations and thirteen leading interdenominational agencies. Its twofold purpose was to try to produce some high-quality dramatic and documentary Christian 16mm films for distribution to various churches, schools, and community groups, and to stimulate and encourage the production of films with positive religious themes from the Hollywood film industry.[127] To help direct these bodies, they released a pamphlet, titled *Teaching Eternal Truths*, that aimed at instructing church groups on basic principles for operating projectors and holding film programs.[128]

The creation of the commission stemmed from three key sources. First, many leaders were bolstered by the success of the Episcopal filmmaker James Friedrich. Second, seeds were planted during a 1943 Missionary Education Movement's Missions Photo Institute in which the American Bible Society's Rome Betts called for representation of Protestants in Hollywood. Finally, the Yale professor Dr. Everett Parker recognized this power of mass media and was prompted to organize an interdenominational Joint Protestant Radio Committee. His organization joined with Sid Mack's PFC of the National Council of Churches to establish a Broadcasting and Film Commission.[129] Numerous other leaders jumped onto the cinematic bandwagon. George Heimrich, who had worked for the PFC, linked with Alex Ferguson, director of visual aids for Congregational Christian Churches, to promote a filmstrip titled *Visual Aids and Their Use in Religious Education* (ca. 1945).[130] Fred Essex of the American Baptist Church and the UMC bishop Gerald Kennedy also committed to produce films on missions, stewardship, Christian education, and evangelism.[131] The most significant set of the BFC would become the *Know Your Neighbor* series, headed up by the producer Alan Shilin in 1957. Targeting a primary audience of young children, the six short films dealt with missions and world brotherhood, featuring such titles as *African Cousins, Bantu Girl,* and *Honshu Holiday*. A film like *Luzon Mountain Boy*, for example, would show how arduously a family in the Philippines worked in the rice paddies, yet also how they would festively give thanks for a good harvest.[132] Various religious traditions contributed to the fertile soil out of which denominational films would sprout.[133]

Newsweek reported that the PFC had been organized in November 1947 to produce high-quality, nontheatrical movies with religious messages and to guide Hollywood studios toward making more moral films.[134] Simultaneously, the PFC realized that churches did not know how to run film programs, and so they enlisted the *Herald* in helping them program their films.[135] In 1947, the PFC announced a series of seven films in both 35mm and 16mm format, the first being *Beyond Our Own*. The producer Jack Chertock proclaimed, "Not only will *Beyond Our Own* be shown in churches, in connection with evening meetings, but in order to give wider distribution it will be released in factories, jails, domestic relations courts, and before clubs and conferences."[136] *Beyond Our Own* was keyed to address the mission theme of worldwide evangelism in 1947/48.[137] Released in November 1947, the famed *Show Boat* dance director Sammy Lee's slick and professional film dealt with two brothers, one who becomes a flashy, ambitious lawyer and the other (DeForest Kelley, of *Star Trek* fame), a humble and idealistic medical missionary in China.[138] The lawyer wins a huge settlement between oil interests, but his son is killed in an automobile accident. Distraught, he visits his brother in China and helps him evacuate children during a bombardment. They suffer the death of their friend, a Chinese Christian whose faith had sustained him during persecution. The humble faith of the Chinese Christians awakens the lawyer to realize the emptiness of his own life and to see the light.[139] He returns home to enlist in benevolent charity and missionary parish work.[140] The story summons viewers to seek a power "beyond our own" (a generic euphemism for Christ) that will enable people to "go home" when their time has come.

According to the *Christian Herald*, the film broke church exhibition records, thanks in large part to its "vital religious message."[141] Two hundred fifty prints quickly recouped the initial investment, with the PFC hoping to raise another million for future works. Distributed through the newly formed RFA, the nontheatrical film was exhibited in scores of American cities and internationally from Manila to London, with the PFC rallying denominations to get on board.[142] *Newsweek* allowed that the "overly ambitious" film was weak on dialogue but still a "significant step toward visual education in the churches."[143] It was praised as a film that actually compared favorably with the quality of Hollywood, and reviewers conceded that "spiritually, the picture stirs."[144]

After having praised many Hollywood industry films, the *Herald* congratulated the PFC and honored *Beyond Our Own* with its "Four (Church) Bells," a distinction recognizing it as "Film of the Month."[145] "The PFC is to be congratulated," chimed in the *New York Herald Tribune*, while the *Religious News Service* called it a "milestone in the history of the religious motivated film."[146] Riding the crest of success, the *Herald* marketed a Bulletin Board Holder designed to slip the title of their "Picture of the Month" from each issue of the magazine under its seal so that people in the churches could see it every week. *Beyond Our Own* earned its own sealed bulletin, the first nontheatrical religious production to do so.

With a preliminary coffer of $250,000 to make seven films, the PFC strategized to produce Christian education, applied Christian living, and humanitarian film projects. Forthcoming films were to deal with racial discrimination, religious intolerance, and mental health. In the postwar era where social concerns trumped theological concerns within several denominations, the PFC sought to erase sectarian differences and focus on common concerns such as the family; personal psychology (coordinating and synthesizing psychology, mental health, and religion); applied ethics (utilizing subtle and persuasive techniques of propaganda, without being "obvious, preachy, moralistic or inept"); social and race relations (the church "cannot be silent on this important question"); labor, democracy, and citizenship; world peace (with the advent of the atomic bomb); and films for children.[147] The PFC moved decisively toward humanistic rather than theological topics.

Addressing the annual meeting of the Associated Church Press in 1946, Paul Heard, executive secretary of the PFC, indicated that the new commission was interested in a formula for constructive films that "make for the better of human life" and enhance the box office returns for the industry.[148] *Variety* reported that the American Bible Society (ABS) was likewise branching out from its straight publication work to map out large-scale film production plans, particularly in its angling for support from Hollywood talent. They planned to shoot 150 half-hour films on the Old and New Testament in color, at the rate of twenty-four a year. They acknowledged that some of the material could be labeled as unfit for children.[149] The trade periodical noted in 1946 that five thousand churches of all denominations were equipped for 16mm screenings, with another seventy-five thousand having 16mm projectors on order. Anson Bond, formerly with the army's motion picture division, was to produce the series with ABS supervision. Involved in Bible distribution since 1821, the ABS furnished its film on equipping Christians for life, *The Whole Armor* (1951), along with more than thirty-three million copies of Scripture, to the armed forces through chaplains.[150] The stickiest challenge of the society's project emerged from a complication in its unique charter that prohibited it from giving any interpretation to the Scriptures, which they recognized would occur in translating the Bible from word to moving image.[151]

The *Herald* announced in 1943 that the ABS "has put the story of the Bible on celluloid—on 16mm film—and made it available to the churches of America," in a film titled *The Book of the World* (1943). The society suggested that freewill offerings be taken at each showing, aiming at an amount of "at least $10.00 to cover distribution expense, cost of prints, and to help build up a fund for future pictures."[152] In the late 1940s, ABS also released *The Word Giveth Light*, a film showing the publication of a braille Bible, and a twenty-minute picture called *The Nativity*, the first reel of a new series of films planned to cover all four Gospels, guaranteed in a King James text narration.[153]

One highly recommended PFC program, produced by Julien Bryan's nonprofit documentary film organization, the International Film Foundation, was *My Name Is Han* (1949), shot in China for exclusive church use. Extremely well photographed and featuring a cast of Chinese amateur actors, it effectively portrayed Christian witness in China with an economy of dialogue and detail. In a neorealist documentary style, the film begins by showing a Chinese farmer returning to a devastated home ruined by war, amid the tremendous suffering and deprivation of refugees.[154] A voice-over explains, "My name is Han. This is my family. I am a farmer, given to keeping my own counsel. But something has happened in my village and to me."

Han's peach orchard had been chopped down and he finds sand rather than good earth. As in Pearl Buck's 1931 novel, common people are set against a cosmic backdrop. The director William Jones (with the executive producer Paul Heard) chronicles the conversion of the family's faith in their own strength and land to the Christian faith. As their little house crumbles, the family stoically surveys the loss. The courageous good wife prays, cooks cheerfully, and offers thanks to the Christian God. Han initially shouts bitterly at his family for this stupid gratitude, seeing them as part of a flock of fools. As the family goes to church, Han responds, "My religion is work." When his little son plays with a bomb, the unexploded cartridge goes off and he is sent to the mission hospital. Han alone is without faith and cannot pray, but the doctors tend his son.

Neighbors from a local Christian mission show Han how to reclaim the ruined land, generously giving him topsoil, but he does not understand their charity. The missionaries then offer education for his daughter. Han concedes that this is like watching a dream; it is a miracle. The pastor explains that

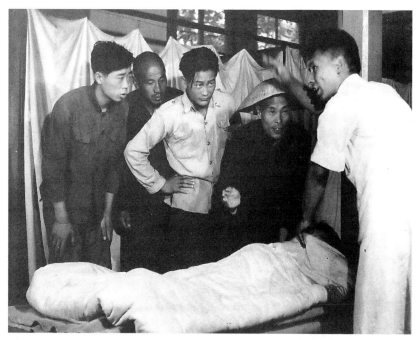

In 1949, a year before Mao Zedong established the People's Republic of China, the Protestant Film Commission produced *My Name Is Han* in China with a completely Chinese cast. Personal collection.

Christian friends must help one another, since the church serves as Christ's hands that fed, healed, and were nailed to the Cross; now the congregation's hands are His to do His deeds. As the church bell rings, Han joins his wife in praying before eating their meal, with the wife grinning at her husband. Han concludes, "A new sun shone in my life and I thought, 'How can I share this thing with others?'" As a photographed docudrama, the film made an eloquent plea for Christian missions with a tribute to the role taken by the younger churches in the spread of the Gospel.[155] The film is "sincere, genuine and appealing," wrote the *Christian Advocate* reviewer, unaware that within a few months a new communist regime would expel American missionaries and introduce collective farming.[156] Some saw the film as motivated by a desire to establish a front line of democracy and the development of young leaders for a new China, as well as a way for American Christians to study China.[157] Nevertheless, Mao had other plans.[158]

The distributor William Rogers of RFA pointed to PFC budgets in 1949 totaling more than $1.5 million, plus another million for distribution, in touting the emergence of a religious film industry. Now that the churches were beginning to spend serious money on film production, Hollywood was keen to take a look at this new phenomenon. Economic investment in religious films in the early 1950s, especially from Hollywood executives, sparked speculation, leading John Adams III, a former college professor and Episcopal churchman, to ask why. Adams explained that Spyros Skouras, president of 20th Century-Fox from 1942 to 1962, decided that Hollywood should perform a service for the religious community. This public service, Adams explained, should not be merely sectarian, but usable by a majority of religious groups. Adams explained that the greatest challenge was finding good subject material that reached across denominational lines.[159]

In an article entitled "What Makes a Religious Movie?," Harry Spencer interviewed Adams, who was also a unit producer at Fox. Adams announced that they had been looking to produce films for church markets and, together with his colleague John Healy, the pair had looked at some 125 pictures already being used by the churches. They decided that the typical subject matter fell into six categories; inspirational, instructional, fund-raising, support for missionary work, promotion of greater church attendance, and entertainment. After reading hundreds of proposed manuscripts, they decided to produce a public-domain short story (in the public domain) by Leo Tolstoy, "Where Love Is, God Is," which they renamed *The Guest*, successfully drafting Academy Award–winning composer Alfred Newman to provide the musical score. In the film, a shoemaker who has been an agnostic since the death of his wife and child is told that Jesus will visit his shop. Waiting all day, he welcomes all manner of visitors. When it appears that Jesus did not show up, he reads Matthew 25:35 and perceives the real meaning of its words: Jesus did, in fact, appear to him incognito through all his visitors, and therefore his faith is restored.

Adams articulated what religious movies could and could not achieve: "The local user must realize that except in the case of strictly inspirational films, a motion picture is only a tool. It is not an end in itself. The local teacher must be prepared to present or discuss his subject as well as show the film." Skouras concurred, "The motion picture industry in general, and our company in particular, can and should perform a service for the religious community by providing it with films of high quality on religious subjects. These films would be in addition to theatrical pictures on religious or social questions, such as *Gentleman's Agreement* (1947) and *I'd Climb the Highest Mountain* (1951)."[160]

20th Century-Fox helped Adams and Healy shoot Tolstoy's story as a parable in a modern urban setting.[161] Spencer recognized a new strategy of investment in religious films like *The Guest*:

> Ten years ago the accusation of technical incompetence might have been leveled at the producer of a church film with ample justification. At that time the movie, usually a silent one, consisted mostly of random shots taken by some missionary in his travels, furious faces, as he aimed the camera like a machine gun at a row of mission workers alternated with long processions of children coming out of Sunday school, each pupil in turn mugging the lens as he walked past. But those days are gone. Today all church motion pictures are in sound, written by professional scriptwriters and photographed by professional cameramen. Before 1940 it was unusual to spend $1,000 on a church film. In 1950 the Protestant churches together invested more than $80,000 in the film *Again . . . Pioneers!* Authorities now agree that it takes more than a spiritual theme and a few random sequences by amateur photographers to produce a convincing religious film.[162]

Spencer envisioned the cinematic retelling of biblical stories like the Good Samaritan, the prodigal son, and the story of Ruth in modern dress, in contrast to Friedrich's recreation of traditional biblical settings. Spencer emphasized that the motion picture was only a tool and not an end in itself; however, he championed its use without too much interference from religious commentators. In the case of an inspirational film, he warned that "the teacher must know when to keep his mouth shut. To talk about or discuss such a film immediately after showing can very easily destroy the effect of the film completely by the attempt to reason out an emotional response."[163]

Jason Joy, director of public relations of the Motion Picture Producers and Distributors Association, was put in charge of the program, with Adams and Healy assigned to the project. They realized they would have to produce films usable by a majority of denominations if the films were to cover costs of production.[164] One such crossover ecumenical film was Paul Heard's PFC documentary *Kenji Comes Home*, nominated for the Best Documentary Feature Academy Award in 1949. *Kenji* contrasted Christian faith with an emergent postwar communism in Japan. The main character, Kenji, is torn between the glowing promises of Communism and the ideals of his girlfriend Aki's religion, Christianity. With the humiliated return of conquered Japanese soldiers after the dropping of the atomic bomb at Hiroshima, young Kenji comes home and there is no one to welcome him. Snapshots remind him of a lost cultural and religious tradition: tea ceremonies, the divine sun emperor, and ancestors. But now the old world of the emperor has been destroyed. Looking for work, Kenji finds none, but he does rescue a dirty-faced orphan and shoeshine boy, Shiro, who had been beaten up and robbed by hooligans. Aki, the younger sister of a dead comrade, surprises him with her talk of a Christian hope for the future. He sees the American military as foreign masters imposing labor unions as a necessary component of democracy. In contrast, a local communist leader emerges, calling for revolution and a rejection of Western culture. When Shiro enrolls in a Japanese Christian school, Kenji discovers that all books are available in the Christian library, even ones on communism and Buddhism. He chooses to read the Bible. In his struggles to find himself, Kenji is torn between a Protestant minister, symbolizing both the Christian faith and democracy, and his comrades. When he discovers the treachery of his union peers, who justify their means for a political end, he loses his job. The film's ending, with his girlfriend praying directly into the camera that there might be something the church could do, directly engages the viewers. Indeed, the film argues that there is something that American church audiences could do . . . for Kenji; and so the film ends with a dramatic and specific appeal for action.

After *Kenji*, the prolific Heard wrote, produced, and directed numerous films for the PFC, including a mystery titled the *Hong Kong Affair* (1958), starring television's Maverick costar Jack Kelly. But one of the more curious directors hired by Heard and the PFC was the former silent film director William Beaudine. Beaudine's work with Mary Pickford in *Sparrows* (1926) was replete with Christian symbols and sentimental Victorian themes that recommended him to the marginal religious industry. Out of work in the late 1930s, Beaudine dabbled in sex hygiene films and PFC message films. According to his biographer Wendy Marshall, Beaudine eschewed the religious life; he dropped his kids off at Christian Science meetings and regularly sprinkled his conversations with "goddamns" when directing.[165] Down on his luck, he had been working cheaply at a smaller independent Hollywood studio on Poverty Row known as Monogram Studios when he accepted work from the PFC, mainly because they doubled his Monogram salary to at least $2,500 per film.

One of his first works for the PFC was shooting a Passion play performance (based on the famous Bavarian play of the last week of Christ) with the citizens of Lawton, Oklahoma, working it into a film titled *The Lawton Story* (1949).[166] The producer Kroger Babb wanted to make a film on this Okie Oberammergau, and he persuaded wealthy Texas and Oklahoma oilmen to bankroll the filmed pageant. The screenplay combined a story of the pageant's founder with a story of two estranged brothers whose lives take different paths. Attending the pageant, the brothers' hearts are softened by its message (along with the catalytic influence of a girl loved by both men). Premiering in Lawton on April 1, 1949, the film sold out the local Ritz theater, with ticket prices for the evening fetching the highest price in Texas movie history at that point, ranging from $5 to $1,000 a seat. But screenings outside Oklahoma and Georgia failed miserably at the box office, where audiences laughed at dialogue between Christ and his disciples thanks to their heavy Southern drawls. "It became the only film that had to be dubbed from English into English," wrote the critic Kenneth Turan.[167] A new campaign renamed the film *Prince of Peace*, redubbed the dialogue with radio talent, and promised that those who saw it would find God inside. This strategy generated enormous profits; the *New York Daily News* called it the "miracle of Broadway," and the film played for eight weeks with every seat sold. To promote the project on its four-walling run (a method of film distribution in which the filmmakers rent the theater themselves and exhibit it directly), the filmmakers and actors would accompany the film. For example, Carl Foreman, one of the characters, would step out on stage to preach mini-sermons and sell stamp-sized copies of the New Testament and eight-by-ten color prints of Christ for two dollars each.

Beaudine directed eleven human interest stories for Heard, usually in only about a week of shooting, between December 1947 and April 1955, and these works were targeted at churches, schools, and religious clubs: "They were designed to connect with wayward or inactive members of the faith and to show them how their lives would be improved if they returned to the fold."[168] Nevertheless, critics thought his films "had the flavor of any good motion picture made for regular consumption."[169] Beaudine wasn't the proselytizing type; he simply had a job to direct films. He viewed religion, and especially the Catholic Church, as his "one big boodoo."[170] In 1948, PFC again sought Beaudine's professional talents for *Second Chance*, the story of a prosperous, middle-aged couple who drifted into dormancy in their church life until a diagnosis of serious illness evokes spiritual reevaluation and persuades them to make a fresh start. Other Beaudine films like *Again . . . Pioneers!*, *City Story* (1950, narrated by the Hollywood actor Glenn Ford), *Each according to His Faith* (1955), and *The Secret of the Gift* (1959), were designated for exclusive religious distribution on the "church circuit." According to Wendy Marshall, "Because of Beaudine's aversion to preaching, he was the perfect choice to create films with a strong story whose message was evident but not overwhelming."[171]

William Beaudine directed *Again . . . Pioneers* for the Protestant Film Commission, emphasizing social action as an extension of one's Christian faith. The Hollywood actress Colleen Townsend reproaches her father (Tom Powers) for siding with the Citizens' Committee against the local migrant workers. Personal collection.

Golda Maud Bader, wife of the ecumenical evangelist Jesse Bader, became the *Herald's* gatekeeper for suitable films, and found films like the previously mentioned *Again . . . Pioneers!* made for the Home Missions Council of North America, quite inspirational. It starred the 20th Century-Fox actress Colleen Townsend (a budding star who had graced a 1948 cover of *Life* magazine)[172] as a student of religion helping Fairview, a typical American community, to recognize the needs of a group of underprivileged migrants who had settled on the outskirts of the city. Tom Powers, a prominent attorney, goes to church on Sunday but tends to take his religion somewhat for granted. His daughter, played by Townsend, believes in putting faith into action. When the city of Fairview wants to rid itself of slum migrants, the daughter needles her father to actually see what is happening. Convinced by her passion, Tom helps the group to rebuild rather than legislating against them, as he and his fellow church members begin a new pioneering task.[173] The film's style, which explored the heart of the American dream as either moral or materialistic, harked back to the classic parallel editing of D. W. Griffith in juxtaposing the affluent family with the poor family, wrapping it up with the upbeat message of seeking to assimilate those who are different rather than "eliminating" them.

Summary

As we have seen, during the late 1940s the ecumenically minded Protestant Film Commission, while seeking to coordinate the visions of its major members (and vigilantly overseeing the work of characters like Beaudine), sparked groundbreaking works that primed denominational pumps. *Beyond Our Own*, *My Name Is Han*, *The Guest*, and *Kenji Comes Home* reveal concerns both for evangelism and for social action, for spreading the Gospel message and for helping others. Positive responses to these films suggested that a Protestant audience existed to support films that essentially "preached to the choir," but a choir that was remarkably diverse. Each of these films contributed to a mainline Protestant vision of living out the message of Jesus and promoted an inclusive, ecumenical spirit, drawing together the various Protestant sects; however, several other denominations, such as the Methodists, envisioned their own ways to make and use films.

Reformed and Dissenting Images

During the 16th-century Reformation, a radical group of icono-
clasts exploded out of the Reformed Church, denouncing what they saw as
the blind veneration of images preserved by the Roman Catholic Church.
In 1566, in the northern, Calvinist provinces of the Netherlands, riots broke
out against "idols in paint," altar paintings, crucifixes, and statuary of saints.
Seeking to obey the Decalogue's prohibition of making or worshipping any
"graven image," the radicals "cleansed" the churches of any potential blas-
phemous art. The German reformer Martin Luther, however, had no sympathy for the image smashers, and he even sought to have his translation of
the Bible illustrated. But before spending money on art, Luther commanded,
one must take care of the poor. This mandate would shape the Christian
film industry of the Lutheran denomination, even as other Reformed and
dissenting churches, such as the Presbyterians and Baptists, would emphasize the words of Scripture in their use of film. These denominations would
explore and experiment with films as historical documents, instructional lessons, evangelistic tracts, and, surprisingly, even as parables in paint.

Lutheran Images

In the 1920s, many Lutherans viewed movies, as much as the steamship and
the piano, as "instruments of service to the Gospel." An amateur filmmaker
and Lutheran pastor, Rev. O. Hagedorn, not too far from Lake Wobegon country in Milwaukee, Wisconsin, produced church films in the early 1920s like
Little Jimmy's Prayer and *After the Fall* (in which he imaginatively incorporated Midrash details in the story of Cain and Abel). For Hagedorn, the dramatic presentation was more important than "absolute historical truth in the
details," in that film stories could "stir the emotions and teach needed lessons."[1]
Lutheran involvement in silent filmmaking culminated in road shows of an
eight-reel German biography of Martin Luther, simply titled *Martin Luther:
His Life and Times* (1923). The film chronicled Luther's reforms and drew

enthusiastic reviews from critics like Rev. Frank Jensen of *Educational Screen* magazine, opining that "art inculcates valuable lessons in a visual form."[2] The success of *Martin Luther* induced other Lutherans to sponsor a second German film on the life of Christ in 1926, entitled *INRI*, distributed in the United States as *Crown of Thorns*, despite earlier protests of the German writer Dr. H. Petri. On the cinematic portrayal of Christ, Petri complained that "efforts to depict the life of Jesus must always fail, as the movies cannot convey religious conviction or edify the soul."[3] Nevertheless, even as the Lutherans splintered into conservative and liberal groups (Lutheran Church–Missouri Synod [LCMS], American Lutheran Church, Lutheran Church of America, respectively), these two films inaugurated the Lutheran Church's foray into film.[4]

By the 1930s, Paul Kiehl, a young Lutheran pastor in St. Louis, envisioned films for children. Rooted in the LCMS, Kiehl pioneered the Lutheran Laymen's League and under its auspices produced a film titled *This Is the Life* (ca. 1935).[5] In 1938, the LCMS invested $50,000 in *The Power of God*, seeking to advance personal evangelism and to entertainingly instruct its audiences on how prayer could help people "meet and feel the Power of God." As one reviewer put it, in finding what is important for life, "prayer wins."[6] Praised as being remarkably orthodox and evangelical, the film was a bold venture by a conservative church, compounded by the fact that the endeavor actually made money.[7] With their Protestant work ethic, Lutherans, it seemed, knew how to invest their hard-earned cash.

Yet Lutherans undertook only sporadic film work. In 1943, the ABS's aforementioned celluloid story of the Bible emphasized the Lutheran tradition on how the Bible came to us by focusing on the persistence and inventiveness of the fifteenth-century German printer Johannes Gutenberg. Beginning with Saint Jerome writing his Vulgate and the odd reception of the Scriptures by the Goths, the ABS communicated the story of the Bible canon and its translation onto 16mm film in *The Book of the World*, asking only for freewill offerings from the churches to offset its cost.[8]

The Evangelical Lutheran's Visual Education Service produced another stimulating, and lucrative, drama, *Reaching from Heaven* (1948), which incorporated romance and pathos in exposing self-complacency. Using lesser Hollywood luminaries (e.g., Regis Toomey), the film highlighted how God utilizes ordinary people to accomplish His purposes. It presented contemporary moral lessons, demonstrating how self-absorbed people could be transformed by tending to the plight of a forsaken stranger or ministering to a lonely man and his little daughter. For the Lutherans, God's purposes were accomplished through changed lives.[9]

Attempting to capture a youth market, the National Lutheran Council promoted *Answer for Anne* (1949), a film focusing on the practical consequences of a high school girl's research essay on displaced persons looking for homes. Writing on the theme of "What Is Liberty?" Anne interviews a recent European immigrant. In her research with her fellow townspeople, she finds mostly negative and prejudiced answers. Her own attitude is significantly affected when she stops by the church and her pastor *shows her a film* about the living conditions of the refugees in Germany (a cunning advertisement and apologetic for using films in churches). As an early film on the problem of homelessness, it conveyed its preachment with the utmost poignancy.[10] *Answer for Anne* received a gold "Oscar" award as the best religious film at the Cleveland Film Festival, being recognized outside its normal exhibition circuit of church venues (which was rare).[11]

Through their films, Lutherans frequently addressed the practical concerns of living the Christian life. Supporting an outreach to high school students, the Lutheran Laymen's League of St. Louis brought out *Youth for the Kingdom* (1948).[12] *Lutheran Stewardship* (1950), directed by John Coyle, told the story of a Pennsylvania coal miner who becomes a Christian, loses his job, and endures resentment and persecution. The topic of stewardship is strangely interwoven in this drama about one layman converting another in a mine shaft.[13] Lutherans worked closely with Cathedral film crews, again with Coyle, in *Like a Mighty Army* (1950). The film emphasized the need for Lutheran churches to move forward in funding church work, while humorously acknowledging that "we're not glowing, not even a spark."[14] Lutheran films centered on church work, on the contributions of the laity in spreading the Gospel, and in doing good works. Lutherans may have been justified by faith, but their films illustrated that faith must bear fruit.

The apotheosis of Lutheran filmmaking occurred in 1953 with another version of *Martin Luther*, the obstreperous Augustinian monk who interfered with the steady flow of ecclesiastical revenues and the collecting of indulgences.[15] In collaboration with Lutheran Church Productions, Louis de Rochemont Associates (an organization that established the practice of the docudrama) hired the director Irving Pichel to translate the historical narrative of Luther (played by Niall MacGinnis)—the story of the German reformer that Pope Leo X had once called "a wild boar invading the vineyards" of the Roman Catholic Church—into a feature-length film.[16] Acknowledged by both the Academy of Motion Picture Arts and Sciences (with two Oscar nominations) and the National Board of Review (rating it as one of the top pictures of the year), the dramatization boasted a balanced schol-

Martin **Luther**   A MAGNIFICENT MOTION PICTURE FOR OUR TIME
Produced by Louis de Rochemont Associates   Distributed by Concordia Films

Irving Pichel directed Niall MacGinnis in a stellar performance of the Lutheran Church Productions' 1953 version of *Martin Luther*. Courtesy of Kathryn G. Gritts and the Lutheran Film Associates.

arly perspective, done in a very reverential manner. On September 10, 1953, the *New York Times* critic Bosley Crowther reviewed the film as "squarely and intelligently embracing" the tough issues of the 16th-century theological crisis occurring in the backwoods of Germany. Crowther acknowledged how excessive discourse, especially with characters incessantly talking about religion, could perilously burden a film; nevertheless, he opined that its clear and cogent conversation engaged the mind with power and passion. Likewise, Manny Farber of the *Nation* called it a "nice, well-behaved little movie" that appealed more to the mind that the eye.[17]

It met with remarkable success, especially in cities like Minneapolis, outdrawing every film being exhibited in the city. The historian Gregory Black pointed to how it was flamboyantly advertised in Houston as the story about "the monk who defied the Catholic Church." And herein was the problem: the film was viewed as provocatively sectarian by local Roman Catholics. Although approved by the Production Code run by the Roman Catholic

Joseph Breen, the Legion of Decency sought to marginalize it with its "special classification," and the Catholic Archdiocese of Chicago successfully blocked an inaugural televised showing of the film in 1956.[18] The film was accused of falsifying history, deliberately twisting the truth, and giving a misleading image of Luther, who was "perhaps the most hysterically-voiced, vehement, immoderate, and foul-mouthed preacher in history," and a communist to boot.[19] Yet for Lutherans, here was an historical documentary par excellence.

On safer topics, the American Lutheran Church Board of Foreign Missions promoted the need for missionaries in the soon-to-be state of Alaska with its sponsorship of *Alaskan Discovery* (1958). The documentary on the Inuit Christian laity was abounding with colorful, spectacular scenery. Its primary problem as a vehicle for engaging spectators, however, reflected the defect of most missionary films, namely, that it lacked a compelling story. Across the Pacific Ocean, *Cry of the China Seas* (1958), also made for the ALC Board of Foreign Mission Films, begins with a brilliant neorealist pre-title sequence: An Asian woman runs down a sand dune along the beach. Her pursuer, a Chinese soldier, raises his gun, takes aim, and fires. The woman falls and we see the contraband she has dropped, a Bible. The film turns out to be a documentary about human rights abuses in Asia, but in light of Mao's communist regime, it potently reflects the Cold War period. The "Christian way" is equated with the American way, and the church seems to be a bulwark against the unrelenting march of communism.

The LCMS would later collaborate with the Episcopal James Friedrich on a more contemporary script that ends in a more ambiguous fashion. For example, *The Lie* (1975) portrays a tough redemptive story about a white cop who accidentally shoots and kills the son of Althea, a black Christian woman. A tense situation is complicated by the cop's wife, police precinct politics, and a meddling media. When the policeman repents and seeks forgiveness in Althea's church, she points him to "someone" else who can provide grace.

Lutherans tended to coproduce many of their films with professionals and other Christian filmmakers. A good number were outsourced to producers like Cathedral and Sam Hersh of Family Films. Usually, Concordia/Lutheran TV Productions of the LCMS commissioned directors like William Claxton to produce children's films, such as *The Cheat* (1953), a tale about Freddy Fisher, who doesn't have enough money to buy his grandpa a birthday gift and so agrees to write someone's English composition in exchange for the dollar he needs. Later he feels guilty for helping a classmate cheat and he prays for help. Freddy then writes his composition about honesty, accepts God's forgiveness, and gets an *A*. In another production for the LCMS's Department of

Visual Education, Claxton directed *All That I Have* (1951), a courtroom drama about stewardship. In a film inspired by Frank Capra's populist comedy *Mr. Deeds Goes to Town* (1936), the relatives of Dr. Charlie Grayson want him declared crazy for giving $10,000 to help the poor and $50,000 for the church missionary program. His angry nephews, who hoped to inherit his money, start court proceedings to prove that their uncle is incompetent.[20] Grayson's lawyer successfully argues that all Charlie has belongs to God anyway. In *A Careless Word* (1954), a LCMS joint venture of Concordia and Family Films, Claxton dramatizes the malicious consequences of gossiping. Moving into more socially relevant material of racial prejudice in the 1960s, the Concordia production of *A Case of Christian Courage* (1966) confronts bigotry when a Christian lawyer reluctantly hires a black secretary.

By 1957, the United Lutheran Church in America would recognize the progress its denomination had made in ten years, especially through its Department of Audio-Visual Aids.[21] Known for the variety and creative diversity of their films, the United Lutheran Church and American Lutheran Church offered a cinematic smorgasbord, from basic documentaries like the aforementioned *Alaskan Discovery* (1958) to *The Difference* (1950), a promotional film pushing the advantage of Christian colleges, to a film documenting the rehabilitation of Germany by the National Lutheran Council, *Two Kingdoms* (ca. 1950).

Described as "a little classic," *The Candlemaker* (1957), an animated film from the famous British Halas/Batchelor studios about a father teaching his son how to make candles for a Christmas Eve service, received an *A+* rating for its teaching on stewardship.[22] Working with Cathedral Films, the Board of Education of the Lutheran Church of America commissioned Coyle to direct *45 Tioga Street: The Use of the Bible in Daily Lives* (1952), an urban drama about a young teenager who returns home from a church confirmation class with a Bible given to him by the minister. Two neighbors, a converted Czech Jewish-Christian and a black Protestant, mentor the fourteen-year-old and share how the Bible helped them confront many temptations and difficulties. When the boy returns home, his father, who vehemently opposes religion, tears the Bible up and throws it out the window.[23] *Question 7* (1961), produced by de Rochemont Associates and directed by Stuart Rosenberg, confronted the Cold War in a drama about a fifteen-year-old musician and son of a Lutheran pastor in communist East Germany, forced to choose between his Christian faith and a scholarship in musical education. Based on actual incidents, the screenwriter Allen Sloane sought to raise issues of the political relevance of living out the Gospel in a totalitarian society.

According to the AP religion writer George Cornell, Rolf Forsberg, who directed the provocative *Parable*, scored with another controversial film, *The Antkeeper* (1966). One Methodist lawyer protested against humans being portrayed as ants by saying "I don't like bugs."[24] The Lutheran Church in America distributed the allegorical film under the auspices of the National Council of Churches, with reactions ranging from the film being too obvious to it being too obscure. The actor Fred Gwynne (later of *The Munsters*)[25] narrated the tale, in which the eponymous character takes on the form of an ant to communicate with warring red and black ants, eventually sacrificing his life. Ants brazenly assert their independence by trying to take over the garden, killing, stealing, and abusing other ants. The antkeeper realizes that they do not understand him, so (in a surrealistic sequence) he sends his son as an ant to communicate his will. They inevitably kill the son as well. Photographed by the professional nature micro-cinematographer Robert Crandall (who shot the mating dance of the scorpions in Disney's *Living Desert*), the film communicates the Fall, Incarnation, and Redemption of rebellious creatures as told to a group of Mexican peasant children. The *Christian Advocate* reviewer James Wall found

> the use of ants as models of men too distasteful to be convincing. There is the suspicion that once we think of men as mere ants in the sight of an omnipotent God, we are more likely to step on—or annihilate—these ant-men when they go against this God. Indeed the extent to which we support capital punishment, wars against "atheistic" communism, or any other form fatal or degrading to man, may be related to our attitude to human life in relationship to God. In any event, this is a film which is technically admirable, but highly questionable in subject matter. If you like biblical allegories that are excessively literal, you might try this one.[26]

Yet it was Wall's interpretation that remained too literal, for there is mischief in Forsberg's film, a strategy that made the viewer think in topsy-turvy ways. Forsberg's film remains more a parable than an allegory and opens up discussion rather than forcing a one-to-one correspondence of image to interpretation. Red ants are not just communists. Nevertheless, *The Antkeeper* fit snugly into the mission of the division of parish education of the American Lutheran Church in Minneapolis, with its "Dialogue Thrust in Films Program."[27] It sparked discussion and debate. Other films stretched the dramatic limits of the status quo. Forsberg's adaptation of Francis Thompson's poem "The Hound of Heaven," titled *Stalked* (1967), triggered resistance in its oppressive and haunting portrayal of a man running from God. Stylistically, *Stalked* owes its grotesque medieval look to Rod Serling's *Twilight Zone*, countering the usual rose-colored, sentimental portrayal of the Christian life. Forsberg explained that his visual theme of human isolation centers on "Christ on the Cross—from the Midway game display of a cheap, chalk crucifix among the Kewpie doll prizes, through the Calvary diorama in the wax museum, through the modernistic crucifix in the church, to the living flesh-and-blood human being who saves The Man from being consumed in the fire."[28] Forsberg's Man prefers "wax to flesh," the simulacra to the real Word made flesh. *Stalked* asks the question "What then *is* the Incarnation of Christ?" Forsberg's film forces the viewer to ponder the unrelenting love of God.

One other timely but controversial film from the Lutheran Film Associates crossed over into the secular market. William Jersey's cinema verité–styled *A Time for Burning* (1967) showcased the attempted integration of a Lutheran minister's white church with a neighboring black ghetto in Omaha, Nebraska. The film frankly chronicled the actual experiences of Lutheran church members, as filmmakers William Jersey and Barbara Connell captured the racial conflict of 1966. Members of the all-white, middle-class Augustana Lutheran Church and their pastor, William Youngdahl, sought to build a bridge of understanding and fellowship with members of Omaha's black community. Again, Wall reviewed it as "an actual report of what happened to one pastor and his congregation when an attempt was made to establish racial dialogue in a transitional urban area. . . . Low-keyed, the resistance to racial co-operation is of the subtle 'the time is not right' variety."[29]

Compelling issues of life, death, and selfishness were humorously addressed in Nicholas Webster's *Number One* (1979), in which the author of a pop psychology book called *Me First* is given an opportunity in the afterlife to make a case for why he should be chosen to return to earth. His competition includes a cop who defended a widow attacked by punks, a young black boy needing a kidney, and an African priest dying of disease. In the debate, the psychologist is indicted for his selfishness. In fact, the only character witness he can summon is a lifeguard who was reading the psychologist's book at the same time that the author was drowning.

One of the most popular and enduring productions of the Lutherans was the television series *Davey and Goliath* (from Clokey Films, the creators of *Gumby*). The church-produced Claymation series directly addressed social issues deemed important to Lutherans as well as ecumenical audiences. The Lutheran Church recognized momentous changes in society itself during the show's span from 1961 to 1971. Most significantly, the series reflected fresh perspectives on blacks, Hispanics, Asians, Native Americans, women, and urban citizens while still emphasizing the central theme that God cares. Davey moved from his rural neighborhood to one that was multiracial and multicultural, and one that dealt with pressing concerns of the environment and poverty.[30]

With the emphasis on the Word of God as a central and potent tenet of the Lutheran tradition, Lutheran filmmaking confronted social conditions and ordinary lives with a bold passion. The story of Martin Luther modeled not only the spiritual struggles of individuals in making sense of God's activity in everyday life, but also the challenge of translating theology into the vernacular. As Luther used Gutenberg's printing press and enlisted the help of woodcut artists like Dürer and Cranach in visualizing the issues of the day, so Lutheran filmmakers stretched into translating what they viewed as key ideas into the medium of film. Whether it was *Question 7* challenging political repression or the animator Art Clokey's clay figures, *Davey and Goliath*, fumbling to find the right way to behave, Lutheran productions took seriously the work of grounding the ordinary lives of people on what the Scriptures said. The Swiss theologian Karl Barth once described reading the Bible as being like a man looking out a window and seeing people in the street below gazing up over the roof above your head, pointing excitedly at something beyond your sight, something you could not see directly. So, the Lutheran films pointed excitedly to God's working in the world, a world of antkeepers, candlemakers, and children called Anne and Davey.

Episcopalians, Presbyterians, and Others

When the Episcopal Rev. James Friedrich began Cathedral Films in 1939, he experienced neither opposition nor concrete support from the bishop of the Diocese of Los Angeles. The bishop William Bertrand Stevens did allow the Episcopal priest the freedom to make Christian films, provided he fulfilled his other obligations to the church, such as performing his sacramental duties of the Eucharist and marriage. Filmmaking thus became an adjunct mission of this Los Angeles clergyman. But several years before, the archbishop of Canterbury investigated how the Anglican Church could contribute more directly to film. Britain thus established its Cinema Christian Council, sponsoring a conference on "The Film and the Church" for younger clergy and theological students at King's College and investigating how much the church could be involved in influencing the history and future of cinema.[31] For the broader Anglican tradition, Friedrich would be at the vanguard in his visual adaptations of the Gospels and the book of Acts.[32]

In 1945, the Episcopal Radio-TV Foundation was established as an independent, nonprofit institution to reinforce the church's educational and evangelistic needs, receiving operating funds from the budget of the General Convention of the Episcopal Church. The Rt. Rev. John Moore Walker, then bishop of the Diocese of Atlanta, working with his administrator, Caroline Rakestraw, inaugurated the foundation and promoted a mission statement that read, "To proclaim and spread the Good News of Jesus Christ with theological discernment and responsibility through the audio-visual media."[33]

The programming fruit that sprouted from this seed included the public television series *Perspectives*, as well as many 16mm films and videocassettes. Its two most popular and critical successes stemmed from the British don and Anglican author C. S. Lewis: the 1979 Holy Week premiere of the director Bill Melendez's rudimentary animated version of *The Lion, the Witch, and the Wardrobe*,[34] and the 1985 joint Episcopal/BBC production of Norman Stone's impressive *Shadowlands*, a ninety-minute made-for-TV biographical movie about Lewis's romance with Joy Gresham, an American Jewish poet who converted to Christianity and married the celebrated writer.[35] (Lewis's interactions with the most proper Rakestraw over the broadcasting of his book *The Four Loves* were not so cordial, as she wanted him to take all the "sex out of *Eros*" and sit before a microphone in silence so that the audience could "feel his presence." When the Episcopalians finally discovered that his talks on Eros were indeed about sex, they cancelled the broadcast.)

In May 1982, the *New Yorker* announced that Episcopalians united with sixteen other churches to present "an historic witness to their faith . . . a statement of the Gospel" for their 1982 World's Fair exhibit.[36] The filmmaker behind this "mind-boggling" project about Creation, the Fall, and Redemption was the renowned Shorty Yeaworth, director of *The Blob* (1958). As producer, director, and president at Valley Forge Films, Yeaworth's resume included more than four hundred educational and motivational films, such as *4D Man* (1959), *Dinosaurus!* (1960), a drug-addiction feature called *Way Out* (1967), and television specials like *Christmas in Bethlehem* (1973, with the Pat Boone family) and *Around the World to China* (ca. 1980, with Billy Graham and Art Linkletter).

In 1984, Paul Wagner Productions and the Smithsonian Institution were given permission to film a documentary on the stone carvers working on the construction of the National Cathedral in Washington, DC; the resulting film, *The Stone Carvers*, won the Academy Award for Best Documentary Short Subject the following year. By the next year, Rev. Louis Schueddig, president and executive director of the Episcopal Radio-TV Foundation, was extolling their creative use of media for the last forty years. Regarding

Shadowlands, Schueddig commented, "This production offers the Episcopal Church an opportunity to be recognized as a leader in quality Christian programming for network television."[37] Of all the denominations, the Episcopal Church achieved the most professional aesthetic quality in this poignantly honest and moving biopic.

On the more subversive and creative side, the advertising work of J. J. Sedelmaier brought a fresh face to the Episcopal Church. In one irreverent short commercial, a father plays catch with his son and suggests that he attend the superannuated Sunday school, where they would have "sword drills" (a speed game for finding Bible verses) and sing "Kumbayah." The son listens in shock and then desperately walks into the middle of the street to welcome an oncoming truck, the preferred alternative to the old-fashioned church experience. The morbidly funny advertisement played on the memory of the parents and rectors rather than on the experience of contemporary youth in warning the church to change or die.

Before Hollywood and Darryl F. Zanuck produced socially relevant films like *Gentleman's Agreement* (1947) and *Pinky* (1949), religious groups dealt with both anti-Semitism and Negroes and poverty in *The World We Want to Live In* (1944) and *One Tenth of Our Nation* (1944).[38] For example, in a similar vein, the Presbyterian Board of National Missions raised ethical concerns about American-Japanese relocation centers.[39]

By the 1950s, Presbyterians settled down to tend their upscale congregations, primarily exhibiting rather than producing films. Rev. Stanley Armstrong Hunter, the nationally known pastor of Saint John's Presbyterian Church in Berkeley, California, announced that "now our children don't like to miss a Sunday" because he had been using a Bell and Howell Filmosound Projector for about three years.[40] As a leader in studying the use of visual aids, the Presbyterian Church (USA) set up a Division of Visual Aids in the early 1930s to assist in developing and prescribing appropriate visual material for its church school curricula.[41] Presbyterians would often purchase the works of Family Films and other production houses to supplement their own meager output of film. For example, Presbyterians would utilize stories of alcoholism, family problems, and a young boy rescuing his father from a crime through prayer in *Yesterday, Today, and Forever* (1949); *Unto Thyself Be True* (1949); and *A Boy and His Prayer* (1949).[42]

An agency known as TRAV (Television, Radio, and Audio-Visuals) coordinated the Presbyterian Church's mass media ministry.[43] Rev. George Wingard, operations manager of TRAV in the early 1970s, stressed the role of media for "dissemination of the gospel during an age of exploding populations."[44] For example, from the Presbyterian Board of Foreign Missions came *Heart of India* (1947), the story of one Indian boy casting his lot with Christ.[45] TRAV's most creative contributions were sixty-second commercials for radio and television from 1964 through 1968 with comedian Stan Freberg. Freberg's spot on the lesson of "Forgive him, it'll teach him a lesson" was animated with its humor and pungent point intact. In the spot, a wealthy Texan discovers that someone has stolen a sheep. "Hang him," he bellows, "it'll teach him a lesson!" After treating his fellow man in such brutal ways, he stands before his Maker, who looks down on him and says, "Forgive him; it'll teach him a lesson." The Presbyterian Church's insertion of humor through the talents of Freberg made a tremendous impact on modernizing its message of grace.

In film, however, TRAV's primary function was to distribute other religious moving pictures rather than produce their own. But the United Presbyterians did produce such "foreign" missionary films as *The Horns of the Crescent* (1956) and *Shining in Darkness* (1956).[46]

Appropriately for the text-centered denomination, several film ventures with the American Bible Society emphasized the Word of God. *Book for the World of Tomorrow* depicted a series of historical sketches of the Bible for the 1964 New York World's Fair time capsule. Having focused on Bible distribution since 1821, it made sense that the ABS film *The Whole Armor* (1951) emphasized the apostle Paul's equipping of the saints for spiritual warfare with the Scriptures.[47]

A distinctly educational, albeit sectarian, film chronicled the history of the Christian Church from a Protestant point of view. The PCUSA's *Fire upon the Earth* (1950, from Norman Langford's book of the same title) mapped key moments from the Pentecost to the formation of the World Council of Churches. This story of Protestant churches documented the developments of Constantine, Augustine, Luther, and others through pictures and limited bits of animation. As a curriculum resource, it offered a leaders' guide lest some feel bogged down, confused, or bored.[48] Seeking to advance interest in missions of social reform in the PCUSA, one of the more timely films was the religious potboiler *The Mark of the Hawk* (1957), which exhibited noticeable political overtones. Starring Sidney Poitier as Obam (with Eartha Kitt as his wife), the film challenges British colonial policies. Obam, imprisoned in a compound, crosses two sticks as an emblematic question of when Africa can again be free and at what cost. *The Mark of the Hawk* soared beyond private devotion in its concern with racial equality and social justice. The film sides more with secular movements of quasi-revolutionary social change than with the mark of the Lord Jesus. In the film, one cannot find a prayer, a Bible, a hymn (although there is a song in a nightclub), or any signs of Christian redemption. The two companies working with the PCUSA, World Horizons Productions and Film Productions International, followed up with the equally political *Saint of Devil's Island* (1961). Similar politically based films formed the core of the National Council of Churches' catalog of free titles, *Our Sunday Best*. This resource listed films under themes of hunger, liberation, ethical issues (amnesty, ecology, multinational corporations, etc.), women in the church, and special ministries such as aging and dying.[49] By 1980, the catalog included a significant section on Eastern religion, listing such films as the Buddhist teacher Alan Watts and the filmmaker Elda Hartley's *The Mood of Zen* (1967).[50]

Other religious groups produced instructional films promoting their own mission work. In *Together WE Serve* (1944), the Salvation Army documented how USO clubs ministered to soldiers, from offering doughnuts and coffee to dealing with more serious emotional, psychological, and spiritual issues.[51] A documentary put out by the Congregational Christian Church and the American Missionary Association, *The Color of Man* (1946), traced the history of interracial relations from a school for Negroes in the antebellum South to the equality of two black and white soldiers in the U.S. Army. While the film preached that God created all humans equal, it also raised questions about present discrimination. The picture closed with a black Boy Scout reciting the Pledge of Allegiance and strategically pausing on "one nation under God, indivisible," posing the challenge of applying Christian doctrines to the education and fellowship of different races.

From the 1950s onward, Episcopal, Presbyterian, and other Protestant denominations contributed minor, though important, film products for the church viewing public; Norman Stone's version of *Shadowlands* stands out as an exemplary model. While they also produced the typical mission and social justice films, these denominations experimented with short films and injected humor (albeit gallows humor at times) into parabolic spots. Such creative work foreshadowed the wildly innovative films that would be created for and distributed on the Internet.

The Baptists and Broadman Press

In his sly, fictionalized biopic of the exploitation director *Ed Wood* (1994), the director Tim Burton portrays a Southern Baptist church being persuaded to invest in one of the worst movies of all time, *Plan 9 from Outer Space* (1958). The fact that Baptists would help subsidize the campy sci-fi/horror film, starring the legendary Bela Lugosi (who would die during shooting), suggests that even this traditionally conservative denomination saw an opportunity for effective communication through this forbidden medium.

In most discussions of cultural antagonism and media battles, Southern Baptists are portrayed as fundamentalists opposed to all forms of modern culture, particularly movies. But in 1938, the Southwestern Baptist Theological Seminary introduced a course on the use of audiovisual materials for church programs. In an uncharacteristic spurt of ecumenical cooperation in 1942, the Sunday School Board of the generally conservative Southern Baptist Convention joined other Protestant denominations in expanding the afore-mentioned RFA to select and distribute their religious films to churches.[52] Southern Baptists invaded the audiovisual world with unexpected abandon, channeling their enthusiasm through the Broadman Press, a Baptist publishing organization that now sponsored films along with its extensive print output. Through its educational bulletins, the Baptist Committee on Visual Education set forth both its vision and a set of rules.[53]

According to Gene Getz, the great impetus in the use of audiovisual media to assist in education "grew out of the circumstances surrounding the Second World War. Rather than using lecture alone, military instructors used visual demonstrations, films, and other media to prepare men for battle. Consequently, warfare techniques and strategy were learned far more quickly through this new approach to education."[54] In 1942, the *Biblical Recorder* reported a debate regarding the positive value of movies, seeking to connect them with the democratic, religious, and moral background of the nation. The editors called for a readjustment of commercial films for an educational or community-minded basis, especially in remaking movies as "a tool of the church, in some cases, to teach Bible, character education, and missions." They found that such a use of film actually made schools and assemblies popular. Motion pictures, they argued, "must be converted by the church" rather than abandoned to pagans. They championed the public-service features of educational films (such as those produced by the federal government).[55] Individual pastors, like one from the Stovall Baptist Church in North Carolina, trumpeted the battle cry, arguing forcibly that the church should be using films in its educational program to help teach its great truths: "The Gospel can be dramatized effectively to have its intended power in the lives of our boys and girls."[56]

As part of the Southern Baptist Convention's centennial celebration in 1945, the Sunday School Board released *The Romance of a Century*, which told the story of the denomination.[57] In 1948, the Southern Baptist Convention assigned all responsibility for producing and distributing Southern Baptist audiovisual aids to that same Sunday School Board. The Southern Baptists' separatist tendencies led the board to discontinue its distribution arrangement with the RFA that year and "set up its own audio-visual libraries in connection with its Baptist Book Stores. The question of film production came before the Convention again in 1949 when the Radio Commission of the Southern Baptist Convention was asked to become the production agency with the Sunday School Board acting as distributor."[58] Thus the Sunday School Board assumed the responsibility for film production and distribution, emphasizing the purpose of film for Baptists as the education of children.

Earl Waldrup's classic 1949 text for the Southern Baptist Convention, *Using Visual Aids in a Church*, addressed the integration of film and other projected and non-projected audiovisual media into Baptist churches. His pragmatic arguments for inclusion echoed those of the silent era, namely, that visual aids were not a substitute for preaching; they were not solely for entertainment; they were not a panacea for attracting crowds; and they were not a substitute for preparation or for the satisfaction of a visual aids enthusiast. They could, however, make learning more permanent and enjoyable, effect change, and enrich other methods in the fields of worship, evangelism, recreation, and teaching.[59] The emphases were thoroughly utilitarian, budgetary, and logistical, assuming that Baptist churches would easily and naturally use such tools for the Kingdom of God; only basic instructions were needed.

After the publication of Waldrup's book, motion picture projectors, filmstrips, slide projectors, tape recorders, and record players became standard equipment in many Southern Baptist churches and Sunday school classrooms. The Southern Baptist Convention then started producing its own motion picture films during the late 1940s.[60] Key to the effective distribution of materials by the Baptist Sunday School Board's Visual Education Service was the network of Baptist bookstores, each possessing evaluative descriptions of films available to rent or buy in the denomination's publication *Focus: A Catalog of Audio-Visual Aids*.[61]

Clergy found vigorous support from women activists advocating their cause. For example, Mrs. W. K. McGee, president of the Raleigh North Carolina Woman's Missionary Union, published reports on acceptable filmstrips and moving pictures for Mission Study Books and Week of Prayer Programs. One twenty-minute film, *The Challenge of the City* (ca. 1958), appealed for a domestic Southern Baptist mission program.[62] A companion film, *In the Circle of His Will* (1959), portrayed the work of two missionaries finding their places in God's plan of redemption.[63]

Distribution of a category of films known as "televangelism," teaching about the concerns of the church through media, originated in the numerous Baptist bookstores. There one could, for example, find a stewardship film, *Treasures of Al Decker* (1959), which exposed the deleterious effects of hoarding money and overconsumption, or *Where Your Heart Is* (1959), in which the Nelson family was torn between buying a new car and giving money for the church building fund. The films emphasized the high priority of the denomination and its goals regarding family concerns, namely, that church tithing trumped personal desires. Biblical lessons of sin and forgiveness were taught in *This Old House* (1958), in which a mother realizes that her beloved son is hypocritical and proud, and in *Tooth for a Tooth* (ca. 1958), showing the detrimental effects of holding a grudge.[64]

In one televangelism film on civic responsibility, a newspaperman tries to stage an all-out improvement campaign based on Christian principles and the Bible, using a headline gimmick to shock the community into action.[65] Baptists partnered with Cathedral, Family, and Coronet Films, coproducing pictures like *Pioneer Home* (1950), which celebrated a traditional home where every family member does his or her part, culminating in a prayer of thanksgiving at mealtime and nightly Bible reading.[66] Other televangelism series addressed Christianity's solutions to modern social problems, such as teenage marriage and marital infidelity (*Feet of Clay*, 1959).[67]

By the early 1950s, the Southern Baptist Department of Radio and Visual Education used religious movies for specific educational programs, offering regional and convention-wide workshops. In 1952, 16mm film uses were taught in workshops designed for pastors, church staff, and leaders of churches, with topics of evangelism and stewardship dominating programs being rented from the Baptist bookstore depositories.[68] By the end of the decade, the denomination promoted summer film programs, advertising five-dollar films such as *Bible on the Table* (1959) and *That They May Hear* (1960).[69]

The Baptist World on Film

In their 1950 annual report, the Department of Visual Education of the Home Mission Board (HMB) stated that if Southern Baptists could "visit their missionaries at work in the field and see the people with whom they labor, it will [would] be easier for them to visualize the needs of the mission fields."[70] In 1950, the Foreign Mission Board produced its first 16mm sound film in color, *Preview of Advance*, which presented "opportunities and responsibilities of Southern Baptists in world missions."[71] In carrying out this vision, the HMB also produced two other motion pictures in the early 1950s (*The Open Door* and *The Baptists of Cuba*) that demonstrated rural and foreign missions. The films continued to be distributed during the early 1950s through Baptist bookstores located in such areas as Dallas, Atlanta, and Fresno.[72]

As part of the missionary education movement, the Christian Film Service advertised a special documentary film titled *South of the Clouds* (1951), which focused on Najla, a wealthy Muslim girl from a cultured and privileged home in Damascus. Najla enrolls at Beirut Christian College for Women and meets her roommate, Suad, a Christian girl from Lebanon. Najla finds it hard to adjust to the democratic atmosphere of a school where girls of all nations, faiths, and economic backgrounds live, study, play, and share their ideas.[73]

Other foreign and home mission films followed, such as *In the Footsteps of the Witch Doctor* (ca. 1951).[74] The denomination highlighted its Foreign Mission Board (with its new synchronous sound production facilities), which not only appealed for increased offerings but also continued to call young people to missions. One specific example, *In the Circle of His Will* (1959), was first screened at Southwestern Baptist Theological Seminary, Wake Forest, and dramatically and vividly told the story of Mr. and Mrs. Zebedee Moss, appointed missionaries to Central Africa.[75] Moreover, in 1954 several motion pictures were released by the Foreign Mission Board for use in overseas missions. These transnational films, like *New Day for Paulo*, whisked church congregations away to other worlds in need of evangelism. In fact, an extensive program sought to "provide essential Biblical motion pictures in national languages."[76] A total of thirty such films were produced for the overseas program in numerous languages, including Spanish, Italian, Japanese, Mandarin, Portuguese, and Yoruba.

Documentary films were made to acquaint Baptists with the needs of international missions. *The Life of Nomad People* (ca. 1951) showed nomadic peoples of North Africa foraging for water, though the film also provided an opportunity to study Bible lands. Working with the RFA, the Northern Baptists financed *Out of the Dust* (ca. 1951), its first dramatic presentation of Latin America. Five separate stories were deftly woven into the theme of missions, portraying how an American engineer became a missionary in Cuba, how a native boy became a doctor, and how an American businessman came to recognize the value of the mission's efforts. With its emphasis on evangelism in a predominantly Roman Catholic country, critics recognized it as a "definitely Protestant film."[77] Another recommended mission film, *An End to Darkness* (1951), conveyed the story of how a native African was converted to Christianity and himself became a missionary to his own people. However, despite their inspired stories, such films did not easily resonate with American congregations, frequently due to production quality. For example, a reviewer complained that in *An End to Darkness*, "the narration was carried in the first person by a man with a native accent. . . . The native narrator is a little hard to understand in certain places."[78]

In 1951, Broadman Films began producing films and filmstrips under the auspices of the Department of Audio-Visual Aids of the Sunday School Board of the Southern Baptist Church (SBC).[79] This audiovisual center was organized to assist religious education teachers in how to use this new medium. Within two years, Broadman would release a series of didactic evangelism films, *A Workman Unashamed, Lift up Your Eyes*, and *As We Forgive* (1952).[80] By 1955, the floodgates had opened, with numerous 16mm films becoming available for rent or purchase at Baptist bookstores. A list of 1950s titles makes clear the topics covered: *All for Him, And Make Disciples, Bible on the Table, The Land I Love, Missionary to Walker's Garage, That They May Hear*, and *What God Hath Wrought* (1955). In case one did not know how to technically use such clearly titled films, one could also rent *Preparing to Use a Film* (1955).[81]

As Hollywood was struggling with how to adapt to the newly emerging television industry, so, too, the Southern Baptists wondered about how to utilize the emerging medium. They produced a pilot film for a proposed half-hour dramatic television series, *This My Son* (1954). The film adapted the parable of the prodigal son for a modern audience, serving as a model for other parable-based films in the series. Eighteen months later, a thirteen-episode run of the series was broadcast, produced by the Sunday School Board. But the producers soon discovered that the production was rather expensive; according to the historian Theodore Lott, the cost of producing *This My Son* was $27,500, with subsequent episodes requiring approximately $25,000 each. In 1955, however, the commission received $200,000 from churches involved in renting the films through a cooperative program of the denomination collecting direct contributions, and another $120,000 in unsolicited donations. While interest in the series escalated (and reactions to the premier showing of the pilot film, *This My Son*, were enthusiastic), producers discovered that the funding they had received was actually insufficient; they were not able to make any follow-up films.[82]

In view of this financial plight, *This My Son* was released for rental through Baptist bookstores until such time as it could be joined on television by other films. In an attempt to help meet this need, the Sunday School Board made six of their previous motion pictures available for revamping to use on television, but even these fell far short of the planned goal of twenty-six films (two runs of thirteen films each). Adequate funding was simply not available to the Radio and Television Commission of the SBC. The $200,000 budget raised by the commission in 1955 for television broadcasting fell far short of what was needed. Because of the lack of funds, the Southern Baptists stumbled in their television broadcasting debut, with the commission recognizing that it would have to distribute the programs to churches to recoup the initial investment.

The Television Venture

During the mid-1950s, the SBC's Home Mission Board developed a visual aids section within its promotion department. Even while the Baptists were producing films that congregations found dull and unwatchable, they continued to publish articles on how to use motion picture films in the church, placing them in key SBC periodicals such as the *Church Library Magazine*, *Sunday School Builder*, *Training Union Magazine*, and *Church Administration*.

Because of the great expense associated with film production, the HMB began to make some films on a cooperative basis with the Sunday School Board. In 1955, the HMB and the Sunday School Board coproduced four motion pictures : *Land I Love*, *What God Hath Wrought*, *Reaching Out* (a film emphasizing church-centered missions), and *The Tenth Man* (a film on mission work to U.S. blacks).[83] In 1960, the Radio and Television Commission boosted its efforts in television evangelism by improving the quality of the films made for a new series, *The Answer* (originally launched in 1956). For thirteen weeks, the series appeared across the country on about a hundred television stations. In one typical film about Christian citizenship, *House of the Wicked* (1960), a district attorney loses his case against a vice czar, suggesting that Christians need to speak out boldly on public moral issues.[84] According to the *1960 Annual Report of the SBC*, these films were "produced in Hollywood, California, by Family Films, Inc., to insure Southern Baptists that the resultant product will be able to successfully compete with secular films on TV."[85] An estimated fifty million viewers watched each installment of *The Answer*, and it was by far the most successful, and expensive, project produced by the Radio and Television Commission at that point. By 1965, *The Answer* had been telecast on about 230 different stations in the United States. The program had become so popular that it was also broadcast on some overseas stations in Spanish, Portuguese, Japanese, Chinese, and Thai.[86]

Film production proved to be a more costly venture for Broadman Films than expected, and during the 1960s the company suffered repeated financial losses. For example, in the *1960 Annual Report of the SBC*, the Sunday School Board documented a net investment of $888,648 in Broadman Films for the production of five films: *About Our Task*, *The Price of Freedom*, *Unto a Full-Grown Christian*, *Planning and Constructing Church Buildings by Units*, and *Better Church Building for Town and Country*, basically the kinds of films only a church committee would invest in. It recouped just about 70 percent of its investment. Five years later, the *1965 Annual Report of the SBC* noted that Broadman Films had creatively branched out with a film for young people, *Iron Hands*, as well as with their Hebrew character films, *Nehemiah*, *Daniel*, and *Moses*, made for leadership-training purposes. Two other films, *Encounter with God* and *Magnificent Heritage*, focused, respectively, on worship and a thrilling, rip-roaring 150 years of Baptist life in the United States. Predictably, as sales for Broadman Films in 1965 reached $220,573, their net loss slipped to a whopping $244,704.[87] In a desperate attempt to stabilize the company, a policy was instituted to secure films through outside professional channels beginning in 1966.[88] Those in charge of selecting Southern Baptist film projects would not know, or care to know, the interests of their intended audiences.

Jots and Tittles

When the children's book author Rev. Wade C. Smith sought a way to illustrate portions of the Bible, his doodles of squiggly, ant-like characters were called into action. In late 1942, Smith published *Little Jetts Bible*, which he followed with engaging Bible lessons to young people published in the *Sunday School Times*, told with a series of dots and dashes. Smith had served as editor of the Southern Presbyterian Church's *Missionary Survey* in Richmond, Virginia, where he developed what he called his JOT characters. They would show, rather than tell, iconic biblical stories, such as how Abraham almost sacrificed his son Isaac. He even aimed at translating *The Pilgrim's Progress* into "simple language." But Smith would not draw a cartoon version of Jesus, instead suggesting Him by a sort of emanation. Smith's creative talents would take flight with the guidance of several Southern Baptist visionaries.[89]

Working for the Southern Baptist Radio and Television Commission in 1959, Ruth Byers and Ted Perry designed an animated television series with a happy, bouncing, anthropomorphic white dot named JOT, who would use the Bible to solve various problems in his four-and-a-half-minute musical episodes. Dr. Paul M. Stevens of the Radio and Television Commission authorized the acquisition of the little dot morality plays. He realized that while the Lutherans had *Davey and Goliath* on television, the Baptists had

The Baptists attracted a broad audience with their animated JOT character, who taught moral lessons with wit and humor. Personal collection.

done nothing for their own children. Smith's delightful little animated stories would be syndicated across the country and broadcast to audiences on Sunday mornings.[90]

In a letter to the "moms and dads," Stevens wrote that JOT "is no ordinary cartoon. It's a wholesome interruption of the stream of pointless mayhem your child normally sees on television."[91] The official explanation on the origin of "The Story of Jot's Father" reveals that the parent is the Southern Baptists Radio and Television Commission. The SBRTC sought to eschew "the proselytizing, the axe-grinding, the propagandizing," that usually pushes a "particular system of dogma or belief." Instead, they sought to "spark an awareness of the spiritual aspect of life."[92]

For Ruth Byers, it was essential that every line of the cartoons be grounded in a theological or philosophical truth: "JOT was a basic circle that changed shape and color depending on his relationship with God."[93] Once the character was designed, his moniker popped up naturally, as a dot whose name could be remembered easily by children. Thirty episodes were produced from its debut in 1968 through a final spot in 1981, at about $20,000 a show. To keep expenses down, JOT's arms and legs appeared only when he was stationary. When he was bouncing around, the animation was very limited. His design owed much to the United Productions of America style of sparse, bold, abstract backgrounds.

Encountering various obstacles, JOT's cheerful face would register darker emotions and undergo metamorphosis. What the dauntless dot reflected, according to its creators, was "a child's personality, sensitive to his inner world of thought and feeling. His conscience acts as a spiritual thermometer, registering thought and actions and calling attention to those that conflict with his spiritual well-being." As JOT's moods changed, so would his shape and colors, corresponding to his level of frustration or confusion. Against stick-figure backgrounds, JOT could become a tree, a rabbit, or even the wind. After finding biblical answers regarding faith in God or forgiveness, JOT, like a more abstract and religious Tom Terrific cartoon character from early television, would resume his normal size and hue.

Within a few weeks of JOT's debut, legions of children wrote more than 175,000 fan letters to their cheery little friend. Not long after, they could receive their own JOT finger puppet and party kit (which included the record game "Make a Joyful Noise," containing two 45 rpm records and a game board, JOT balloons, JOT whistles, and JOT party hats). There were also JOT puzzles and storybooks that taught moral lessons in fair play, obedience, honesty, and respect for Mom and Dad, all packed into a short format. In the first episode, JOT steals a one of his mother's dessert cupcakes, lies about it, and suffers the pangs of conscience in a surreal hallucination in which he is squashed, dissolved, and relentlessly pursued by his lie, "NO MAM." Like the narrator of an Aesop's Fable, JOT's mother sums it all up by telling him that "lying Lips are an abomination to the Lord."

The animation historian Hal Erickson noted how the spiritual and moral lessons were "deliberately soft-pedaled in the cartoon."[94] Yet religiously grounded propaganda lay embedded in the comic images. Following his early spiritual lessons, JOT dared to address issues of racial tolerance or bullying. For a tumultuous era of civil rights and racial unrest, JOT reminded children that all people were created in the image of God.

Summary

Denominational films remained a mixed bag of ecumenical and sectarian products. Throughout the second half of the 20th century, denominational boards and commissions were set up to conceive and implement ways to use the media, particularly film. Because organizational decision makers were rarely filmmakers, they would generally green-light films that fulfilled some aspect of the denomination's core mission, such as producing instructional films on foreign missions, tithing, or evangelism. Like the Methodists did in their features on John Wesley, Lutherans would release their own hagiographic pictures on their founders and the Episcopalians would feature the Anglican author and scholar C. S. Lewis.

Forays into dramatic films were usually less than compelling. Yet these story films revealed as much about the denomination as did their promotional films. The more socially liberal groups would promote films on racial equality and social justice, such as the Presbyterians' *Mark of the Hawk* or the Lutherans' *A Time for Burning*. Ironically, the one Protestant group that developed its own cottage industry with energy and fervor was the autonomous and sectarian Southern Baptist denomination, whose voluntary congregational polity cooperated to give birth to Broadman Films. Working with the producer Sam Hersh's Family Films, the Baptists demonstrated their concern for evangelism in pictures addressed to both home and foreign missions, but also with films aimed primarily at young audiences. In particular, the animated JOT series inaugurated a major development in marketing entertainment for children, with Baptist leaders realizing that competing visual attractions were necessary weapons in the growing war of mediated messages. For the Baptists, however, it would be one of their own Southern evangelists, Rev. Billy Graham, who would later organize one of the largest cinematic outreaches of the century with his World Wide Pictures.

Denominational films were also marginalized in several ways. Their primary exhibition venues remained most frequently church basements, relegated to Sunday nights, or in Sunday school classes, all part of general Christian education programs. But that wasn't the only problem for such religious films. A 1959 statistical study on media audiences and religion conducted by LeRoy Ford for *Educational Screen* investigated the actual use of these motion pictures. Most were used in parochial religious education (primarily in assemblies, rarely in classrooms), with only 0.7 percent of respondents using films regularly in the classroom.[95] More than one-third of the churches, predominantly the larger ones, felt that the films were too long for effective use.[96] As most films were documentary, missionary, or moral and evangelistic tales, they could become hackneyed, formulaic, and too predictable. For example, in one editorial review, the film critic William Hockman drolly announced that the "missionary study themes for 1959–1960 are Africa and The Church in Town and Country."[97] A 1958 cartoon by "Zanco" captured the younger generation's rejection of church films. The image shows four kids wearing Mickey Mouse ears and announcing to the church film director, "As a committee of four, we have chosen the following films for viewing," a sly reference to the preference of young people for Disney films over typical church productions.[98]

Since the early 1960s, reviewers have consistently panned Christian films. In his forecast for 1960, the educator George Ammon confessed, "We are beginning to realize that the Bible is difficult to visualize."[99] Admitting a bias against message films, Kyle Haselden, managing editor of the *Christian Century*, opined that most of the films produced for church consumption were "maudlin, moralistic, sermonic, and artistically poor."[100] The film critic and USC professor Arthur Knight echoed this sentiment, noting that such films "rarely had the stamina to make it on their own in the movie houses. Too often they have been weakly produced, concentrating on messages designed for a specific flock rather than raising their sights to matters of broad, general interest."[101] The problem as Knight saw it was that denominations could not command either artistic competence or the necessary economic resources to compete.

The enthusiasm for making and using films had spread throughout numerous denominations like the Methodists and Lutherans. Each group was able to tailor the content of their films for specific purposes, such as evangelism or the promotion of social justice. Each had a method for their making of visual media for congregations and a larger world. Lutherans, in particular, reformed typical church film images and adapted Jesus's method of telling parables with such films as *The Antkeeper* and *Parable*. But denominational budgets would demand that more money be designated to other, more pressing concerns of the church than cinematic sermons. Thus dramatic motion pictures that might reach wider audiences would have to come from companies and studios whose exclusive mission was to produce films.

—————————————————————————————— 5 ——

The Studio Era of Christian Films

—————————————————————————————————————

In David Prill's lackluster satire of the Christian film industry *Second Coming Attractions*, the author tried to capture some of the amateur wackiness of true believers engaged in making films for the Kingdom of God.[1] But his creation of a fictional Christian film producer of Good Samaritan Films, Leviticus Speck, pales in comparison with the actual characters involved in the mission of making films as Christians. Individuals like the Gospel Films producer Billy Zeoli and director Mel White would prove to be more fascinating, complex, and hilarious than any novelistic construction. As Lord Chesterfield once observed, "You will often meet with characters in nature, so extravagant, that a discreet poet would not venture to set them upon the stage."[2] Many of these curious characters emerged during the studio era of Christian films.

During the golden era of Hollywood, from the early 1930s to the mid-1950s, studio moguls controlled various modes of production. For the Christian film industry, after the pioneer days of Friedrich and Baptista, and concurrent with the efforts of various denominations, the 1950s ushered in a studio era controlled by the godfathers of religious films. Under the auspices of these personalities, the movement of Christian filmmaking erupted in a disconnected, serendipitous fashion. Yet Family Films, Gospel Films, and Ken Anderson Films would cross-fertilize the work of major denominations and shape the imaginations of a generation of churchgoing youth.

The Jewish Christian Studio

Sam Hersh was undoubtedly one of the most colorful and unexpected characters to join the Christian film industry. The founder of Family Films (1948–85), Hersh instinctively knew the film business better than any one else, making deals with other companies and denominations to secure a hold on the market. In particular, many, if not most, of Broadman Films (1951–75) productions from the Baptist denomination up until the 1970s were coproductions with Family Films. Hersh had a canny eye for talent and a savvy intuition for marketing that energized the Christian film industry. One of his most memorable catches was the freshly innovative filmmaker and Fuller Theological Seminary professor Mel White.

Marking the end of the conformist 1950s, White's *Charlie Churchman* films were unequivocally the funniest ever made for the church market. *Charlie Churchman and the Clowns* (1960) and *Charlie Churchman and the Teenage Masquerade* (1968) delightfully ripped off the silent comedies of Charlie Chaplin, with the requisite slapstick and pathos. But when White tried to sell them to Sam Hersh, he found the negotiations quite frustrating. "Hersh was not a Christian at the time," White noted, "but he knew what fundamentalist Christians wanted.

> When you go into his office, he had a commode up behind his desk. He would go in and do a bowel movement sitting on the john with the conference room door open. So I said: "I have films you've got to see and you keep turning me down."
>
> And Hersh said: "Well, I'll get somebody in there to see them in my conference room, but I don't have time to see your films. I make my own films."
>
> And I said: "Well you better show them to somebody." He called about three of his executives down, and they were laughing from the beginning. Halfway through, he heard them laughing and said to "cut them off."
>
> He had me come in and he said: "What do you want for them?" He hadn't seen anything. He'd just heard his men laughing.
>
> I'd made them for about $3,000 each, so I said: "I'd like $75,000 for them, $25,000 a piece." And I thought if I can get $75,000 for them, I will be the richest man on the face of planet earth.
>
> He said: "Give them to me." Years later, Sam Hersh told me: "You know, I made enough money to build La Cienega Towers out of your damn films. You should have asked for royalties." But I had no idea about royalties then.[3]

In the 1930s, Sam Hersh had been, among other things, a real estate magnate, entrepreneur, and bootlegger. As regards Christian films, the most important thing about him was that he was Jewish. As such, he had no interest in such sectarian concerns as Christian films. But around 1940, a man who owed him a large sum of money was unable to repay his debt. In lieu of money, the man offered Hersh the distribution rights to a series of films based on the life of the American composer Stephen Foster. Realizing there was no other option, Hersh agreed and his film business started. With *The*

Life and Songs of Stephen Foster (a series of thirteen films, ca. 1940), Hersh soon discovered a profitable market for patriotic and value-oriented films; he soon realized that religious films could be a lucrative supplement to his family-oriented films.[4]

When Sam Hersh founded Family Films in 1948, he was not thinking of producing "Christian films," but rather films for the whole family. According to the historian Harvey Marks, "Hersh was not a Christian when he founded the company; he was an opportunist. But he became a Christian and began to produce films with a strong Christian message."[5] Family Films' first three projects—*A Boy and His Prayer*; *Yesterday, Today, and Forever*; and *Unto Thyself Be True*—were completed in 1949 at the Occidental and Hal Roach Studios.[6] *A Boy and His Prayer* dramatically portrays some loan sharks threatening to corrupt a boy's father, until the young son prays desperately for divine help and receives it in the form of a deus ex machina, the death of the criminals in a holdup. But Family Films usually focused on mundane social crises facing church members: ordinary family problems were addressed in *Unto Thyself Be True*, while alcoholism underlay *Yesterday, Today, and Forever.*[7] The emphasis became entertaining and effective moral teaching films for the family.[8] A typical Family Films project is *In His Name* (1950), in which a boy throws a baseball through the stained-glass window of a church, shattering the face of Christ. The boy sends an anonymous note with eight cents as a down payment, and when he is caught, the pastor forgives him and decides to establish a recreational center for children, which includes a playground, club room, library, and other community amenities. Such an act inspires the contrite young vandal, who eventually, and conveniently, decides to enter the ministry.

Using Friedrich's distribution techniques, Hersh tucked his three films under his arm and traveled across the country to the Bible Belt, knocking on church doors to sell the pictures. Within a year, his aggressive entrepreneurship paid off. In 1950, Family Films received denominational acceptance with a contract from the Southern Baptists to produce *Dedicated Men* and *Bible on the Table* (1950), the latter one of the most successful films in the church market over the years.[9] In it, a grocery boy notices in his delivery to one particular house that a Bible is "always on the table. I wonder why." Such an opening question allows the father to explain that the Bible is essential furniture in their home and is needed in the kitchen just as much as a stove or icebox.

In the early 1950s, Hersh would identify himself with his nom de plume, S. M. Hershey, in such films as *Speak No Evil* (1950) and *Rim of the Wheel* (ca. 1950, with Gail Storm) so that none of his Hollywood associates would discover that he was making religious films. His standard director remained William F. Claxton, later to produce and direct numerous episodes of *Little House on the Prairie* (1974–82). Claxton shepherded several open-ended films, which would allow some ambiguity and provoke discussion among the viewers. Claxton produced *Talents* (ca. 1953, with Monte Blue), taken from a *Guideposts* story; and *Our Children: King of the Block* (1958, with Alan Hale Jr.). Claxton's atypical, even odd (and uncredited) production included the actor Jack Elam in the murder mystery *Lure of the Swamp* (1957), in which a cruel and wicked female villain sinks under quicksand with hell as her destination. Less bizarre was his *God Is My Partner* (1957), featuring Marion Ross and the irascible Walter Brennan. A typical plot was that of *I'll Give My Life* (1960, featuring Angie Dickinson), which involved a child and his father, a businessman who chooses overseas missionary work ahead of a promising engineering job.

Hersh employed well-known directors like Sam White, who oversaw Darryl Hickman (from *The Many Loves of Dobie Gillis*) and the Whitworth University choir for his social engagement film *As We Forgive* (1952). The story involves Lakewood Community Church's mission to keep youngsters off the street and out of mischief. Two juvenile delinquents are caught stealing a cornet. The arresting officer, a Christian, takes them into custody and, with a local minister, finds them jobs and helps to rehabilitate them.[10]

Hersh's success would come with his ability to partner and cosponsor various religious films, building a remarkably respectable practice. When the Lutheran Church–Missouri Synod wanted to expand its film ministry, it turned to Family Films for assistance in the production of the television series *This Is the Life*. Family Films would produce the series for twenty-three years. Developing a smaller division called Concordia Films, Hersh contracted Edward (Eddie) Dew (*Living Bible*, 1952) to join as a key director, along with Claxton, in producing for the Lutherans. In addition, Hersh negotiated with the Southern Baptists to produce films for their television program *This Is the Answer*. Methodists likewise engaged Family Films to help with their series *The Way*.[11]

Family Films proved to be one of the most fruitful production houses, issuing more than 150 films and 800 filmstrips in the 1950s and 1960s, and providing church libraries with a much-needed variety of films to help church leaders in their selections. Similar to Cathedral Films' emphasis on Bible stories, Family Films produced a twenty-six part series of short films titled *The Living Bible* (1952). Work on a sequel resulted in *The Book of Acts Series* (1957). The ubiquitous Nelson Leigh, who had acted as Paul and Christ for Cathedral Films, again portrayed Christ. These modest but sincere films, directed by Dew, polished a model of dramatic recreations done economically in bathrobes, with an unabashedly didactic editorial style. *Thy Sins Are Forgiven* (1955), for example, features Jesus curing a man with palsy and then turns the miracle into a lesson on forgiveness. In *I Am the Resurrection* (1955), Jesus restores the lives of both the son of the widow at Nain, Jairus's daughter, and Lazarus, bringing them together for a happy reunion.

In 1980, Family Films released a contemporary video series aimed at a teenage audience, *The Goosehill Gang*. A modern Hardy Boys, the Goosehill Gang solved mysteries just in the nick of time. After Sam Hersh died in 1969, his two sons, Melvin and Stanley, continued the work at Family Films and eventually transferred the studio to Concordia Publishing. In a tribute to Sam Hersh, the *Educational Screen* columnist William S. Hockman acknowledged that his harsh criticisms of Hersh's films never bothered Hersh, who wanted candor: "I never saw a man who was more eager to provide a good and useful product for the church."[12] For Hockman, Hersh was a friend with a most practical mind-set, in that he made money as he practiced his craft and distributed a shared vision for family films that offered moral advice for social problems.

A World Vision of Film

An influential event involving a young filmmaker occurred during the onset of the Korean War and prefigured the 1950s boom of evangelical filmmaking. Bob Pierce, founder of the international relief organization World Vision, had utilized film for Christian social action and humanitarian propaganda. Pierce's early work experimented with "the thoughts of men which would otherwise be forgotten," often showing the background stories of hymns. However, in 1948, a year before Mao's Communist Party would triumph in China's civil war, Pierce produced his seminal thirty-minute-film *China Challenge*, illustrating missionary work with orphans, refugees, and the needy in Asia. He had shot some raw footage of his meetings in the Orient that he then incorporated into traveling lectures with silent films, much like the silent film traveling exhibitor Lyman Howe, who had taken a similar approach some forty years before with his travelogues in various church settings. Like a Japanese *benshi* (a lecturer who would explain silent films), Pierce would narrate the pictures, which he projected himself.

He extended "the evangelical film to the area of social consciousness, using documentary and dramatic techniques," and stunning viewers with newsreel footage regarding "disaster relief, hunger alleviation, child care, refugee aid, indigenous national development, and evangelism."[13] His heart broken with compassion over the devastation among the poor in Korea, Pierce shot footage of the haunting faces of needy orphans and widows during the early 1950s, establishing a holistic ministry. His vision to serve the Kingdom of God encompassed making films for numerous programs of social justice, peace, liberation, and hunger issues, usually distributed under the auspices of the Mennonite Church's Central Committee.[14] Pierce presented stark, poignant, and compelling films that dealt more with the Great Commandment of loving your neighbor than emphasizing the Great Commission's call to spread the Gospel story and make disciples.

In 1949, Pierce was joined by the talented pioneer producer/director Dick Ross, who had worked with the Moody Institute of Science Films. After leaving Moon, Ross had established his own film company, Great Commission Films, under whose auspices *China Challenge* was completed. (Ross's media endeavors would include television work with the Pentecostal evangelists Kathryn Kuhlman and Oral Roberts, and eventually to the evangelical Christian breakthrough feature film of 1970, *The Cross and the Switchblade*.)[15] The first words spoken in *China Challenge* were those of Pierce, who announced the maxim "One picture is worth ten thousand words."[16] The pictures with which he shocked spectators reveal the excessive poverty, misery, and suffering of Chinese peasants. He shows blind women begging and a "bloated boy dying of starvation in the street" with no help. As disease-ridden and rejected children are presented, Pierce asks, "How can the children smile at the camera, you ask? Well, remember they have never known a time when the dead did not lie unburied in the streets and when someone in their family did not lie sick and dying from lack of food or care."[17]

The reality of the squalor and sickness reveals a stark "drama of the street," just as the Italian neorealists sought to capture after World War II. Evoking pathos was the primary tactic of Pierce and Ross, as they awakened the sympathy and concern of the congregations to whom they exhibited their film. The prevailing theme of all of Bob Pierce's films is evident even in this early work, namely, the words of Jesus in Matthew 25:35–36, 40 (NAS): "For I was hungry, and you gave me something to eat; I was thirsty and you gave Me drink; I was a stranger, and you invited Me in; naked, and you clothed Me; I was sick, and you visited Me; I was in prison, and you came to Me. . . . Truly I say unto you, to the extent that you did it to one of these brothers of Mine, even the least of them, you did it to Me."[18]

In 1948, Pierce had also been involved with a newly formed ministry to young adults, Youth for Christ, and he invited Ken Anderson, the editor of its primary publication, to join him in preaching to thousands in China. Acknowledged as the "father of the evangelical Christian film industry," Anderson learned to write scripts, teach missionaries filmmaking, and help start new production companies in the 1940s. Out of his experiences in China, Anderson produced a short documentary titled *This Way to the Harvest* (ca. 1949).[19]

China Challenge affected the entire Anderson family. Ken's wife, Doris, recalled, "That was the film that opened our eyes to what films could do to the human heart."[20] After working on *China Challenge,* Pierce had gone on to build the international relief organization World Vision, and Anderson then decided to move from the mecca of evangelical organizations in Wheaton, Illinois, to the Youth Haven Boy's Home in Michigan. Youth Haven provided a fertile setting for a budding writer, and the director of the home, Maury Carlson, opened his camp facilities to the Andersons. After Anderson wrote a book based on the Youth Haven boys, Carlos Baptista visited the camp in 1949. Baptista proposed a film adaptation of Anderson's book, and the two began collaborating. Not knowing how to write a script, Anderson borrowed one to use as a guide. Out of his modest attempts emerged his first full production, *That Kid Buck* (1949), a film stemming from actual cases of adolescent boys at the Youth Haven Boys Home in Muskegon.[21] Much like the 1938 Spencer Tracy film *Boys Town, That Kid Buck* portrays boys with dirty faces in need of spiritual guidance. A rebellious young burglar is apprehended and offered the choice of doing time or going to the outdoor camp, where he meets other young convicts whose lives have been transformed. When his life is saved by a bunk mate, Buck realizes that a "friend" sacrifices his own safety to care for others. The lesson is explained more fully and didactically in chapel talks and around the campfire, which stress that it "takes real red-blooded he-men" to be Christians. This small moral tale sparked Anderson's imagination, and he shared his concept of a film production company with several Christian businesspeople.[22] And from this work, the formation of the nonprofit Gospel Films (incorporated as Gospel Communications International in 1998) would ensue.

Gospel Films

Opening its first studio in the Eisenhower election year of 1952, Gospel Films stepped into a conservative church market that was still characterized by general skepticism or even hostility to the idea that God could use "movies."[23] Up until the late 1960s, many Christian colleges, such as Vanguard University, Calvin College, and Wheaton College, contained a moral clause that forbade attendance at movies, along with taboos on dancing, drinking, smoking, and going with girls who did such things.[24] The screenwriter Leonard Schrader, elder brother to writer-director Paul Schrader, did not attend his first movie until he was seventeen; his stern Calvinist parents forbade him to watch movies or television. "I wanted to see one movie in my life as an act of sin," he recalled, but having bought a ticket, he then ran away in terror of Judgment Day: "I saw the Lord God Jehovah and hosts of Angels coming down, and I was gonna burn in hell forever." Later, he recovered and went back to see the movie, *Anatomy of a Murder* (1959), but, of course, he never told his parents, lest he get yet another whipping: "I got whipped, six, seven days a week. . . . I took off my Sunday shirt, my father leaned me over the kitchen table, took the extension cord from his electric shaver, and he whipped my back with the plug so I'd get little pinpricks of blood, a nice little pattern of dots up and down my back."[25] While the typical evangelical family's reaction to Hollywood films rarely deteriorated to such violence, it remained a constant source of tension and conflict between conservative parents and their children.

With a central concern about young people and their leisure activities, Ken Anderson coordinated the original committee for the creation of Gospel Films, which included Maury Carlson (Youth Haven Camp worker and Zondervan Publishing salesman), Chuck Peterman (businessman and Youth for Christ founder), Ted Essenburg (businessman), Ted Engstrom (Zondervan Publishing, Youth for Christ founder, and later president of World Vision), and Jack Sonneveltz (businessman). Engstrom served as the first president, followed by Sonneveltz. The six board members handled virtually all work for the first eight to ten years. They raised the finances for productions among themselves, bought the equipment, and ran the company with a "hands-on" approach. Each contributed individual gifts and talents, practicing habits "of accountability, spiritually and financially. It was a close-knit group." Sonneveltz even took a one-year leave of absence from his business to concentrate on Gospel Films.

From Muskegon, Anderson and his first full-time employee, Chuck Peterman, moved in 1952 to Indiana, where they set up shop using a basement and garage as office space. In their first year of operations, Peterman acquired the distribution rights for *Martin Luther*. Even though the contract guaranteed only one year, it brought instant credibility and visibility to the new company. With virtually no salary and no money for film budgets, the first productions were very amateurish, yet still effective. For example, *Captured by the Indians* (1951), a short Western filmed on the Youth Haven ranch, had numerous scenes with modern telephone poles in the background.[26] Both *Going Steady* and *Silent Witness* (1952) were produced, directed, and written by Anderson as low-budget films. Most significant, the films wielded a tremendous synergistic impact on the emerging Christian youth movement, the ministry of Youth for Christ (YFC).

Anderson realized that they needed a distribution network and they turned to YFC for help. Most of the board members had been associated with YFC, and, in fact, for the first five years Gospel Films was unofficially considered the film production arm of YFC. One YFC board member, Bob Pierce, ran his own film production company (as we have seen) and was thus opposed to any official ties between the two ministries. Nevertheless, when a distribution system of Gospel Film Libraries was organized, ten of the first dozen "librarians" were recruited from YFC personnel. For example, Henry Grosh, a proprietor of Gospel Witness Films in Atlanta, continued to be a film librarian and a director of YFC Atlanta until 1985. YFC personnel, interested in using all the available means of media to reach the youth of their area, were quick to involve themselves in running or supporting these libraries.

Using his sales and marketing background, Peterman established guidelines for Gospel Films Libraries. Rather than sell films to the churches, as had been practiced in the silent era, they established a rental network. Consistent monthly cash flow from rentals would prove beneficial for further investment. Peterman's terms introduced the one-third/two-thirds rental income formula that remained the standard for several decades. Gospel Films would provide member libraries with advertising literature and film prints. The church or youth group would call on the library for the material and would rent the film from them. The library would keep one-third of the rental money and send two-thirds back to Gospel Films.

With what appeared to be the profitable operation of rental film libraries, a new studio was built on the Youth Haven site. But by 1954, after the completion of the teenage film *Seventeen*, Gospel had an outstanding debt of $100,000. According to Sonneveltz, those involved interpreted what happened as a direct intervention by God:

> We had a prayer meeting in Wheaton one day at the Wheaton Evangelical Free Church and someone came up with the concept of showing films free of charge to high schools. On the face of it that must have been the stupidest thing we can do. The only asset we had was the film in the can [*Seventeen*] and no cash. Here we were with all of this debt and yet we knew the Lord was speaking to us, so we instituted the program and within three months the Lord paid off the entire debt because the film was a major success and had a great impact since tens of thousands received the Lord from the film.[27]

The new high school policy was set up as its own division of Gospel Films, called Youth Films. To head up the program the board brought in a young and passionate Youth for Christ club leader from Indianapolis, the mesmerizing Billy Zeoli. With the 1950s marking an era of rebellious youth and rock and roll, Zeoli instituted a new strategy for Gospel Films, broadening the base of the company to reach more teenagers and college students. A bimonthly publication titled *Free Films* became an indispensable tool for youth workers in learning how to attract and engage this untapped market.[28]

Three years after the tragic automobile wreck that killed the troubled cultural icon James Dean, Zeoli helped secure the rights for a biography of a popular teen-recording artist who had converted to Christianity after his own near-fatal car accident. *The Tony Fontane Story* (1963) became Gospel's most ambitious project to date. Zeoli steered the studio to employ a professional Hollywood crew and the former Cathedral director Jan Sadlo. For three years, Tony Fontane, his glamorous wife, Kerry Vaughn, and Billy Zeoli hit the conference circuit, promoting the film in a musical road show.[29] The motto of the company became "People reaching people reaching people," a multilayered form of evangelism.

But this new direction for Gospel Films away from direct evangelistic films into dramatic narratives had created strains in the leadership before Zeoli's film would be shot. Anderson wished to make conservative and mission-oriented films, while Zeoli aggressively pursued youth-oriented films. In 1957, Anderson went to Singapore to produce and direct the predictably evangelistic *Something to Live For* (1957), a film that was dubbed into thirty languages and claimed "close to a million souls saved." Competitively, Zeoli argued that his *Tony Fontane Story* project could carry the same impact as Anderson's conventional evangelistic films. Disagreements ensued.

A quiet power struggle erupted in 1959, when Ken Anderson sought to obtain the presidency of Gospel Films, with Jack Sonneveltz remaining as chairman of the board. According to Ken's wife, Doris, "Ken had been the driving force of Gospel, and for ten years we worked night and day with them. We saw what films could do in the church market, how important they were in changing lives. We felt as though Gospel Films was very successful. They had a complete board that was the ruling body and Ken felt a bit pinned in, and he felt as though he would go back into writing as an author."[30] Sonneveltz agreed, acknowledging that "Ken Anderson was an amazing man personally. He would challenge everybody to be something better than they are. He made people great thinkers. He took the average businessman and challenged us to get new ideas; he would spend three hours at a time with us with his blackboard and chalk."

Nevertheless, the election process was suspect, as Anderson believed that he had sufficient votes from board members to guarantee his appointment. After an anonymous vote, however, Zeoli, master promoter and backroom salesman, emerged as the winner. While some suspected that Zeoli had manipulated the election, Anderson humbly submitted to the vote and left Gospel in December 1960, starting Ken Anderson Films the following year.

In 1965, Rich DeVos, CEO and cofounder of Amway, became chairman of the board, with Zeoli as president of the company.[31] By that time, Gospel was by far the largest Christian film production and distribution center in the world, having built a state-of-the-art film studio on their lot in Michigan. With Zeoli's emphasis on youth, Gospel intentionally opted to become a distributor as much as a producer, encouraging young talent to make films and submit them for distribution deals.

Called a slick, modish, and flamboyant preacher to the stars, and especially to pro athletes, Zeoli was also the personal pastor to President Gerald R. Ford.[32] His fellow Michigan native Ford wrote, "Your organization is making a major impact upon America and the world as it builds Christian principles and moral fibre into the lives of people." Even though he wore tacky outfits (deep, open-collared shirts and three-piece suits), he cultivated friendships with numerous celebrities, such as the Dallas Cowboys head coach Tom Landry, who wrote testimonials for Gospel. According to Landry, Gospel Films like *A Man and His Men* (1990) "have been a great inspiration to me personally, and to the Dallas Cowboys . . . in our chapel services."[33] The Italian-German "Z" constructed himself as a colorful caricature, seeking to reign as the king—or, more appropriately, the godfather—of Christian filmmaking.

Several notable successes came about under the new leadership. The Christian film industry's first self-effacing satire, *The Gospel Blimp* (1967), was based on the Christian author Joseph Bayly's popular short story of the same name. Shorty Yeaworth directed this sly comedy about misguided evangelism conducted from a zeppelin, which hauled Bible verse banners, broadcast Christian music from above, and dropped Gospel "firebomb" tracts on the unsuspecting victims of Middletown, Anywhere. Once the church has established the International Gospel Blimps Incorporated, a clever satire on the growing bureaucracy of Gospel Films itself, an ordinary Christian realizes that being a good neighbor may be a more effective mode of sharing one's faith than any media blitz.

Gospel also picked up the controversial filmmaker Rolf Forsberg's remarkable adaptation of Don Richardson's *Peace Child* in 1972. Shot in Papua, New

Shorty Yeaworth's adaptation of the Joe Bayly satire *The Gospel Blimp* made fun of modern methods of evangelism, which incidentally included film. Personal collection.

Guinea, Forsberg's film captured how the sacrificial myth embedded in foreign cultures served as a metaphoric bridge for communicating the death of Christ. Forsberg would later direct *The Miracle Goes On* (1976); and two precursors to the *Left Behind* series, the dramatic sequences for the dispensational best seller by the end-times pop author Hal Lindsey, *The Late Great Planet Earth* (1979), with Orson Welles; and *Years of the Beast* (1981), in which a college professor meets the Antichrist.

Gospel Films became known among many librarians as a hard-edged, professional organization. Whereas Anderson had allowed libraries to keep 40 percent of the gross, the one-third policy took full effect under Zeoli. Another Gospel policy, "use or lose," fueled by the need for strict business transactions, placed more pressure on the libraries to market their films. Libraries had to use the films they were offered in a sort of block booking, or else lose the opportunity to secure the next popular release.

The prime rental time for libraries to market their films, particularly in Baptist churches, was Sunday nights. Other holidays, especially New Year's Eve, offered special opportunities to rent out a group of films. However, with the demise of Sunday evening services in the late 1950s, and with family shows like *Bonanza* and *The Wonderful World of Disney* dominating television, rentals fell off considerably.[34]

By 1971, J. R. Whitby assumed the presidency of outreach, or evangelistic, films for Gospel and served as CEO for seventeen years; by 1998, Gospel Films would evolve into Gospel Communications International. In the late 1960s, however, the company struggled for survival. Whitby is said to have saved the studio as it teetered on the edge of bankruptcy. Gospel Films burgeoned into the most expansive Christian film rental outlet in the nation, grossing more than $1 million annually. What enabled Whitby and Gospel to profit was the emergence of a new phenomenon, the teaching film/video series, which would transform the industry. The first series to arrive would originate from a modest group of culturally engaged Christians in L'Abri, Switzerland, led by the philosopher/theologian Francis Schaeffer, trying to bridge the divide between Christianity and secular culture.

The Schaeffer Phenomenon

In 1976, Gospel released director Franky Schaeffer's remarkably successful set of films, *How Should We Then Live? The Rise and Decline of Western Thought and Culture*.[35] Like the historian Edward Gibbon's classic history of the downward trajectory of Roman civilization, in this project the Schaeffer family sought to visually trace the decline and fall of Western (Christian) culture from ancient Rome to the new modern elite. Franky and his father, the reformed evangelical apologist Francis Schaeffer, sought to excavate the past as a judgment on the present. As a documentary filmmaker, Franky explored the wilderness of visual polemics, producing one of the most notable series for engaging the cultural wars before such a topic had become fashionable.[36]

A friend of Franky's, Ray Cioni, who was to become a codirector with him, had heard a Francis Schaeffer lecture at the Moody Bible Institute and decided that he would try to communicate Schaeffer's ideas without just filming a presentation: "We wanted to be funny, to make an entertaining film that would appeal to more than the sympathetic Christian audience. We wanted to make people think and laugh at the same time."[37] Another friend of Franky Schaeffer, Jim Buchfuehrer, was brother-in-law to a Gospel vice president, Wendell Collins, who was able to promote the project.

At first, a Swiss American filmmaker had been contracted to direct it, but as his incompetence became evident with the film falling behind schedule and budget, Franky's two friends, Cioni and Buchfuehrer, encouraged the younger Schaeffer to confiscate the directorial duties from him. They finished the five-part film series *How Should We Then Live?* and then initiated a three-month touring show.[38] In 1979, Franky, known as the enfant terrible of the Christian world,[39] and his father produced a second series in conjunction with the soon-to-be Surgeon General C. Everett Koop, *Whatever Happened to the Human Race?*, in an effort to spark a cultural and political engagement with the world.

The five-episode series with Koop altered the typical look of an evangelical film series. In contrast to flat, lecturing heads, Franky utilized surreal images of hundreds of "dead" baby dolls surrounding Koop standing by the Dead Sea, images of the elderly harshly disposed of in banal nursing institutions, babies imprisoned as nonhumans in wired cages, and broken baby carriages stuck in the mud. All were designed as an assault on the senses in an attempt to convince the viewer of the horror and insanity of abortion and euthanasia. Whatever its faults in sound, performance, and editing, the film experimented with the domain of the prophetic, of shocking, shaming, and horrifying audiences into action. It is almost as if the surreal filmmakers Luis Buñuel and Salvador Dali coproduced the film with the evangelical apologists.[40] A special showing was held at the home of the presidential hopeful Jack Kemp, who saw the possibilities for a pro-life movement in the Republican Party. According to Schaeffer, a small hullabaloo broke out when the film critic for the *Washington Post*, Judy Mann, allegedly plagiarized a brief sent out by Planned Parenthood condemning the film as part of her film review, fueling accusations of liberal collusion.[41]

Bishop Fulton Sheen viewed the film as underscoring Pope Paul VI's *Humanae vitae*, an encyclical letter on the sanctity of all life, and recognized that it would make abortion more than an exclusively Roman Catholic issue. Sheen noted that after the *Roe v. Wade* Supreme Court decision, "the unborn need more friends." He suggested that perhaps more than any other single event, the release of the film series roused an evangelical awakening to the controversy, putting the issue of abortion onto the front lines of the nation's political struggles.[42]

A ten-part series on *Reclaiming the World* followed the format of a television interview show, in which Schaeffer as a theologian/philosopher was able to articulate why he was a Christian, to probe definitions of "humanism," and to challenge the idea of the "separation of church and state." In the final films in the series, the elder Schaeffer explored experiences of conversion, suffering, and God's sovereignty, especially in the context of the Christian intellectual community he established in Switzerland (the L'Abri Fellowship).[43]

Not one to mince his words, Franky castigated previous Christian efforts in filmmaking as an "illiterate repetitive hash of Christian drama." He bashed the "few simple categories that are endlessly and timidly reshuffled: the sob story, the dramatic conversion, before and after ('I used to be high on drugs, but now I am high on the Lord'), the narrow escape, the testimony (always famous and infamous people), the how to [live the Christian life or overcome addiction, etc.] in three easy lessons, and so forth."[44]

Challenging the status quo of the Christian film industry, Franky spewed forth a diatribe against what he saw as its pervasive mediocrity.[45] Franky joined with Buchfuehrer and the executive producer Paul McGuire to form Schaeffer/Buchfuehrer/McGuire Productions and release several other features, "commercial films with certain integrity." "We don't want to do teen-age exploitation films," said McGuire, announcing the development of what the *Hollywood Reporter* described as a teen comedy, *Booby Trap*, the working title of *Wired to Kill* (1986).[46] But Franky followed his own incendiary rhetoric with this less-than-praiseworthy film based more on Nietzschean than Christian themes. *Wired to Kill* did win him the award for best director from the Academy of Science Fiction, Fantasy, and Horror Film and garnered the distinction of being the best-selling independent film presented at the 1986 Cannes Film Festival. The filmmaker Eric Karson called the movie a "reaffirmation of fundamental American principles" and a "challenge to confront evil."[47] While it foregrounded a pious grandmother as a Christian martyr in a *Road Warrior*–type futurist world, the maverick film dealt more in sadism and torture, such as when a villain is impaled on the seat of his motorcycle. Schaeffer defended his use of ultraviolence by comparing it to that of Shakespeare, Homer, and the story of "King David chopping off the foreskins of a hundred Philistines and putting them in a pile in a field."[48] The point of *Wired to Kill* is encapsulated in the final line, when the protagonist tells his girlfriend, "Well, we kicked some ass. . . . If you want history, you gotta make your own." The movie didn't connect with Christian audiences, except perhaps a few right-wing militia groups. Franky's films went from mediocre to poor. His later works, *Headhunter* (1989) and *Rebel Storm* (1990), are remembered as abysmal, with rock and roll defeating a television evangelist in the latter and a demon erupting from a public pool and interrupting a baptismal service in the former.

Evidence of the growing rift between Franky and the evangelical world can be seen in the filmmaker's production of an animated film with Ray Cioni in 1984 based on his father's work *The Great Evangelical Disaster*. Franky's view of film as a weapon in the culture wars elicited public criticism. The Indiana State University history professor Richard V. Pierard viewed Franky as an evangelist rather than an intellectual apologist, and found *The Great Evangelical Disaster* marked by "cheap shots, *non sequitor* [*sic*], *ad hominem* [*sic*], and rhetorical flourishes." For Pierard, the film was "so absurd that no one with any artistic sensitivity took it seriously."[49] Franky's defense centered on the fact that the film was not a simple adaptation of his father's book as much as a playful satire inspired by the Monty Python troupe.

The initial success of the Schaeffers' Gospel-distributed films opened the doors for other serial films, such as the Christian educator James Dobson's series *Focus on the Family*, which sought to teach young parents how to raise their children in a world that the Schaeffers had painted as culturally corrupt and degenerate. Teaching series would dominate the market. The film reviewer Mark H. Senter III argued that Christian filmmakers had quickly learned the profitable lesson that "serials make money. . . . [They] can create repeat audiences, multiply ministries, and frequently increase revenues."[50] The numerous series on various topics were all to be subsumed under the category of teaching films and would hit their peak with Dobson's instructional family videos, leading the industry to tag the phenomenon the "Dobson effect."

The Dobson Effect

The instructional films that began to dominate the market in the early 1970s were rooted in the Greek words for teaching and preaching, *didache* and *kerygma*. The emphasis was on conveying propositional truth and engendering discipleship. Their generic style was one of unencumbered instruction, which fit with much Sunday morning preaching.

The instructional film, also known as the "talking-head" or "rent-a-preacher" film, promoted a particular personality to provide a teaching or inspiration. Rather inexpensive to produce, these films capitalized on a speaker's popularity, expertise, and charisma. Most of these works dealt with fashionable topics or controversial issues. *Turn Your Heart toward Home* (1986), *Hooked on Life* (1985), and about two dozen others provided audiences with many hours of instruction. Apologetics such as Josh McDowell's *Evidence for Faith* (1984) also became fashionable instructional series.

But the champion of instructional series was the widely rented *Focus on the Family* (1979), Dr. James Dobson's presentation of his pop-psychology Christian teachings on family issues, which positioned him as the new Dr. Benjamin Spock. For a production cost of about $30,000, Dobson's seven-part series established a norm of biblical instruction regarding raising children and communicating with one's spouse. *The Strong-Willed Child, Christian Fathering, What Wives Wish Their Husbands Knew about Women*, and other films resonated with congregations when they debuted nationally. Dobson, an educational psychologist from the University of Southern California, addressed sensitive areas of counseling with which ill-equipped pastors had struggled for years.

Incorporating a nonprofit, evangelical, para-church organization, Dobson extended his ministry based in Colorado Springs, Colorado, into various media, distributing a daily radio broadcast as well as producing teaching films. Synergistically, the twelve hundred radio stations that carried Dr. Dobson's ministry became an instant source of advertising for his new film series. Within one month of the first film's release, the radio programs had effectively communicated to virtually every film-renting church in the country: In an article on *Focus on the Family*, Chris Franzen quoted an anonymous executive as saying that "we have an excellent opportunity here to test the effectiveness of messages and messengers through our radio broadcast—to know whether anybody cares or not about what we've said—by virtue of the public response to the broadcasts. When an individual comes along with a message for the family that we think might be very effective, we put it on. Then we watch the mailbox. With 125,000 pieces of mail arriving every month from listeners, Focus has its own instant audience poll."[51]

The film series was such a phenomenal success that it drastically altered the Christian film industry in what became known as the "Dobson effect,"[52] namely, launching an avalanche of similar instructional talking heads. Edward Flanagan, one of three producers for Focus in the 1980s, felt that the talking-head genre had realized its fullest potential in the Dobson series by establishing a "close on-camera relationship between the audience and speaker and by intercutting dramatic segments that drive home the message."[53] It cost more than $400 for a church to rent the whole seven-part *Focus on the Family* series, a figure that consumed most of the annual film exhibition budget for at least 90 percent of the churches. Churches chose the Dobson films over the more dramatic films, causing exhibition of the latter category to wane. But Van Moore of Zondervan Films opined that "some in the film libraries are saying Dobson widened the market."[54]

At the beginning of 1986, Word Publishers then released Dobson's second series, *Turn Your Heart toward Home*, which provided more practical counsel, not only recommending how to discipline teens but also analyzing why American culture made it so difficult to do so. With six hundred prints released simultaneously, the second series broke all the showing records for a first film set. Dobson's first series "rewrote the history of religious films. Nobody knew, back in 1978, if churches would rent a film series featuring a man standing and talking, . . . but Hitler almost conquered the world, and one of the things that stopped him was Churchill's oratory—his ability to stand up and say we will never, never, never quit. Oratory has the capacity to capture the imagination of people, to move their hearts."[55]

In its ministry to support traditional marriage and families, Focus on the Family expanded into more creative, youth-oriented programming with a clever and engaging animated/live-action video series, *McGee and Me* (1990), created by Ken C. Johnson and Bill Myers about a normal boy named Nick who shares adventures with an imaginary cartoon character named McGee. Typically, in each episode, the two buddies learn biblical maxims about lying ("The Big Lie") or bullying ("Skate Expectations"). Mary Stevens of the *Chicago Tribune* found the series exceptional and not too "preachy."[56] Another home video series developed by Focus on the Family (first as a radio project in 1987) was their character-building *Adventures in Odyssey* (1991), addressing issues of faith, friendship, and forgiveness at a place called Whit's End, in Odyssey, the "town where anything that's remotely possible becomes probable."[57]

Other evangelical celebrities, such as the Presbyterian minister Charlie Shedd and his wife, Martha, capitalized on their wisdom and wit in marriage workshops to produce an interactive film series, *Fun in Marriage Workshop* (ca. 1970). The instructional and anecdotal films were designed to foster gender communication and relational help in marriage encounters. Like the *Alpha Course*, a video series on basic doctrines of the Anglican tradition taught by the curate Nicky Gumbel, this series was designed so that significant dialogue and debate would occur after viewings.[58]

The didactic video series proved to be not only financially profitable, but also effective in drawing groups of people together to talk about salient issues that impinged on their lives, such as marriage and parenting. It transformed the ways the church used media, now not merely for entertainment but also for engagement, for stimulating thought and action among viewers. Watching was no longer a mere spectator sport.

Gospel Distribution

As Gospel Films found considerable success in marketing the Schaeffer and Dobson series, it pressed them to expand its organization considerably. The full-time staff of Gospel Films reached about forty people around 1979, with additional personnel hired during periods of in-house production. In 1973,

Zeoli had opened communication lines with independent Christian producers and set policy guidelines for Gospel Films to acquire outside films for distribution. As a savvy "natural" marketer, Zeoli felt he could gauge the latest trends in Christian film, reaffirming that film had become a "major tool in the ministry" of the church, one that enhanced but did not supplant the Bible. He averred that the scarcity of Christian films was no longer a problem, with the number of producers multiplying and a diversity of themes being addressed.[59] Within a decade, he would recruit a bright cadre of creative filmmakers as part of the newly expanded Gospel family. From 1980 to 1986, of the sixty-four productions released by the company, only two were even coproduced by Gospel. In fact, more than two dozen independent filmmakers produced works specifically for Gospel, including Heinz Fussle, Mel White, John Schmidt, Rick Garside, Eric Jacobsen, Mike Evans, and Steve Zeoli (Billy's son).

After attending the film historian Arthur Knight's classes at USC, Mel White began his work in Christian filmmaking while he worked with Youth for Christ, the organization that gave rise to Gospel Films. White, seeing himself as a "gadfly," sought to change the image of religious films, which had a "reputation of being notoriously dull."[60] His first film, *The Moral Choice* (1965), is an odd, propagandistic melodrama about two kids spending a summer near Dream Island who are tempted to have premarital sex. Father, a skipper, narrates the evangelistic story of a headstrong young man who tries to rendezvous with a girl on a deserted island, only to see the girl drown, punctuating the moralistic tone that the "wages of sin (especially sexual sin) is death" (Romans 6:23). White then wisely turned to comedy, as discussed in prior chapters, and working with Dr. Winfield Arn in the early 1960s he produced the hilarious *Charlie Churchman* series. White shot in grainy black-and-white and sped up the action to match "those wonderful high-speed, slapstick performances by early Charlie Chaplin, Buster Keaton, and the Keystone Kops."[61]

After working for several other Christian producers, White made his way back to the Youth for Christ "mafia" at Gospel Films. His strained encounters with Billy Zeoli came to be legendary. Zeoli, as the head of Gospel Films, designated himself "godfather" of Christian films. He even claimed to have delivered "messages" to religious leaders like Jerry Falwell and Charles Colson at religious conventions by sneaking imitation horse heads into their hotel rooms (alluding to the famous scene in 1972's *The Godfather*). Years after White had finished his work with Hersh, he got a call from Zeoli. White remembered that Zeoli "was so aggressive and sounded so much like a Mafia don":

As an homage to the great silent comedies, Mel White inserted gentle satiric laughter into church auditoriums with his *Charlie Church-man* series. Courtesy of Mel White.

Zeoli demanded: "I want the next Charlie Churchman film for Gospel Films!"

White explained he wasn't making any more.

Billy retorted: "Oh, yes you are. You're going to make those Charlie Churchman films. You're going to make them for me. And you should have come to me for the first one. I'm coming into town and I want you to meet me at the steam room of the Hilton at the airport." So I met Billy Zeoli and we immediately took all our clothes off and ended up in this steam room. We had massages and steams and swimming pools, because he was always reducing. And he'd say: "What do you want? What do you want? What would it take me to get a Charlie Churchman series for Gospel Films in color?"

And I'd say, "Well, you see, it was a genre we were trying to imitate. It was Charlie Churchman in black and white." And Billy replied: "Those days are past. You need to do it in color." And I replied: "that would take away from it." Billy replied: "I don't care. Do it in color." We did *Charlie Churchman and the Youth Quake* and two or three others for him.[62]

White's favorite film, *The Circus* (ca. 1968), had been a flop. The parabolic story concerns a young crippled boy who joins other children in following a kind of pied piper through darkened streets to the edge of a circus. Dressing in colorful costumes, the children frolic on the high wires, until adults arrive and snatch them back to their customary roles. White explained that this parable expressed his joy that "there are all kinds of people that need to have an active role in Christ's kingdom; old and young, new and long term, and the kingdom is for all of us, and let's all be active in the kingdom. Let's celebrate the kingdom together."[63]

The film failed to connect with his spectators. But White grew up along with his audience and left his delightful teenage comedies and parables to focus on a more substantial and mature series on the twenty-third psalm for Gospel Films. This provocative group of biographical films centered on faithful Christians who had suffered tremendously. Each individual story was matched with a particular phrase from the psalm. For example, *In the Presence of Mine Enemies* (ca. 1974), the dramatic story of the Vietnam POW prisoner Howard Rutledge and his persevering wife, Phyliss, launched the series. *Though I Walk through the Valley* (1972) traced the courageous struggle of a Christian college professor, Tony Brouwer, living with terminal cancer, editing together interviews with him and his family throughout the ordeal and after the funeral. It was one of the "first films in history to document the last year in the life of a dying man and his family." *He Restoreth My Soul* (1975) probed the anguish of Merrill and Virginia Womach after Merrill's horrible disfigurement in a plane accident. *He Leadeth Me* (1978) documented and celebrated the buoyant, inspiring, and triumphant life of the blind composer/singer Ken Medema.

Evangelical reactions to these cinematic psalms of suffering combined amazement and gratitude. The documentary on Tony Brouwer's life and death, for example, struck one reviewer with a sense of ambivalence, horrified and humbled as "the brazen camera intrudes on the intensely private suffering of a family watching the husband and father die of cancer."[64] The real characters exposing their lives, their suffering, and their spiritual doubts for the camera borders on voyeurism and morbidity, yet one watches their vulnerable lives as inspirational stories of true saints.

The horror of the Jim Jones cult was also exposed in White's *Deceived: The Jonestown Tragedy* (1980), which stitched together the appalling and poignant memories of survivors with rare footage of the cult leader preaching and directing his ministry. Ann McMath discerned what she called "the problem of pain" in White's personal documentaries, a crisis of incomprehensible suffering that laid human anger, frustration, anxiety, fear, and desperation at the feet of God.[65] Yet White's films also captured sources of triumph and inspiration paralleling the thinking of C. S. Lewis's writings on the subject: "God whispers to us in our pleasures, speaks to us in our conscience, but shouts to us in our pain: it is His megaphone to rouse a deaf world." For White, the communication of such tribulations was necessary for Christian transformation, as he believed that when evangelical Christians "come up against tragedy, their simple faith hadn't really equipped them to face that horror. . . . All I am trying to do is make the Christian faith a little more full-orbed, a little more honest." The lessons gleaned from a medical doctor who worked with lepers, Dr. Paul Brand, head of the leprosarium in Carville, Louisiana, taught White that "pain, whether it is psychological or physical, is a tremendous gift of God."[66]

Close to the early comic work of Mel White, another Southern California filmmaker used humor to spread the Gospel. The director John Schmidt, gleaning a broader understanding of film history from his academic studies at UCLA, set out to parody popular Hollywood products while also inculcating biblical messages. Schmidt delivered several snappy presentations of humorous stories within suburban Christian communities. *Super Christian* (1980), *The Greatest Story Never Told* (1983), and *Kevin Can Wait* (1983) topped the list of his bright, glossy, entertaining films. Spoofing the Hollywood style, Schmidt intelligently addressed issues of hypocrisy, evangelism, and prejudice among evangelicals in a gentle, Horatian satirical mode.

The parodic style also caught on with Dave and Rich Christiano's version of *The Twilight Zone*, titled *The Daylight Zone* (1986). The film cleverly opens with the narrator intoning, "Meet Carl Smith, a thirty-five-year-old schoolteacher on his way home to Johnson City, Texas. . . . Before he reaches Johnson City, he'll make one brief stop in *The Daylight Zone*." In *The Pretender* (1987), the twin Christiano brothers directed the story of a cunning knave who feigns to be a Christian in order to date an unsuspecting Christian girl.

By 1989, Gospel Films had acquired Thomas Nelson Communications film distribution, bringing in Fred Carpenter's Mars Hill Productions, Son Pictures, and Chuck Warren's Life Productions. This group of young, earnest, and talented filmmakers sought to erase the stigma attached to making religious movies, which had continued despite the success of filmmakers like Mel White. After twelve years of Christian filmmaking, Fred Carpenter was asked when he was going to make "real movies." Rather than becoming miffed, Carpenter split his focus among Hollywood movies, "church movies," and his kind of films, shorter and open-ended narratives. He explained that his task was to facilitate legitimate relationships, "taking the whole message of Christ into the whole of creation, but not at the expense of the highest quality."[67]

Gospel Films catalogs presented the wide range of films available. In 1984, for example, it highlighted the early teen movies of Heinz Fussle, *My Brother's Keeper* and *The Winning Circle*, while Mike Meece received a lively "Producer Profile" for his MDM Productions, featuring his children's series *Sunshine Factory* ("It's going to be happy, it's going to be great. / I've got to hurry—don't want to be late. / I can learn to be the best that I can possibly be. / Where? Down at the Sunshine Factory").[68]

Continually expanding since its inception in 1950, Gospel Films grew into Gospel Communications International in 1998, dedicated to spreading the Gospel through film, the Internet, and other emerging technologies. For a film company on the verge of bankruptcy in 1954, it has made a major impact on the cultural mind-set of the evangelical community. According to Zeoli, more than eighty thousand free showings of Gospel films took place in high schools during the 1988/89 school year, and it is estimated that 2.5 million high school students viewed at least one of their productions that year.[69] By 1994, Gospel had added videos to its distribution offerings of 16mm films. But in 2008, while Amway President Doug DeVos and Billy Zeoli remained cochairmen of the board (with J. R. Whitby serving as president and CEO), financial difficulties strained the corporation's resources. Zondervan purchased its internet holdings, and Gospel put its other operations, including Gospel Communications, up for sale.

Ken Anderson Films

The Anderson family left Gospel Films in 1960 and moved to Indiana, supported by several key investors who remained personally committed to Anderson's vision. As Gospel Films had broadened its scope in producing various kinds of projects, Anderson established his own company, Ken Anderson Films, with a more focused and definitive motto: "The message is always first." Every Ken Anderson Film catalog opens with this axiom, asserting an unequivocal modus operandi. Promotional pencils were designed with erasers on both ends, punctuating the idea that "this pencil has no point, but there's always a point to a Ken Anderson film." The company's primary aim was to produce films that were able to reach the youth and church community with the Gospel and teach the basics of biblical truth and Christian living. For Anderson, evangelism was only the initial step; audiences needed to be instructed in the things of God. He continually saw his films as a means of training and discipleship: "We have basically two purposes here. One is to produce films in the United States, to be used here. Secondly, the financial returns from these films make it possible for us to do things in other parts of the world. We are very much more interested in the evangelization and ministry opportunities oversees. . . . It is just that the United States has the ability to pay the bills."[70]

When the Andersons first married, they had planned to be missionaries and they applied to their denomination's foreign mission board. Their message films became an extension of their physical presence in a global mission field. In fact, their first film as a new entity, *The Family That Changed the World* (1961), was about serving God as missionaries, and it was instrumental in generating interest in global missions. Testimonies from Christians in response to *The Harvester* (1963) and *In His Steps* (1964) led many to seek opportunities to serve abroad. In an interview, Doris Anderson explained:

> We've done many missionary films, unfortunately missionary films are not the key thing that people want nowadays. But we keep on making them because we feel that the missionary spirit is what God has put into the world, into the hearts of real Christians. . . . Every December we have a seminar at our studio where missionaries on furlough come in and we teach them how not to make films. Our whole production team goes into operation and we teach them how to manage their cameras, how to get the very best they can when they go back to the mission field.[71]

Criticisms of Anderson's films centered on the fact that he was simply "producing radio drama on film"; one reviewer suggested that they just make their films on audiocassettes. Anderson responded that they were "much more concerned with message impact than screen prowess, although we tried to make our films as good quality as possible."[72]

Anderson envisioned a greater calling to produce a global mission, organizing International Films to create films for other nations in the early 1970s. Language problems remained a barrier in overseas filmmaking. In one film done with Tibetans in North India, which featured a cameo by the Dalai Lama, Anderson could only find a few Tibetans who understood English. Anderson remembered that they contracted a Tibetan to synchronize lip movements to dubbed English: "Oh, said the man, I see, I am only a parrot."[73] Anderson coined a term "AVangelism" to describe the process of translating their domestic audiovisual products into scores of other languages.

Heinz Fussle had worked in Swiss TV news when he was invited by Ken Anderson to join him on film projects in the Far East. Fussle produced both dramatic and documentary films for Anderson Films, such as *Cry for Freedom* (1987), a startling film dealing with the problem of cocaine use and the role of the Teen Challenge organization in ministering to addicts. It won both a CINE Golden Eagle and a Silver Screen Award. Fussle explained his twofold vision as "evangelistic—challenging teenagers to a relationship with Jesus and teaching," and second, as practical, "helping them to deal with issues such as drugs and peer pressures."[74] The topicality of his films, coupled with the donation of films to high schools, enabled him to infiltrate the education system. Fussle's films reveal a continental aesthetic, a sense of form and structure that marked them from ordinary religious films. For example, his *Bamboo in Winter* (1991) was as much atmospheric as evangelistic, evoking a mood of exotic appeal amid a story about the discovery of faith in communist China.

Ken Anderson Films was an innovator in the 1950s, becoming the first Christian film company to become a for-profit organization, and the first to communicate internationally via InterComm Media, a means for translating films into other languages. At the time, many other Christian filmmakers questioned whether one could combine ministry and business. Yet while Ken Anderson Films theoretically was established as a profit-making company, it operated more like a mom-and-pop nonprofit company. They even self-labeled themselves "Poverty Productions," signifying low budgets, with virtually all profits channeled to finance new productions.

The staple plot of Ken Anderson's films revolves around individual transformation or the conversion of stock characters, with a critical "moment of decision" requiring a person (usually young) to face God and confront the meaning of his or her life. When a rowdy teenager drinks too much and falls from a window in *Man of Steel* (1970), his friends must soberly reassess their lives. Another student is paralyzed from a car accident in *Senior Year* (1976), which provokes his fellow students to rethink their priorities and their relationship to God. Unexpected pregnancy occurs in *Footprints* (1975). Though most of the films seem to have been made with conservative church audiences in mind, two films produced by the company stirred a great deal of discussion and controversy with conservative church markets. *The Enemy* (1975) dramatized the testimony of a young Christian couple confronted by a pair of demon-possessed teenagers. Exploiting the firestorm over *The Exorcist* (1973), the director Jim Grant wanted Christians to "realize that Satan is real [and that] demons are at work in the world today."[75] The film employs suspenseful horror techniques of chiaroscuro, abrupt sound effects, and sinister music. An even more provocative sacred terror film, *The Deceiver* (1976), deals with the role of demons in the lives of evangelical Christians. Both films disturbed elder church members, thinking that even by acknowledging the topic they were opening the gates of hell itself. Nevertheless, the films stirred much interest and rented quite profitably.

Anderson undertook several ambitious projects, the most memorable being *Pilgrim's Progress* (1977), shot in Northern Ireland and featuring a young Liam Neeson in his first film. Narrated by the gospel singer George Beverly Shea in a sort of reader's theater production, it devotedly recreated John Bunyan's allegory of Christian's journey to the Celestial City. Each actor appears on the screen and recites their portion of the original text. *Christiana* (1979) followed, a two-part sequel dealing with the pilgrimage of Pilgrim Christian's wife to the Celestial City, and though not as popular as the original, it shared its didactic tendencies. In a completely different vein, a four-part animated series featured a young teenager, Sparky, and followed him on numerous adventures that taught children about trusting God. In *The Lost Gold Mine* (1983), for example, Sparky and his gang of helpers learn to pray when threatened by a villain. Sparky would later explore the *Legend of Sunshine Mountain* (1984) and *Lasers from Space* (1984).

Perhaps the studio's two most impressive projects were Anderson's hagiographic studies of *Hudson Taylor* (1981) and *Fanny Crosby* (1984). The former proved to be the studio's most expensive production, dealing with the first dozen years of the missionary's life in China. Set in 19th-century Shanghai,

Hudson Taylor followed the pioneer work of the founder of the China Inland Mission, who began as a frail, frustrated missionary. The film dramatically captures Taylor's quiet rejection of the cultural imperialism of his native British society, symbolized by his abandonment of Western clothes for Chinese attire. Taylor's Pauline strategy of becoming all things to all people transformed the arrogance of much mission work into a humbler service to all humanity. For Anderson, it affirmed all he believed in adapting film AVangelism for international audiences.

Probably one of the more fruitful influences of Ken Anderson comes from his encouragement of the other Christian film companies that have directly or indirectly emanated from Ken Anderson Films. Doris Anderson recalled that "many of the actual film companies you hear about were influenced by Ken Anderson Films. Mark IV Films came to us, wanting us to help them get started. We helped them to get the scriptwriter, get all the things. Quadras Films is composed of one of our sons and a production crew that was one of ours, [and] they decided that they wanted to get into Christian films. International Films is a direct product of ours. It was our dream."[76]

The priority of Anderson's Christian filmmaking remained on the message, even as he planted the seeds for other film studios. These offshoots, particularly the apocalypse-oriented Mark IV Pictures, were more likely to emphasize evangelistic aspects of the Gospel message than to explore human dramas.

Summary

The studio work of Sam Hersh, Ken Anderson, and Billy Zeoli, along with the efforts of their stable of independent producers and directors, provided the bulk of Christian film products for church and school use from the 1950s through the 1980s. Each filled a particular niche in the growing market and contributed to the building of a community of Christian filmmakers. Hersh brought a savvy, intuitive sense of audience analysis to the cottage industry of Christian filmmaking, recruiting other key characters into the business, like the creative director Mel White. Hersh, as we have seen, also bolstered the growth of denominational films, particularly the Baptist studio Broadman Films.

Billy Zeoli, playing the role of "godfather" of the film fellowship, frustrated some producers and filmmakers with his backroom deals and internal politics. But he would not only open doors for budding filmmakers like John Schmidt, but also would build Gospel Films into a successful enterprise that would enjoy an economic boom with the instructional series of Franky Schaeffer and James Dobson. The Dobson effect would fill the producers' coffers, but it also stymied creative work, as investors would find it easier and more profitable to underwrite guaranteed-success instructional films over financially risky dramatic projects. After being passed over for leadership at Gospel Films, Ken Anderson ventured into international film work, maintaining his integrity as a Christian evangelist more concerned about spreading the Gospel message than entertaining. Faithfully adhering to his motto—"The message is always first"—Anderson would produce didactic classics like *Pilgrim's Progress* that preached unequivocally clear sermons. As each of these producers added their bricks to the building of an international Christian film industry, they contributed, directly and indirectly, to the use of films by various Protestant groups. Their general evangelical film work would spark studios with greater economic resources, commitment to film ministries, and innovative scholarly visions to serve as master filmmakers for wider Christian audiences. Billy Graham's World Wide Pictures and Ken Curtis's Gateway Films would fill this vacuum.

6

The Master Filmmakers

On September 21, 1969, CBS broadcast *Woody's First Special* in which Woody Allen interviewed the evangelist Billy Graham, whom the comedian and film director called "charming and provocative." Allen introduced his guest by announcing that he disagreed with Graham on a significant number of issues (Graham's favorite commandment at the time was to honor thy father and mother, which was Woody's least favorite as he was saving up money to put his parents in a home; Graham hoped it would be in a home with Woody). As they squared off, Woody wondered which of the two would be converted, as he sought to cajole Graham into agnosticism. Woody acknowledged that when he looked in the mirror in the morning, he found it hard to believe that God was perfect. Graham responded that God had created Woody "beautiful" but that he needed God's redemptive help to become the person God intended him to be. Graham confessed that he had not seen any of Woody's movies, but with a free pass or ticket, he might go see one. Woody agreed that if Graham went to one of his movies, he would go a Billy Graham revival: "That is a deal!," quipped Graham.

The meeting between these two worlds, entertainment and religion, suggested more than a simple interview between representatives of the sacred and the profane; it recognized that the two realms had become blended in ways that some separatist ministers would never have imagined. Entertainment and revival religion would be combined in the products of one of the major studios of the Christian film industry, while a lesser-known group would employ entertainment as education.

Two distinctly different organizations made their mark as significant contributors to the history of Christian filmmaking, World Wide Pictures and Gateway Films. At first glance they appear to have little in common: the first being a larger, synergistic corporate entity with global tentacles, and the latter being a Pennsylvania cottage industry run by an educator. Both WWP and Gateway found a niche—evangelism and religious education, respectively—that they pursued with perseverance and a desire to present professional quality beyond that found in typical religious film productions.

World Wide Pictures

The mythic theme of journey functions as a staple of many classic narratives. Seeking a compelling narrative structure, numerous Hollywood producers turned to Christopher Vogler's book *The Writer's Journey* to exploit his model of the spiritual journey, a mythic odyssey that a character must travel to arrive at some point of revelation or redemption.[1] The stages of the journey include such aspects as the call out of the ordinary, an encounter with a wise mentor, enduring and overcoming various tests, enemies, and ordeals, and a threshold experience in which characters are transformed and "resurrected." Rooted in Joseph Campbell's famous study *The Hero with a Thousand Faces*, this "hero's journey," with its archetypes and variations, has formed the skeletal framework for many Hollywood films, including those of George Lucas and Steven Spielberg.

If one replaces the hero with the sinner, the formula finds its home in many WWP films. Even the title of the studio's first foray into comedy suggested this journey structure, *Road to Redemption* (2001). These Christian filmmakers open up the paradigm of film as a pilgrimage, adding the concept of sin as a central motif within the journey. The children of Israel were condemned to wander in the wilderness because of their sin, even as they sought a promised land of milk and honey. Disobedience was the cause of their detours. As the religious film critics Ernest Ferlita and John May observed, to sin is "to miss the road (*hata*) or to wander away from it (*avon*). To repent is to return (*shuv*)."[2]

As a pervasive symbol in Christian mystical literature, the spiritual journey usually follows a threefold path of ascent, descent, and redemption. In both Vogler's heroic adventure and the spiritual quest journey, the hero undergoes an adventure and matures; in Vogler's model, he usually returns home much wealthier and married to a princess. For the spiritual journey, one is chosen for a higher calling and is radically transformed. One leaves the old life behind. As with the persecutor Saul on the road to Damascus, an encounter and calling occurs that overturns a prior map.

Western journeys usually adhere to *via affirmativa*, a positive movement toward the divine. Both Augustine's *Confessions* and Bonaventura's soul adventure trace several steps forward with one step back, yet continually onward.[3] Eastern patterns, such as that of the 14th-century mystic Meister Eckhart, call for one to strip away, to be purged *via negativa*. What is key for both, however, is the ritual stage of liminality, that internal moment, however brief, when the past is suspended and the moment of potentiality is set before the protagonist. The liminal state is one of threshold, wherein one opens oneself to risk and radical change.[4] It is the moment of conversion that underlies most WWP films. What concludes such a crisis of the soul is the spontaneous *communitas*, that utopian vision of community and personal wholeness/holiness. Generally the hero meets a character who helps him or her along the way. This mentor can be crusty or irascible but is always old and wise, and offers sound guidance against the diversions that would tempt one to go astray. The protagonist in many WWP productions encounters the actual founder of WWP, the evangelist Billy Graham himself, either through an open-air crusade, a television program, or on the radio, receiving his wisdom and guidance through a public or mediated ministry.

Even before the famous Los Angeles tent crusades of 1949, when the publishing magnate William Randolph Hearst ordered his *Los Angeles Times* reporters to "puff Graham," Rev. Billy Graham, along with the singer Cliff Barrows and other close advisers, envisioned films being shown all over the world in schools, courtyards, hospitals, and missions. In conjunction with their crusades around the country, the Graham association engaged many churches that would never have a chance to be involved in a crusade. The plan was to film preparations for the crusade and then film the crusade itself, allowing churches to have some insight into what was happening and share in some of the results.[5]

It would take over a decade for such documentary records to be filmed (and then televised), but the first steps for the Billy Graham Evangelistic Association (BGEA) to provide dramatic motion pictures for the furtherance of the Gospel had been taken. The global vision, epigrammatically condensed in a slick promotional ad provided for pastors, prophetically announced, "A WWP film showing is started somewhere in the world every 19 minutes around the clock."

Touted as "the granddaddy of evangelical filmmakers" (having produced twenty-five feature films between 1953 and 2004), WWP was officially formed in 1952 as the Billy Graham Evangelistic Film Ministry, when the entrepreneur Dick Ross's Great Commission Films was incorporated into the BGEA.[6] In 1950, Ross had filmed a Graham crusade in Portland, Oregon, and suggested incorporating footage into a dramatic feature film. The broad landscape of Texas mapped out the spiritual geography for their first three dramatic films. The first, *Mr. Texas* (1951), shot during the Fort Worth Crusade, featured Red Harper in the leading role and premiered at the prestigious Hollywood Bowl.

None other than the great director Cecil B. DeMille attended the record-breaking premiere in the Hollywood Bowl in 1951 to see the first Billy Graham feature film, *Mr. Texas*. In a publicity photo, DeMille is pictured posed with Graham and a copy of *The Ten Commandments* script, which was to be the director's next spectacular. In the same pictorial review, Graham remembered the projector breaking down and wondered at his audacity to invite Hollywood celebrities to a film that had cost only $25,000 dollars to make: "It took that amount of money just to turn on their lights."[7]

The next year, *Fort Worth* (1954) debuted and found its way into the newly formed film libraries of Gospel Films. *Oiltown, USA* (1953) also exploited Texas locations, using documentary footage of oil-drilling rigs to produce a musical melodrama, scored by the renowned composer Ralph Carmichael. The Hollywood actor Paul Power starred as the jaded, shrewd oil manipulator Manning. When Manning's daughter Christine and a friend of hers return home from college "up north" in Houston, the girls undergo a spiritual struggle, even in amid their Texas paradise of wealth and social prominence. Christine declares, "I'll be out of school next year and I want to know where I am going . . . and where I've come from too." The theme of homecoming is echoed as the choir sings, "Lord, I'm coming home." Along with nine minutes of Billy Graham preaching, the songwriter Red Harper supplied the generic Christian testimony during the filmed crusade, while George Beverly Shea, Cliff Barrows, and the Sons of the Pioneers filled the plains of Texas with their music.

Setting up headquarters in Burbank, California, WWP turned out numerous features, including a groundbreaking popular and commercial success with *The Restless Ones* (1965, with Kim Darby). This watershed film was followed by *For Pete's Sake* (1968, with Teri Garr), *Time to Run* (1973, with the Oscar-winning Charles Rosher as director of photography), *The Hiding Place* (1975), *Joni* (1980), and *The Prodigal* (1983), marking two decades of reliably consistent productions of quality religious filmmaking. WWP set up its own distribution process out of Minneapolis, established by the thousands of pastors and church leaders already in support of the BGEA.[8] They produced what Ken Engstrom called the "Billy Graham signature series, pure and simple and evangelistic, true to the Gospel."[9] These films would usually insert the protagonist into a Billy Graham crusade, where he or she would come to Christ. According to a 1966 article in *Christianity Today*, more than 120,000 conversions from the films had been recorded. WWP President William (Bill) F. Brown explained that "the central purpose of all our films, whether dramatic or documentary, is to *demonstrate* that Jesus Christ, and He alone, is the answer to mankind's problems and needs—that a personal, vital relationship with Him is not only possible, but necessary, if we are to fulfill the purpose for which we are created."[10]

Most of their early films were exhibited primarily in churches or youth rallies; yet WWP also recognized the need to show the films where they could be viewed by people who would not normally go into a church service. Thus they adopted the aforementioned practice of "four-walling" to exhibit their films. The plan involved buying the rights to all performances for an agreed sum from local theaters, which meant that exhibitors did not have to worry about ticket sales; their profits were already guaranteed, regardless of whether the public came to the Billy Graham picture showing there. Like Wesleyan circuit riders, advance teams hopped from city to city. Advance marketing would invade a city six months before the showing, alerting sympathetic churches of this coming attraction, seeking to sell as many tickets as possible before the local premiere. Church members were encouraged to invite nonchurch friends, and counselors were present to pray with anyone seeking spiritual guidance after having seen the film. Using this four-walling technique, backed by extensive marketing and advertising support, WWP was able to blanket theaters across the country with mediated evangelism.

This method became the model for every BGEA message motion picture release in the secular theatrical field, a pioneering step for the Christian film industry rarely copied until the late 1990s. The BGEA applied professional marketing techniques to insure success. According to Ken Engstrom, newspaper advertising was coordinated

> in conjunction with the run of the film in any given city; we do television and radio spots; and quite a lot of direct mail to people who have been part of the Billy Graham organization in one way or another. But probably the key thing with our major theater releases we go into a city only if there is a local committee of people made up of a broad cross section of the churches who are the ones who do all the organizing necessary for that release in their city. . . . We just provide the advice and counseling.[11]

Attending movie theaters remained a cultural taboo for some conservative denominations. To remedy the problem of acceptable viewing venues, Harry Bristow of Ambler, Pennsylvania, established his own Christian cinema for families. In the mid-1980s, teenagers would converge every weekend night to see new Christian movies and old, "clean" Hollywood favorites.[12] The highlight was always a Billy Graham film.

When James Collier scripted Ross's *The Heart Is a Rebel* in 1958, he indirectly introduced racial concerns to the evangelical world through the inclusion of the black musical artist Ethel Waters. The film, however, deals with modern skepticism regarding the divine, emphasizing that one is called to trust God even when one does not "feel" His presence. Nevertheless, the film follows a formulaic pattern, with the protagonist being forced to confront God in relation to a personal crisis (the terminal illness of a child). The film also suffers from the typical WWP faults, in that the narrative stops whenever a sermon is preached or a song is sung; the static, almost stagnant, religious moments contrast with the tumultuous journey of the normal life.

The BGEA's ability to attract a young audience peaked with *The Restless Ones* (1965), a film that took the viewer into the world of a teenager struggling with doubt, parental interference, and peer pressure. The marketing and advertising plan for the film became the model of virtually every "message motion picture" to be released in the secular theatrical market: "*The Restless Ones* opened a previously closed door and many teenagers came to the Lord. Secular junior and senior high schools would sell tickets for one dollar and allow students go to special student showings during the school day. When *Two a Penny* (1967) came to Hurst, Texas, half of my junior high school went forward in the theater after the program and received the Lord."[13]

On *The Restless Ones*, Collier had served as associate producer; *For Pete's Sake* was his first crack at directing a feature: "I created *For Pete's Sake* because I felt it was the unanswered question. They'd always done all these formula pictures where there was a crusade and Billy Graham came to town and everybody got saved and then he left. And I said the drama is when he leaves town. What happens to people when he's gone? I wanted to show a meat-and-potatoes guy."[14]

Having started in the film industry as a page boy for NBC, Collier was first noticed by WWP when he produced and directed an independent film titled *Woman of Sychar*, a picture that Collier acknowledged "was a shock to the status quo of the time because it was so natural."[15] Ross, then president of WWP, needed a "gofer," and when he saw the film he asked Collier to join the team. After he rose through the ranks, the studio eventually offered him the opportunity to become a full director in 1966. *Two a Penny* (1967) and the popular *For Pete's Sake* (1968) saw the emergence of Collier as one of WWP's key directors. Collier articulated the organizational vision when he described WWP as standing as "a lighthouse in a great storm [during] a power failure." After previewing *For Pete's Sake* at the Director's Guild Theater, however, Collier incurred the hostility of his professional colleagues. They complained that he put too much "deep *light* in a film." Its preachiness was too explicit, even if the film did explore what happened to a family after a conversion at a Billy Graham crusade, instead of the film conveniently ending with the conversion itself.[16]

Between 1966 and 1988, Collier would write four of WWP's feature productions and direct eight. *Two a Penny,* filmed in swinging London, starred Britain's most popular Christian pop music star, Cliff Richard. Trumpeted as a truly unique Christian film, and "definitely the best release yet from the studios of Billy Graham" (according to the reviewer David Coombes), it portrayed "believable people searching for convincing answers to contemporary problems" and was not an "anemic version of an evangelical fairy tale."[17] But this film musical harked back to Victorian melodrama with the good, converted Christian girl, Carol, seeking to help her unredeemed boyfriend, Jamie, played by Cliff Richard. Coombes found the hero's spiritual progress limited but refreshingly genuine. Rather than an overnight dramatic conversion, he moves from defiance ("If you want me, God, you've got to stand in line like everyone else") to sincere openness ("God, if you're real, if you're there at all, show me").[18]

In 1973, WWP released *Time to Run,* a film little different in theme, character, and structure from *The Restless Ones.* In the WWP's ongoing attempt to bridge the cultural gap between evangelicals and the larger cultural world, rock concerts and hitchhiking replaced churchgoing. In its attempts to adapt the ephemeral fashions of miniskirts, long hair, hip generational jargon, and kids singing "Kumbayah," the film stands as a marker for the 1970s as much as the dated disco films. With the scriptwriter Alan Sloane, Collier built the film around Francis Thompson's classic poem "The Hound of Heaven," but the spiritual journey drama did not compel fellow travelers to follow or notice the haunting hound snapping at one's heels. The reviewer Cheryl Forbes acknowledged that "making a believable Christian film is a difficult task."[19] Yet for Forbes, the problem was not in mere resources or technical expertise. The critical, even insuperable, problem of credibility as she and others saw it was framed in the actual strength of film: "The celluloid medium is the vehicle of illusion *par excellence*: can it believably convey spiritual truth?"[20]

The two most successful feature films from WWP in terms of critical response, audience reception, and evangelism were *The Hiding Place* and *Joni.*[21] Both were written and directed by Collier, who had become convinced that true-life stories offered the most effective means for communicating faith. But it was Ruth Graham who convinced everyone that Corrie ten Boom's autobiographical story about a family involved with the underground resistance during the Nazi occupation of the Netherlands needed to be a feature production.[22] *The Hiding Place* started a new trend for the company in that a number of influential Christians joined to underwrite the cost of production. With fund-raising appeals sent to various churches, gifts trickled in for the film to be produced, including donations of as little as one or two dollars. Prior to this, WWP received its financial support from the evangelistic ministry's base of donors and from the limited proceeds generated from previous WWP productions.

Starring Julie Harris, Arthur O'Connell, and Eileen Heckart, *The Hiding Place* recounts the true story of the ten Booms, a Dutch Christian family who cooperated with the underground in saving the lives of countless Jewish families during World War II. While it is one of the few films not to include Billy Graham preaching in a crusade, the evangelist and author Corrie ten Boom, who survived the concentration camp, contributed a powerful epilogue. Two separate endings were released, one for general audiences, in which Corrie walks from the Ravensbrück concentration camp through the snow, reflecting on a thirty-year spiritual journey. In an alternative ending for churches and religious audiences, ten Boom appears on the screen and appeals directly to the audience: "For a period of time [I] really questioned who the audience was for *The Hiding Place* until I read a review written by the movie critic of the *Boston Globe* newspaper: 'I wept in scene after scene, wept not only for the plight of the ten Booms and the Jews they tried to save, but wept within my own agnostic floundering for the surety of their beliefs.'"[23]

Even with its preachy coda, the film tremendously affected reviewers, including the influential Rex Reed.[24] Christian audiences also adored the film; *Christianity Today*'s two-page review gushed, "Christian filmmaking has come of age. It should get recognition not only from churches but from the secular film world and the academy as well."[25] Kevin Thomas of the *Los Angeles Times* concurred, calling it "that rarest of rarities, a film of shining, triumphant spirituality."[26]

Like *The Hiding Place*, *Joni* transformed the conversion formula movie into a genuine and evocative drama of suffering. The film chronicled the true story of Joni Eareckson, a young woman who at the age of seventeen was paralyzed when she snapped her neck in an automobile accident. Playing herself, Joni conveyed the intense pain, doubt, and bitter confusion of being confined to a wheelchair. Collier reluctantly wrote the script and directed the film: "I didn't want to have anything to do with it. I died a few deaths before it was finished because it was extremely difficult for me personally to do."[27] In avoiding any fictional melodramatic elements, Collier showed restraint and managed to let the biographical material provide the drama and Joni herself supply a transcendent performance. The film was a major success and was widely acclaimed for its authenticity.

The WWP director Irving Rapper and the executive producer Robert Munger didn't succeed nearly as well in adapting the spiritual autobiography of President Richard Nixon's hatchet man, Charles Colson, in *Born Again* (1978). The impish reviewer John Lawing pointed out a marketing ploy in the release of the film. On the Sunday before the world premiere, a television network showcased Disney's earlier feature, *The Shaggy D.A.* (1976), since both films starred Dean Jones as a villain.[28] The key problem of the film, Lawing posed, was how to treat the "old man" during his pre-conversion phase. "Conversion to Christ changes the theological content and direction of a person's life," Lawing noted, but it "does not usually change his personality." Thus how can one show dramatic change while preserving the personality?[29] Another problem was such Christian films struggle with making God-talk genuine and non-God-talk realistic. The script seemed too scrubbed and sanitized.

With the producer Ken Wales, Collier returned to write and direct the quintessential Billy Graham conversion/journey picture, *The Prodigal*. The contemporary version of Christ's parable of the wayward son expands to the overlapping tales of three desultory pilgrims: son, brother, and now the father's own wife. Each gropes for meaning along his or her own road.[30]

The film, however, sparked a spirited defense of Christian filmmaking by the two executives. In a dual interview conducted by the filmmaker Mel White, Collier and Wales reflected on the problems and challenges confronting Christian film.[31] A recurring objection for WWP was the ubiquitous nature of Billy Graham and the explicitly and unapologetically evangelistic tenor of the films. Yet these films were intended and designed to serve audiences as "a catalyst in their spiritual journey." And as a result of viewing a WWP picture, Collier points out, "over 400,000 people indicated some sort of first-time commitment to Christ."[32]

According to Wales, a second complaint haunting Christian filmmakers is whether to make evil explicit or implicit. For Wales, the latter option allowed audiences to bring to the film "all their imagination, their biases, their prejudices . . . and forced the director to be creative and imaginative and to come up with some way to say what was happening [especially sexually]." Collier felt *The Prodigal* was daring in that he was able to "imply that people have sexual lives," although he stopped short of provoking the voyeurism of most Hollywood films. He still felt pigeonholed by Hollywood executives who joked that "any script that came into a major studio that had 'God' in it and didn't have 'damn' behind it was immediately sent to World Wide."[33]

The Prodigal addressed issues of hypocrisy, masquerading, identity, pretense, and genuine Christianity to a churched audience even more than an unchurched one. On one level, Collier noted, "it's a spiritual odyssey of one young man," a contemporary prodigal. For Wales, it was also the dissection of an entire family and so could have been titled *The Prodigals*.

The two basic philosophies of Christian filmmaking had been set on a continuum between Baptista and Friedrich. The former believed that Christian films should be shot with born-again Christians; the latter thought that one needed to use the best Hollywood talent around to minister to the non-Christians. Opting to go with Friedrich's view, Collier and Wales sought out all the outstanding professionals they could find, hiring fully union crews, which made for some "earthy" encounters with those who did not understand the Christian motives and purposes but nonetheless saw the work as "worthwhile."[34]

One final prevailing problem in Christian filmmaking concerned the narrative structure in which crises are usually resolved in the last reel with a trip to the altar at a Billy Graham meeting. But in *The Prodigal*, the filmmakers chose not to apply "a Band-aid or an easy cure"; rather, they wanted audience members to recognize that other problems remained. Harry Cheney acknowledged that "religious conversion is . . . perhaps the most difficult human experience to duplicate in a dramatic setting. It is often like listening to one side of a two-way argument." He argued, effectively, that an encounter with God should "propel the action, not end it." Nor could Cheney approve the rebellious lifestyle of the protagonist, as it appeared to him to be a "sanctified view of sin," a squeaky clean portrayal of the deeply gritty and selfish human heart of darkness. He also faulted the film on its "strange absence of awe . . . of a visual grammar that communicates the brooding presence of a transcendent being. There is a sense of Jesus, but never of his presence."[35]

WWP produced and distributed more than one hundred Christian films in the last thirty-five years, claiming that more than 1.5 million people experienced conversion as a result of the showings. But a crisis point occurred in 1986, with huge production overheads weighing down the studio. Films had become too expensive to produce in-house and kept the studio and its personnel quite busy. As a result, the following year the Burbank studio house was shut down. Nevertheless, WWP continued to sponsor films, and in 1988 it released what some thought would be its last film, a stark production centering around the 1986 International Conference on Itinerant Evangelists in Amsterdam, *Caught* (1988).

Written and directed by Collier, *Caught* bursts on the screen with drug trafficking, murder, male prostitution, and a young man's search for his unknown father. The quest of Tim Devon (played by the *Friday the 13th* actor John Shepherd) begins in California and winds up in the morally corrupt city of Amsterdam. Simultaneous with Devon's troubles with drug dealers and pimps is the arrival of a young, naïve, but sincere (and kung-fu fighting) Indian evangelist, Rajhad, who has lost his own Hindu parents by becoming a Christian. At the international conference Billy Graham reiterates the theme of various spiritual journeys: "We have come from more countries and territories than probably any event in the history of the world. . . . Your minds are weary from long travel but your hearts are here."

Graham punctuates the film's sermon by saying that "choosing our own way is separation from Christ," a reference to Devon's and Rajhad's aimless and frantic pursuit and flight throughout the canalled city. Rajhad, after confessing to God his own incompetence in guiding others, becomes the vehicle God uses to lead the prodigal American away from the wages of his life and into the home (and veterinarian clinic) of his birth father. Rajhad would proclaim that "God has brought us to Amsterdam to fulfill the work of an evangelist." Rather than the blind leading the blind, the film follows the reformer Martin Luther's adage that one Christian is merely a beggar showing other beggars where to find the bread of life.[36]

The huge debt of the Burbank studio headquarters, its numerous worldwide centers, and its astronomical operating costs compounded to pressure for a shutdown. Theaters had changed as well, with distribution becoming more difficult to obtain from major exhibition sites. The task of raising donor money for films (practiced since *The Hiding Place*) was reassessed, with more films being produced specifically for church markets, as was the case with Friedrich's and Moon's pictures. Films meant to "reach the lost or teach the church," said Barry Werner, director of operations for WWP, were now used simply to "entertain the choir."[37] After more than thirty years of owning their studios in Burbank, the ministry finally closed down the operation. In anticipation of Billy Graham's retirement, the board considered trimming or phasing out numerous other ministry functions as well.

From 1965 through 1986, the product had been driven by theater exhibition. A decade later, in 1997, a dormant WWP began a decisive move back into media evangelism and national television. The team that turned WWP around, "rescuing film out of the ashes," was headed by BGEA President Dr. John Corts, operating under a snappy, dynamic new motto: "More future than history." A new executive, Roger Flessing, joined WWP and asked Corts how much money they had, and the answer was $1.9 million. They agreed to spend these last funds, hiring John Shepherd's Shepgroup, a creative production team with the Make-a-Wish Foundation, and found a mutually agreeable project, the Western-themed feature *The Ride* (1997). The board of directors stamped their internal confirmation on the plan and WWP was revived.[38] With Corts and Flessing's vision, a WWP renaissance would take place in the 1990s while keeping within the corporate mission statement of the BGEA. Every film was run through the screen of the mission statement, checking its evangelical orthodoxy, before it was made more compelling. But films were intentionally conceived as "seed planters," rather than trying to plant ideas in audiences *and* trying to compel them to convert. The harvesting of souls would be left to the Graham crusades. These films would function more as parables than as sermons.

The narrative arc familiar to classic Hollywood filmmaking was baptized and adopted for evangelistic purposes by the WWP. Developing a character with a fatal flaw was seen as the equivalent to presenting the lost condition of human beings, of drawing characters in desperate need of God's grace. The character curve or trajectory also found its parallel in the outside forces and turning points of life being set in the sufficiency and sovereignty of God. The critical moment of human choice became the decision moment, with central characters confronted with the message of Jesus as the Christ through some public or mediated presentation from Billy Graham himself. Finally, the evidence of a changed life and the film's resolution was expressed in the character's transformation. One not only saw the conversion but also witnessed a life changed for the better. The script patterns provided a structure not unlike the famous Campus Crusade for Christ tract of the four spiritual laws.[39]

The process of acquiring new screenplays was streamlined as WWP entertained various two-page treatment ideas. Treatments would then be distributed around the BGEA and engender various responses. The writer would then serve as the creative genius, expanding the treatment, testing its correspondence to the Christian faith and mission statement throughout. A beat sheet (an efficient record of key events designed to tell the story) would assess the entire film for administrative team, with a single sentence per scene, no longer than 120 lines total. If the Gospel appeared slim or inadequate, action would be taken to enhance it.[40]

Collier argued that WWP deserved "honor for its place in history." He pointed to Billy Graham's vision of film's potential; while the BGEA didn't understand the relationship of screen to audience in its development years, it became more sophisticated and professional as the organization experimented and evolved.[41] The standards for success for WWP work did not correspond to how many people saw the film or how much money came in at the box office, nor were they measured by critical reviews. As Wales put it, the studio was more concerned "about its impact upon the people who see it. Will it change their lives?"[42] The films' impact for evangelism was paramount, taking audiences on a journey with "little bumps along the way" and ending at a crusade.

Collier observed that WWP "is in the business of offering people new beginnings. . . . We see our responsibility to offer the folks sitting out there in a darkened theater the chance to start again. That is the gospel."[43] In keeping both with their vision of engaging audiences to begin their journeys, and with the Danish philosopher Søren Kierkegaard's dictum that art (and preaching) not distract from personal, existential confrontation, the motion picture ministry of the Billy Graham Evangelistic Association set forth a list of six ideas to plot their evangelistic outreach.[44] Their first two criteria focus on spiritual preparation, namely, "Pray with us for the impact this will have on your community for Christ!," and "Make sure the opportunity for evangelism is presented to everyone possible in your church." The other four suggestions lean toward a full-fledged local marketing campaign: "'Adopt' the nearest theater as 'yours,'" "Have your church fill one or more nights at a theater" (which may be accomplished by busing them in), "Encourage people to bring unchurched family, friends and neighbors to the theater" (with youth groups competing to see who can bring in the most guests, presenting skits as church announcements, and giving away prizes and rewards), and "Remind people that they can have fun with this!" (such as serving desserts to help promote "follow-up" discussions). The biblical counsel to be as wise as serpents (Matthew 10:16) compels the film's sponsor to become all things to all people in order to win some converts; it is evangelism informed by simple public relations techniques.

WWP provided the hallmark of excellence for evangelical filmmakers. The films were professionally made, professionally acted, and, above all, professionally distributed. But they still remained exercises in film persuasion, or as the Roman Catholics liked to term it, film propaganda. Many smaller companies tended to follow WWP's approach to evangelical outreach. But one company, Gateway, was different; it branched out to Roman Catholic as well as Protestant groups and emphasized the importance of church history and education in reaching other audiences with Christian messages.

Gateway Films

Classic Hollywood cinema painted historical characters like heroes in biopics such as *The Story of Louis Pasteur* (1936), *Yankee Doodle Dandy* (1942), or *Wilson* (1944). A movement to produce pictures on historical saints, appropriately called "hagiopics," for Christians was coordinated by an ordained American Baptist minister with a background in television, Ken Curtis. As a student at Gordon Divinity School, Curtis secured a job with the CBS affiliate WHDH and helped to develop *Young World*, a local program for the Boston area.[45] His arrival into the world of Christian film was unexpected, thorny, and providential.

In 1968, Curtis got entangled in the complicated production of a feature film titled *The Cross and the Switchblade* (1970). Back in 1959, the *New York Times* reporter John McCandlish Phillips stumbled across a story of God's Spirit and a crusading preacher from Pennsylvania invading the urban jungle of the Big Apple. Pastor David Wilkerson's dogged determination to work with drug addicts and gang members provided a story of local color and daunting challenges. The spiritual challenge between icons of sacrifice and violence resulted in a 1963 autobiographical best seller on Wilkerson about his experiences with the feared gang leader of the Mau-Maus, Nicky Cruz. Dick Ross, former president and founder of World Wide Pictures, had wanted to film the story of Cruz's radical conversion. Ross coordinated various limited partnerships with the American Baptist Convention and private Baptist investors to underwrite his own corporation, Dick Ross Associates. Needing additional resources and contacts, Ross approached Curtis and persuaded him to come in as a limited partner, serve as associate producer of the drama, and recruit several other American Baptist investors to join the project.

Problems continually beset the *Cross* production. Both legal and tax troubles hounded Dick Ross Associates, which suffered from undercapitalization and little management discipline. Remarkably, *The Cross and the Switchblade* set house records in about a third of its first two hundred cities of release in 1970. Still, the threat of bankruptcy hovered over the project, and Ross's company eventually went into receivership. But even before this first film had been paid off, Ross initiated a second project, *The Late Liz* (1971, starring the Oscar winner Anne Baxter).[46]

Ross had previously developed the presale strategy of four-walling with George Wilson of WWP, and thought that he could effectively distribute his films. However, two major complications ensued that set his company back.

First, Spyros Skouras, president of Twentieth Century-Fox, who had green-lit a film project on the life of Saint Paul and had authorized $1.2 million to the film, passed away on August 16, 1971. Second, Ross had withheld taxes on the film, and the IRS subsequently began an investigation in which they would eventually seize all properties, even inadvertently auctioning off the company's books and records.

Then the National Film Service shut down Dick Ross Associates even though their main source of income, *The Cross and the Switchblade*, still had several hundred play dates on its calendar. In 1972, Phillips realized the quandary he was in and looked for a way out. He approached a newly organized Gateway Films to pick up the film from Dick Ross Associates and explore how they together might crack the metropolitan New York City market with a saturation exhibition strategy.[47]

Curtis, who was teaching a course at Eastern College at the time, got a call one night asking him to run the company. Yet it was too little too late; Dick Ross Associates had to file for bankruptcy. According to Curtis, "The company got in over its head and went into Chapter 11. The reorganization plan called for the formation of a new distribution company to help in the transition period, namely, Gateway Films. I had gotten the major part of the investors into the Dick Ross Company and they were looking to me. The majority of them were saying, 'You're the one that got us into this. You're the guy that has to get us out.'"[48]

The courts agreed. Early in 1973, however, Phillips was investigating the production for the *Times* to see if it was a scam fleecing money from Christians and so he called Curtis. Curtis acknowledged that the company was in over its head, crippled by business incompetence, but that there was no fraud. He entreated the reporter to hold the story, as they were trying to get a multiple opening in New York theaters. Rather than jeopardize a budding media ministry, Phillips accepted and delayed the background story.[49]

The court's federal receiver had ordered that the name of the company be changed. Curtis had to think of a new name quickly, and "Gateway" just popped into his mind. The name was derived, however, not from some symbolic idea of the company becoming a gateway into heaven, or even into the spectators' minds; actually, the evening that Curtis was reconfiguring the company, he ate dinner at a greasy spoon in Norristown, Pennsylvania, called the Gateway Diner. Thus Curtis found himself at the helm of a new distribution company. In 1972, offices were moved from Columbus Circle in New York City to the rural environs of Valley Forge, Pennsylvania, where Gateway became a nontheatrical distribution company. Curtis was not daunted by the transition; in fact, he had been inspired by a 1972 cover of *Esquire* magazine, emblazoned with a photograph of a cathedral superimposed with a movie marquee announcing "Faith of Our Children." Curtis realized he could magnify the proclamation of the Gospel by using film, noting that "the motion picture theatre is a central place where the values and views of life of young Americans are shaped, and we think that we ought to be in that arena."[50]

With the temporary help of his denomination, the American Baptists, his new company was able to continue the distribution of *The Cross and the Switchblade* and stabilize the situation until Gateway acquired new investors and a new board of directors. Fortunately, the film continued to be a profitable rental product, despite the corny but sincere acting of Pat Boone and Erik Estrada.

What enabled the distribution to succeed, however, was a strategy of multiple openings in scores of theaters, beginning in New York City and then mostly in minor markets with simultaneous and widespread media coverage. Curtis himself represented the film in Lancaster, California, where local media covered the film and area churches rallied to support the exhibitions. Radio and television talk shows invited the principal players for interviews. Critics did not see the film until it opened, and when they did, many responded with remarkable generosity. Although one New York exhibitor deemed it "too violent," the *New York Times* reporter Howard Thompson provided a modest but glowing review, and *Newsday*, the *Daily News*, and a host of small papers joined the bandwagon of puffing the film.[51] For Thompson, it didn't offer any savagely blistering realism, but rather earnestness and a "pungent savvy edge," which raised the script above the usual mire. Philips even secured the quotation of the day on the front page in June 1972, and others acted to persuade critics to postpone negative reviews.

Directed by Don Murray, *The Cross and the Switchblade* succeeded enormously at the box office, despite its tumultuous beginnings, because of its compelling human drama. *Cross* was distributed in more than thirty languages and in more than 150 countries, and inaugurated both the ministries of Rev. David Wilkerson and the former gang member Nicky Cruz.[52] Mixed reviews came from Christian critics. One lambasted it for its "poor use of actors and script, an unbelievable human situation, and dishonest manipulation of the original true-life story material."[53] The satiric Baptist critic Joe Bob Briggs called the docudrama about the life of David Wilkerson the "Gospel according to Pat Boone." Playing the evangelist, Boone "wanders through the slums in neon red-stocking feet because his shoes are stolen [and] screaming 'I love you and God loves you' at the Mau-Mau war council." Unfortunately, according to Briggs, all the gang members, led by Erik Estrada, look "like they were recruited from the Southwestern Baptist Theological Seminary and the wild sex party consists of a lot of smoke, two miniskirts, and a hanging-bead doorway."[54] But Thompson credited Estrada as demonstrating enormous acting potential in a scene in which he undergoes the agony of his drug cravings. For John Everson of *Christianity Today*, the film suffered from the usual schizophrenia of Christian movies, trying vainly to be both evangelistic and entertaining.[55]

Nevertheless, the film became the foundation for Gateway's ministry, sustaining the company as its best-selling title. The arrival of video sales would provide necessary financial funding for other projects, enabling Gateway to maintain a ministry that was not market-driven, but rather focused solely on distributing stories of the Gospel.

Because productions were expensive, Gateway's early releases were acquired from independent American producers. Governed in large part by the American Baptist Convention, Gateway took on true stories with a sense of history, social consciousness, or human responsibility, like that of a mobster's conversion in *The Confession of Tom Harris* (1969). Don Murray wrote and produced this reality-based drama of rape and violence based on the exploits of Tom Harris and his Christian victim Pat Jennings, whom he eventually married.[56] *Confessions* challenged the status quo of biopics in its use of impressionist symbolism and creative editing. (In classic Hitchcockesque style, Jennings screams during the rape sequence on a wharf, with the sound fusing into the strident cry of a seagull.) But in this daring first venture, Curtis quickly discovered that the church market was not ready for too much reality. In the grand spirit of a DeMille production, Murray had adamantly insisted that you must show a little debauchery if you are going to demonstrate a conversion from sinner to Christian.[57] His presentation, however, was not acceptable to most churches in Gateway's distribution network. Despite decent acting from John Derrick, Linda Evans, and Tommy Harris, brutal boxing scenes and other forms of violence resulted in the movie being deemed "too hard" for the church audiences, and it did not do well financially. In discussing the film, the reviewer Cheryl Forbes was particularly acute in her critique of the Christian film industry, recognizing the difficulty in balancing "edification with entertainment," and concluding that the scales usually tipped in favor of edification: "Too many Christian films are mere excuses for the final sermon—and from the first frame we know that the heavy is heading for conversion."[58] The consequence of such an unabashed confrontation is that secular critics cringed at the blatant Christian themes;

Pat Boone played David Wilkerson and Erik Estrada played Nicky Cruz, the gang leader, in the Gateway production of *The Cross and the Switchblade*. Courtesy of Ken Curtis and Vision Video.

in equal measure, church leaders refused to support such films because they did not portray their particular brand of piety, but rather pandered to more suggestive and offensive elements. Curtis quickly learned from this abortive experiment and concluded that Gateway Films was not equipped for effective theatrical distribution.[59]

Twentieth Century-Fox contacted Curtis regarding the 1955 film *A Man Called Peter*, proposing that "maybe it would help you out."[60] The inspiring story tells of the Scottish immigrant Peter Marshall who became the Senate chaplain, offering an intimate portrait of a man who "enjoyed" God. In addition, Curtis picked up a slew of forgettable films such as *Hazel's People* (1973, aka *Happy as the Grass Was Green*) and a cornball Western produced through a Grand Rapids, Michigan, Reformed Church crowd, *The Ballad of Billie Blue* (1972). Charles Davis's *Hazel's People*, starring Geraldine Page, showed the personal transformation of an activist who observed the authentic Christian lives of a Mennonite community.[61] Underwritten in part by a local dentist, Ken Osborne's *The Ballad of Billie Blue* ironically warned of the temptations of show business, as Billie Blue goes from country music celebrity to jail to gospel music stardom. An opening country musical number previews the entire narrative through its campy lyrics, and the nightclub comedian Marty Allen appears as a sleazy press agent. Theatrical exhibitions fell flat. Remarkably, *Christianity Today* reviewed the film as a "realistic and believable story" that shows both the sinfulness of man and the hope of salvation. *Insight* magazine indicated that the "gutsy film" was the kind you wanted to "rap" about once it was over, while the *Banner* found it "technically indistinguishable from an MGM production."[62]

Two thoughts occurred to Curtis. First, as he researched the success of WWP distribution, he discovered the potential 16mm market and inaugurated his work in this medium with three films: The first two were the Seventh Day Adventist production of the self-explanatory *About Addiction* (ca. 1975), and a clever warning against secular media manipulation in the director Jan Doward's *So Many Voices* (1975). The latter was a humorous take on communicating Christian living to youth amid the cacophony of media voices, which provoked laughter and introspection with funny sketches, including one about a caveman family trying to figure out what to do with a television set, ultimately destroying it with their clubs and returning to a more peaceful family dinner. Lastly, *Sound of Light* (1978) focused on a disabled person coping with selfishness. All three films helped Gateway expand its distribution ministry.

Most significant for Gateway, however, was Curtis's vision to appeal to all Christian traditions, not just the evangelical Protestant market. Curtis picked up films aimed more directly at Roman Catholics, like *Rain for a Dusty Summer* (1975), which told of a solitary priest's work to keep the faith during the 1917 Mexican Revolution, a story similar to Graham Greene's famous 1940 novel *The Power and the Glory*. For Protestant evangelicals, he released films like *The Girl Who Ran out of Night* (1975), which dealt with teenage female runaways.[63]

American Baptist Films decided to cut Gateway loose from the denomination, so Gateway sought its own core group of independent investors to help acquire other productions. As a student of history, Curtis had discerned a Christian ignorance in the contemporary church, so he decided to build "a collection of films depicting God's activity throughout history in the lives of those who have been especially called out to serve, and in many cases gave their lives for the cause of Jesus Christ." Stories gleaned from church history would dramatize the "found stories" of the Gospel in action.[64] According to Curtis, such a vision was crucial for the health of the church: "The public perception of Christianity, especially in the United States, is tragically distorted. We desperately need a historical perspective to understand where we have come from, who we are as Christians in the church, how we got here and where we should be headed."[65]

After a decade of desertlike experiences, in 1979 Curtis found his way, establishing his Christian Heritage collection of dramatic historical films. The significant event was the acquisition of the American rights to the Seventh Day Adventist production of Michael Economou's *John Hus*, about the early 15th-century Bohemian reformer. Originally, the film contained some anti-Catholic propaganda that Curtis felt would be detrimental to building up the Christian community, so the SDA prudently edited it. In this film Curtis discovered his own personal mission, historically informed films enhanced with accompanying study guides. Produced by the BBC, *John Hus* was awarded the Christian Film Distributors Association's Best Film of the Year Award. *John Hus* provided the Christian film industry product from Europe and established Gateway as a key emerging distributor, legitimizing their presence among Christian libraries. It also inaugurated Gateway's collection of films on church history.

Gateway then collaborated with the BBC Everyman series on great preachers for such films as *Bunyan the Preacher* (1981) and *John Wesley, Preacher* (1983).[66] BBC executives Norman Stone and David Thompson were impressed with the distribution system of Gateway, which ably rented out 16mm prints of the BBC films to nontraditional markets. *Bunyan the Preacher* was produced for European television as a dramatic presentation on

In its work to reintroduce church tradition to audiences, Gateway Films released the epony-mous story of the Bohemian reformer John Hus. Courtesy of Ken Curtis and Vision Video.

the author's life, and Gateway provided distribution in the United States. The BBC had been working with Films Incorporated to release their films, but when they saw the profits coming from their sublicensing agreement with Gateway, they began to contract Gateway directly. Gateway had established rental relations with pastors' conferences, adult education classes, and Sunday schools, all groups that looked to Gateway for additional period films.

Released by Gospel Films thirty years earlier, Gateway rereleased the Academy Award–nominated *Martin Luther* as part of its heritage series. This initial stream of films from across the Atlantic continued with *First Fruits* (1982). In 1978, a group of Moravian leaders looked forward to the group's 250th anniversary in 1982 and wanted a film to commemorate the birth of its missions. With a modest budget of $96,000, Gateway undertook the story of early Moravian missionaries to the New World. The biblical idea of first fruits involved the theme of God's providence, of recognizing that the "Lord is already there ahead of you; your task is to identify what God has already prepared." The narrative chronicled the travels of two bright and dedicated young missionaries from their community in Herrnhut, Germany, who endured suffering and deprivation in their journey to the West Indies to bring the Gospel to the "heathens." *First Fruits* won a second Best Film of the Year Award from the Christian Film Distributors Association for Gateway.

Investigating the viability of the video market (and incorporating a side company, Vision Video, in 1981), Curtis selected Grenville Film Productions to develop coproductions. The small British independent company was run by the filmmaker Tony Tew, who was to direct the developing genre of hagiopics. Tew masterminded three such films for Gateway, *John Wycliffe: The Morning Star* (1983), *Nikolai* (1986), and *God's Outlaw* (1988, about William Tyndale). Tew specialized in documentary and dramatic film productions for BBC Channel 4 in England and shot many films in association with outside organizations, most of which were Christian, such as Youth with a Mission and World Wide Pictures.[67]

Gateway's interest in historical films led to the development *Christian History* magazine, which began with the publication of a sixteen-page study guide to accompany an edited version of *John Hus*, a film produced by Faith for Today, a Seventh Day Adventist organization. A second issue of *Christian History* provided background and cultural context on John Wesley to accompany the new production on the founder of Methodism. The intellectually rich periodical supplied supplemental information on many the films that Gateway released. Curtis explained that "all we are feeding the church is contemporary; our calling is Christian history." The magazine would teach what the films portrayed.[68]

One of Gateway's most challenging productions was *Candle in the Dark: The Story of William Carey* (1998), which spent twelve years in preparation and two in production. The film explored the life of the father of modern missions and a key leader in outlawing the practice of suttee (widow burning) in India. Professor Michael Korpi of Baylor University believed that a film on Carey would help to demonstrate to the Texas Baptist constituency Baylor's commitment to the Baptist mission. President Herbert Reynolds sent out fund-raising appeals on behalf of the university to Southern Baptist churches and encouraged the development of the film. Amid the televangelist scandals of the 1980s becoming more and more prominent, Korpi was invited to comment on an episode of *Nightline*. When he quipped that the Southern Baptist televangelist Jerry Falwell was raising money in questionable ways, Baylor clamped down on their professor. Since Korpi was the coordinator for the Carey project, the university administration also stopped the film project. Based on a good faith agreement, Gateway assumed that they would be reimbursed for their investment in hiring a scriptwriter, but the university lawyers denied liability. The film appeared to be dead in the water.

When Curtis attended a conference on Christian history at Samford University, however, President Tom Corts discovered the project, asked to review the materials, and had copies of the script passed around. One of the nation's most respected evangelical church historians, the Samford faculty member Dr. Timothy George, had written a book on Carey, which aided tremendously in conceptualizing the narrative arc of the script. Tom Corts, brother to the BGEA executive John Corts, asked Curtis about the status of the film. Curtis indicated they needed $150,000 to continue the film. Corts generously replied that he could put Samford down for $200,000. Another major donor, the visionary lawyer Gordon Severance, found that he couldn't raise money from Baptists for the film, and so he put up his own retirement funds to make certain the project would be completed. One of his clients, a Hindu businessman, then helped provide entree into key areas of India for location shooting. Despite the many years in production and the numerous financial and logistical challenges, *Candle in the Dark* was an indisputable success.

Tony Tew portrayed Carey, who had been caricatured as a moonstruck fanatic by the East India Trade Company, as the respected friend of the Hindu leader Rama Ray, and therefore a friend of India. Carey's work consistently honored Indian culture: not only as a missionary, but also as an advocate for the outlawing of infant sacrifice and suttee practice, and for the founding of the Agricultural and Horticultural Society of India. Providentially, the actor who played Carey, Richard Attlee, was the grandson of Clement Attlee, the British prime minister who oversaw the transition to Indian independence. Julie-Kate Olivier, daughter of Sir Laurence Olivier and Dame Joan Plowright, played Kitty. The motto of Carey's life, "Expect great things from God; attempt great things for God," stood as a tribute to the success of the film, which had its premiere in Bombay. Expecting to be clobbered for not recognizing the subtle nuances of cultural difference in the film, Curtis found an "incredible response" from the appreciative audience. Rather than a tool of cultural imperialism, the film stood as recognition of an influential Christian who had done much to help India.

One profitable series for teaching was the *Discovering the Bible* (1982) set of documentary films, developed using sophisticated instructional material. In a similar vein, the next year, Gateway released a daring twelve-part series shot on video, *Jesus Then and Now* (1983). Produced by Lella Video, the ambitious film series was hosted by the noted British evangelist and author David Watson and the BBC's Tina Heath. Produced in the Churches Radio and Television Centre by Andrew Quicke, this video series explored the events of Jesus's life and their relevance to today's world. Each program was highly innovative for its time, using a talk show format with frequent cutaways to biblical narration, dramatic vignettes, and interviews with key figures, such as the bishop of Uganda. For the serious student, a 189-page study guide was made available. Curtis realized that the transfer of video to 16mm would be financially strapping and so didn't expect to break even, but the value of the theological insights for the church overrode such cost considerations.

Gateway's crowning achievement occurred in 1985 when it coproduced the first version of the aforementioned *Shadowlands* (1985), a dramatic biopic by William Nicholson concerning romance and grief in the life of C. S. Lewis. Coproduced by the BBC Religious Department, Gateway, the Episcopal Radio-TV Foundation, and EO, the evangelical Dutch TV station, the director Norman Stone's film poignantly portrayed the brief marriage of Lewis and the American poet and divorcée Joy Davidman.[69] Winner of the International Emmy for Best Drama and numerous other awards, as well as two British Academy Awards for Best Single Drama and Best Actress for Claire Bloom, no other Christian film had ever been honored so highly. (Subsequently, the story became a successful play in the Queen's Theatre in London in 1989, with Nigel Hawthorne winning the Tony Award for Best Actor, and then a glossy Hollywood movie starring Anthony Hopkins and Deborah Winger and directed by Richard Attenborough.) Critical consensus opted for Norman Stone's earlier version as a superior movie over Attenborough's historically inaccurate tearjerker. Attenborough's worst distortion was that he implied that C. S. Lewis lost his faith after the tragic death of Joy. Lewis's works published after her death, *A Grief Observed* and *Letters to Malcolm*, do not hide his spiritual struggles, but they also reveal an enduring orthodox faith. Stone's more subtle film conveyed the authenticity and humor of the actual relationship. *Shadowlands* did, however, suffer from a fundamentalist backlash, as Baptists blackballed Lewis, who smoked and drank, and a televangelist even accused him, falsely and ignorantly, of being a "British homosexual." Nevertheless, the film inspired a new generation of young Christian intellectuals to explore a calling in filmmaking.

Another adventure took Curtis into communist-occupied Czechoslovakia, when a friend, Professor Jerry Zeman of Arcadia Theological Seminary, obtained a print of *Standing in the Storm* (ca. 1984), a three-hour communist propaganda drama on the 17th-century "father of modern education," John Amos Comenius. After trying to get rights through the state agencies, Curtis finally made contact with Italian licensees. Receiving permission to distribute the film in the United States in 1986, Curtis realized that it would have to be edited down for American audiences. One Moravian sponsor wanted Curtis to insert aspects of Comenius's Christian witness and life when the

In Norman Stone's award-winning *Shadowlands*, Joss Ackland and Claire Bloom play C. S. and Joy Lewis, respectively. Courtesy of Ken Curtis and Vision Video.

film was translated, but the official Soviet sponsors refused. Curtis countered with a proposal that he could incorporate additional material, but only from Comenius's writings, in adapting the film for Christian audiences, which was agreed to by all parties. The edited Czech film took on its own ironic life, as the playwright Václav Havel became the new president of the Czech Republic and sparked a Comenius revival. With the thawing of Soviet hegemony, Prague hosted an international conference of educators. To showcase Comenius's work, the Czechs chose to exhibit Gateway's version over the original for two reasons: it was in English and it was shorter. Curtis was told, "We want what you did [with the movie]. We know what you have done. It is our choice to have what you have."[70] Unexpectedly, Gateway's evangelical version of the Comenius narrative would thus enjoy a second life in the new Czech Republic.

Gateway's difficulty financing new Christian movies was remedied by securing different organizations to underwrite the projects. The press release for *God's Outlaw* sounds like a roll call of religious film and television organizations: a Grenville Film Production in association with Channel 4 Television, the Focus Trust, the Bible Society, Churches Radio and Television Centre, Mezzo Two (New Zealand), Gateway Films (USA), EO Television (Holland), and the International Bible Society. Ken Curtis explained how his strategy of coordinating projects with the BBC, Channel 4 Television, and other groups like EO Dutch TV turned to everyone's advantage: "We have a similar interest in certain programs. They have to do a certain amount of religious programs. So we discuss and develop projects together on what is called a co-production basis. That means that the projects are developed from scratch. We work together on scripts, approve the cast, the production personnel, etc. They provide the production facilities, which is a tremendous resource to draw on. It's all pre-agreed, what the financial responsibilities each party has, and what territories are shared, based on the financial input."[71]

Through the coming decades, Gateway would coproduce some provocative and creative works, including Norman Stone's exquisitely edgy *Tales from the Madhouse* (2000) for the BBC about characters whose encounters with Jesus alter them markedly, *The Fourth Wise Man* (2000, with Martin Sheen), and *Test of Time* (2001) with the BBC, which won the British Academy Award for Best Youth Television Program, triumphing over three Channel 4 productions. Most powerfully, however, Ken Curtis's diagnosis of cancer led to a courageous and inspirational film series on a holistic view of dealing with the disease, *You Don't Have to Be Afraid Anymore: Reflections on Psalm 23 for People with Cancer* (2006).

Gateway has continued to distribute church history media (*The Story of George Muller*, 2006) with steady success, continuing to rely on European production facilities and European coproductions to provide new material. What has marked their creative work, albeit with limited budgets, has been the meticulous research afforded each project, as well as a drive for narrative authenticity (e.g., shooting scenes in original locations). Curtis emphasized that while Gateway strove to be good stewards, the purpose of the company remained ministry, not commercial success. Market research and an undue focus on net profits could divert attention from what is most important and become a form of idolatry. What was relevant was whether the story was needed. Paraphrasing the Spanish philosopher George Santayana, Curtis emphasized that those who cannot remember the past, which includes the past of Christian film history, are condemned to repeat it. For Curtis and Gateway, the mission must remain paramount lest one be distracted from the holy vocation.

Summary

Unlike the mini-studios of Gospel Films and Family Films, World Wide Pictures and Gateway reached beyond the evangelical ghettos. While not compromising their theological purposes, the films were not embarrassing church-basement productions, but rather carefully conceptualized and professionally developed. Following metaphors of spiritual journey and histories of God's saints, the two organizations set out to bring evangelistic and historical films to churches. They each achieved their aims, respectively, to bring individuals to recognize God's presence in their lives and to revive an understanding of God's work in history. Their hagiographic films, from *The Hiding Place* to *Candle in the Dark*, evoked thought as well as emotion. They taught as they entertained. Finally, their films also crossed denominational boundaries and promoted religious unity through shared narratives about grace, hope, and healing. In stark contrast, another genre, the apocalyptic film, would bring terror, thrills, and urgency into churches, literally trying to "scare the hell out of people."

7

Mark IV and Apocalyptic Film

The Puritan divine Jonathan Edwards recommended a sort of salutary terror in the communication of the Gospel. Although delivered in a staid monotone, his classic jeremiad sermon, "Sinners in the Hands of an Angry God," goaded sinners into repentance and toward a great awakening. The threat of God's wrath on unrepentant sinners, dangling like spiders over the raging fires of hell, has been an efficacious tool in the hands of prophets and evangelists for centuries, particularly with regard to impending end-times terror. While the use of shock aesthetic techniques of the horror genre in Christian films has been criticized, scholars like Will Rockett and Michael Lieb find a fascinating interrelationship among Christian faith, the eschatological, the technological, and the fantastic.[1] From the wild *merkabah* chariot literature of Ezekiel to the enduring presence of evil and the devil in popular culture, all with an impending sense of imminent political, ecological, and cosmic disaster in a secular Armageddon, the seemingly bizarre links of Christian faith and horror film are not as far-fetched as one might think.[2] Rockett identifies a terrible "downward" transcendence of evil in Hollywood cinema, a discovery not only of a "heart of darkness" but of evil itself, which parallels a similar strand in the Christian film industry. Dim and foreboding echoes of Rudolf Otto's *The Idea of the Holy*, as well as the fire-and-brimstone sermon of Edwards, reverberate in the "Rapture" productions of Mark IV Pictures.

The 19th-century development of the notion of the rapture is rooted in the traditional and orthodox doctrine of the Second Coming of Jesus Christ, an apocalypse of judgment and reward. In the parable of the separation of sheep from goats, it is at the end of time that some are welcomed into eternal bliss and others sent (or choose to go) into eternal torment. Around 1830, a New England sect led by John Newton Darby, a former member of the Plymouth Brethren, published the idea that the church would escape a future season of tribulation by being literally plucked out of the world, believing Christians would be raptured (i.e., abruptly transported from earth to heaven with the second coming of Jesus) and thus escape the suffering of an impending apocalyptic time of tribulation. Fundamentalists rallied to the impending judgment on this world and embraced the idea of being rescued from the cataclysms of the last days, leading to the spread of a pre-millennial and pre-tribulation hope. In contrast to the post-millennial idea of creating the Kingdom of God on earth through progressive Social Gospel programs, the pre-tribulation devotees feared being left behind.

Predicting the end of the world still requires a distribution network to attract congregants to your message, something beyond the kind of sandwich board signs of *New Yorker* cartoons warning of the end of the world and calling for repentance. The visual rhetoric scholar David Morgan documented how various eschatological messages of the 19th-century were disseminated through various pictorial charts of the prophet Daniel's visions, illustrated prophecies of the beasts of Revelation, and the visual pedagogy diagrams chronicling the end days (e.g., Clarence Larkin's well-circulated dispensational chart of the "Great Tribulation").[3] Just as efforts of spreading visual apocalyptic tracts and charts throughout fundamentalist churches in the 19th century were coordinated by savvy distributors, conservative Christians would utilize a synchronized system for distributing the apocalyptic films of the 20th century. The organization that would systematize and manage the need for films to be spread throughout the nation would be the Christian Film Distributors Association.

Mark IV Pictures and Heartland Productions

A key part of the apocalyptic narrative involves the setting up of an Antichrist, whose government will mark those left behind with the numbers 666 on their forehead or hand. Such riveting devices of pre-millennial tropes provided screenwriters with a fertile field for the dramatic invention of suspense and terror. While Carlos Baptista had produced *The Rapture* (1941) and *Blessed Hope* (1943) during the war, the first Christian filmmaker to effectively employ such shock-and-awe narrative techniques was Russell S. Doughten Jr., a creative young man from Drake University who had studied at Yale and USC. At Good News Productions (becoming the more visible Valley Forge Studios) in Chester Springs, Pennsylvania, Doughten providentially met up with Shorty Yeaworth, who trained him in filmmaking. As director of the 1958 cult classic *The Blob*, starring Steve McQueen, Yeaworth brought on Doughten as one of his producers, breaking him into the world of independent filmmaking.

In 1965, after a brief stint teaching in South Pasadena and then freelancing with Cathedral Films, Doughten returned to Des Moines, Iowa, where he formed his own Heartland Productions. His goal to cheaply put out low-budget B movies along the lines of Roger Corman's successes (e.g., 1960's *The Little Shop of Horrors* and the Edgar Allan Poe/Vincent Price *Tales of Terror* series) produced two films shot on 35mm, *The Hostage* (1966) and *Fever Heat* (1969). Both recouped their initial investments as he sold them to Crown International and Paramount Pictures.[4] For the next five years he remained active as an exhibitor, running eight moving picture theaters that he owned and operated.

His direction of these cheap B films taught him to build gripping and suspenseful narratives. The screenplay for *The Hostage* had been adapted from a Henry Farrell novel, the same author of the film *Hush . . . Hush, Sweet Charlotte* (1964) and the novel *Whatever Happened to Baby Jane?* (1960). Marked by a leisurely, sinister atmosphere, the film starred classic Hollywood character actors like John Carradine and Harry Dean Stanton, and was built on the story of a psychopathic killer and his dimwitted assistant accidently kidnapping a young boy. *Fever Heat* did less well two years later since the market for B movies was dying fast, with television quickly replacing them in American viewing habits. Few prospects for Heartland's pictures existed in light of this fading demand.

In 1972, Doughten saw tremendous potential in the fledgling Christian film market as an opportunity to return to the craft of making films, as an evangelistic outlet to express his fervent faith, and as an alternative cinematic product for the church. He unequivocally defined his purpose as producing "films that illustrate the saving power of the Gospel to families in today's world."[5]

Around the same time, Doughten's future partner, Don Thompson, was making television shows for Paramount Pictures through the creative services division of an educational network. Years earlier, he had encountered Doughten at Paramount and been struck with a vivid impression of him as "a kind of a Moses-type of character. I mean the type of guy you just really respect."[6] The impression contributed to Thompson's own spiritual journey in becoming a Christian. Noticing a Christian book in a bookstore, Thompson imagined making pictures that promoted Christ and approached Doughten:

> I went over to his office and asked him, "If I were to make a (Christian) film like this, I would want to direct it; would you produce it?" I told him that I was a born-again Christian. And he said, "What do you mean, a 'born-again' Christian?" So I gave him my testimony and he wept, and he

said, "Well, I was going to talk to you about that when you came by here today, because I am too." We prayed together and we knew, right then and there, that God had put us together for something big.[7]

Shortly after that meeting, Thompson went to Ken Anderson Films to ask if they would help them organize. Anderson charitably opened his books and explained the whole operation of running a Christian film company, pointing out the unique difficulties of providing film products for the church market. Thompson remained convinced of the feasibility of such a venture, thinking their first order of business was to give the company a name. Heartland decided to differentiate its audiences, specifically targeting a teenage market with a spin-off company. Thompson wanted his brand to be both commercially viable and rooted in the Bible. Since the plan was to produce dramatic action-adventures for the youth church market, he wanted a name that would intrigue audiences. "And so I came across Corinthians VI, which sounded like a Dixieland band, and I came to Mark VII; that was Jack Webb's logo, and I came to Mark IV and I called Russ on the phone and said, "What do you think of Mark IV?" He said, "What does it mean?" And I said it was a whole chapter in the Bible. He called me back and told me to read Mark 4:33 which was exactly the thing we were looking for."[8]

Mark IV Pictures determined to release their films based on the model of Jesus's communication recorded in this passage: "With many such parables he spoke the word unto them, as they were able to hear it" (ESV).[9] The two filmmakers grounded their purpose on this genre of parables, believing that their films might speak indirectly to congregations. But the central theme of their most successful films dealt unabashedly with overt end-times narratives, stories rooted in literal dispensational perspectives, namely, "the Rapture" and "the Tribulation." Mark 13, with the Olivet discourse on the signs of the times, wars and rumors of wars, and the shaking of the heavens, would have been more apt as the corporate name.

Thompson had only been a Christian for six months when he wrote the seminal apocalyptic classic *A Thief in the Night* (1972), depending on Doughten to provide his dispensational eschatology. From the opening shot of the alarm clock ringing, the script rushes into the intense fear of a young woman named Patty who has been "left behind" after the Rapture. The concept was so powerful that, according to Doughten, it became the most publicized, most watched, and most rented Christian film in the thirty-five-year history of the industry, with his estimate that more than two million people converted immediately after watching the film.[10]

A significant aspect of the film's appeal was its musical score, arranged by the man known as the "father of contemporary Christian music," Ralph Carmichael. He would later compose scores for Graham's World Wide Pictures, but *Thief* gave him an opportunity to pull out all the stops, making him the Bernard Herrmann to the Christian film industry's *Psycho*.

Thompson and Doughten raised money as they produced the film, completing the rough cut for around $68,000. They called Ken Anderson to see their edited version and ask him to distribute the film. Thompson remembered that "Ken kept saying we had a hit on our hands. He kept handing me a pen but [also advised that] I shouldn't sign that [distribution agreement with him]," as Doughten would make a lot more money distributing it himself.[11] Doughten's ownership of some theaters enabled him to start the distribution of Mark IV Pictures all by himself. It was common practice at the time to make 40 prints of Christian films, but the demand for *A Thief* through word of mouth skyrocketed, reaching 1,500 bookings a month. After such success, Mark IV would release their next eleven films with 250 prints each.

Local film libraries stocked as many as fifteen prints of the film in order to keep up with the demand. Some churches would rent it several times a year (especially for Halloween and New Year's Eve services). It was *the* film for evangelistic rallies and evening services, as it would "literally scare the hell out of sinners." Its cinematic manipulation of fear was worthy of horror film maestros like George Romero or Wes Craven. Patty's commitment to Christianity is lukewarm and nominal; she thinks that if she is a good person and goes to church, she need not fear God's wrath. In a self-effacing role, Doughten himself plays a liberal pastor seeking to allay the hysteria of the characters. But Patty wakes one morning to find that her Christian husband and others have disappeared.

While rushing about trying to find out what has happened, Patty continually stumbles into deception, danger, and paranoia with authorities and alleged friends. Guillotines stand ready to execute those who do not take the mark of the beast—a threefold set of binary numbers, "0110," equating 666—on their hand or forehead. The hauntingly evocative strains of the Christian folk musician Larry Norman's "I Wish We'd All Been Ready" reminded spectators that they too could be left behind.

During the Tribulation, UNITE (United Nations Imperium for Total Emergency, marking a fundamentalist reaction to the United Nations and one-world governments) hunts down instances of noncompliance. Patty is chased and trapped on a bridge, from which she seemingly falls to her death; however, she wakes and we realize it has all been a dream. Just then, the radio alarm starts, with the announcement that millions have disappeared and she has this time been left behind for real. This surprise, O'Henry ending startled many and opened the door to altar calls to all who were not sure they were ready for the Rapture.

A snatch of dialogue reveals the incipient fear engendered by the film, which is essentially a fear of abandonment:

> JENNY: Sue, could you run next door and ask Mrs. Thompson if I could borrow a stick of butter?
> SUE: Okay, but you be sure to be here when I get back.
> JENNY: Don't worry, sweetie, if I'm gone, you'll be gone, too.

One respondent on the film's *IMDB* page reflected that "perhaps because I was so young, innocent and brainwashed when I saw it, this movie was the cause of many sleepless nights for me. . . . I was particularly terrified of what the newly converted post-rapture Christians had to endure when not receiving the mark of the beast." One of the most astute observers of the Christian film subculure, Heather Hendershot, noted the conspicuous import the film had on evangelical culture, where even the satanic rocker Marilyn Manson acknowledged the mark of sacred terror left on him growing up as a fundamentalist Christian:

> Just as most Christians have an anecdote about *A Thief in the Night*, they also have at least one about thinking they missed the Rapture. There's a little girl in the movie who comes home to an empty house and thinks the same thing. And there were a couple times after I saw *Thief* that I woke up on a Saturday morning to find a completely empty house. I was in a mad panic until I ran out to the garage and breathed a sigh of relief when I saw that the car was gone too.[12]

Designed to scare spectators into the Kingdom of God, the film was criticized for traumatizing younger viewers, manipulating them into altar call conversions.[13] As the filmmaker Andrew Quicke quipped, "Thanks to this film whole generations of impressionable pre-teen Christian girls now worry every time their mothers take longer than usual to return from shopping."[14]

Conservative churches nevertheless enthused that Doughten was an effective evangelistic storyteller, in that he

> developed the message of salvation in two important ways. First he shows us through action the reality of Jesus Christ's sacrifice for our sake. This is achieved in a subplot where the zookeeper is bit by a poisonous snake and nearly dies. The only cure is blood from someone who is immune from

the snake poison. The poison is like sin, the cure like Christ's blood, shed on the cross. Second the filmmaker also develops the message of salvation through dialog. He has various characters explain the truth about human sin and the need for salvation through faith in Christ. So the moviemaker uses both action and dialog to tell his story. . . . The fact that a movie produced by evangelical Christians actually contains dialog and scenes that convey a clearly delineated message of salvation, couched in specifically evangelical Christian language, imagery and theology, is perfectly acceptable. To criticize this film for being specifically Christian is absurd: it's akin to criticizing a Nike commercial for promoting sport-wear.[15]

To make certain the propaganda element was not missed in later films, Doughten would appear as a wise, hoary prophet hidden in a cave, with a giant wall chart that illumined the puzzles and riddles of biblical prophecy. The action of the films would stop for his inserted lectures.

The response among fundamentalists was phenomenal, as the film attracted large audiences for evening services. Followed by the "come to Jesus" evangelistic rhetoric, the film swayed thousands, haunting many and terrorizing a few. Both authors have stark memories of watching this film in crowded churches and witnessing flocks of teenagers rushing to the altar lest they be left behind.

Though not as popular as the original, the sequel films—*A Distant Thunder* (1978), *Image of the Beast* (1981), and *Prodigal Planet* (1983)—created similar interest and controversy. Certain groups of Christians felt that many people were becoming born-again because of the use of "scare tactics," and that fear should not be an instrument of the Gospel. Thompson responded thus: "I tried to write [scare tactics] into *Distant Thunder* and in *Image of the Beast*. You can go ahead and be nice to the people, and when you're gone in the Rapture, let them stay behind, scared to death and they can't do anything about it. The whole purpose is to scare them now if they've got to be scared, so they can make a decision before it's too late."[16]

The interest in *Thief in the Night*, which generated over $1 million in rental revenue, led Doughten to create Mustard Seeds International. Set up as a nonprofit arm of their commercial ventures, the company was dedicated to providing film prints for evangelists to use and dubbing them into different languages. Thompson told the story of a particular problem with an entrepreneur in Mexico who was showing the four Rapture films without paying royalties. Thompson sent someone to confront him, and the messenger came back with the news that the man in Mexico was showing the films as evangelism tools and had made seven hundred converts. So they made him a distributor.[17]

Recognizing such uses of their films, the team created the Telecrusade Ministry in 1973. Community organizations (local churches and para-church groups) would come together in selected cities to telecast the film on a local station. Mass advertising was set up, phone lines were installed, and counselors would handle calls as a number would come on the screen during the film's showing. In Kansas City, one such crusade with forty phone lines stayed busy for an entire weekend ministering to people who had seen the program.[18] In 1984, a similar crusade for the Heartland film *The Healing* (1984) gathered five hundred volunteers from area churches in Des Moines for counseling and telemarketing support.

Heartland provided films that communicated the Gospel differently from the apocalyptic films of Mark IV. *Nightsong* (1978) dealt with alcohol and drug abuse, while *Brother Enemy* (1981) and *Face in the Mirror* (1982) addressed the generational gap between teenagers and their parents.

Because Mark IV and Heartland Productions used Screen Actors Guild members and union crews for filming, after *A Thief in the Night*, their average cost of production soared to between $4,000 and $5,000, only a quarter of the production costs regularly spent by WWP but still double the amount spent by other small film companies. Excluding the *Prodigal Planet* films, the most expensive production was Heartland's *The Shepherd*, which cost $600,000, about ten times the budget of *Thief in the Night* while only generating one-tenth the rental revenue. The companies' commitment to high-quality production hampered growth, and by the year 2000, Heartland and Mark IV reduced their filmmaking operations, after having produced twenty films.

While still pursuing film projects, Doughten shifted his emphasis, running filmmaking seminars on "Putting Christian Messages in Dramatic Films." He argued that a motion picture does not deserve the "label Christian unless it presents the gospel message in a complete enough way for the average person to be challenged to make a commitment for Christ."[19] Yet ironically, Doughten discouraged young Christian filmmakers from going to Hollywood, warning that there are few "signs that the establishment there would be open to making uncompromising Christian films."[20] Nevertheless, in the Christian film industry, Doughten and Thompson's pioneering efforts in exploiting the paranoia and fear of being left behind during a rapture would be bequeathed to another generation of filmmakers. But while their Christian horror films attracted young filmmakers such as Danny Carrales, Wes Llewellyn, and Matt Crouch, a more gruesome tradition of evoking terror had taken root down south.

The Burning Hell

After exploiting women and car chases in drive-in movies like *White Lightnin' Road* (1967), the schlock filmmakers Ron and June Ormond, along with their son Tim, experienced a life-changing catastrophe when their plane crashed in a cow pasture. Emerging from the wreckage and believing that the Lord spared them for a purpose, the Ormond Organization changed their ways and began making "exploitation pictures for Jesus."[21]

Ron Ormond then went to a meeting of the Hollywood Christian Association (with stars like Jane Russell in attendance) and an altar call resulted in his raising his hand and asking for prayer. The next morning, June joined him in this taste of heaven: "The Lord comes into you. I got down on the floor. The tears were coming out of me. And all these deacons got around me. It was the middle of this shopping mall. It was the greatest feeling I've ever had in my life. Like somebody had given me 10,000 baths."[22]

In an earlier film, *Girl from Tobacco Row* (1966), the preacher Tex Ritter warns an ex-con that he is standing at a crossroads. So, too, the Ormonds stood at a juncture, deciding what kinds of films the Lord would have them make. They decided to transform their exploitative blood fests into spiritual lessons. The film that would set the world of Southern fundamentalists on fire was *The Burning Hell* (1974). As June Ormond claimed, "*The Burning Hell* is the most potent, soul-winning picture that has ever played a church. It cost about $60,000 and . . . it showed a profit of two million dollars."[23]

When a hippie motorcyclist neglects the warning of a preacher that he needs to be "saved," he dies in a violent accident, with his head being cut off. His friend, played by Tim, returns to the minister and hears a sulfurous sermon on judgment and hell. The film's primary investor was an anonymous hell-and-damnation preacher. June pointed out that "he wanted to show the maggots. The Bible tells you about the worm that never dies. What is the worm that never dies? Do you know? Your conscience. It eats on you from within—the worm that never dies. So this preacher, the producer, put real maggots on the people. Plugged up their ears and put maggots all over their faces. . . . People would throw up at church when they saw this stuff."[24]

While people under red lights are seen burning in hell, surrounded by seemingly inflammable maggots to accentuate the tortures of the damned, the film provides an opportunity for an altar call. As June opined, "The Baptists don't even *want* a picture unless there's an altar call." The Ormonds left the drive-in circuit for church halls with their graphic and shocking "soul-winning picture." They would continue to make dramatic movies, some even involving famous ministers like Jerry Falwell in cameos. While some of their films—like *The Grim Reaper* (1976), a wildly delirious story about a father and his son who stop going to church, dabble in the occult and stock car racing, and end up in hell—would get "a lotta bookings for Halloween," they also produced films like *The Land Where Jesus Walked* (1975), a documentary tour of the Holy Land, and *The Second Coming* (1984), a mix of sci-fi, dispensational prophecy, and special effects, with the return of Jesus on an horse coming down from the clouds.[25]

Toward a More Polished Apocalypse

Certain apocalyptic and surreal films provided audiences with prophetic possibilities concerning the future, with their generic visual roots stretching back not only to the mass-mediated visual images of the Millerites and Adventist Church of the 19th century, but also to the apocalyptic imagery of Hieronymus Bosch, Albrecht Durer, and William Blake.[26] The ubiquitous use of engravings and lithographs to communicate the dread and horror of the beasts of Daniel and Revelation and the imminent judgment of God marked much of the woodcut wars of the Reformation. Such pictorial propaganda inaugurated a tradition of holy fear that gave credence to Samuel Johnson's observation that nothing focuses the mind like a hanging.[27]

Even as Mark IV capitalized on this form, related films came from other production companies. Other ministries affiliated with Doughten sought to expand the field of apocalyptic Christian films, such as *The Return* (1987) by Mark Evans Ministry Productions, a fast-paced drama about the Tribulation and the Advent of the Lord. *There's a New World Coming* (1975), written by Hal Lindsey for the church market, was followed by his 35mm theatrical release *The Late Great Plant Earth* (1979), a pseudo-documentary dramatization of Lindsey's best-selling book. By the 1980s, plenty of Christian films about dreams, visions, and the end of the world proliferated.[28] As *A Thief in the Night* established a model of apocalyptic evangelistic film, others such as Fred Carpenter's *Without Reservations* (1989) would imitate its success, combining surrealism and evangelism in predictable ways. The apocalyptic genre generated intense interest among conservative Christians, with the top four renting videos in the Christian Film and Video Association in the 1970s being Mark IV films.[29]

With the arrival of the millennium, and its attendant fears of Y2K and other "eschatological signs" threatening human existence, the doctrine of the Second Coming (and especially its controversial and dispensational forms of "Rapture") sparked a rash of topical products. Exploiting the sudden and unexpected return of Jesus Christ as "a thief in the night" to gather His saints, films struck resonant chords of urgency and holy dread.

The success of the Mark IV/Heartland end-times 16mm films in the 1970s augured a boom in the 1990s, with the heavily funded Cloud Ten Productions and the Trinity Broadcasting Network entering the field with both theatrical and video releases. Simultaneously, Hollywood exploited the genre around the turn of the millennium (e.g., Peter Hyam's *End of Days*, 1999). Three Prophecy Partners films (from the Jack Van Impe and John Hagee Ministries), *Apocalypse* (1998), *Revelation* (1999), and *Tribulation* (2000), were marketed with stunning professionalism by Peter and Paul Lalonde of Cloud Ten Pictures. In *Revelation*, Jeff Fahey, from the television series *The Marshal* and films like *The Lawnmower Man* (1992), stood in the eye of the tribulation storm, being confronted by the Antichrist, played with suave menace by Nick Mancuso. Transported to a virtual world, people are confronted with the choice of whether to take the mark of the beast. Consistent with earlier films, the chosen instrument of torment and gruesome death remains the guillotine rather than injections or gas chambers. If one rejects the mark, one must literally give up one's head.

Of the three, *Tribulation* is the most innovative. While it does include the stock narrative inserts of evangelists (in this case, Jack Van Impe, John Hagee, and T. D. Jakes, interrupting the story with sponsorship messages, mostly because they helped underwrite the films and sought to advertise their theology), the suspense, action, and humor are well scripted. Converted Hollywood second-stringers like Margot Kidder and Howard Mandel dot the landscape, providing a minor celebrity presence. But it is the middle-age romance of Gary Busey and Sherry Miller that evokes true sympathy and enjoyment. To watch an overweight Busey elude the minions of the devil provides a self-reflexive pleasure, playfully straining the suspension of disbelief concerning a flabby, unfit, and notoriously hedonistic hero. Yet it works to convey the idea that it is grace that rescues the flaccid Busey and not any of his own good works, "lest he should boast."

The Christian Film Distributors Association

Fortunately, the films of Mark IV and the other studios found a more direct outlet to congregations through a new organization, one that attempted to connect and coordinate the business between production and exhibition. This group, known as the Christian Film Distributors Association (CFDA), was established in 1974, two years after the release of *A Thief in the Night*. Under the association, a functional fellowship of Christian Film and Video Libraries were formed to serve the churches. In its guidelines, the CFDA described itself as "more than a business, it is a ministry. It is established for the purpose of serving the churches in its area with films and videos that will help that church present the Gospel of Jesus Christ in a more potent and effective manner."[30] In an attempt to analyze what kind of films might be profitable, a New Life Films market research study in July 1988 investigated the types of films needed for a vibrant business. According to CFDA records, a hierarchy of preferences indicated that most libraries sought dramatic narrative films, followed by documentaries, animated films, talking-head seminars, and music concerts. A second questionnaire determined a hierarchy of desired genres, listed in descending order evangelistic films, entertainment films with moral messages, family issue films, church social films, church growth films, mission-oriented films, biographical films, and historical films. The study concluded that conservative churches renting films would most likely choose dramatic, evangelistic, and message-oriented entertainments for their congregations and outreach. The CFDA recruited and promoted films that fit this prioritized list and generally ignored the more educational historical films.

The founder of the CFDA, Harry Bristow of Christian Cinema Inc. in Glenside, Pennsylvania, was not only the largest Christian film distributor, but also the owner and operator of one of the few exclusively Christian movie theaters, the Christian Cinema in Ambler, Pennsylvania. He was primarily responsible for coordinating the burgeoning business in film rentals. Bristow formed the CFDA so that distributors and librarians would not be bullied by producers, being forced to acquiesce to block booking or blind bidding (i.e., libraries would not have to take all the films offered by a producer or to buy films that they had not seen). Bristow essentially unionized the Christian film industry. In the late 1970s, the CFDA would include eighty distribution libraries, a significant market force. Bristow's own distribution library would send out around four hundred films a month, mainly to evangelical churches, with dramatic end-times films being the most popular.[31] In particular, he insisted that producers start making films for young people, citing marketing figures that 85 percent of film audiences were under twenty-five years old. (Nonetheless, he disparaged films like International Films' cleverly animated *Humpty Dumpty* [ca.1979], as they "watered down the Christian message so much they are worthless. . . . Where is Jesus in that film?")[32]

Other figures contributed to the building of the industry. As a student at Naperville College in the 1930s, Harvey W. Marks had written a paper on the future of audiovisual materials for the church. By 1945, he had established a ministry called the Visual Aid Center for securing films. In 1961, he had risen to the presidency of the National Audio-Visual Association. By the 1970s, he was editing the official publication of the CFDA, the *News 'N Views*, which would provide helpful hints for film libraries, handle the nuts and bolts of the distribution industry, and preview workshops and conventions.[33] By 1983, the monthly newsletter had become *News of Reel People*, edited by Dick Hayford, and included updates on the annual convention, calls for volunteerism, cartoons, and miscellaneous materials.[34] From 1976 to 1984, Hayford would serve as executive secretary of the CFDA.

In an effort to acknowledge and spur excellence in the field, the CFDA pushed for its own award system, inaugurating in 1974 what became known as the Crown Awards, or the Christian Oscars, a none-too-subtle take on Hollywood's own glitzy self-advertisement. The more visible Angel Awards (founded by its executive director Mary Dorr) were presented in Hollywood annually, with more fanfare and publicity.[35] For example, the 1987 Angel Award for Best Picture went to World Wide Pictures' *The Prodigal* and the trade magazine *Variety* publicized the list of winners.[36] The Angel Awards were also issued to television, radio, music albums, and print/press media. As more of a cottage industry, on the other hand, the CFDA limited their awards to 16mm films. In 1979, for example, the CFDA had given their Academy of Christian Cinema Arts Best Series of the Year Award to Word Productions' *Focus on the Family*, and the Best Film of the Year Award to Gateway's *John Hus*.

In the late 1980s, the organization evolved through the Christian Film Producers Fellowship, to the Christian Film and Video Association, and finally to the more inclusive Christian Visual Media Association. The emphasis remained with the film medium, acknowledging the dominance of the National Religious Broadcasters in dealing with television programming. At the group's annual conventions, typical seminar meetings would include panels on "Film Evangelism around the World" (offered by John Gilman) and "Maximizing the Profitability of Films" (offered by Dave Anderson and Chuck Warren), interspersed with premieres of new 16mm releases.[37]

The film librarians functioned as mediators between the filmmakers and the consuming publics. Certain producers like Ken Anderson treated the filmmakers professionally and generously, allowing them to keep 40 percent of a film's gross. Other production studios like Gospel Films adopted a 70/30 ratio in their favor. As front-line dealers, the film librarians were also the primary targets of public criticism for the films themselves. Libraries had to balance the predilections of various groups, from liberal Congregationalists such as the United Church of Christ wanting "great films that didn't say anything" to Southern Baptist fundamentalists voicing displeasure at someone with long hair or smoking, even in a crowd scene. The film librarian Paul Marks, son of Harvey Marks, remembered that certain audiences had a problem a scene in Gospel Films' *Big Blast* (ca. 1975), a panning shot across a crowd in a baseball crowd revealed a young man behind a fence "giving the finger." In another problematic film, *Flipside* (ca. 1973), the effect of drugs on a young man was shown by his vomiting into a toilet, except that the point of view for the audience was from the toilet. *Gates of Splendor* (1967) offended congregations because of *National Geographic*–style nudity among the natives of Ecuador. Some audiences even expressed their disbelief over Moon's pronouncement in *Red River of Life* (1957) that "someday in the future we may be doing heart transplants," which had to be edited out of the film.[38]

The creative ministry of Youth for Christ turned out numerous characters who became involved with the fledgling film industry. Brice Fennig, for example, took Baptista films into the streets, using sheets as screens. Evangelistic rallies were conducted in the open air, showing a film like *The Rapture* (which, while it was so shoddily made that audiences could see the wires hoisting saints into heaven, still had its desired effect of drawing a crowd for a public performance). As evidence of the mutually beneficial relations between the Youth for Christ organization and Christian films, Fennig points to the fact that the young librarians would net more than $100,000 a year for the youth ministry from its circuit-riding church exhibitions.

A chief value of the CFDA has been its judgment regarding the sales and marketing potential of Christian films. Ascertaining the vagaries of public taste is a risky business, but the librarians were remarkably prescient through most of their history. Various eras were marked by the release of certain films. *Seventeen* (ca. 1959), for example, turned Gospel Films around financially with its *Rebel without a Cause* style, showcasing "chicken races" among troubled teenage drivers.[39] So, too, the phenomenally successful *A Thief in the Night* had churches lining up to rent it. While the *Focus on the Family* series kept most libraries financially afloat in the mid-1980s, the most popular rentals of the 1980s remained *A Thief in the Night*, followed by Ken Anderson's *Centerville Awakening* (ca. 1980) on church renewal, and a film for teens, *Without Onion* (ca. 1979), which some felt to be corny but others considered quite campy.

By 1989, CFDA industry experts could see the writing on the walls of churches in the coming collapse of the Christian 16mm film rental libraries, and the consequent collapse of the industry as it had been structured. Randy Petersen, writing in a trade magazine, saw that the "Dobson effect" had changed the film rental business forever. He accurately predicted the demise of all Christian drama films, mostly because the churches now demanded higher production values but were unwilling to pay higher rental fees.[40] Film genre categories were about to change dramatically, moving away from expensive dramatic productions and toward low-cost instructional films.[41]

By 1989, film libraries sensed the waves of change. With fewer dramatic films being played on Saturday or Sunday nights as part of evangelistic outreach, film rentals decreased significantly. The Christian film industry resisted advances in technology such as video and rarely altered their content relating to what churches actually wanted to utilize.

As we have seen, the technological factor in the late 1980s was rooted in the birth of videocassettes, which were so much cheaper to make and so much easier to use. If a 16mm drama film cost $300 to duplicate, a videocassette of the same movie could be copied for a couple of dollars. Church leaders saw no point in renting films that cost between $50 and $150 in rental fees when they could find a Hollywood movie at a video rental outlet for three dollars, which was less than the cost of return postage for a 16mm film.

The change in content was due to the huge surge in popularity of a refreshed and compelling series of didactic films. The films, such as the works by Dobson, emphasized the meaning and significance of the Gospel message for the daily lives and spiritual maturity of their spectators. They accented the role of discipleship and daily living, offering propositions and teaching, but they were achieved through translating biblical principles into the common language of their audiences. Dobson's first series rewrote the history of religious films. Back in 1978, nobody knew that churches would rent a film series featuring a man standing and talking, but across the nation churches wanted to rent this new series that met felt needs. Congregations wanted clear teaching by a Christian psychologist on raising children and other challenges. But the effect on the Christian film industry was catastrophic; not only the production companies but also the film libraries, after the first rush of profit on the *Focus* series, found themselves without the necessary diversity of film product to meet future demand.

The next twenty years would bring great changes as the Christian film industry sought to find a general audience and make money doing so. The Christian film industry would revive in the new century, with novel distribution techniques and much bigger budgets to make more ambitious films for the general theatrical market. Many more mixed characters and colorful filmmakers, from Mel Gibson (*The Passion of the Christ*) to Phil Vischer (*VeggieTales*), would emerge to push these changes forward.

Summary

Russ Doughten and Don Thompson are credited for developing a whole new genre, the apocalyptic or Christian horror picture, and for making suspenseful films that still rent widely today. Their phenomenal success with *A Thief in the Night* was followed by such offspring as *Future Tense* (1990), *End of the Harvest* (1995), *The Gathering* (1998), *The Moment After* (1999), and *Escape from Hell* (2000). The popularity and originality of the *Thief* films inspired Christian film school graduates to enter the field, particularly from Pat Robertson's Regent University. Its film school produced two highly trained independent filmmakers, Wes Llewellyn and Danny Carrales, who dedicated their professional lives to making low-cost apocalyptic films, often using fellow alumni as crew members. Llewellyn's first feature, *The Moment After*, follows two FBI agents investigating the mass disappearance of Christians that occurred in the "twinkling of an eye." Working in association with the Christiano Film Group, Llewellyn's film associated the evil of a new world order with the emergence of a paramilitary organization that seeks to suppress certain truths of the books of Revelation and Daniel and instead pushes its own totalitarian agenda.

Carrales initially directed a documentary for EO Dutch television on the Washington, DC, African American churches. He then conspired with his fellow alumnus, the maverick screenwriter Michael Martin, to create several harrowing end-times videos that raised issues of faith, good works, and salvation, all released under the rubric of DRC Productions. The films dealt with Judgment Day (*Final Exit*) and the Rapture (*The Gathering*) in unpredictable and effective ways. While not avoiding evangelistic presentations of the Gospel message, Carrales vividly and convincingly dramatized the personal lives of individual characters. In the third film of this eschatological thriller trilogy, *Escape from Hell*, he exploited the interest in near-death experiences (long tunnels of light and peace), portraying them as wide paths leading to the destruction of hell. Jerry Falwell loved the film, testifying that "if this doesn't get a non-believer to think about life without Christ, nothing will."[42]

The trend would continue into the next decade, not only with the Tim LaHaye pop-fiction phenomenon of the *Left Behind* series and Trinity Broadcasting's *Omega Code* franchise, but with Hollywood blockbusters like the Arnold Schwarzenegger vehicle *End of Days* (1999). Rapture fiction appealed not only to dispensational fundamentalists but to Roman Catholics as well.[43] Unfortunately for the CFDA, these later films would bypass the local Christian libraries and develop new strategies for distributing their products to the churches.

Finally, these films situate the political and geographical nation of Israel as the enduring chosen people of God whose conversion will serve as a harbinger of the apocalypse.[44] Less time is given to exegeting and interpreting the sacred texts and more to reading the cinematic signs of the times. With the dramatic tendency among end-times filmmakers, echoing and exploiting Darby's 19th-century notion of the Rapture, this apocalyptic genre attracted an anxious and gullible audience. In contrast to the early Christian belief of the blessed hope of the Second Coming, these cinematic interpretations triggered fear and restlessness.[45] But while these films portraying sacred terrors would have a lasting evangelistic impact, the historical story of Jesus would be revived in global productions to claim the honorific status as the "most seen film in the world."

8

Global Film Evangelism

While much of the Christian film industry settled into domestic production, several visionary producers looked across the seas. Realizing that a media-saturated market in the United States limited their appeal, they envisioned multiplying their investments and their effectiveness in communicating to the world. Grounded in the Great Commission—the call of Jesus in the Gospel of Matthew to preach the Gospel throughout the world—these producers sought to adapt the medium to other cultures, with mixed results. As communicators, they were little concerned with cross-cultural communication problems; even when these filmmakers produced their films in foreign countries, their product was clearly a Western, Christian view of the world, with mostly Caucasian actors and Western music.

Often unexpected events enlivened the filming process. Not many film companies can claim to have converted a bank robber while he was about to carry out a heist. During the course of filming *The Caged* (Holland, 1974) for International Films, the director Don Ross was shooting a scene where an evangelist is preaching in the street. Not knowing a movie was being filmed, a bank robber was on his way to rob a bank when he heard the message of the actor and he received the Lord. Later he turned himself in to the police.[1]

Films Afield

As we have seen in earlier chapters, the Baptists, Methodists, Lutherans, and Presbyterians were able to chronicle documentary footage of their overseas missionary work from 1930 onward. Many of these were filmed by missionaries who were amateur camera operators, but these "home movies" found an audience among their denominational supporters. These films were not part of "global film evangelism"; rather, they were promotional films to encourage American Christians to give to denominational mission projects.

One early pioneer of global film evangelism was Tom Hotchkiss, who incorporated his own company, Films Afield. Originally a radio announcer,

Hotchkiss had served as a deck officer in the Merchant Marine during World War II, crisscrossing the Pacific making the supply runs to the China-Burma-India theater. Against this setting he had the opportunity to see firsthand the Third World. After the war Hotchkiss began his own film company, noticing that many mission organizations were becoming interested in employing film as a new medium for evangelism and for raising support. In the early 1950s, he and his company produced their first documentary missions film, *Light of the Sun* (1957). Julius Bergstrom, a veteran China missionary reassigned to Japan after the communist takeover of China, shot the 16mm pictures for their first overseas production assignments for the Conservative Baptist Foreign Mission Society (CBFMS). Ten films were made in a four-month tour in 1957, and eventually that figure rose to thirty films for CBFMS. According to Hotchkiss, "A virtual flood of films followed as scores of foreign missions signed contracts and we became recognized as global film makers."[2]

Hotchkiss and his wife, Carol, zealously produced dramatic evangelistic films overseas for distribution in those same countries. An early effort in the 1970s was *Suzanne* (1972), shot in the French-speaking Ivory Coast and featuring an all-African cast. A very explicit salvation message is intertwined with a tale of love, jealousy, and intrigue; eventually, more than two hundred 16mm prints of the film were used by various mission groups in Africa. Most Films Afield projects were thought provoking and serious in nature. For example, a popular urban ministry film, *Pourquoi Moi? (Why Me?)* (1974), dealt with the terminal illness of a young African photojournalist, who must accept the reality of his dying as he seeks guidance through his spiritual and mental confusion. The film *Chidi* (1985), set in the Nigeria-Biafra Civil War, told the story of African Christian heroes. One of the most widely exhibited films, *It Happened to Shankar* (1987), was shot in India with a cast of boys in their early teens. By the 1990s, the goal of the company was to produce two dramatic evangelistic films a year in Africa, Asia, and Latin America, respectively.

A charge leveled at missions and mission films by their opponents is that they are financed by foreign interests, not by indigenous supporters. Mission films are almost always financed by donors from Western countries who are directly funding missionary activity inside the target country. Films Afield became a totally owned subsidiary of a "for profit" business called Tri Media Communications, and each missionary film was made as a limited partnership whose profits were applied to new productions. This business model failed to ensure the long-term survival of the Films Afield, and later film companies succeeded through charitable donations, not business profits.

International Films

Ken Anderson formed International Films in 1963 to create films that would communicate the Gospel to global audiences. But it was another visionary, Ray Carlson, who fulfilled Anderson's dream. Ray Carlson had become a Christian thanks to the performances of Robert Mitchum and Deborah Kerr in the Hollywood movie *Quo Vadis* (1951). Carlson confesses, "When my wife and I saw this movie about the Christians of Rome being martyred in the arenas . . . it so gripped us that they could have such faith; when Joy and I got home, we knelt for the first time and we asked God to reveal that kind of faith to us." Carlson then heard Ken Anderson describe the making of *Something to Die For* (1960), his movie made in Singapore; immediately he knew that what he most wanted to do was to make Christian films for other cultures.[3]

Carlson felt called overseas, where he introduced a new production policy as he became convinced of the importance of films being not only photographed but also produced in the same country as the target audience. With the help of Youth for Christ he set up indigenous partner companies of International Films in England, Holland, and Germany. Between 1965 and 1985 International Films produced and distributed some twenty films outside the United States, each one a culturally sensitive movie made in the country where it would be shown. This list includes *The Accuser* (Germany, 1965), *Carnival of Pretense* (Brazil, 1966), *The Lost Gamble* (Korea, 1970) *Getting It Together* (Italy, 1973), *The Caged* (Holland, 1974), *Treasures of the Snow* (Switzerland, 1980), and *The Pearl* (India, 1985).

Their first European film, *The Accused*, was directed by the Swiss director Heinz Fussle, who had already worked extensively with Ken Anderson in the United States. The central goal of International Films was that it should become the first Christian film company formed for the specific purpose of creating indigenously produced films using local writers and camera operators. International Films UK was set up with an office in London, run by Nigel Cooke and Ray Carlson, who left his Swedish oil company to go full-time with International Films in Europe. Their first English director was the talented cameraman Mike Pritchard, who produced two of Patricia St. John's books, first *Tanglewood's Secrets* and then *Treasures of the Snow*. This two-hour 16mm Christian movie made for less than $180,000 proved incredibly successful in secular markets in the United States and Europe, being bought and replayed many times by HBO, Showtime, and ten other cable channels, and has repaid its investment many times over.

Carlson wanted each European country to produce their own Christian films, and with financial help from EO (Evangelische Omroep), the evangelical Dutch television station, International Films produced their first overseas movie in Dutch. *The Caged* (1974) was an interracial teenage drama about a relationship between a white Dutch girl and her very white Dutch family, and an Indonesian boy and his Indonesian mother. The movie dealt with the drug culture, which was relevant, as Amsterdam had become a European center for narcotics. Unfortunately the film was never released; because some of the actors were not Christians, the fundamentalist board members of EO banned it. Carlson said sadly, "It was tragic. After we had gone to all this effort to produce it: to my knowledge, to this day, it has never been aired, but bits and pieces have been aired by the Youth Department."[4]

International Films next opened up in South Africa, with Don Ross making two films with the help of South African Youth for Christ. The first was *Little Lost Fisherman* (1974), an interracial film for children, made with the help of a black African pastor, Andrew Ballentine, and his congregation in Cape Town. The second film, *Love Is a Quiet Thing* (1975), was a daring story of how a black African's heart was transplanted into a white man. The black African dies, but the donor's widow witnesses to the white man's wife. It was a very moving story, but its theme was quite unpopular with the many South Africans who supported apartheid, so the film flopped. Carlson commented, "Every time I see it I get all choked up because it's so beautiful, so real and I think that's what, of course, the whites just couldn't stand in South Africa."[5]

Next International Films expanded into three Asian countries, Vietnam, India, and Japan. With Americans fighting in Vietnam, it was natural to produce their films in English and Vietnamese, but by the time the films were finished, U.S. forces had withdrawn. Instead, the Vietnamese versions of the films were shown inside the large Vietnamese refugee camps in the United States. Carlson was also keen to produce Christian films in India: for three years International Films ran monthlong film training programs at the Catholic Xavier Institute of Communications in Bombay. Out of these training sessions one Indian Christian film from Cephas International emerged, C. D. Jebasingh's *The Pearl* (1985).

The third Asian country chosen for film production was Japan, with director Don Ross developing a film for Japanese children, *Mysterious Books* (1973), and *Yoneko* (1974), a true story about a girl who attempted suicide and lost her limbs but later received Christ. The production qualities were good, though in both films the acting was less convincing. The film with the most exotic location was *The Book That Would Not Burn* (1976), filmed on the

African island nation of Madagascar. This sixty-seven minute 16mm feature, made in the Malagasy language, tells the story of the 19th-century queen of Madagascar who tried to destroy all the Christians and their Bibles. Carlson explained that "the movie is basically a primer on how to martyr Christians; it shows all the ways of doing it. . . . When the first copy came to the censor of Madagascar, the guy had never seen a film in his own language and he just wept." Whenever the film is shown in Madagascar, Bible sales go up and church attendance increases.[6]

International Films was the first to try to produce films with indigenous talent and crews, eschewing American cultural influences. But as the director for nearly all these films was Don Ross, an American, it was difficult to avoid a Western slant on the events portrayed. To their credit, however, International Films involved nationals of the countries concerned with the screenwriting process; for each production, one of the crew positions was a cultural consultant and dialogue director. International Films then distributed their films through missionary agencies that, in turn, supplied individual film evangelists with prints. At other times, International Films used state-run television services, but it soon became clear that Hindu and Muslim governments did not want their people to hear about Jesus Christ. Opposition to Christian movies in the Middle East, India, and some Asian countries would escalate, even becoming a matter of life and death for some exhibitors who showed *The Jesus Film*.

"The Most Seen Film in the World"

An early Christian strategist proposed using film as a worldwide tool in order to fulfill the Great Commission; the missionary John R. Mott recognized in 1926 how missionary films were mostly addressed to the home audience. He pleaded with the church to broaden its vision for a global use of films to spread the Gospel message to other cultures; he believed that in just a few short weeks the cinema could influence more people than missionaries could physically expect to reach in a lifetime. The church took up the challenge but missed the point; it did not make motion pictures for the mission field. Instead, it made films about missions for the people back home. This was good, but the film medium, with few exceptions, had yet to really be harnessed.[7]

The culmination of Baptist activity in film production occurred in 1980, when its International Mission Board partnered with the Genesis Film Project, an extension of Campus Crusade for Christ, to give birth to what has become known as "the most seen film in the world," namely, the Jesus Film

Project. Beginning in 1945, Bill Bright, president of Campus Crusade, had considered the creation of a biblically accurate motion picture biography of Jesus, which was realized more than thirty years later in 1979 and would garner praise from prominent evangelical Christian leaders like Rick Warren, who called it the "most effective evangelistic tool ever invented."[8] According to its promoters, since 1979 *The Jesus Film* has been seen six billion times and is "responsible for saving some 225,873,100 souls," claiming that "every four seconds, somewhere in the world, someone becomes a Christian as a result of seeing *The Jesus Film*."[9]

As the script developed out of a literal reading from the Gospel of Luke, it was filmed on location in Israel with "authentic Biblical settings" and employing more than five thousand Israelis and Arabs as cast members in the movie. Realizing that hundreds of Southern Baptist missionaries were already using the docudrama media for outreach in foreign lands with great success, *The Jesus Film* director Paul Eshleman met with the SBC International Mission Board leaders in early 1979. In order to expand the use of *The Jesus Film* on the mission field, the SBC International Mission Board formed a partnership with the distributors of the Jesus Film Project. This agreement has magnified the film's impact throughout the world, with Southern Baptist International Mission Board missionaries distributing and exhibiting it internationally. Southern Baptist missionaries found the film useful for both outreach and discipleship, providing a visual and oral presentation of God's plan of salvation to all peoples of the earth.

The film actually started out on its path to extraordinary success because of the floundering of another film venture. When John Heyman, the famous English film producer of *A Passage to India* (1984), became a Christian in the mid-1970s, he dreamed of putting the entire Bible on film. Heyman had a string of movie credits to his name, such as *The Go-Between* (1970), starring Julie Christie and Alan Bates. Born a German Jew in 1933, Heyman came to Britain and as a young man spent his Sabbaths teaching the Hebrew Bible at his local synagogue, where he conceived the idea of putting the sacred texts on film. His dream eventually became the Genesis Project's New Media Bible, which translated biblical stories into visual forms. Beginning with a series of fifteen-minute shorts, he had hoped to film the entire Bible, but funding proved an obstacle. Interviewed by the *New York Times* in 1976, Heyman described his motivation as financial: "I believed the best-selling book in the world would sell a lot of 8mm and 16mm films."[10] Befriended by Paul Eshleman, the former U.S. field director for Campus Crusade for Christ, the two men spent a year trying to market Heyman's New Media Bible to churches. In 1978, Eshleman remembers Heyman remarking that they needed to make a longer feature to earn money for the project. "Let's do the first one on Jesus," Heyman said.[11]

Oklahoma-born Bill Bright, who had spent part of his early career in Los Angeles "trying to convert Hollywood stars," had planned to produce the film on the life of Jesus, even once approaching Cecil B. DeMille to remake his silent classic *The King of Kings* (DeMille declined).[12] But the Jewish Heyman and the evangelical Bright joined forces as partners, with Heyman needing financial backing and Bright wanting a movie about Jesus. After numerous Hollywood studios rejected their idea of a Jesus movie, the partners roped in the Dallas businessman Bunker Hunt, who put up $3 million to underwrite much of the film's $6 million production costs. Several investors in Israel supplied another $2 million, and finally Warner Bros. opted to put up $3 million for distribution and advertising.

The film had to appeal to all denominations, lest some sectarian doctrine alienate certain groups; therefore Bright and Heyman chose to ensure textual and visual accuracy, which conveniently suggested the Southern Baptist emphasis on the inerrancy of Scripture. Almost every word in the movie derived from the *Good News for Modern Man* translation of the Gospel of Luke, but key passages, like the Lord's Prayer and the Beatitudes, were taken from the King James authorized version. A panel of biblical scholars were invited to participate in every stage of the production; Heyman recalled that "we were required to refilm three days' work because we had shown Eucalyptus trees in a variety of shots and Eucalyptus trees were introduced to Palestine very much later."[13]

Shot in Israel, the producers opted for a predominantly Jewish cast to avoid the critical reception given to Nicholas Ray's blue-eyed Gentile Jeffrey Hunter Jesus of *King of Kings* (1961). The crowd scenes were provided by a group of Yemenite Jews who, according to Eshleman, offered ethnic "facial features that had changed the least over 2000 years."[14] Jewish actors were given the speaking roles, with Rivka Neuman playing Mary, Leonid Weinstein playing James, and Eli Cohen as John the Baptist. The search for the actor to play the role of Christ took several months. More than 250 actors were screened, and finally Brian Deacon, a relatively unknown British Shakespearean actor, was chosen to play Jesus, partly because of his ethnically correct olive complexion (although his visage was compromised by his piercingly blue eyes). Brian memorized whole chapters of Saint Luke's Gospel and read it twenty-two times before filming began. He was so convincing as Jesus that bystanders often broke out in applause at the end of one of his speeches, and many asked to be healed by him after the healing scenes were filmed.[15]

Claiming to be the "most seen film in the world," Campus Crusade's *The Jesus Film* was translated into hundreds of languages and imported to play on huge screens in places like Nigeria. Courtesy of the JESUS Film Project®/Mick Haupt.

On-location shooting proved challenging as the project encountered production difficulties, from cases of pneumonia suffered from inclement weather to the purchasing of more than forty sheep, thirty goats, twenty chickens, ten donkeys, and a host of other assorted animals as extras, and hunting for a herd of pigs. The cinematographers wasted more than ninety minutes of film stock attempting to shoot a dove landing on the shoulder of Deacon during the baptism sequence (the birds kept landing on his head).[16] Another difficulty came with the pigs playing the Gerasene swine: it was quite difficult to simulate their stampede over a cliff, since they proved reluctant to run anywhere, much less over a cliff. So the production manager decided to explode a few grenades around to encourage them to move in the right direction. Unfortunately, as pigs tend to eat everything, one swine ate a grenade; it exploded into a thousand pieces and the entire cast and crew were drenched with particles of pig.[17]

Worldwide Reaction

In the United States, the Warner Bros. theatrical release in October 1979 earned a modest $4 million and some lukewarm criticism. But the evangelical Christian community welcomed this literal version of Saint Luke's Gospel;

in fact, some churches bought out entire movie theaters and filled every seat. For Bill Bright, the real audience waited in the developing world; he planned to distribute the film pro bono through missions and churches worldwide as a powerful evangelistic tool, dubbing the picture into many languages. He sent out Campus Crusade teams in advance to visit many countries in 1979 to record audio versions of the film commentary and dialogue in fifty different languages. Over the following thirty years, the number of foreign-language versions of *The Jesus Film* would exceed a thousand.

The start of the dubbing process was full of drama. Inspirational Films, the Campus Crusade for Christ subsidiary initially responsible for worldwide distribution of the film, was in a hurry to get the foreign versions out to their evangelistic teams in South East Asia. But back in 1979 the technology for producing foreign-language versions of films, called "looping," was both expensive and time-consuming. Crusade teams in the various counties had already recorded different language versions of Luke, using the formula of six different male voice tracks: one for the Luke commentary, one for Jesus, two for various disciples, soldiers, and priests, and two female voice tracks for the two Marys plus other women and children. The work had to be carried out in London for copyright reasons, but the quotations from British professional film recording companies for doing each foreign language were very high, far more than the Jesus Film Project could then afford to pay.

Language version editors Andrew Quicke (one of this book's authors) and Gordon Woodside came up with a very low-cost solution to the problem; because the Crusade teams had recorded the different translations in precisely the same order as the narration and dialogue of the Gospel, it appeared possible to lay in the sound tracks accurately using a film editing table, despite the film editors' ignorance of what was being said and inability to read the various scripts provided in Thai, Chinese, and so on. Quicke placed film-editing machines in virtually every room in his London apartment, including the bedrooms and the nursery. A team of inspired film editors aligned the 16mm sound tracks to the 16mm pictures by hand, working twelve hours day to keep up with the needs of the Crusade teams in South East Asia that were already showing the film at evangelistic rallies.[18]

The films recorded for the South Pacific islands were the first in history recorded in Tongan, Nauru, and other rare Pacific Island languages. Nationals from the countries concerned checked the translations in the author's London apartment. The princess of Tonga greeted her first viewing with gales of laughter and the production team asked anxiously what had gone wrong. "Nothing, but the modes of address are not the ones we aristocrats use," she replied cheerfully; the translation recorded in Tonga used the phraseology of the common people throughout, but in Tonga there are special ways of addressing God and nobles. Using the common modes of address for Jesus seemed hilarious to the aristocratic princess, though she approved of it as appropriate for the film. Reactions worldwide to the first fifty language versions of *The Jesus Film* were very enthusiastic. Missionaries took projectors, generators, and film cans to remote areas in Asia, Africa, and Latin America, and conversion stories flooded in from the world over.

The distributor, the Jesus Film Project, published many stories detailing the success of the film. The provost of Calvin College in Grand Rapids, Michigan, told of an evangelist in Nigeria who in a single summer of *Jesus Film* showings created thirty churches in a predominantly Muslim area. The provost commented, "In Nigeria, people consume most of their media in English. When people see Jesus speaking in their tongue, they instantly identify with him. He seems sent to them."[19] Many mission groups besides the Campus Crusade teams used the film as an evangelistic tool. Brian Helstrom of the Church of the Nazarene missions described a typical screening in Phaphamani, a town without electricity in South Africa. The team fired up their generator, turned on their five floodlights, and projected the film on a large screen. The crowd of 350 people had never seen a film in their own language before. Helstrom recalled, "You could see them physically jump back at the sight of the serpent tempting Jesus; when the soldiers whip Jesus, you could hear grown adults crying." After the crucifixion scene, but before the resurrection, a black South African missionary told the crowd they had the chance to walk forward into the light and pray to accept Christ. "One hundred and fifty people walked out of the darkness into light," said Helstrom.[20]

A special edition, devised to be a millennial tribute broadcast globally, drafted former presidents Jimmy Carter, George H. W. Bush, and Gerald Ford, the singer Naomi Judd, and the tennis player Michael Chang to testify to its significance. According to the Baptist news agency, billions of people in more than 220 countries saw *The Jesus Film* in theaters, on television, via video, or—still the most common method—watching 16mm reels projected onto portable screens, sheets, or walls. More than seventy-three million people have publicly declared their decision to follow Christ after seeing the film. *The Jesus Film* has been dubbed into more than 450 languages, making it the most widely translated production in film history.[21]

Even though *The Jesus Film* became the most widely distributed film in the history of cinema, its tremendous success also led to increasingly articulate opposition from political and religious groups in India and in Muslim countries. But another film would sneak in the backdoor to evangelize in Hindu and Muslim villages.

The Other Jesus Film

Some missionary strategists have wondered whether, despite its many language versions, *The Jesus Film* remains too Western in its conception, music, and editing. Certainly it has been shown across the Indian subcontinent since 1979 with great success. Campus Crusade claims particular success in some of the remote areas. "Our film evangelism among extremely backward tribal groups in India is proving stunningly successful," claimed a Crusade spokesman from the Bangalore headquarters of the India Campus Crusade Ministry.[22] But in India it has a serious rival.

In 1978, an Indian film about Jesus was made in the Telugu language called *Karunamayudu* (in Hindi *Daya Sagar*, or in English *Man of Mercy*). It is a full-length, 160-minute motion picture about the life of Jesus, featuring an entirely Indian cast and produced by Vijay Chander, who also takes the part of Jesus himself. Originally recorded in Telugu, it has now been dubbed into fifteen different languages of the India subcontinent and won national commercial distribution in India. But the film became widely seen when John E. Gilman, an American television producer, was seeking to make a film in India about the life of Christ and discovered that such a movie from an Indian perspective had already been produced.[23] Gillman explained, "Here was a Hindu whom God was using to present the story of His Son to the unconverted peoples of India. . . . It simply meant that God is not limited to our traditional means. He uses whomever He wills—even a Hindu filmmaker.[24]

Ever since the age of twelve, John Gilman had had a desire to minister and go to India. After thirteen years with the Christian Broadcasting Network, John knew he wanted to spread the Gospel in India through the cinema.[25] He resigned and took a plane to Bombay. As he was riding in a taxi he came across a billboard depicting Christ at different points during the crucifixion. The driver told him that the billboard was about a new film playing in the theaters. Gilman remembers, "'Oh, Lord,' I prayed, half in joy and half in shock. 'I have come halfway around the world to bring the message of Jesus through motion pictures to the people of India. And you are already doing it!'" Gilman lost no time in locating the film's producer, Vijay Chander: "To my astonishment, Vijay agreed that God had sent me to him."[26]

Gilman further explains his fascination with the film:

What makes this motion picture unique in spreading the Gospel by the use of the film industry is the fact that Jesus in this film is not a "white man's" Messiah. Via this film, Jesus walks out of Nazareth into a typical Indian village. He is one of them—with Asiatic features, wearing very similar clothes, drawing water from a well, walking the dusty roads as they do today. This film breaks down cultural barriers that would probably not be possible if it were a Western production. The Indian villagers relate to the film when Jesus is ministering to the poor. They understand when Barabbas (a leading figure in the film) attempts to persuade Jesus into helping him overthrow the oppressive Romans by force. And they can feel the agony on Barabbas' face when he watches Jesus dying on the cross he should be dying on. An American producer would not even think about having Barabbas as a leading actor in a film on the life of Christ. The Indians cheered when He drove out the moneychangers from the temple. They wept when He was beaten. When He was crucified, I heard cries of anguish. And when He rose from the dead, the audience applauded, cheered, and whistled. When the three-hour movie concluded with Christ's ascension, I realized I had viewed an incredible tool of evangelism, perhaps the most powerful witness to the Gospel presented in India in 2,000 years.[27]

Soon Gilman formed his own ministry, Dayspring International, and helped by a $40,000 donation from Jim Bakker of the ill-fated Praise the Lord (PTL) television ministry, began showing *Karunamayudu* throughout India. Dayspring formed mobile film teams to travel throughout the villages, and by 2009 they had shown their film in 190,000 villages. In just ten years, they estimate, 120 million people have seen this film, and 7 million have made public confessions of belief in Jesus.[28] Seminars were set up in order to train potential film evangelists who needed to learn how to run and maintain portable generators, how to use the movie projectors, how to go into a village and prepare for the viewing, how to work with (not against) established local Christian work and churches, and how to disciple the new converts after each viewing.[29]

Gilman views his main responsibility as ensuring that the Dayspring ministry is being conducted according to the original goals and policies, which were to show *Man of Mercy* as widely as possible, to train Indian Christian leaders in the techniques of film evangelism so that they might be able to train others, and to raise funds. There is a board of advisers who are experts in their knowledge of India's land and people and who are committed to evangelism. In order to comply with the Indian government's laws and regulations, Dayspring Enterprises of India was formed in 1985, an eight-person board of directors combining ministry experiences in church planting, education, hospital building and management, orphanage operations, and evangelism.

How Dayspring and Crusade Differ

The Jesus Film Project teams had concentrated on spreading the Word; they were not, and are not, concerned with the political and social structures of Indian society. With only 2 percent of the Indian population identifying as Christian, they at first encountered little opposition to their showings. From the start, the Dayspring teams had a different approach; their films were thoroughly Indian in culture and conception, and so fundamentally more subversive to the rigid class structures of Hindu society. John Gilman spent a good deal of time in India himself, and therefore became well acquainted with the class hierarchy so different from his American ideas of equality. He wrote fearlessly that

> for 3,500 years Hindu's caste system has oppressed the majority of its people, calling them untouchables. Today these nearly 250 million Dalits [untouchables] are being led by their leaders to publicly renounce Hinduism and look for hope and dignity elsewhere. The worship of a hundred million gods will disappear. Idolatry will be cast down, but what will replace it? Dalit leaders plead to the [Christian] church saying, "Come and tell us about your Jesus. Teach us your scriptures." They believe that this is the only hope for India, a nation that could be on the eve of a bloody civil war, or on the brink of an outpouring of the Holy Spirit unlike any in history.[30]

Gilman continues to believe that "there has never been a better soul-winning opportunity than right now in India." Toward that end, he has been helped by other American organizations like Operation Mobilization, whose film teams have already visited 85,000 villages and plan to visit another 650,000. Gilman's message is clear: "A revolution has begun in the nation of India that will transform the society forever."[31]

This revolution has two aims; first, to "stir up an insatiable thirst for God in the hearts of Christians around the world"; and second, "to strive to do our part to help those who cannot help themselves, and to be a voice for those who have no voice. . . . The goal is to break the cycle of poverty."[32] Dayspring has become much more than a film ministry; besides providing food, shelter, and medical care, it also provides for social change through multilevel intervention programs like job training, education scholarships, and grants, together with seeds and equipment for farming. Dayspring wants to liberate the untouchables from their desperately underprivileged situation.

Hindu Backlash

The Hindu intellectual Dr. Gautam Sen wrote that "evangelical activity has become a political vehicle for self-proclaimed Christian states like the US that regard it as a useful adjunct to more obvious economic, political and cultural means of controlling other countries and cultures. . . . The fact that such religious conversions precipitate social tensions and conflict by dividing families and communities does not appear to trouble evangelists. . . . The myriad variants of American Protestantism, but also the papacy, are essentially business corporations striving to enlarge market share and revenues."[33] Dr. Sen pointed to the success of Christians in the state of Kerala, commenting that "superior numbers and higher educational levels proved decisive for Christian evangelical activity . . . once they had reached an understanding with communists and Muslims to disempower the nominal Hindu majority." And in a grudging tribute to evangelical success, he concluded, "India south of the Vindhyas is politically Christianized on a scale that will be difficult to reverse."[34]

Summary

While it may seem surprising that showing evangelistic films should lead to ethnic tensions and even murderous violence, their impact has greatly increased Indian persecution of the Christian minority. At the same time, *The Jesus Film* and *Karunamayudu* have proved very powerful evangelistic tools and have converted many Hindus. American and European Christians have been determined to fulfill the Great Commission for the past 150 years, and so have increasingly targeted the developing world with missionary groups. During colonial times there was nothing that subject nations could do to stop this active missionizing. With independence everything changed; though the Indian constitution guarantees freedom of religion, India has demanded that foreign missionaries withdraw while still allowing indigenous Indian Christians freedom of worship.

So in 2011 the situation now exists in India that *The Jesus Film* is regarded by Hindus as a provocative Western import, with distribution paid for by Westerners, that spreads disaffection with the dominant Hindu culture and seeks to empower the 250 million untouchables who might wield real voting power in years to come. The powerful Hindu national party, the BVP, feels threatened by an indigenous Christian movement. What will happen in the future is unclear; all we can be certain of is that American and European Christians will continue to finance film evangelism in India and throughout the developing world.

—————————————————————————————————— 9 ——

Conclusion

A Modest Renaissance before the End

———

In 1979, a group of graduate film students at Regent University were given twelve hours in a television studio to shoot a documentary on the history of the Christian film movement. Titled *We've Come a Long Way Baby*, the hour-long presentation featured the former Gospel Films vice president Dave Anderson as its host, reflecting on key people and films over the previous forty years. Even with a noticeable fatigue overcoming the host after the long shoot, with his eyes and shoulders drooping and his words becoming slurred, the crew managed to capture the early energy and the tentative hope of the Christian film industry on the verge of a new decade.[1] But after half a century of development in sound pictures, the Christian film industry actually seemed to stagnate as much as Anderson drooped on camera. With a few exceptions, film products produced for the church now followed predictable patterns. Yet in the early 1980s, the industry was to experience its own mini-revival, particularly with an influx of young Christians who had studied filmmaking in universities and sought to express their own visions through the 16mm format. Many were mavericks itching to forge ahead with innovative products, new wine into new wineskins. In the early 1980s, the future looked bright for these young directors and producers.

When this new generation of Christian filmmakers arrived to offer interesting and challenging films, a modest renaissance flowered, as progressive (and sometimes desperate) distributors were looking for fresh products. This rebirth would be short-lived, however, due to the impending demise of the 16mm Christian film distribution network and the subsequent rise of videotape.

The New Auteurs

By the late 1970s, most of the Christian film pioneers had retired or died. Simultaneously, a fresh new generation of filmmakers came into the Christian film industry, sparked not only by exposure to Christian films, but also by a cultural renaissance among evangelicals, finding a call to be leaven in the world rather than to be a judge of that world. By 1980, the Protestant scholar Edward Berckman observed the changing attitudes of Protestant churches to movies. Many conservative colleges that had condemned films as generally lewd and immoral, offering a deceptive illusion of life, and being a spiritual distraction ("the Hollywood road runs nearer Babylon than Sinai") now relaxed their evangelical taboos.[2] Many of those who flocked to Hollywood's films were young college students ready to engage culture rather than merely condemn it.

Young Christians began to attend film schools such as USC, even as institutions like Fuller Theological Seminary in Pasadena, California, offered seminars in "Theology and Film." The vanguard evangelical periodical, *Christianity Today*, had been reviewing films since December 10, 1956 (with its first review being on DeMille's *The Ten Commandments*), both Christian and secular, which opened the door for young Christians to experiment with the medium. Super-8 film formats allowed these entrepreneurs to easily tinker with telling stories on celluloid.

The Christian film industry was about to start a fresh generation with innovative films like *Super Christian* (1980) and *The Music Box* (1980), sprinkled liberally with music and humor. As we have seen, because of the work of the pioneers, a distribution system had been established with the film librarians. Unlike in the early days, these young Christian filmmakers didn't have to be concerned about whether churches had projectors. Their prime concerns centered on production issues, on both the logistical challenges of budgets and equipment and the creative options of scriptwriting and cinematography. Their modest renaissance came about because of their better training, innovative opportunities for alternative genres of Christian film, and increased savvy regarding the importance of marketing.

John Schmidt, one of the most ingenious and resourceful auteurs of the new generation, emerged out of the UCLA film school and Fuller Theological Seminary with his inaugural thesis film, *Super Christian*, a mixed satire and parody, released in 1980. With his brother Jim starring as the eponymous hero, the mild-mannered Clark Kant, Schmidt's film gently and humorously poked fun at the plastic image of Christian youth and their artificial culture removed from real life. On Sundays, Clark Kant would become the model Christian while he took the rest of the week off. A clever sequel, *Super Christian 2*, appeared in 1986, puncturing the sacred cows of religious hypocrisy and the masks Christians wear to camouflage sin, pain, and fear.

In *Super Christian*, John Schmidt provided a remarkably clever parody of the Hollywood film while spoofing hypocritical posturing in churches. Courtesy of John Schmidt.

As writer, director, producer, and editor, Schmidt controlled all aspects of his personal film visions. Having attended a mission conference in Urbana, Illinois, in 1981, Schmidt wrote and directed several films dealing with foreign and home missions. He critiqued themes of idealized and romantic visions of foreign missionary work with funny, satirical jabs, pointing to the overlooked practical evangelization of next-door neighbors in *Kevin Can Wait* (1981) and *The Greatest Story Never Told* (1983). His films parodied Hollywood features like *Superman*, *Heaven Can Wait*, and *The Greatest Story Ever Told*, but infused with Christian messages. He then wrote and shot *The Wait of the World* (1986) and *Guess Who's Coming to America* (1992), in part to investigate problems with international missionary work, dealing candidly with the challenges of Muslim conversions. In late 1999, he was tapped to direct and produce a feature for World Wide Pictures titled *A Vow to Cherish*, in which a Billy Graham crusade would emphasize faithfulness and forgiveness during seasons of physical and spiritual testing. Rather than simply focusing on Graham's evangelistic rally, the film dealt with delicate family issues surrounding a spouse with Alzheimer's disease. With the presence of an accomplished actor like Ossie Davis, the film demonstrated a maturing of the Billy Graham films, with Schmidt weaving his professional competence into the remarkably poignant story. As a university-trained filmmaker, Schmidt marked the transition from religious visionaries who wanted to use film to professional filmmakers who expressed their Christian visions through celluloid.

Jim Robinson, another of the notable filmmakers of this new generation, studied cinema at Trinity University and later at the American Institute for Foreign Study in Paris, which brought a Continental style to his work. His premiere film could have come from the fantasies of an Italian director like Federico Fellini, as Robinson invented the genre of the visual psalm with *The Music Box*, an exuberant film of lament, praise, and celebration. A listless factory worker stumbles across a surprise in an alley, five singing and dancing angels, both black and white, dressed in white tuxedos with little wings on their backs. They break out in infectious music singing about the King of Kings, which causes the awkward factory worker to smile and then dance with the angels. He tries to keep the gift from his coworkers and even from his bored and languid family, but he discovers the parabolic lesson that one cannot keep the gift of joy a secret—it embarrassingly breaks out in hilarity and music at inopportune times, arousing suspicion from those around him. The angels reappear to set him straight. While he and his wife are sleeping, the angels begin to dance and sing in the bedroom, resulting in his wife having a similar life-changing experience with the gift of joy. After learning his lesson, the man begins to share his contagious gift with his coworkers, who are also transformed.

With the producers Wendell and Marge Moody, Robinson shot this unique film in Chicago with a budget of about $85,000. He felt called to craft enigmatic parable films that were entertaining as well as instructional. In 1982, the prestigious Cannes International Film Festival bestowed on *The Music Box* an award for its original creativity. With this fresh boost of confidence, Robinson set out to release the film into the Christian film market. After having been rejected by the largest Christian production house, Gospel Films, because "Gospel felt that the Christian community was not ready for dancing and little wings," he approached the Christian Film Distributors Association.³ At their annual conference, however, Robinson realized that there was no chance of placing *The Music Box* in the Christian film market. Christian distributors, aware of the conservative nature of their audience, declined to distribute the film, finding it too uninhibited and wondering what to do with both white and black angelic beings who seemed a bit gay. None of the seventy distributors placed the film in their libraries. Still believing that his style of filmmaking contained an important message for the Christian community, Robinson began to search for alternative means of placing his film inside the churches. He formed White Lion Pictograph and virtually went door-to-door, sharing his film with individual congregations. He acknowledged that, "basically, it was a word-of-mouth situation." *The Music Box* was shown in one, two, and then multiple churches. After a few months White Lion began to send out the film by mail to churches, free of charge. Each showing was totally dependent upon a freewill, "love" offering basis. Robinson recalled that many times the love offering gifts did not even cover the postage required to send out the film. But the word began to spread because the film was so popular with the churches, and particularly the youth, who had viewed it. Church leaders began to call their local distributors inquiring about renting *The Music Box*. But, of course, none of the distributors had copies. Robinson explained, "The distributors began to get so many calls that one by one they asked us to send the film to them." White Lion Pictograph became not just a film company on an address label but also an active ministry with real-life people. It also developed a core network of churches for all future productions from White Lion, for whom the production house began a program of training church leadership on how to use Christian films effectively. Robinson's *6 P's to Successful Film Ministry* (ca. 1985) would teach media literacy to Christian leaders, instructing on not just how to show a film, as they had been doing for years, but also how to use a film effectively.

A third player in the mini-revival of Christian film was Fred Carpenter. Having graduated with honors from the Department of Radio, Television, and Film at the University of Texas, Carpenter brought both an inquisitive mind and a social conscience rarely seen in the church film market. His company, Mars Hill Productions, derived its name from the story in the book of Acts in which the apostle Paul arrives in Athens and challenges the philosophers of the city by preaching the truth of the Gospel before their statue to the "unknown god." Carpenter's films, likewise, attempt to engage nonbelievers and skeptics through what he calls "discussion-starter" films. At the

In Jim Robinson's *Music Box*, the musical group the Sensational Nightingales appear as angels of joy every time the protagonist opens the music box sent by God. Courtesy of Jim Robinson.

Areopagus (i.e., Mars Hill), some listeners had ridiculed Paul, while others wanted to hear more. So Carpenter adopted this passage as his modus operandi. When he graduated from the University of Texas he wanted to use film for youth evangelism as part of his involvement with Youth for Christ. Like Billy Zeoli of Gospel Films thirty-five years earlier, Carpenter made his first four films as part of the Youth for Christ ministry in Houston. What he discovered, however, changed the nature of his films: "Churches can best use media to get people to interact with each other. Films are by nature incomplete without personal interaction and ministry. My goal was to provide a springboard for meaningful discussion after the lights come back on."[4]

Provocatively, his film *The Question* (1983) opens on a suspenseful note with a college student considering suicide. The film cuts back and forth from that scene to a high school commencement exercise, where the senior class president is the brother of the suicidal student. In a series of flashbacks during commencement, we see the events of the last week unfold: the brother's joy of graduating and practicing his speech; his older brother committing suicide; the grief of the family; the last week of school following the funeral; a letter coming in the mail sent by the brother before his death. The pressing question of the letter resounds: "Why keep living?" The film intentionally did not answer the question, focusing instead on just raising the sensitive issue. Carpenter felt that these were questions many pastors did not want to answer or want their youth group to ask, but he believed that his films had to move from the priestly role of tending spiritual needs to a prophetic role of afflicting those too comfortable in the church.

In 1986, Mars Hill produced *Angel of Light*, a dramatic film that takes the viewers on a journey into the psychic world. Sara, a college student, shares her experiences and escape from spiritualism. The film focused on the reality of the occult, suggesting that spiritual warfare is not a game, that "tampering with the supernatural is dangerous and that spiritism is no joke."⁵ Carpenter's next film, *Without Reservations* (1988), also dealt with the supernatural and dying. In this narrative, after several young adults are all killed in an automobile accident, they are suspended in purgatorial time, waiting for judgment. The film asks why these students did not choose to become Christians before their death. The twist comes when we learn that one of the boys in the car was a Christian but had failed to tell the others about his faith. Carpenter continually stretched the comfort zone of a conservative audience, pleading with his viewers to attend to the fundamental questions with which his generation wrestled. Significantly, he recognized that just showing a film did not suffice. Spiritual growth and community came from the interaction after a film was shown. For Carpenter, film was a mere tool, useful for provoking spectators to reflect on what was eternally important.

Another filmmaker of the modest 1980s renaissance, Chuck Warren, had an educational background in political science, first entering film when producing political commercials. In 1980, Warren started Life Productions with a sports/evangelism film called *More Than Winning*, featuring sports celebrities like Coach Tom Landry, Kyle Rote Jr., and Bobby Jones. In 1983, he made *Believing God for the Best in You*, a fast-paced, graphics-filled production aimed at addressing a central problem for youth: self-image. Combining drama and interviews, the protagonist Robert drifts in and out of the "Identity Zone" (a takeoff on the *Twilight Zone*). Shots of cover-girl photos lead into an interview with Cheryl Prewitt, Miss America 1980, who tells how winning the crown made her feel even more lonely and alienated. Later on, the Christian pop singer Stormie Omartian relates a message for healing poor self-images. Continuing his onslaught on how culture brands its consumers, Warren's next film, *They Lied to Us* (1984), unmasked the permissive philosophies he felt were brainwashing society. His film sought to expose a lie that happiness could be found in possessions, beauty, and sex (and generated a tiny controversy by showing a full cover of *Playboy* magazine). Warren's interest in questions of social ministry led him to produce *And Justice for All* (1988), confronting the poverty and injustice that Christians too frequently ignore.

Another transitional figure, the director Ed McDougal, intersected with many of the industry's key figures. McDougal had been teaching high school when he sensed God calling him to the Christian film industry. His very first film experience came through work on a documentary on the Salvation Army summer program at a camp in Wisconsin. From there he studied film production under Ken Anderson and then migrated to Russ Doughten of Heartland/Mark IV, who mentored him on producing dramatic films for the Christian rental market. Trying to innovate, McDougal's philosophy encompassed looking at things "crooked"; he quipped that the "first thing that comes into your mind is usually the first thing that comes into your audience's mind." In 1984, McDougall premiered his first Christian feature, *Never Ashamed*, which won the Best Film of the Year Award at the Christian Film Distributors annual conference. The picture, grappling with problems of sharing one's faith, explored how young Christians relate to a non-Christian world, with a Capra-esque touch. Beginning with the eager zeal of a newly converted Christian trying to communicate the Gospel amid hostile peer pressure from old friends, the film contrasts the enthusiasm of first love versus the compromising character of lukewarm faith. McDougall's *Gold through the Fire* (1988) retained the evangelistic message of *Never Ashamed* but added a new twist, that of American Christianity's insensitivity to the cultural differences of immigrants. *Gold through the Fire* stands as the first film produced for the Christian market where it is the foreigner who has a more mature faith than the American Christians he meets.

In the early 1980s, national media outlets (e.g., the *Chicago Tribune* and the *Los Angeles Times*) and academic journals focused public attention on the embryonic Christian graduate filmmaking program at Regent University in Virginia Beach.[6] In 1981, Dan Georgakas, editor of the Marxist film journal *Cineaste*, prophesied that a new film school generation of conservative Christian filmmakers might well bloom out of what was then CBN University, now Regent University.[7] As a fashionable symbol of industry acceptance, even the pop-news show *Entertainment Tonight* did a special feature on Regent's film program.[8]

Regent's students competed impressively with their secular counterparts at NYU, USC, and UCLA. For the next decade, Regent's students not only won awards from CINE and at numerous film festivals, but they received a dozen student film finalist nominations at the Student Academy Awards.

Their films included the pencil object animation of Andy Rowe, *A Parable* (1983), and Dave Wilcox's wickedly funny animated religious satire, *If Your Eye Offendz Thee* (1986), mocking the hypocrisy of television evangelists. In 1986, the Regent student Antonio Zarro won the Best Dramatic Picture Student Academy Award for *Bird in a Cage*, inspired by Charlie Chaplin's *The Pilgrim* and Max Beerbohm's "The Happy Hypocrite," about a thief pretending to be a new preacher in town. Ironically, the thief's playacting hypocrisy leads to his own radical transformation and redemption. The following year, the director Jim Lincoln and the producer Lisa Swain adapted a Jeannie Burns-Hardy script about a coach, his runner with Down syndrome, a competitive female athlete, and the Special Olympics to win the Silver Student Academy Award for *Turtle Races* (1987). Rather than opting for hard-hitting evangelism or apologetics, the Regent students, like Chaucer's pilgrims on the way to Canterbury, essayed to tell vivid and compelling stories packed with humor and pathos.[9] Many Regent University films were sold to HBO, Showtime, and Fox, including Bill Harris's *All Things Fanged and Carnivorous* (1984), while several were picked up by the Christian film librarians, including Steve Baldwin's historical drama of John Fawcett's composition of his famous hymn in *The Tie That Binds* (1994) and Rick Settoon's interracial drama *Lighthouse* (1989). This student trend bucked the old industry formula of message coming first; now story and characters predominated.[10] These films were crafted to focus on compelling narratives rather than to propagate a religious message.

Unfortunately for the nascent renaissance, the introduction of the videocassette, combined with the "Dobson effect," handicapped the old Christian film rental libraries. As these libraries went out of business, many small film production companies simply collapsed. Some hoped that it would be possible to switch to selling Christian films on video as opposed to renting out 16mm copies, but the transition proved difficult. Selling videocassettes in sufficient numbers to defray the cost of production and return a profit proved impossible for most Christian filmmakers, who were forced to find other employment. Even a mail-order catalog of religious films, ROA, suffered from the vicissitudes of the business. Until June 1986, ROA Films had rented out religious films under categories ranging from evangelism and church history to themes of aging, ecology, and personal values, with large sections reserved for films for children and youth. But a declining church market for films meant less funding for productions like these.[11] "Unfortunately," Vice President and General Manager Ronald E. Reed wrote in 1986, ROA "found it necessary to close our religious film rental and sales library. The economics are such that we cannot compete with bookstores and other low costs of video."[12] A few were fortunate enough to be able to self-distribute their product; among this select group were Danny Carrales and the Christiano brothers, with Dave Christiano recognizing that no one wanted to "rent third-rate stuff. It has to be a work of art."[13] These young filmmakers were as adaptable as they were ambitious. Despite the declining church market and lack of funding, they found ways to distribute their own films, but many saw these difficulties as signs of the necessity to infiltrate the Hollywood industry, marking the coming shift to box office Christianity. As Jim Robinson would celebrate, "The whole industry is in flux. It's like going from the horse and buggy to the automobile."[14]

Summary

Back in 1930, the British author Evelyn Waugh in his cleverly satiric novel *Vile Bodies* made sport of an entrepreneur trying to make a Methodist film.[15] Not only did Waugh's send-up of Britain's decadently bright young things skewer the generation between the wars, but the hilarious satire spoofed the ambitions and naiveté of ersatz religious filmmakers, here known as the Wonderfilm Company of Great Britain, trying to make a buck off the church. In the novel, a filmmaker called Mr. Isaacs tries to capture the life of the social and religious reformer John Wesley in his movie *A Brand from the Burning*. He inserts plenty of movie stuff, such as gambling scenes, minuet dancers, American "Red Indians," and a fictional fencing duel between Wesley and the evangelist George Whitefield to provide exciting drama. When it is pointed out that the two never fought a duel, he retorts that "it's known that they quarreled and there was only one way of settling quarrels in those days. They're both in love with Selina, Countess of Huntingdon. She comes to stop them, but arrives too late. Whitefield has escaped in the coach and Wesley is lying wounded. That's a scene that'll go over big."

A character in the book explains that the trouble with *A Brand from the Burning* is that "we haven't enough capital. It's heart-breaking. Here we have a first-rate company, first-rate producer, first-rate scene, first-rate story, and the whole thing's being hung up for want of a few hundred pounds." In Waugh's satire, this fictional religious filmmaker, trying to produce the "most important All-Talkie super-religious film," reflected the state of the early Christian film industry. It was not enough to just make the films; one had to recognize the importance of audience, market, and the economic realities of the business. Waugh's fictional filmmaker tells his potential investors, "D'you know what the Wesleyan population of the British Isles is? Well, nor do I, but I've been told and *you'd be surprised.* Well, every one of them is going to come and see this film and there's going to be discussion about it in all the chapels. We're recording extracts from Wesley's sermons and we're singing all his own hymns."[16]

Presciently, Waugh mocks the "meticulous accuracy" of the religious film-maker who is making a truly amateur production (with his pupils and camera operators learning on the job) that he hopes to market to the mass of British Methodists. It is an incompetently directed and ineptly produced film that will never be seen. In a similar vein, the feisty editor and critic John Alexander complained about the quality of real films made by Christians. For Alexander, "Christians make lousy movies." He asked, "Why have Christians—who say they know the truth—made such a wretched showing in the arts?"[17]

The charge of poor filmmaking has dogged Christian filmmakers for decades; the reason for the lack of aesthetic "success" of Christian films most frequently revolves around the substandard artistic quality and content of the Christian film. Yet for the filmmakers, the films did succeed in conveying their messages, in preaching to their tribal congregations or in imparting a moral message. Others have criticized what they saw as an oversimplistic evangelization, which seemed crassly manipulative. Spectators are told what to see and believe. For the French Roman Catholic critic Amédée Ayfre, "the bigger danger would certainly be to want to take greater care of God's interests than He does himself by trying to direct events by force and constrain the audience to read in them a meaning which is only accessible to those who discover it freely."[18] The French theologian Blaise Pascal had observed centuries earlier that we are more fully persuaded by the reasons we discover for ourselves.[19] For some critics, the audience itself needs to hunt for the redemptive message, much like disciples puzzled over Jesus's parables. Christian filmmakers in the past had seldom trusted viewers to come to the correct interpretations. Subtlety has largely escaped the typical Christian film-maker, as "their films are populated with ill-formed ideals rather than with drama, often short on candor, imagination, and technical skill."[20]

The WWP producer Ken Wales described what he believes is an answer to the failure of the Christian film industry: "I think it is important for everybody—WWP and all of us as Christian communicators—to realize that we need to understand the bases of psychological and theological communication. People are so much more attuned to reality and real answers. They want to know where the hurt comes from, and they don't want a Band-Aid or an easy cure."[21] In calling for messages that illuminated the texture of normal living, Wales and others sought films that functioned as parables rather than lectures.[22]

In contrast to Waugh's mercenary and bungling filmmaking and Alexander's critique, the emerging Christian film industry produced, often effectively, celluloid sermons as a corpus of film work generated to evangelize, preach, teach, provoke, and sometimes entertain. These films were successful in *what they were intended to be*. From the 1930s and 1940s—with the emergence of sound movies for the church in the United States and the work of the three church film pioneers, James Friedrich, Carlos Baptista, and Irwin Moon—laying the foundation, the Christian film industry blossomed in the studio period of the 1950s and 1960s as an effective system of production, distribution, and exhibition was established. A downpour of ecumenical and sectarian films followed, with Methodists and Baptists leading the way. As we have seen, two distinctly different organizations demonstrated a larger vision of the place of Christian filmmaking: World Wide Pictures dedicated itself to providing well-funded, professionally made evangelistic films, strongly Baptist in content, from their own Hollywood studios, while Gateway Films, a much smaller organization nestled in the hills of Pennsylvania, concentrated on assembling a library of educational and historical films that appealed to all Christian denominations, including Roman Catholics. Christian film rental libraries proliferated in the 1970s, becoming unified under the banner of the Christian Film Distributors Association in 1974. The most popular genre rented by churches were end-times apocalyptic films, with the Christian horror film *A Thief in the Night* earning over $1 million in rental fees, an enormous sum for an industry that normally assessed its earnings at a fraction of that total. Few anticipated the tremendous impact that an evangelistic film translated into more than a thousand different language versions would have around the world. *The Jesus Film* (1979) became the most widely seen film in cinema history, viewed by millions, while the indigenous *Karunamayudu* (1978) proclaimed the Gospel story in remote villages and in the vernacular of the Indian culture.

As a subterranean movement of filmmaking, the emerging Christian film industry sought to adopt all the available means of production to communicate distinctive religious and moral messages amid Hollywood's prolific output. While both liberal and conservative Protestant churches dabbled in filmmaking, scripting social issue and salvation message films, respectively, it was the evangelical use of film that created a cottage industry that spread around the world. The use of movies by the church effectively accelerated its missions of evangelistic outreach and religious education. Although much of this work smacked of amateurism, it revealed a zeal for translating the

Christian faith into the vernacular of visual media; in short, it showed how the church sought to communicate in a new tongue, a visual glossolalia, producing volumes of celluloid sermons for the world to see and hear. The next generation of Christians in the film arts would move into the mainstream, creating a world where box office profits would supplant church-basement prophets.

In 1981, the "dean of distribution" for Warner Bros., Barry Reardon, staged an early premiere in Virginia Beach of a film that radically changed the Christian film industry. The producer David Puttnam and the director Hugh Hudson translated the hagiographic story of Eric Liddell, the Olympic runner and devout Christian martyr, in *Chariots of Fire*. Liddell's purpose to run for the glory of God lit another spark in the new generation of young filmmakers, as they witnessed an award-winning film that neither compromised its faith nor sacrificed aesthetic quality. This picture, made outside the confines of the Christian film industry, promoted a higher calling for Christian filmmakers. In his review of the film, Harry Cheney, critic for *Christianity Today*, observed that Christian films often violated "a cardinal rule of good drama, that character, not ideology, dictates plot and action."[23] In contrast, *Chariots of Fire* succeeded because it created identification with characters of integrity and presented a story that connected to audiences' own crises of soul.[24] *Chariots of Fire* would become the model to which the next generation would aspire, making films for public consumption at the Hollywood box office. Celluloid sermons would seek to reach beyond the church market, preaching with parables to a larger world.

The significance of Protestant films in the mid-to-late 20th century inheres both in the history of the church and in the history of film. Their visual sermons stand in that historic Christian tradition of Saint John of Damascus and Pope Gregory the Great, who argued for the importance of visual images for audiences who were generally illiterate, slothful, and forgetful. Like stories in stained glass windows, cathedral stones, and mystery plays, Christian films roused spectators who wept before *The Jesus Film* in a Tanzanian village or trembled before *A Thief in the Night* in an old Baptist church. As the media scholar Quentin Schultze demonstrated in the fields of publishing and radio broadcasting, Protestants readily immersed themselves in new media technologies to spread the word of God, yet they were not always tech savvy.[25] In one very apt example, a 1958 Charles M. Schulz cartoon in the *Young Pillars* series, three church-group kids sit around a film projector as one confesses, "When I was twelve years old I was almost converted by a church movie, but the projector broke down."

"WHEN I WAS TWELVE YEARS OLD, I WAS ALMOST
CONVERTED BY A CHURCH MOVIE, BUT THE
PROJECTOR BROKE DOWN."

Charles M. Schulz's *Young Pillars* comic captured the mix of hope and frustration of those involved in film evangelism. From *Reach* by Charles M. Schulz, © 1969 Warner Press. All rights reserved. Used by permission.

Protestant filmmakers, grounded in a tradition of the Word, of preaching and teaching, gambled on communicating their faith through images, investing time and a little money to show the acts of the apostles and the parables on ants and clowns. While rarely reaching the aesthetic or technical quality of their Hollywood counterparts, these films fulfilled and gratified their congregations, reaffirming traditions, beliefs, and values. They taught, as in *Answer for Anne*, that one should love one's neighbor, even when your neighbor was of a different race or economic class. They effectively communicated the Providence of God over all creation in the Moody science films and within the crucibles of suffering in *He Leadeth Me*, and they even satirized their own evangelistic technophilia in *The Gospel Blimp*. Protestant films fulfilled a cultural purpose in disseminating their messages in teaching and mission work. With various media teams hauling projectors and films around in Africa and India, they translated the Gospel message into images that spectators could comprehend. Likewise, Social Gospel films provoked discussions, transformed prejudices, and prodded people into broader acts of charity and tolerance. Inadvertently, however, the films also exerted a secondary cultural influence on congregations, nudging conservative groups opposed to Hollywood to recognize the value of films, and then, in seeming support of a domino theory of cultural assimilation, to adapt more liberal moviegoing habits in general. Ironically, conservative Christian colleges that had exhibited films in their chapels, for example, now acquiesced in permitting their students to attend Hollywood movies.

Indeed, one of the unexpected side effects of the Christian embrace of films was to modernize churches; even among conservatives these films betrayed a tendency to teach character and morality rather than doctrine. Their films were exemplary parables rather than revelatory ones, showing congregations how to behave rather than what to believe. As a more emotive form of religious discourse, appealing to the dominant sense of sight and calling for a visceral response, films conveyed narratives of modeling behavior, recommending kindness to neighbors or reading of your Bible. Even World Wide Pictures, which centered on the Billy Graham revival services with evangelistic preaching, tended to *show* how one's life could be mended by simply coming forward at a rally rather than wrestling with the nature of the Incarnation. Perhaps in this regard the investment in film production for mainline denominations in the 1950s and 1960s paralleled what some have called their own theological secularization, with church attendance plummeting and historical Protestantism in retreat.[26] The medium became, in the media critic Marshall McLuhan's terms, the message, the sacred texts were reduced to movies.[27] The warnings of a social critic like Jacques Ellul— haranguing against the technological tyranny of the image over the Word, of *technique* replacing Scripture, of a facile and naive faith believing that media could be more efficient in propagating the Gospel—went unheeded.[28] To put one's faith in films qua films, without fully understanding the complex impact of the medium, was to surrender truth to a propaganda industry and to propagate a false, superficial, and even illusory presence of the Kingdom of God.

But certain Christian films did successfully mediate a new consciousness in various communities. Films that introduced new teaching or fresh perspectives (e.g., Moon's *City of the Bees, My Name Is Han*), those dealing with suffering (e.g., Mel White's *Though I Walk through the Valley*), those requiring dialogue on their meaning or significance (e.g., *Parable, How Should We Then Live?, The Music Box*), and even those that demanded a personal religious response, for good or ill (e.g., *The Jesus Film, The Hiding Place, A*

Thief in the Night), functioned to make certain ideas or images dominant. At the end of the 20th century, for instance, marriage and family life issues had been indelibly shaped by James Dobson's Focus on the Family, mediated through his numerous Christian video productions.

The general adherents of a denomination are likely more acquainted with their history through viewing cinematic narratives of their founders than through personal study. For example, films on Martin Luther or John Wesley, however abridged or biased, have contributed to shared congregational memories, reinforcing the dramatic traditions that permeate the community's awareness of itself. More than in-depth study of the biblical books of Daniel or Revelation, end-times films bolster the dispensational eschatology of true believers, even haunting the popular imagination with the imprinting of 666 on human hands or with ominous guillotines being constructed in public squares. It is worth reiterating here that such inexpensively produced films as *A Thief in the Night* would culminate in major features on the end of the world, from the *Left Behind* series to the Arnold Schwarzenegger blockbuster *End of Days*.

While the Christian film market maintained its separation from Hollywood, it was aware of the trends in the larger industry. Nevertheless, rather than imitating the secular behemoth, it generally aimed at preaching sermons, reporting on missions, and teaching the faithful, using the goals of communication practiced by the church for millennia. But with the educating of film school graduates in the 1980s, Christian filmmakers tapped into technical and narrative strategies practiced by Hollywood. John Schmidt, for example, had wrapped his messages about missions into parodies of Hollywood features.

Yet Christian filmmaking lingered in the outer courts of cultural impact, rarely inviting either broader critical awareness or economic clout. During this era, Christian films were also off the radar screen of Hollywood producers, either as competition or as models. Religious audiences had not yet become a segment of the market that could be targeted. But these films were sown as seeds that would bloom into later box office successes, as more professional visions of Christian filmmaking moved outside the camp to communicate to other tribes. Where denominations and Christian studios would surrender the work of filmmaking, individuals would capture a vision to be, like Daniel in Babylon, a presence that might not only interpret the dreams of Nebuchadnezzar, but one who might have its own dreams communicated as well. Christians in the film industry like Tom Shadyac, Ralph Winter, Ken Wales, Scott Derrickson, Tyler Perry, Denzel Washington, and even Mel Gibson would take up the mantle and produce parables that would have amazed Friedrich, Moon, and Baptista. But that is the next part of the story.

Appendix

Chronology of Christian Film History

1927	The Harmon Foundation founded
1927	*The King of Kings* released, directed by Cecil B. DeMille
1929	Aimee Semple McPherson of Foursquare Angelus Temple forms her own film company, Angelus Productions
1931	*The Spirit of Christ at Work in India* and *The Moslem World* produced by the Harmon Foundation
1932	John Wesley Picture Foundation established
1933	Better Films Council sponsored by the Federal Council of Churches
1934	The Roman Catholic cardinal of Philadelphia orders his diocesan flock to stay away from all movies
1936	The Religious Motion Picture Foundation produces film catalog
1938	*The Power of God*, made to promote personal evangelism, sponsored by the evangelical Lutheran Synod of Missouri
1939	*The Great Commandment* feature film released, produced by James Friedrich and directed Irving Pichel for Cathedral Films
1939	*If a Boy Needs a Friend*, produced by Yale Divinity School, promotes tolerance
1940	Cathedral Films releases *A Certain Nobleman*, *The Child of Bethlehem*, *The Prodigal Son*, and *No Greater Power*
1942	Baptista's Scriptures Visualized Institute (SVI) releases *The Story of a Fountain Pen*
1942	*Variety* announces, "Wave of Religious Movies Is Due."
1943	American Bible Society announces plans to put the Bible on 16mm film
1944	SVI manufactures the 16mm "Miracle" projector, which weighs only twenty-five pounds
1945	Episcopal Radio-TV Foundation established as an independent, nonprofit organization

1945	Protestant Film Commission formed, coordinating the efforts of nineteen religious denominations
1945	*The Romance of a Century* produced by Baptist Sunday School Board to celebrate one hundred years of the Southern Baptist Convention
1946	Family Films founded by Sam Hersh with release of *The Life and Songs of Stephen Foster* series
1946	Methodist Publishing House establishes eight film libraries
1946	Moody Institute of Science releases *The God of Creation*
1946	*Variety* notes that five thousand churches equipped for 16mm film screenings, and another seventy-five thousand had 16mm projectors on order
1947	*Beyond Our Own* released, the first of seven films made by the Protestant Film Commission
1948	The *Christian Advocate*, the official paper of the Methodist Church, begins publishing short film reviews on a regular basis
1948	Religious Film Association formed as a distribution organization for Protestant films
1948	Southern Baptist Convention establishes Broadman Films
1949	*Answer for Anne* produced by National Lutheran Council
1949	*China Challenge* made by Bob Pierce, who later founded World Vision
1949	*Kenji Comes Home* nominated for Best Documentary Feature at Academy Awards
1949	*The Prince of Peace* released, one of eleven films directed by William Beaudine for the Protestant Films Commission
1949	*Using Visual Aids in a Church* booklet published by Earl Waldrup for the Southern Baptist Convention
1949–52	Cathedral Films releases the *Life of St. Paul* series
1950	Coronet Films created by the Methodist Publishing House for younger audiences
1950	SVI releases *The Pilgrim's Progress*, the first one-hour, color, animated religious film
1951	*The Guest* produced by Twentieth Century-Fox
1951	*Mr. Texas* released, the initial offering from Billy Graham's evangelistic film ministry, World Wide Pictures
1952	The General Conference of the Methodist Church creates its Television, Radio, and Film Commission
1952	Gospel Films founded in Muskegon, Michigan, by Ken Anderson

1953	*Martin Luther* directed by Irving Pichel, financed by Lutheran Church Productions and Louis de Rochement Associates
1951–57	*Living Christ* twelve-part series produced by Cathedral Films
1956	TRAFCO (Television, Radio, and Film Commission of the Methodist Church) takes over the Methodist Radio and Film Commission
1957	*Light of the Sun* made by Tom Hotchkiss of Films Afield
1959	Premier of JOT, a thirty-episode series of animated films sponsored by TRAFCO
1960	Ken Anderson leaves Gospel Films to start Ken Anderson Films
1961–71	*Davey and Goliath*, a Claymation television series confronting social problems, produced by the Lutheran Church–Missouri Synod
1962	*Sermons from Science* pavilion at the Seattle World's Fair showcases Moody Institute of Science movies
1963	*The Tony Fontane Story* released, a Hollywood-made Christian message film produced by Billy Zeoli
1964	The controversial *Parable* released, directed by Rolf Forsberg for the Communication Commission of the National Council of Churches
1964–65	*Sermons from Science* pavilion at the New York World's Fair reaches an estimated audience of 1.5 million
1965	*The Accused* released, the first of some twenty films made outside the United States for foreign audiences by Ray Carlson's International Films
1966	*The Antkeeper* released, another controversial film directed by Rolf Forsberg for Lutheran audiences
1967	*The Gospel Blimp* released, a Christian satire from Shorty Yeaworth.
1968	First Assembly of the World Association of Christian Communication meets in Nairobi, Kenya
1970	*The Cross and the Switchblade* released, starring Pat Boone and Erik Estrada and directed by Don Murray; this is the first film acquired by Ken Curtis's Gateway Films
1972	*A Thief in the Night*, released Russ Doughten's Mark IV end-times movie
1974	Christian Film Distributors Association founded by Harry Bristow of Christian Cinema Inc.
1975	*The Hiding Place* released, starring Julie Harris and Arthur O'Connell and directed by James Collier

1976   *How Should We Then Live?* by Dr. Francis Schaeffer and Franky Schaeffer released by Gospel Films

1977   *Pilgrim's Progress* from Ken Anderson Films released, featuring Liam Neeson

1978   *Karunamayudu (Man of Mercy)* released, an Indian-made film on the life of Jesus

1979   *Focus on the Family* teaching series from Dr. James Dobson released

1979   *John Hus* launches the Gateway Films Christian Heritage collection

1979   *The Lion, the Witch, and the Wardrobe* animated film released by the Episcopal Media Center (formerly Episcopal Radio-TV Foundation)

1979   *The Music Box* released; directed by Jim Robinson, the film eventually wins a 1982 Cannes Film Festival award

1979   The Jesus Film Project established by the Campus Crusade for Christ

1980   *The Goosehill Gang* series released by Family Films in an attempt to attract the teen market

1980   *Super Christian* released, a parody of evangelical subculture directed by John Schmidt

1980–86 Gospel Films acquires sixty-two independently produced productions from other filmmakers

1983   *The Question*, directed by Fred Carpenter, released by Mars Hill Productions

1984   *Never Ashamed* released, directed by Ed McDougal

1985   *Shadowlands* released, Norman Stone's brilliant portrait of C. S. Lewis

1986   The Regent University film *Bird in a Cage* wins the Best Dramatic Picture Student Academy Award

1986   World Wide Pictures closes its Burbank studios

Notes

NOTES TO THE PREFACE

1. Opie, Thomas, "Sermons in Pictures" *National Board of Review Magazine* (January 1927), 15.

2. Sumner, Robert, *Hollywood Cesspool: A Startling Survey of Movieland Lives and Morals* (Sword of the Lord Publishers, 1955).

3. Sumner lamented that he could not update his book, as contemporary details of Hollywood would now make the work nearly pornographic. See http://screenresearch.ning.com/group/bookclub/forum/topics/hollywood-cesspool.

4. Thorp, Margaret, *America at the Movies* (Yale UP, 1939), 52–53.

5. Anderson, Milton, *The Modern Goliath* (David Press, 1935), 17.

6. Ibid., 72. *Old Truths in New Garments* (1936) was an experimental film that recorded the first talking picture church service.

7. Stout, Harry, *The New England Soul: Preaching and Religious Culture in Colonial New England* (Oxford UP, 1986).

8. The turbulent era from the late 1960s to the early 1980s fostered the growth of interest in film studies by theology scholars and young Christians. A plethora of film-related books triggered engagement and would set the stage for technically trained and film-educated students to usher in their own renaissance of Christian filmmaking. See Kahle, Roger and Robert Lee, *Popcorn and Parable: A New Look at the Movies* (Augsburg, 1971); Jones, William, *Sunday Night at the Movies* (John Knox Press, 1967); Konzelman, Robert, *Marquee Ministry: The Movie Theater as Church and Community Forum* (Harper and Row, 1972); Schillaci, Anthony, *Movies and Morals* (Fides, 1968); Wall, James, *Church and Cinema* (Eerdmans, 1971).

9. We are deeply indebted to Schulze's work, particularly "A Rhetoric of Conversion" in his *Christianity and the Mass Media in America* (Michigan State UP, 2003); however, he does not deal with film as much as print and broadcast journalism.

NOTES TO CHAPTER 1

1. Dougherty, Cardinal Dennis, "Legion of Decency" *Catholic Standard* (May 25, 1934), 1.

2. As a Presbyterian elder, Hays sensed his calling as divine. See Ross, Clyde, "A Presbyterian Elder, a Church Crusade, and the Period of 'Family Movies'" *Fides et Historia* (Fall 1993), 80–90. By 1933, Edward Edkahl denounced him thus: "As the Master of the Movies, I pronounce you, Will Hays, a complete failure. Your cameras are all out of focus." "The Screen" *Christian Advocate* (June 15, 1933), 573 (*Christian Advocate* hereafter cited as *CA*).

3. "Taking It on the Jaw" *Hollywood Reporter* (July 12, 1934), 1.

4. The International Catholic Film Organization (OCIC) was established in 1928, primarily to establish dialogue among filmmakers and theologians. The Catholic educator Jan Hes argued that the OCIC also aimed at supporting initiatives for church film production, creating a wider international basis for such projects and developing contacts with film professionals. See Hes, Jan, "Notes from the Diary of a Stepchild" *Media Development* (February 1980), 3. Hes's article is based on a quotation from Dr. Hans Florin: "Film is the stepchild of Christian communication." A second group, INTERFILM (International Interchurch Film Association) began in Paris in 1955.

5. Black, Gregory, *Hollywood Censored: Morality Codes, Catholics, and the Movies* (Cambridge UP, 1996), 170.

6. Skinner, James, *The Cross and the Cinema: The Legion of Decency and the National Catholic Office for Motion Pictures, 1933–1970* (Praeger, 1993), 35.

7. Couvares, Francis, "Hollywood, Main Street, and the Church: Trying to Censor the Movies before the Production Code" *Movie Censorship and American Culture*, ed. Francis Couvares (Smithsonian Institute Press, 1996), 129–58.

8. Beardsley, A. H., "I Went to the Picture Show" *CA* (February 1933), 103.

9. Chesterton, G. K., *As I Was Saying* (Eerdmans, 1985), 37–38. More than sixty years later, Chesterton's cultural observation was echoed by the independent filmmaker John Sayles, who envisioned a "democratizing of the filmmaking process." Through a decentralization of financing, distribution, and delivery systems, he hoped for more demographically narrow casting of film audiences. John Sayles, "The Big Picture" *American Film* (June 1985), 10.

10. Krows, Arthur, "So the Pictures Went to Church" *Educational Screen* (October 1938), 252–53 (*Educational Screen* hereafter cited as *ES*). See also Rick Prelinger, *Field Guide to Sponsored Films* (National Film Preservation Foundation, 2006).

11. See the following pieces by Arthur Krows: "A Quarter-Century of Non-theatrical Films" *ES* (June 1936), 169; "Motion Pictures—Not for Theatres" *ES* (September 1938), 211–14; "Motion Pictures—Not for Theatres" *ES* (October 1938), 249–53, "Motion Pictures—Not For Theatres" *ES* (January 1939), 13–16; "Motion Pictures—Not for Theatres" *ES* (September 1941), 333; "Motion Pictures—Not For Theatres" *ES* (May 1942), 180–82.

12. Brady, Mary Beattie, "A New Era for the Church" *ES* (December 1935), 289–90.

13. "Motion Picture for the Church" *Christian Statesman* (January 1927), 8.

14. See Clements, Keith, *Friedrich Schleiermacher: Pioneer of Modern Theology* (Collins, 1987); and Schleiermacher, Friedrich, *On Religion: Addresses in Response to Its Cultured Critics*, trans. Terrence Tice (John Knox Press, 1969).

15. Schleiermacher, Friedrich, *On Religion: Speeches to the Cultured Despisers*, trans. John Oman (John Knox Press, 1994), 18, 138–39. I am indebted to Ryan Parker for this insight.

16. Anne Morey, *Hollywood Outsiders: The Adaptation of the Film Industry, 1913–1934* (University of Minnesota Press, 2003), 145.

17. Andrews, George Reid, "The Church and the Motion Picture" *National Board of Review Magazine* (March/April 1926), 9–10; cited in Morey, op. cit., 145.

18. Janes, H. Paul, *How to Stimulate Greater Activity in Your Church through Motion Pictures* (Religious Motion Picture Foundation, 1932).

19. "Sources of Religious Films" *Religious Motion Picture Foundation* (May 15, 1936), 2; Johnson, R. F. H., "Suggestions from the Religious Motion Picture Foundation" *ES* (February 1933), 56–57 (italics added).

20. Janes, H. Paul, "Using the Direct Route to the Feelings: A Character Education Project" *ES* (February 1934), 42–43.

21. Janes, H. Paul, "Changing the Emotional Potential" *ES* (October 1934), 212, 219.

22. "How the Alert Minister Can Use a Life Situation Picture" *ES* (October 1936), 247, 261.

23. See Benjamin, Walter, "The Work of Art in the Age of Mechanical Reproduction" (1936), in *Illuminations*, trans. Hannah Arendt (Schocken, 1968); and Federal Council of Churches of Christ in America, *Public Relations of the Motion Picture Industry* (1931; Jerome Ozer, 1971).

24. Boyd Gatewood, "Girl, Dumb Eight Years, Speaks after Seeing Thrilling Moving Picture" *Los Angeles Times* (December 14, 1919), 4, 13.

25. "Harry Levey Company to Furnish Pictures to Churches Everywhere" *Moving Picture World* (August 26, 1922), 660. Hays did propose an experiment to test the popularity and financial viability of religious pictures by monitoring the demand among twelve churches in twelve towns (near New York City) over twelve consecutive Sundays. See "Films in Churches" *Motion Picture News* (July 4, 1925), 32.

26. Morrow, Mrs., "The Cinema: I Make a Discovery" *Christian Herald* (June 1934), 18, 35 (*Christian Herald* hereafter cited as *CH*).

27. "Have You Sent Yours Yet?" *CH* (April 1946), 69. The monthly would highlight positive cinematic treatments of Protestant ministers and what were viewed as devotional films. Selections included *Anna and the King of Siam* (August 1946), 66; *Henry V* (September 1946), 74; *Sister Kenny* (October 1946), 100; and *Angel on My Shoulder* (November 1946), 102.

28. Robinson, Harold, *Better Films Council* (Federal Council of the Churches of Christ in America, 1933).

29. Ibid., 4.

30. Stidger, William, "Berries for the King's Plate" *CH* (April 1937), 14.

31. Vandercook, Anna Jean, "Motion Pictures Bring Life to Conferences" *International Journal of Religious Education* (October 1936), 18–19, 40 (*International Journal of Religious Education* hereafter cited as *IJRE*).

32. In 1947, Vieth would pen his classic work, *The Church and Christian Education* (Bethany Press), as he guided denominations in putting together curricular series.

33. Vieth, Paul, "Movies and Slides as Teaching Aids" *IJRE* (July 1935), 17–18.

34. Hopkins, Robert, Jr., "Where Materials in Visual Education May Be Secured" *IJRE* (November 1937), 16–17.

35. Tippy, Worth, "The Supporting Church Interest in Community Motion Picture Organization" *National Board of Review Magazine* (June 1934), 5–7, 10.

36. "An Informational Pamphlet for Pastors" *ES* (September 1934), 139.

37. Bortz, Dorothy Fritsch, "Motion Pictures for the Church" *Church Management* (February 1936), 235–36.

38. "New Mission Films" *ES* (January 1933), 23.

39. Toulouse, Mark, "Socializing Capitalism: The *Century* during the Great Depression" *Christian Century* (April 12, 2001), 418.

40. "The Movies Last Chance" *Christian Century* (June 20, 1934), 822–24 (*Christian Century* hereafter be cited as *CC*).

41. "Exposing Another Attempt at Camouflage" *CC* (March 5, 1930), 293.

42. LeSourd, Howard, "Church Use of Moving Pictures" *CC* (March 19, 1930), 37.

43. See the following articles by Eastman: "The Menace of the Movies" *CC* (January 15, 1930), 75–78; "Who Controls the Movies" *CC* (February 5, 1930), 173–75.

44. See the following articles by Eastman: "Social Issues in Movie Code" *CC* (September 20, 1933), 1170–71; "Chances the Movies Are Missing" *CC* (May 12, 1937), 617–18.

45. Eastman, Fred, "What Can We Do about the Movies?" *Parents' Magazine* (November 1931), 19, 52–54. In the same issue, Eastman lauds the magazine's Movie Guide as the best aid in previewing services for reliable moviegoing guidance.

46. Hellbeck, Robert, "The Film and Protestantism" *International Review of Educational Cinematography* (October 3, 1931), 923–25.

47. Cited by Hopkins, op. cit., 16–17.

48. His general manager, George Reid Andrews, divided them as "The Bible," "Religious Biography," "Church History," "World Friendship or Missionary," "Religious Pedagogical Pictures," and a large class of wholesome pictures for Sunday night services. Andrews, op. cit., 10.

49. Hayward, P. R., "*The King of Kings*" *IJRE* (April 1928), 7. A *New Yorker* cartoon by I. Klein (December 21, 1929) showed a couple sitting in a movie theater watching a prosecutor harangue a witness, with the wife whispering, "Sure that's H. B. Warner. Don't you remember Jesus in the *King of Kings*?"

50. See Maltby, Richard, "*The King of Kings* and the Czar of All the Rushes: The Propriety of the Christ Story" *Screen* (Summer 1990), 188ff.

51. Of course, not everyone saw DeMille's religious spectacle as laudatory. The Marxist critic Harry Alan Potamkin quipped, "It has not been observed that the American movie has produced a single 'sacred' film comparable to *The Passion of Joan of Arc*, made in France. *The King of Kings* is a product of this sycophancy—it is the pimple of sanctimony." Cited in Jacobs, Lewis, ed., *The Compound Cinema: The Film Writings of Harry Alan Potamkin* (Teachers College Press, 1977), 156.

52. Palmer, Gretta, "Greatest Movie Success" *CH* (April 1944), 23.

53. DeMille, Cecil B., "The Screen as a Religious Teacher" *Theatre Magazine* (June 1927), 45.

54. At the same conference, Judge Lindsey of Denver said that there were more incentives to misdirected passion and immorality in the Song of Solomon than in all the motion pictures ever produced: "And more girls have been led astray on their way home from Sunday school than in 4,000,000 cinema palaces!" "Conference on Movies" *Banner* (March 19, 1926), 168.

55. Cressey, Paul Frederick, "Influence of Moving Pictures on Students in India" *American Journal of Sociology* (November 1935), 341–50. The American Trading Association promoted the 16mm version of *Jerusalem: Cradle of Faith*, which was available in both a synchronized sound version and a silent copy with descriptive titles. Likewise, they advertised *The Passion Play: The Story of Jesus of Nazareth* with "sacred songs sung by the Roxy Chorus and Emil Velazco at the Organ," and also "narrada en espanol, musica y cantos." Biblical narratives remained universal in interest and in outreach. No sound American version of the Christ story would be made until George Steven's mammoth *The Greatest Story Ever Told* (also known as the longest story ever told) in 1965.

56. A one-reel Indian version of the New Testament parable, *The Good Samaritan* (1950), was also performed by students of Leonard Theological College in Jubbulpore, introducing the customs, colors, and flavors of a contemporary Indian countryside.

Incorporating the colorful clothing of South India and various customs such as women carrying water pots on their shoulders, the film resonated with both native and foreign audiences. See *Visual Materials for Your Program* pamphlet, n.d., Division of Visual Experiment, Harmon Foundation, Manuscripts Division, Library of Congress.

57. The latter was made in conjunction with the Visualization Committee of the Missionary Education Movement, with Harry Myers of Northern Baptist Convention and William Rogers of Harmon Foundation scripting their scenario from the 1937 book *Mecca and Beyond*, assembled by the Central Committee on the United Study of Foreign Missions and the Missionary Education Movement of the U.S. and Canada.

58. See Ernst, R. A. and Vivien Cooper pamphlet, March 28, 1977, 3, Harmon Foundation Gift Collection Catalogue, Archival Manuscripts, Library of Congress.

59. "Motion Pictures in Mission Work" and "Evangelizing Films" *ES* (September 1934), 139.

60. Tanis, Rev. E. J., "Timely Topics: The Movies" *Banner* (January 24, 1930), 80.

61. "Motion Picture on India's *Untouchables*" *CA* (April 28, 1938), 406. On the domestic side, Methodist Home Missions captured the need for social work in U.S. urban centers in their film *Children of the Crowded Streets*. "New City Motion Picture" *CA* (August 11, 1938), 842.

62. Joy, James, "A School That Never Closes" *CA* (September 10, 1931), 1102–3.

63. "Mission Work to Be Dramatized in Motion Pictures" *ES* (January 1936), 11. Another media-savvy school, the Moody Bible Institute, also documented *Life at MBI* (n.d.) in 16mm film.

64. "Japan in Motion Pictures" *CA* (February 25, 1937), 198.

65. At home, the Board of Missionary Cooperation of the Northern Baptist Convention acquired both 16mm projectors and the eight-reel film *A Michigan Miracle*, about a rural church in southwestern Michigan, to show among its churches. "Clergyman 'Shoots' Camp Movie" *ES* (February 1933), 57; "Priest Makes Travel Film" and "Film Announcements" *ES* (February 1933), 57.

66. "Baptist Women's Foreign Mission Society Uses Movies" *ES* (May 1933), 139.

67. "Missionaries and the Cinema" *International Review of Educational Cinematography* (July 1932), 557–58; and Ford, J. T., "Motion Pictures and Foreign Missions" *Missionary Review of the World* (August 1931), 611–12. The journal also investigated how Christ would make a difference in the lives of youth and missions. See "The Child—Movies—Missions" *Missionary Review of the World* (July 1933), 348–49.

68. "New Mission Films" *ES* (January 1933), 23.

69. "Missions in Syria to Be Filmed" *ES* (May 1936), 145. Presbyterians emphasized "educational answers" to native problems in such films as *New Indian Trails* (ca. 1936) about North India missions.

70. "Film Activities among the Denominations" *ES* (January 1936), 12.

71. "Missionaries and Motion Pictures" *Missionary Review of the World* (February 1936), 86.

72. "Editorial" *CA* (March 19, 1936), 267.

73. Forsher, James, *Hollywood Chronicles: The Search for God, Grails, and Profits* (MPI Home Video, 1991).

74. Morey, op. cit., 117.

75. Krows, Arthur, "Motion Pictures—Not For Theatres" *ES* (June 1944), 248–50; Anderson, op. cit., 90.

76. Ironically, Fosdick, the Social Gospel pulpiteer and old dean of liberal preachers, gave a sermon in 1935 at the Riverside Church titled "The Church Must Go Beyond Modernism," challenging culture while at the same time using it.

77. "Clergyman Interested in 16mm Talkies" *ES* (January 1933), 23.

78. "Motion Pictures for Catholic Audiences" *ES* (January 1934), 21.

79. Buehrer, Edwin, "A New Deal for the Sunday School" *ES* (April 1934), 104–5.

80. It also cooperated with the Missionary Education Movement to launch the Africa Motion Picture Project in 1939. The secretary of the American Mission to Lepers, Dr. Emery Ross, oversaw the work. See Rogers, William L. and Paul H. Vieth, *Visual Aids in the Church* (Christian Education Press, 1946), 16.

81. "Editorial" *CA* (October 11, 1934), 829.

82. "Editorial" *CA* (February 20, 1936), 172.

83. Nall, Otto, "Our Advancing World: Movie Tip" *CA* (August 18, 1938), 846.

84. See "The Religious Film: Religious Cinematography in India" *International Review of Educational Cinema* (August 1929), 162–69. See also "Religion: *Padre Sahib*" *Time* (September 19, 1949).

85. Robins, Michela, "Films for the Church" *Hollywood Quarterly* (Winter 1947/48), 178–84. See also Reynolds, Glenn, "'Africa Joins the World': The Missionary Imagination and the Africa Motion Picture Project in Central Africa, 1937–39" *Journal of Social History* (Winter 2010), 459–479.

NOTES TO CHAPTER 2

1. Friedrich, Rev. James, "His Pulpit Is a Movie Screen" *Virginia Seminary Journal* (November 1988), 1–13.

2. Anderson, Dave and Terry Lindvall, executive producers, Ned Vankevich, producer, *We've Come a Long Way Baby: 40 Years of Christian Film* (CBN/Regent University, 1979).

3. Friedrich, James, "A Producer Serves the Church" *ES* (December 1942), 389. In the article, Friedrich explains, "This drama in Paul's life . . . aroused my desire to use my amateur 16mm experience for the good of the church. I began in my second year at the Seminary at Alexandria, Virginia, to work toward this end with three other students in volunteer collaboration. The scenario was used as my graduation thesis. The fact that the professor under whom I worked had never seen a scenario probably accounted for its acceptance."

4. Ibid., 401.

5. Friedrich, James, Jr., interview by Kent DeVoll, May 13, 1985, 1, Regent University Religious Film Archives, Virginia Beach (Regent University Religious Film Archives, Virginia Beach, hereafter cited as RURFA).

6. When the writer Dolph Sharp visited the set of *The Calling of Matthew*, one of a dozen pictures released by Friedrich's Cathedral Films in 1947, he noted, "Its films reach all of the 2,000 plus American churches equipped with sound projectors—an important and growing factor in the hectic 16-millimeter field." "The Reverend Makes a Movie" *Pageant* (June 1947), 104–11 See also "Little Movies with a Big Future" *Pageant* (September 1946).

7. Friedrich, James, interview, Better Film Council/National Council of Churches Fourth International Christian Film Workshop in Green Lake, Wisconsin (1947), collection 327, Billy Graham Center Archives, Wheaton College, Illinois.

8. Davidson, Herbert, "Religion in Films" *CA* (October 5, 1939), 956.

9. Friedrich, James, "Adventures in Film-making" *CH* (February 1948): "My experience in visual aids began in my early Sunday school classes when the teacher ended the lesson by giving each of us a brightly colored picture of a Bible scene. I can still remember some of these distinctly. Pictures of any kind make a lasting impression on young minds" (40).

10. Rushmore, Howard, "Motion Picture Commentator: The Great Commandment" *CH* (February 1941), 44; "Cathedral Films Began as 'Church-Craft Pictures'" *CH* (October 1946), 52.

11. "Religious Classes in Film" *Newsweek* (December 23, 1940), 44.

12. Friedrich, interview by DeVoll, op. cit.

13. According to Friedrich, "I called it *The Great Commandment* because that was its subject: 'Thou shalt love the Lord thy God with all thy heart and all thy strength and thy neighbor as thyself.'" "A Producer Serves the Church" op. cit., 400.

14. Neal, Wesley, "Minister without a Pulpit" *CA* (July 21, 1949), 8–10, 31. Joe Bridges argues that Friedrich began as an assistant rector at St. Mark's Episcopal Church in Van Nuys. Bridges, Joseph Lewis, "A Historical Study of Cooperative Protestant Religious Film in America from 1914 to 1972" (PhD diss., University of Southern California, Los Angeles, 1975), 93.

15. "Dark Laughter" *Time* (April 29, 1940).

16. Marshall, Wendy, *William Beaudine: From Silents to Television* (Scarecrow, 2004).

17. Fanning, Leah Irene, "A Study of the Use of Motion Pictures in the Program of Certain Protestant Churches" (master's thesis, University of Southern California, 1932).

18. Friedrich, Elaine, "Biography of Jim Friedrich" (unpublished manuscript, 1975). Courtesy of Elaine Friedrich.

19. "*The Great Commandment*" *CH* (January 1942), 29.

20. Fanning, op. cit., 70. See also "Cinema and the Church" *New York Times* (March 19, 1939).

21. Frakes, Margaret, "Something Plus in Pictures—A Director Who Sees the Way" *Motive* (April 1942), 37–38.

22. The ranch belonged to a Mr. Iverson, who had "devout Christian interests." Bridges, op. cit., 96.

23. Friedrich, James, "*The Greatest Commandment*" *ES* (December, 1942), 388.

24. Hunt, Candice, director of marketing, Cathedral Films, recorded interview by Carlton Edwards, 1989, RURFA, transcript 3.

25. Eddy, Don, "The Movies Go to Church" *This Week* (January 27, 1946), 4–5.

26. "Rev. James Friedrich" *CH* (December 1947), 14; Brady, Thomas, "7 Films on St. Paul Will Be Produced" *New York Times* (December 9, 1948), 48.

27. Friedrich, James, "Teaching Can Be Pleasure" *Christianity Today* (February 27, 1961), 8 (*Christianity Today* hereafter cited as *CT*).

28. "Visual Aids for the Church" *CH* (February 1949), 45.

29. See "Church Builder: 16mm Sound Motion Pictures" *CH* (November 16, 1950), 20; and Hockman, Williams, "How to Visualize Your Teaching" *CH* (November 16, 1950), 19–23. In the same issue, a photograph of children, a few men, and women in hats watching films in church appeared with the following caption: "What enters the eyes is usually better retained than that which enters the ears." Films were distributed by United World Films and rented for eight dollars each.

30. Friedrich, interview by DeVoll, op. cit., 4. Various well-known actors and film artists worked on Cathedral films: Lee J. Cobb and Joanne Dru in *Day of Triumph* (1954); George Macready in *I Beheld His Glory* (1953); Hugh Beaumont in *Indian American* (1955); Walter Brennan in *Don't Blame Me* (1962); John Alton shot (with backlighting, halo effects, and sharp contrasts of light and darkness) a story about Zaccheus, *No Greater Power* (1942), four years before his stylized film noir work on Robert Siodmak's *The Killers* (1946); and Sven Nykvist shot *In the Footsteps of the Witch Doctor* (1950) and *Africa and Schweitzer* (1961), which were bracketed around his tremendous success with Ingmar Bergman's *The Seventh Seal* (1954) and *Wild Strawberries* (1957) (years later, in 1991, Nykvist would direct his own powerfully religious film, *The Ox*).

31. Bader, Golda Maud, "Visual Aids for the Church" *CH* (October 1951), 58.

32. "Movies in Church" *Newsweek* (February 11, 1946), 74; Friedrich, Rev. James, "Pamphlet on *The Conversion*," n.d., RURFA.

33. Friedrich, "Adventures in Film-making" op. cit.

34. The United Lutheran Church underwrote Cathedral's *And Now I See* (ca. 1947), a film on Christian stewardship, with Ralph Morgan starring. See "Programming with Visual Aids" *CH* (October 1947), 40–45.

35. "We see a great mission in the field of audio-visual aids. We know we are on the right path when pastors write: 'Your pictures are giving our Sunday-school children a better concept of the stories of Jesus than they ever had before!'" Ibid., 44. Friedrich acknowledged that while production and acting talent was selected on the basis of competence and not on a confession of faith, "every production is begun with an opening prayer for God's guidance and help. . . . In our early productions we hired professional scriptwriters, but found that while they did an expert job technically, they didn't know enough about the Christian religion and the church. Mr. Coyle and I, therefore, went into scriptwriting ourselves. We realize our first efforts were crude in some respects, but experience has helped us smooth out the stories and give first-rate productions" (42).

36. Ibid., 43. Said Friedrich, "It was a thrilling experience to hear a boy answer that 'Jesus died for all of us so that our sins would be forgiven.'"

37. "16mm Film Sources" *CH* (February 1948), 45.

38. *Audio-Visual Resource Guide*, 9th ed. (National Council of Churches, 1972).

39. Vernon, Walter, "For Church Showings: *The Pilgrimage Play*" *CA* (December 21, 1950), 1614; Leigh, whose real name was Sidney Christy, played the role of Jesus in most Bible films.

40. *Audio-Visual Resource Guide*, op. cit.

41. The flavor of the writing adumbrates the emotional tone of a later Jesus film, *Jesus Christ Superstar* (1973), where Mary Magdalene confesses that she doesn't "know how to love him."

42. "*Day of Triumph*" *Newsweek* (December 20 1954), 50; Schallert, Edwin, "*Day of Triumph* Offers Beauty and Inspiration" *Los Angeles Times* (December 25, 1954), 10.

43. Friedrich, "His Pulpit Is a Movie Screen" op. cit., 10.

44. Dymmel, Ken, interview by Terry Lindvall and Andrew Quicke, July 13, 2001, International Christian Visual Media Conference, Atlanta.

45. This was followed up with *The Difference* (1950) about the need for Christian colleges, especially a Lutheran one, where ethics and business are integrated. The fictional narrative was framed and bracketed by a pastor presenting the case from behind a pulpit, saying, "So, you see, there is a difference in Christian higher education."

46. While students at Assemblies of God colleges were not allowed to attend movie theaters in the 1960s, one of the sponsored colleges, Vanguard University (aka Southern California College), produced *Whatever Happened to Dudley* (1969), a lighthearted campus recruitment film, starring the author Terry Lindvall's brother-in-law, Ron Nipper, with a cameo by the author's twin sister, Tessy Lindvall, as the coed who catches his eye.

47. Friedrich, interview by DeVoll, op. cit.

48. Friedrich, "Teaching Can Be Pleasure" op. cit., 8.

49. Marks, Harvey, "A Brief History of Church Films" *Christian Film and Video Review* (January/February 1985), 8.

50. Eddy, op. cit., 4. Eddy also pointed to another religious motion picture producer, Anson Bond, the son of clothing millionaire. The Presbyterian Bond worried that movies were jammed while churches were abandoned on Sunday nights, and so he made *The Birth of Jesus* (n.d.) to remedy attendance problems.

51. Anderson, *We've Come a Long Way Baby*, op. cit.

52. Buchholz, Harold, "Baptista Films: Pioneer of the Christian Film Industry" *Film Witness* (February 1990), 8–9.

53. Baptista, Carlos, newspaper interview (source unknown), 1945, 2, RURFA.

54. Baptista quoted in Anderson, *We've Come a Long Way Baby,* op. cit. Baptista said, "Although mediocre, it was the first clear indication from the Lord that we could put the Gospel on film" (Baptista interview, op. cit., 22).

55. "Gospel Sound Films" *CH* (December 1940), 64.

56. Miller, Wilford, telephone interview by Terry Lindvall's class, August 2, 1989, RURFA.

57. Marks, Harvey, interview, quoted in Brian Hess, "A Brief History of Christian Films: 1918-2002" *A/V Geeks*, (2011), http://www.avgeeks.com/wp2/a-brief-history-of-christian-films-1918-2002-by-brian-hess-phd/.

58. Anderson, op. cit.

59. Miller interview, op. cit. Miller explained that "The project was so secret that none of us were allowed into the room in which the projector was being built in. In fact, we did not even know about the Miracle projector until it was finished. However, when Carlos claimed the invention to himself, the creator [Max Kerr] quit the company."

60. *How the Miracle Came About* (promotional brochure, Baptista Company, n.d.), RURFA. Along with Kerr, the former Bell and Howell designer Stephen Platt helped to engineer the sprocket-type mechanism and high-fidelity sound system.

61. "Yesterday They Said It Couldn't Be Done, Today, It's a Miracle" advertisement, *IJRE* (October 1950), 58.

62. Baptista interview, op. cit.

63. Kerr salvaged and collected his films, and secured them for the archives at Regent University. See Marks, Harvey, "CFDA Letter on Archives for Christian Films to Terry Lindvall" (May 4, 1982), RURFA.

64. Piper, John and Jonathan Edwards, *God's Passion for His Glory: Living the Vision with Jonathan Edwards* (Crossway Books, 2006), 112.

65. *Sermons from Science: A Story of God at Work* (Moody Institute of Science, 1976), Moody Institute of Science Archives, Chicago (Moody Institute of Science Archives, Chicago, hereafter cited as MIS Archives); Gene Getz, *MBI: The Story of the Moody Bible Institute* (Moody Press, 1969).

66. Gilbert, James, *Redeeming Culture: American Religion in an Age of Science* (University of Chicago Press, 1997), 125. In an article on "The Man on the Coil," the author Gary Wall explained how the shock of the high voltage did not harm the recipient, and pointed out that "no other illustration shows so vividly how one can be in tune or out of tune with his source of power. If you are not in tune with God, you cannot tap into his source of power." Wall, Gary, "The Man on the Coil" *Moody Monthly* (March 1979) (*Moody Monthly* hereafter cited as *MM*).

67. "Drama in Film Evangelism," videotape 184, Moody Bible Institute Video Collection (1978), quoted in Hendershot, Heather, *Shaking the World for Jesus: Media and Conservative Evangelical Culture* (University of Chicago Press, 2004), 151.

68. Orgeron, Marsha and Skip Elsheimer, "'Something Different in Science Films': The Moody Institute of Science and the Canned Missionary Movement" *Moving Image* (Spring 2007), 1–26.

69. *Sermons from Science*, op. cit., 4.

70. "The Greatest Thing of Its Kind in the World" *CH* (June 1944).

71. Marks, "Brief History of Church Films" op. cit., 4.

72. Flood, Robert and Jerry Jenkins, *Teaching the Word, Reaching the World: The Moody Bible Institute, the First 100 Years* (Moody Press, 1985), 200.

73. Gilbert, op. cit., 131.

74. Hansen, Rip, "*God of Creation*" *Santa Monica Independent/Ocean Park Independent* (September 1948).

75. Gilbert, op. cit., 137.

76. See also the 1947 Wartburg Press film *Way of Peace*, with the famous pacifist and Hollywood actor Lew Ayres narrating a combination of animated puppets, model sets, and heavenly perspectives (of a burning Earth that is ultimately consumed by fire). The film displays a literal wall between God and humans, one that can be removed only by personal intervention from God.

77. Gilbert, op. cit., 350n36: "The official history of the air force chaplains suggests that the Moody films were the most popular films used by the chaplains." As one who grew up on military bases in the fifties and early sixties, the author Terry Lindvall remembers well the tremendous excitement among fellow school kids who tinkered with rockets and chemistry sets when a Moody Science film was coming to the base chapel. See Bailey, Faith Coxe, "Reel Science . . . Wins the Airmen" *MM* (July 1949), 774.

78. Cited in Ellis, Don Carlos and Laura Thornborough, *Motion Pictures in Education: A Practical Handbook for Users of Visual Aids* (Thomas Crowell, 1923), 65.

79. Gilbert, op. cit., 137.

80. Ibid., 140.

81. *Sermons from Science*, op. cit., 8.

82. Everest, Alton and Elva Everest, *Moody Films in Foreign Lands, 1963–1968* (Moody Institute of Science, 1994).

83. "Publicity Statement," Moody Institute of Science (1949), 2, MIS Archives.

84. Everest, F. Alton, "Can Christians Be Scientific?" *Moody Monthly* (May 1947), 663.

85. See Mitman, Gregg, *Reel Nature: America's Romance with Wildlife on Film* (Harvard UP, 1999), 127–28.

86. Gilbert points out that not only did universities began to consider that religion and science were antithetical, but that "churches that once opposed showing any movies now welcomed Moon's documentaries." Op. cit., 140.

87. Everest, F. Alton, "Can Christians Be Scientific?" *MM* (May 1947), 663. See also his book *Hidden Treasures* (Moody Press, 1951); and Crew, Wayne, "Our Laboratory Is a Pulpit" *MM* (February 1957), 27.

88. The author Terry Lindvall grew up on military bases in the 1950s and 1960s tinkered with chemistry sets, and launched rockets from Monterey, California, beach dunes; thus the MIS films at the base chapels would stir tremendous excitement.

89. *Analysis of Some Aspects of the Results of Sermons from Science Presentations: Seattle World's Fair* pamphlet (April 21 to October 21, 1962), Moody Institute of Science, Los Angeles; press release, July 4, 1965, MIS Archives; "Drama in Film Evangelism" (1978), videotape 184 in Moody Bible Institute Video Collection, MIS Archives

90. Flood and Jenkins, op. cit., 202. See also Jack Houston, "City of the Bees" *MM* (April 1963).

91. "Scientific Gospel Films" *CH* (February 1950), 83.

92. "Dr. Irwin Moon Receives Highest Kodak Award" *Moody Alumni* (Spring 1981), cited in Flood and Jenkins, op. cit., 202.

93. Cooperative film libraries had been set up by a number of city councils of churches (e.g., in Louisville and Denver) that provided mainline churches with religious education films. See Hockman, William, "The Film in Religious Education" *Film and Education: A Symposium on the Role of the Film in the Field of Education*, ed. Godfrey Monroe Elliott (Philosophical Library, 1948), 349.

94. Flood and Jenkins, op. cit., 200. Gilbert argues convincingly that the *Sermons from Science* and MIS films constituted "one of the most crucial elements in a developing religious popular culture," utilizing science as a persuasive vehicle for presenting traditional Christian ideas. Op. cit., 144.

95. Internal memo, n.d., MIS Archives; *Film World and A-V News* (September 1964), MIS Archives.

96. Hargett, Keith, "Letter on Rental Policy" to Hillsdale Health Museum, June 4, 1958, MIS Archives.

97. *World Reports of the Moody Institute of Science*, April 1970, MIS Archives.

98. "Eastman Kodak Gold Medal Award Winners" SMPTE.org (2011), http://www.smpte.org/about/awards_program/east_kodak_winners (accessed January 30, 2011); "Rev. Irwin Moon, 78, Science Film Producer" *Chicago Tribune* (May 24, 1986), 9.

99. Everest, F. Alton, "Can Christians Be Scientific?" *Moody Monthly* (May 1947), 663; "Irwin A. Moon Dies; Made Religious Films" *Los Angeles Times* (May 15, 1986).

100. Getz, Gene, *Audio-Visual Media in Christian Education* (Moody Press, 1958); Proverbs 20:12 ESV.

101. See Comenius, John Amos, *The Great Didactic*, trans. M. W. Keating (Black, 1896), 291–92.

NOTES TO CHAPTER 3

1. Bierce, Ambrose, *The Unabridged Devil's Dictionary* (Feather Trail Press, 2009), 53. Bierce had already observed among his diabolical definitions that a Presbyterian was "one who holds the conviction that the government authorities of the Church should be called presbyters" (72).

2. Troeltsch, Ernst, *The Social Teaching of the Christian Churches*, trans. Olive Wyon (Allen and Unwin, 1912), 2:461. See also Morris, Jeremy, *The Church in the Modern Age* (I. B. Tauris, 2007), 41–43.

3. Mencken, H. L., *The American Language* (1919; Knopf, 1977), 230.

4. Young, Stephen, "Movies as Equipment for Living: A Developmental Analysis of the Importance of Film in Everyday Life" *Critical Studies in Media Communication* (December 2000), 460.

5. Janes, H. Paul, *Screen and Projector in Christian Education: How to Use Motion Pictures and Projected Still Pictures in Worship, Study, and Recreation* (Westminster Press, 1933), 50 (emphasis added).

6. Hintz, William and Stephen Tebes, *Children of the Light: Cinema and the Apostolate, a Guide to Short Films* (Regina Cleri Graphic Arts, 1967), 296.

7. "Griffith to Advise Church on Films" *New York Times* (May 11, 1919), 22.

8. "Methodism in Pictures" *CH* (January 3, 1920), 40.

9. "Taking Films to Heathens" *New York Times* (June 27, 1920), 1.

10. Coffin, Helen Lockwood, "A Minster as a Movie Maker" *National Board of Review Magazine* (June 1931), 8–9, cited in Morey, op. cit.

11. "Methodist Talkies" *CA* (February 4, 1932), 186. James K. Shields also had a project on Francis Asbury in preproduction, but it also evaporated. Shields's son, Wendell, persisted in trying to get his father to add sound to his classic silent *Stream of Life*.

12. "Around the Methodist World" *CA* (March 5, 1936), 221; "A Methodist Movie" *CA* (January 9, 1936), 46.

13. "Committee for Films" *CA* (June 29, 1933), 603–4.

14. "Methodist Talkies" *CA* (May 17, 1934), 460.

15. Brady, Mary Beattie, "The Church Field: News Notes" *ES* (November 1936), 277.

16. Taylor, David, "In Christian Education—Seeing Is Believing" *CA* (January 8, 1948), 4; Vernon, Walter "Seeing Is Believing—Sometimes" *CA* (March 3, 1949), 507.

17. "Good Films for Good People" *CA* (November 4, 1948), 1413.

18. Board of Managers, "Theological Understanding That Guides Our Work of Communication" (April 1975), 2, in *Theological Statement and Role of United Methodist Communications* (United Methodist Communications, 1998). The great impetus for Methodist moviemaking emerged out of the work of British producer Lord Arthur Rank. For a fuller portrait of this remarkable and devout media mogul, see Wood, Alan, *Mr. Rank: A Study of J. Arthur Rank and British Films* (Hodder and Stoughton, 1952); Smith, Rebecca, "J. Arthur Rank" *Films in Review* (May/June 1996), 2–11.

19. Frakes, Margaret, "Religion on the Screen" *Motive* (December 1941), 41.

20. Ibid., 38. See her articles "A Screen-Issues Roll Call" *Motive* (September 1942), 31; "What of Religion on the Screen?" *Motive* (April 1945), 44; and "Religion according to Hollywood" *Motive* (May 1946), 40.

21. "New Film Libraries . . . Coast to Coast" Methodist Publishing House advertisement, *CA* (August 26, 1946), 31.

22. "Center for Protestants" *CA* (February 26, 1948), 275; "Photos" *CA* (April 1, 1948), 422.

23. Jackson, Glen, "Seeing Is Believing" *CA* (January 1, 1948), 4.

24. "Good Films for Good People" *CA* (November 4, 1948), 1413.

25. Wall, James, *Church and Cinema: A Way of Viewing Film* (Eerdmans, 1971).

26. Around 1953, the World Association of Christian Communication began publishing its journal, *Media Development*, to explore how the church related to various initiatives, themes, technologies, and issues in communication industries that were salient to the church at large. In his editorials, Michael Traber would reiterate the significance and relevance of the cinema for the church. "In the history of communication," he noted, "the image can be said to pre-date the written word." With the religious image becoming firmly established in the heritage of Europe, it has also evolved out of a "mystical, almost pagan, belief in the intrinsic force of that image." Cinema, the modern art form of the image, he argued, assumed a "spiritual role" in holding up a mirror to a global humanity. Traber, Michael, "Editorial: Film in Christian Communication" *Media Development* (February 1980), 1–2.

27. "Eutychus and His Kin" *CT* (February 3, 1958), 25–26.

28. Vernon, Walter, "For Church Showings: *Two Thousand Years Ago*" *CA* (February 10, 1949), 190.

29. "Canned, Ready to Serve" *Time* (November 17, 1947), 69. Later, *Time* would report the religious film success of the Methodist J. Arthur Rank in "Shot in the Arm" (December 6, 1948), 52. *Time* also had noted the sudden resurgence of religious films after the war, due to increased church attendance and Hollywood recognizing potential profits. See "Celluloid Revival" *Time* (April 24, 1944), 48–49.

30. Vernon, Walter, "For Church Showings: *Crossroads*" *CA* (September 7, 1950), 1094.

31. Ellis, Howard, director, Department of Public Evangelism, in *Annual Report of the Joint Staff to the Radio and Film Commission of the Methodist Church* (United Methodist Communications, 1951).

32. Vernon, Walter, "For Church Showings: *The Dislocated*" *CA* (June 5, 1952), 770.

33. "Religion: Protesting Protestant" *Time* (January 21, 1946). Paul Frederic Heard was designated as secretary for the newly established PFC, charged with helping foster the "Protestant point of view."

34. "Protestant Film Board Head Cites Studios' Help" *Hollywood Citizen-News* (February 11, 1950), 8.

35. Heard, Paul, "Protestant-Made Films" *CA* (September 5, 1946).

36. Ibid.

37. "The Brotherhood of Man" *CA* (January 13, 1949), 62.

38. Smith, Ken, *Mental Hygiene: Classroom Films, 1945–1970* (Blast Books, 1999), 208–9. In the field of animation, the General Board of Temperance of the Methodist Church would later commission the Creative Arts Studios to produce *Stop Driving Us Crazy* (1961), the "world's only religious-sci-fi highway safety cartoon," preaching that "reckless driving is a sin."

39. "The Color of a Man" *CA* (January 13, 1949), 2.

40. "Prejudice" *CA* (July 7, 1949), 902.

41. "100 Cities to Premier Race Film by Protestant Church" *New York Daily News* (October 19, 1949).

42. "Movies for the Family—*We've a Story to Tell*" *CA* (March 3, 1949), 506. *Reaching from Heaven* (ca. 1952) preached about personal evangelism, seemingly less of a concern for Methodists than social missions. See "Don't Let Your Summer Church Programs Lag—Methodist Publishing House" *CA* (June 5, 1952), 770.

43. Vernon, Walter, "Movies for the Family—*From across the Border*" *CA* (March 17, 1949), 370.

44. Vernon, Walter, *"The Wrong Way Out" CA* (May 5, 1949), 614.

45. Vernon, Walter, *"Between Two Worlds* aka *That Boy Joe" CA* (June 9, 1949), 774.

46. Vernon, Walter, *"Unto Thyself Be True" CA* (June 6, 1949), 838.

47. "Wave of Religious Movies Is Due" *Variety* (September 1942), 10.

48. *"The Parson of Panamint" CH* (September 1941), 40.

49. Rushmore, Howard, "Motion Picture Commentator" *CH* (September 1940), 44.

50. Poling, Daniel, "Hollywood: Halo or Hellfire?" *CH* (October 1942), 29, 61.

51. Maynard, Paul, "Just Between Ourselves: Letters on *One Foot in Heaven* for Warner Bros" *CH* (February 1941), 76; Peale, Norman Vincent, "Motion Pictures Can Be Constructive" *CH* (April 1941), 27, 67.

52. Rushmore, Howard, "Motion Picture Commentator on *One Foot in Heaven*" *CH* (November 1941), 44.

53. "Winston Churchill on *One Foot in Heaven*—Take It Back to England" *CH* (March 1942), 16.

54. Spencer, Harry, "Movies for the Family—*Stars in My Crown*" *CA* (March 9, 1950), 318.

55. Brown, Marel, "Circuit Rider in Technicolor" *CA* (November 11, 1950), 1426.

56. *"Again . . . Pioneers!" CA* (September 7, 1950), 1094.

57. Vernon, Walter, *"What Happened to Jo Jo?" CA* (September 28, 1950), 1191.

58. Numerous films echo this point: In *Love Thy Neighbor* (1950), a postman named Lem practices Christ's command on his busy city mail route. When customers start following his example, startling changes come about. DeForest Kelley appears in a parable about gossip, *Speak No Evil* (1950), in which a veteran ends jealousy and dissension by living the Christian faith he gained in combat. *The Road Back* (ca. 1950) concerns a modern advertising man who wonders whether Christ's commands are practical in business today. *Rolling Stones* (ca. 1950) is described as the story of a boy whose "family traveled too much to sink roots . . . or think much about real values. A sexton, a minister and their church help him find himself." "Movies for the Family—*The Pilgrimage Play*" *CA* (December 21, 1950), 1614.

59. "Announcing Coronet Films" Methodist advertisement, *CA* (December 28, 1950), 1646. Titles, all produced in 1950, included *Are You Popular?, Are You Ready for Marriage?,* and *How Do You Know It's Love?*

60. *"Birthday Party" CA* (February 15, 1951), 222.

61. Cristina, Diana, manager of EcuFilm, interview by Carl McLellan, Fall 1986, RURFA.

62. It also offered twenty-six "talk-back" film programs, which consisted of one-reel dramas with a panel of ministers and laity engaging various issues. See Burke, Emory Stevens, ed., *History of American Methodism* (Abingdon Press, 1964), 3:531–32.

63. Through their BFC, the NCC founded the Visual Education Fellowship and developed the International Workshop in Audio-Visual Education in 1943. Pearl Rosser was the guiding light for drawing in film producers, editors, scriptwriters, critics, and film aficionados to the Green Lake Workshop at the Baptist Conference Grounds in Wisconsin. See Marks, "Brief History of Church Films" op. cit., 8.

64. See Spencer, Harry, "Pick of the Week for Church Showings: *Into the Good Ground*" *CA* (November 1, 1949), 30. Pathescope produced *Into the Good Ground* about the Bible as a revelatory source for daily living, for the Presbyterian Church (USA). An architect, Dan Gardner, humbly accepts the Scriptures' truth and becomes a new man. According to

Spencer, "The story line is confused. The motivation of the characters is weak. Too often the events are told by narration instead of pictures on the screen."

65. Ibid., 17. Other producers included John Ott Films, Encyclopedia Britannica, the Religious Film Association, the American Bible Society, and Foundation Films.

66. "Easter Movies" *CA* (May 5, 1953), 318.

67. "*Fire upon the Earth*" *CA* (March 20, 1952), 382.

68. PFC films were usually short, but *Second Chance* (1950)—boasting the Hollywood stars Ruth Warrick and Hugh Beaumont and written by Robert Presnell (*What Price Hollywood?* [1932], *My Man Godfrey* [1936], and *Meet John Doe* [1941])—offered a full-length feature about "backsliding Christians" and one woman's dream of her former life, which propels her to the realization that "she should start anew, and maintain a Christian home."

69. Vernon, Walter, "For Church Showings: *Family Next Door*" *CA* (October 4, 1951), 1242.

70. "Movies for the Family—*The Family Next Door*" *CA* (October 4, 1951), 1242; "*The Family Next Door*" *CA* (October 11, 1951), 1264–65.

71. "*The Family Next Door*" op. cit., 1264–65.

72. "*John Wesley*" *CH* (April 28, 1951), 4.

73. "*John Wesley*" *CA* (May 13, 1954), 602; "Movies for the Family—*Wesley* Film" *CA* (June 25, 1953), 26.

74. "Museum of Modern Art" *CA* (March 25, 1954), 378.

75. "Radio and Film Commission" *CA* (February 17, 1955), 199.

76. "*I Beheld His Glory*" *CA* (April 23, 1953), 527.

77. Reed, Ron, "The Lost Films of Rolf Forsberg" *Filmwell* (June 3, 2009), http://www.filmwell.org/2009/06/03/the-lost-films-of-rolf-forsberg/.

78. Personal correspondence with Rolf Forsberg, September 10, 2010. Forsberg called this the "Green Lake Treatment."

79. See Schillaci, op. cit., 122–27.

80. Ibid., 57.

81. "The Gospel in Disguise" *CT* (1963), n.p.

82. Forsberg personal correspondence, op. cit.

83. "Pavilions" *Time* (June 19, 1964).

84. Ibid. Unexpectedly, a letter to the Church Federation calling for them to exhibit the film came from the Association of Rabbis of the City of New York: "Show it! It is a work of art." Forsberg Files, RURFA.

85. White, Mel, interview by Andrew Quicke, Summer 2000, RURFA.

86. Hartman, Rachel, "What's Happening in Church Films?" *CH* (February 1969), 64, 65.

87. Forsberg personal correspondence, op. cit.

88. Larson, Lawrence, "The Church as Producer" *CA* (June 18, 1964), 14–15. *Martin Luther*, however, he believed was a lasting religious film, along with *Moment to Act* (ca. 1960), a film sponsored by the Commission on Missionary Education of the NCC.

89. Heard, Paul, "Protestant-Made Films" *CA* (September 5, 1946). For example, the short morality play film *First Steps* (ca. 1953) concerned a widower whose ten-year-old son, Tommy, throws rocks through church windows with his gang before joining a church group and putting his faith in God. One reviewer commented that "a weakness of the film is that Tommy's reason for wanting to join the church seems to be little more than peer pressure." "*First Steps*" *CA* (November 13, 1953), 1430.

90. "Church Film Needs Reforming" *CA* (January 12, 1967), 12–13.

91. Wall, James, *"A Man for All Seasons" CA* (March 9, 1967), 11.

92. Wall, James, "Short Film Summaries" *CA* (January 11, 1968), 19–20.

93. Wall, James, *"The Eighth Day" CA* (February 8, 1968), 20.

94. "Film Awards" *CA* (March 21, 1968), 12–14.

95. Ibid.

96. *Communications in the United Methodist Church: Report to the General Conference* (United Methodist Communications, 1979), 1.

97. Pilkington, James Penn, *The Methodist Publishing House: A History*, vol. 1 (Abingdon Press, 1968).

98. Maynard, Edwin, "Working Paper on Communications in the United Methodist Church" (September 18, 1978), in *Communications in the United Methodist Church*, op. cit. The purpose of United Methodist Communications was to develop and maintain a comprehensive, holistic, communications system through the *Interpreter*, a magazine for clergy.

99. Miller astutely deconstructed the religious spectaculars in noting that they "make abundant use of biblical and religious themes, figures, symbols, names and words—but they are not religious in content. They are the wind, the earthquake, and the fire, but there is no still, small Voice. They are made up entirely of externals; religion necessarily involves the internal. Their emphasis is all on quantity; religion is a matter of quality . . . In movies like these it seems that Hollywood exploits the religious allegiances of its audiences. These films are religious only in name, not in content. The content of the movie is distinctly pagan." Miller, William, "Hollywood and Religion" *Religion in Life* (Spring, 1952), 273. See also Jones, William, *Sunday Night at the Movies* (John Knox Press, 1967); Wall, James, "What Makes a Movie Religious?" *Face to Face* (September 1969), 25; Winston, Kenneth, "Films and the Faith" *Face to Face* (September 1969), 3; and Crowther, Bosley, "Peril in Film Trends" *Motive* (November 1947), 46.

100. Jones, William, "The Church and Secular Films" *CA* (June 18, 1964), 7–8.

101. Boyd, Malcolm, "For Adults Only" *CA* (June 18, 1964), 9–10; Tower, Howard, "Motion Pictures: Enemy or Ally" *CA* (June 18, 1964), 11; Schreiner, George, "Film Reviews" *CA* (June 18, 1964), 12–13. A group of Episcopal clergymen headed by Sidney Lanier and Malcolm Boyd designed guides to aid churches in the use of such contemporary films.

102. Dalglish, Rev. William, ed., *Media for Christian Formation: A Guide to AV Resources* (Pflaum, 1969).

103. "Minutes of the Meeting of the Executive Committee R & F C of UMC" (September 7, 1952), in *Communications in the United Methodist Church*, op. cit.

104. "Trumpets in the Morning" *Time* (April 11, 1960).

105. McMurry, Glenn, *The Autobiography of an Unimportant Important Man* (University of Southern California, 1995).

106. Gerbner, George, "Communication in Christian Education" *ES* (February 1957), 78–80.

107. Friedrich, James F., "Cathedral's USC Workshop" *ES* (July 1957), 382.

108. Smith, Lyndell, *A Brief History of United Methodist Communications and Its Predecessors* (United Methodist Communications, 1977), 3–7.

109. McLellan interview, op. cit.

110. Agee, Bill, "The Historical Position of the Methodist Church on Motion Pictures and Their Relation to the Church" (March 31, 1986), 11, RURFA. See also the *Encyclopedia of World Methodism* (United Methodist Communications, 1979), 2320–21.

111. In a self-defining brochure, EcuFilm identified itself as a "media distribution service for church and secular audiences. It is the consolidation of the film and video resources previously contained in several of the major Protestant denominational resource centers of those of the National Council of Churches' TV film library." *Presenting EcuFilm: An Ecumenical Film/Video Distribution Service* (EcuFilm Catalogue, 1982), 2.

112. See Hyland, Jack, *Evangelism's First Modern Media Star* (Cooper Square Press, 2002).

113. Stidger, William, "Berries for the King's Plate" *CH* (April 1937), 12, 13, 14, 56.

114. Stott, Roscoe Gilmore, "What's Right with the Movies?" *CH* (October 1944), 33, 34, 74–76.

115. "A Militant Protestant Voice" *CH* (February 1945), 37.

116. Ibid.

117. Lucille and George Heimrich, the backbones of PFC, continued to promote Hollywood films like *Ben Hur*, *The Greatest Story Ever Told*, *A Man Called Peter*, and *The Ten Commandments*, and behind the scenes served as ambassadors for Christian movies.

118. The PMPC was created almost simultaneously alongside the Johnston Office, where Eric Johnston served as president of the Motion Picture Association of America Production Code enforcement from 1945 to 1963. The PMPC seemed to have been transferred to the National Council of Churches Broadcasting and Film Commission in 1950, which distributed reviews to numerous periodicals.

119. "After Two Years" *CH* (January 1947), 28, 29, 83.

120. In 1932, the Harvard professor Hocking published *Re-Thinking Missions: A Laymen's Inquiry after One Hundred Years* (Harper and Bros.), celebrating the good that had been done, but also critiquing the Western methods. See Olmstead, Clifton, *History of Religion in the United States* (Prentice-Hall, 1960), 555.

121. Hockman, William, "First Church Builds Its Dream Program" *CH* (June 1948), 33–39. He also included Hoban's *Movies that Teach* and Strauss's *Look, Listen, and Learn* (39). See also Linnel, Greg, "'Applauding the Good and Condemning the Bad': The *Christian Herald* and Varieties of Protestant Response to Hollywood in the 1950s" *Journal of Religion and Popular Culture* (Spring 2006), http://www.usask.ca/relst/jrpc/art12-goodandbad-print.html.

122. "So That All May Hear" *CH* (October 1945), 58–59; "New Aid to Religious Educators . . . Free! Bell and Howell" *CH* (January 1946), 43; Coelln, O. H., Jr., "How to Install the New Visual Aids" *CH* (February 1946), 41–46.

123. "Let Motion Pictures Aid Religious Education" Bell and Howell advertisement, *CH* (January 1945), 49.

124. Strauss, Harry "Motion Pictures in the Church" *CH* (October 1946), 49.

125. Miles's excoriating rhetoric grew out of the fundamentalist John Rice's *What's Wrong with the Movies?* (Zondervan Press, 1938), which issued a radical call to quit the movies altogether.

126. Miles, Herbert, *Movies and Morals* (Zondervan Press, 1949), 119–20.

127. Hockman, William, "The Film in Religious Education" *Film and Education: A Symposium on the Role of the Film in the Field of Education*, ed. Godfrey Monroe Elliott (Philosophical Library, 1948), 339.

128. *"Teaching Eternal Truths"* advertisement, *CH* (August 1948), 35.

129. From 1949 to 1954, Parker headed the Communications Research Project of the Yale Divinity School and the NCC.

130. Ferguson, Alexander, "How to Start Using Visual Aids" *IJRE* (April 1945), 9–10.

131. Fore, William, NCC Communications Division, interview by Jean Fagnilli, June 21, 1981, 1, RURFA. Fore—former head of the Broadcasting and Film Commission of the NCC from 1964 to 1988, and later president of the Foundation for United Methodist Communications (following Rev. Thomas Trotter)—defined the films not as "Christian films," but as works "made by people who are Christians that reflect their perspective on issues of concern and interest."

132. Hockman, William, "Church Department: *Know Your Neighbor* Series" *ES* (February 1957), 84.

133. In June 1938, Leah Irene Fanning received her master's degree for the University of Southern California, Department of Religion, with her thesis "A Study of the Use of Motion Pictures in the Programs of Certain Protestant Churches," finding its primary employment as a mode of teaching, worship, recreation, and service. In June 1950, Ralph Marion Nichols presented a thesis, "A Survey of the Production of Religious Motion Pictures," to the Department of Cinema at USC. He noted that since 1939, religious pictures have "branched off from the main river of theatrical productions and are wending a course all their own" (32).

134. "Sermons in Films" *Newsweek* (November 10, 1947), 68.

135. "Programming with Visual Aids" op. cit.

136. *"Beyond Our Own"* CA (December 4, 1947), 1537.

137. "Religious Pictures on the Way" *CA* (April 1, 1948), 419; "Sermons in Films" *Newsweek* (November 10, 1947), 68.

138. *"Beyond Our Own"* op. cit., 1537.

139. "Programming with Visual Aids" op. cit.

140. "Non-theatrical Films: *Beyond Our Own*" *National Board of Review Magazine* (1947), 22.

141. "Programming with Visual Aids" op. cit.

142. Robins, op. cit.

143. "Sermons in Films" op. cit., 68.

144. *"Beyond Our Own"* op. cit., 1542.

145. *"Beyond Our Own"* CH (December 1947), 46; "Visual Aids for the Church" *CH* (April 1948), 24.

146. "By the Churches, for the Churches" *CH* (October 1948), 67.

147. A prewar Federal Council of Churches had sought to spank the movies for not doing enough good, for glorifying the army and navy, and for pushing indecorous drawing-room antics. See "Spanking the Movies" *Literary Digest* (July 11, 1936), 20.

148. "Protestant View Slated on Films" *CH* (May 1, 1946), 5.

149. "Bible Society Woos Top Names for Filming Old and New Testaments" *Variety* (May 15, 1946), 1, 18.

150. Bader, op. cit., 58.

151. "Bible Society Woos Top Names" op. cit., 18.

152. "A Motion Picture of the Bible" *CH* (February 1943), 29.

153. "Suitable for Church Showings" *CH* (September 1947), 77. ABS also released its historical depictions of the King James Bible, along with its 1939 New York World's Fair

exhibit, *Book for the World of Tomorrow*, in a time capsule, sponsored by Westinghouse Electric.

154. "Visual Aids for the Church" *CH* (October 1949), 64.

155. Vernon, Walter, "*My Name Is Han*" *CA* (March 24, 1949), 402; Hockman, "First Church Builds Its Dream Program" op. cit.; "Visual Aids for the Church" op. cit., 64.

156. "Movies for the Family—*My Name Is Han*" *CA* (March 24, 1949), 402.

157. "For Church Showings" *CA* (November 4, 1948), 1439; Forsyth, N. F., "Using Films in Methodist Churches Now" *CA* (November 11, 1948), 1470; Vernon, Walter, "Films for Use in Studying China" *CA* (November 18, 1948), 1502.

158. Dramatic cinematic references to Communism were frequent in early 1950s BFC films, such as *In the Face of Jeopardy* (in China) and *What Price Freedom* (in East Berlin). See Hockman's articles "For a Deeper Understanding of the Place of Religion in the Life of Refugees" *ES* (February 1957), 84; and "Church Department: As We See It" *ES* (June 1956), 65–66.

159. Spencer, Harry, "What Makes a Religious Movie?" *CA* (December 27, 1951).

160. Ibid.

161. "Films of the Month: *The Guest*" *CH* (December 1951), 76.

162. Spencer, "What Makes a Religious Movie?," op. cit., 1630.

163. Ibid., 1647.

164. Spencer, Harry, "What Makes a Religious Movie?" op. cit., 1647. Healy and Adams would be nominated for an Academy Award for their short documentary *The Word* in 1953.

165. Marshall, op. cit.

166. Beaudine's lover, the newspaper film critic Mildred Horne, authored the screenplays for *The Lawton Story* (aka *The Prince of Peace*, 1951) and the moral hygiene story *Mom and Dad* (1944).

167. Turan, Kenneth, "'You've Got to Tell 'em to Sell 'em,' Said Kroger Babb, and Did He Sell 'em" *Washington Post* (August 1, 1977), B1.

168. Bader, Golda Maud, "Films for Your Church" *CH* (April 1951), 48.

169. "Second Chance Good for Special Release" *Hollywood Reporter*, Beaudine Scrapbook, cited in Marshall, op. cit., 248n4.

170. Marshall, op. cit., 241.

171. See Friedman, David, *A Youth in Babylon: Confessions of a Trash-Film King* (Prometheus, 1990).

172. Townsend would also star in two World Wide Pictures films and become the first female chair of the Billy Graham Crusade.

173. Spencer, Harry, "*Again . . . Pioneers!*" (December 7, 1950), 1550; Bader, "Films for Your Church" op. cit., 50.

NOTES TO CHAPTER 4

1. Hagedorn, Rev. Otto., "The Film as a Messenger of the Gospel" *Educational Film Magazine* (August 1920), 13, 22.

2. Jensen, Frank, "The Church and Pictures—Church Film Review, *Martin Luther: His Life and Times*" *ES* (June 1925), 368; see also MacRae, James, "An Exceptional Opportunity for Co-operation by the Church" *ES* (October 1925), 486.

3. "The Life of Christ as Shown in the Movies" *Current Opinion* (September 1914), 192; see also Muckermann, Richard, "Religion and the Film" *International Review of Educational Cinematography* (January 1930), 476; Hellbeck, op. cit., 924.

4. Pannkoke, O. H., "Living Pictures to Bring the Church at Large to Its Members" *American Lutheran* (February 1924), 15–16; Nickelsburg, J. F. E., "A Successful Publicity Tour" *American Lutheran* (February 1926), 8–9.

5. Marks, "Brief History of Church Films" op. cit., 8.

6. "Religion in the Films" *CH* (May 1943), 37.

7. "Christianity in Action" *CH* (February 1947), 54; Rogers, op. cit., 19.

8. "A Motion Picture of the Bible" *CH* (February 1943), 29.

9. "Visual Aids for the Church" *CH* (April 1948), 24; "*Reaching from Heaven*" *CH* (April 1948), 71; *Reaching from Heaven* advertisement *CH* (May 1948), 70; "Stirring Motion Pictures with a Message for Every Christian Community" *IJRE* (March 1950), 64. Designated as "Christian drama and romance," *Reaching from Heaven* (1947) was released out of Concordia Publishing House. Gred Linnell Keenly noted how *The Christian Herald* valorized films. See "'Applauding the Good and Condemning the Bad': *The Christian Herald* and Varieties of Protestant Responses to Hollywood in 1950s" *Journal of Religion and Popular Culture* (Spring 2006). http://www.usask.ca/relst/jrpc/art12-goodandbad-print.html (accessed March 5, 2011).

10. "Visual Aids for the Church" *CH* (June 1949), 46.

11. "*An Answer for Anne*" *IJRE* (February 1950), 76.

12. "Visual Aids for the Church" *CH* (June 1948), 37–38; "*Reaching from Heaven*" *CH* (October 1948), 86.

13. A second stewardship film from the United Lutheran Church, *And Now I See* (1949), contracted Ralph Morgan as narrator.

14. Coyle, John, *Like a Mighty Army* (Cathedral Films, 1950).

15. See also Pichel, Irving, "*Martin Luther*: The Problem of Documentation," *Quarterly of Film, Radio, & Television* 8 (Winter 1953), 172-185. Of course, no film has communicated a history of Luther as effectively as Sam Mulberry's hilarious online animated short *The Reformation Polka*, with its chorus of "Papal bulls, indulgences, and transubstantiation." See http://www.youtube.com/watch?v=b4TeJJmQJqU (accessed July 17, 2010).

16. "The Bible Goes to Press: From the Motion Picture, *Our Bible—How It Came to Us*" *The Church and the Fine Arts*, ed. Cynthia Pearl Maus (Harper and Bros., 1960), 410–12; see also De Groot, Dr. A. T., "Scenes of the Protestant Reformation" in *Christian-Evangelist* (Bethany Press, 1954), 1032–40.

17. Crowther, Bosley, "*Martin Luther*" *New York Times* (September 10, 1953), 22; Farber, Manny, "*Martin Luther*" *Nation* (September 19, 1953), 108.

18. See Black, Gregory, *The Catholic Crusade against the Movies, 1940–1975* (Cambridge UP, 1997), 128–32; Klauser, Alfred, "*Martin Luther*—The Story of a Film" *Christian Century* (October 21, 1953), 1195–97; and "The *Martin Luther* Controversy" *Commonweal* (March 15, 1957), 615–19.

19. Cited by Black, op. cit., 131. Black points out that this film drew a wedge of opposition between the Legion of Decency and its Lutheran allies.

20. "*First Steps* and *All That I Have*" *CA* (November 13, 1953), 1430; see also "Don't Let Your Summer Church Programs Lag—Methodist Publishing House" *CA* (June 5, 1952), 770.

21. Ammon, Rev. George, "The Audio-Visual Story in the United Lutheran Church in America" *ES & AV Guide* (May 1957), 252–53. Ammon celebrated the work of Rev. E. O. Armbruster, who also helped set up the interchurch distribution agency RFA and its successor, the Religious Film Libraries. See also Oscar Rumpf, "AV in the Evangelical and Reformed Church" *ES & AV Guide* (February 1957), 82.

22. Hockman, William, "Church Department" *ES* (March 1958), 144.

23. Vernon, Walter, "For Church Showings: *45 Tioga Street*" *CA* (November 6, 1952), 1398.

24. Cornell, George, "Artful TV Allegory about Ants' Antics Stirs Controversy as Church Vehicle" (September 10, 2010), Forsberg Files, RURFA.

25. Trying to get a known "name" for the film, Gwynne proved to be a disappointment, speaking in an insincere and condescending voice. Forsberg personal correspondence, op. cit.

26. Wall, James, "Review of *The Antkeeper*" *CA* (May 30, 1968), 18.

27. Konzelman, Robert, *Marquee Ministry: The Movie Theater as Church and Community Forum* (Harper and Row, 1972), 35.

28. Forsberg personal correspondence, op. cit.

29. Wall, James M., *Church and Cinema: A Way of Viewing Film* (Eerdmans, 1971), 21.

30. Wolff, Rich, "*Davey and Goliath*: The Response of a Church-Produced Children's Television Program to Emerging Social Issues" *Journal of Popular Film and Television* (Fall 1990), 112–21; Crescenti, Peter, "Yabba-Dabba-David-and-Goliath" *CT* (October 3, 1986), 49.

31. "Church Films" *CA* (April 1937), 312.

32. The Episcopal scholar G. William Jones keenly recognized that church and screen had been friends in the first decades of the century, whereas other saw in these relations ambivalence, enmity, and mutual hostility. See Jones, G. William, *Sunday Night at the Movies* (John Knox Press, 1967), 25; and Haselden, Kyle, *Morality and the Mass Media* (Broadman Press, 1968).

33. Schueddig, Rev. Louis, "History of the Episcopal Radio-TV Foundation, Inc.," letter/bulletin from the president and executive director of the Episcopal Radio-TV Foundation (September 1985), 1, RURFA.

34. Also known as "Good Grief, Aslan!," in light of Melendez's prior work directing *A Charlie Brown Christmas* (1965).

35. Written by William Nicholson, produced by David Thompson, and directed by Norman Stone, the film stands, in the opinion of these authors, as a superior production to Sir Richard Attenborough's later Hollywood film of the same title.

36. "The Religious Life" *New Yorker* (September 13, 1982), 102. Theodore Baehr, then president of the Episcopal Radio-TV Foundation and executive producer of the exhibition, described it thus: "Using the most advanced, modern technology available, visitors to the exhibit of the churches enter into a space vehicle and travel back to the beginning of time, where they find that God created the heavens and the earth. Then they travel to paradise, where they turn away from God, and are kicked out into a room which represents our search for a means to overcome our alienation through power, energy, politics, sex, war, and do-it-yourself religions. Finally, in the midst of the chaos, Jesus appears and leads the audience through the cross into his body. Here they are filled with his power and joined together to sing the Lord's Prayer, and then go out into the world to worship and serve God." Cited in

the brochure *The Power: The Church's Presence at the 1982 World's Fair* (Association of Christian Denominations, 1982), 1, RURFA. Baehr subsequently published a biblical periodical guide on movies and entertainment, *Movieguide*, to both challenge Christians to examine their viewing habits and to lobby the entertainment industry to set higher standards. See Thigpen, Paul, "Cleaning Up Hollywood" *Charisma* (December 1991), 34–42.

37. "Claire Bloom to Star in TV Special on Life of C. S. Lewis" press release, Episcopal Radio-TV Foundation (September 12, 1985), 2.

38. "*The World We Want to Live In*" *IJRE* (January 1944), 25; "*One Tenth of Our Nation*" *IJRE* (April 1944), 26.

39. "War Films" *IJRE* (June 1944), 23.

40. Hunter, Rev. Stanley Armstrong, "Now Our Children Don't Like to Miss a Sunday" *CH* (May 1950), 11.

41. Janes, "Using the Direct Route to Feelings" op. cit., 41.

42. "Visual Aids for the Church" *CH* (October 1949), 42.

43. For a more thorough study of Presbyterian communication, see Hormell, Sidney James, "The Presbyterian System: An Examination of the Formal Mass Communication System of the United Presbyterian Church, USA" (PhD diss., University of Illinois, 1966).

44. Wingard, George, "TRAV and the Media" *ES & AV Guide* (February 1970), 197.

45. "Suitable for Church Showings" *CH* (September 1947), 77.

46. Kuhn, Rev. Orville, "The United Presbyterian AV Story" *ES & AV Guide* (November 1956), 428.

47. Bader, Golda Maud, "Visual Aids For the Church" *CH* (October 1951), 58.

48. Vernon, Walter, "For Church Showings: *Fire upon the Earth*" *CA* (March 20, 1952), 382.

49. National Council of Churches, *Our Sunday Best* (TV Film Library, 1979).

50. National Council of Churches, *CC Films for 1980–81* (Communication Commission of NCC, 1981). In 1972, the Seventh-Day Adventist Church produced Mel White's *So Many Voices*, a fifty-minute film warning against the worldly exploitation of movies, the battleground where Satan seeks to conquer the human heart. Ironically, its intentionally humorous portrayal of the battle for the soul against media was produced on film.

51. "*Together WE Serve*" *IJRE* (July/August 1944), 25. *Army Chaplain* (ca. 1944), part of RKO's *This Is America* series, followed a new Roman Catholic chaplain, Father Hart, joining other ministers, priests, and rabbis into the jungle to minister to the wounded and dying and to bring food, medicine, and cigarettes to soldiers. See "*Army Chaplain*" *IJRE* (July/August 1944), 25.

52. Waldrup, Earl, "Audio-Visual Aids" *Encyclopedia of Southern Baptists*, ed. James W. Merritt (Broadman Press, 1958), 1:94.

53. Waldrup, Earl, *Using Visual Aids in a Church* (Broadman Press, 1949).

54. Getz, op. cit., 13.

55. Prejudice and anxiety persisted in their concern that movies be taken out of the hands of "freelance capitalists" and other disreputable persons—in other words, Jewish producers.

56. Walker, Marshall, "A Possible Attitude toward Movies" *Biblical Recorder* (September 26, 1945), 4–5 (*Biblical Recorder* hereafter cited as *BR*).

57. Allen, Clifton J., "The Sunday School Board" *Encyclopedia of Southern Baptists*, op. cit., 2:1327.

58. Waldrup, "Audio-Visual Aids" op. cit., 95.

59. Marshall, op. cit., 12–13.

60. Getz, op. cit., 13.

61. Several periodicals recommended acceptable visual aid products, such as *Audio-Visual Aids, Baptist Program, Baptist Student, Baptist Training Union Magazine,* and *Sunday School Builder.* See Waldrup, *Using Visual Aids in a Church,* op. cit., 173. See also Dent, Ellsworth, *The Audio-Visual Handbook* (Society for Visual Education, 1949); Dale, Edgar, *Audio-Visual Methods in Teaching* (Dryden Press, 1946).

62. McGee, Mrs. W. K., "Woman's Missionary Union: Filmstrips and Motion Pictures" *BR* (January 11, 1958), 15; McGee, Mrs. W. K. "Home Missions Books and Teaching Aids" *BR* (January 23, 1960), 15.

63. "World Evangelism: Overseas" *BR* (October 10, 1959), 15.

64. "Televangelism Stewardship Films" *BR* (October 22, 1959), 15; "Televangelism Stewardship Films" *BR* (October 11, 1959), 15; "Televangelism Stewardship Films" *BR* (October 15, 1958), 15.

65. "Televangelism Films on Civic Responsibility" *BR* (September 29, 1959), 14.

66. "The Best from Outstanding Producers" *BR* (April 22, 1950).

67. "Films Presenting Christianity's Solution to Problems of Our Times" *BR* (June 6, 1959).

68. Morris, L. J., "Audio Visual Aid Workshop Announced" *BR* (February 5, 1955).

69. "$5 Films for Summer Programs" *BR* (May 30, 1959), 213; see also the American Bible Society's *So Great the Light* in "New Film Features Bibles for Blind" *BR* (March 12, 1960).

70. Ibid., 213.

71. Merritt, James W., ed., *Annual of the Southern Baptist Convention* (Broadman Press, 1950), 161.

72. Allen, Clifton, "The Sunday School Board" *Encyclopedia of Southern Baptists,* op. cit., 2:213.

73. Vernon, Walter, "Movies for the Family—*South of the Clouds*" *CA* (December 28, 1950), 1646.

74. "Films with a Message—1950–1951" *BR* (October 9, 1950).

75. "Baptist Hospital Promotion Aids Now Available, in 16mm and 35mm" *BR* (April 16, 1960); "Mission Call Portrayed in New Motion Picture" *BR* (August 15, 1959); "Pointing toward 30,000" *BR* (September 30, 1958).

76. Merritt, James W., ed., *Annual of the SBC* (Broadman Press, 1955), 179.

77. Vernon, Walter, "For Church Showings: *Out of the Dust*" *CA* (March 22, 1951), 402.

78. "Movies for the Family—*Out of the Dust*" *CA* (March 22, 1951), 402l; see also "Movies for the Family—*An End to Darkness*" *CA* (May 3, 1951), 594.

79. Robbe, Adrian, "Southern Baptist Convention's Use of Motion Picture Film—Historical Insights" (research paper, March 25, 2003), RURFA.

80. "Broadman Evangelism Films" *BR* (November 14, 1953), 22.

81. *Annual of the SBC* (Broadman Press, 1955), 238.

82. Lott, Theodore, "The Radio and Television Commission" *Encyclopedia of Southern Baptists,* op. cit., 2:1131: "On the basis of $25,000 a film, full-time television ministry would cost the commission $1,300,000 a year, exclusive of handling and extra film prints."

83. Merritt, James W. ed., *Annual of the Southern Baptist Convention* (Executive Committee, Southern Baptist Convention, 1955), 205.

84. "*House of the Wicked*" *Biblical Recorder* (December 24, 1960).

85. *Annual of SBC* (Broadman Press, 1960), 269.

86. *Annual of SBC* Annual of the Southern Baptist Convention - 1965, 108th Session, 120th Year Dallas Texas, June 1–4, 1965. Ed., Clifton J. Allen, Recording Secretary of the Convention (Executive Committee, Southern Baptist Convention, Broadman Press, 1965), 261.

87. Allen, Clifton, J., ed., *Annual of the SBC* (Broadman Press, 1965), 186.

88. Fallis, William and Herman King, "Broadman Press" *Encyclopedia of Southern Baptists*, op. cit., 1:1620.

89. Smith, Wade, *The Little Jetts Bible* (W. A. Wilde, 1942), v.

90. Sandstrom, Harry, "Father of the 'Little Jetts'" *CH* (August 1951), 29, 64.

91. Stevens, Paul, "JOT Official Letter," n.d., RURFA.

92. *The Story of Jot's Father* (brochure, Southern Baptist Radio and Television Commission, March 11, 1964), 1.

93. "JOT," *Toonerific*, http://www.toonarific.com/show.php?show_id=1881 (accessed July 18, 2008).

94. Erickson, Hal, *Television Cartoon Shows: An Illustrated Encyclopedia, 1949–1993* (McFarland, 1995), 284.

95. Corbett, Gordon, "TV-Radio and Religion" *ES & AV Guide* (May 1956), 180; Parker, E. C., D. W. Barry, and D. W. Smythe, *The Television-Radio Audience and Religion* (Harper Bros., 1955).

96. Hockman, William, "AV in the Church Field" *ES & AV Guide* (April 1959), 204–5.

97. Hockman, William, "AV in the Church Field" *ES & AV Guide* (June 1959), 304.

98. Zanco, "Cartoon" *ES & AV Guide* (January 1958), 41.

99. Ammon, George, "AV Education in the Church" *ES & AV Guide* (December 1959), 652.

100. Haselden, op. cit., 160. Haselden castigated the church for a warped view of Hollywood films, quoting the jingle "The film is under official ban / because the hero utters 'damn.' / Well, we will go to see another / and watch a gangster shoot his mother" (166). To Haselden, it seemed that the church excused violence but maintained a strict taboo on language.

101. Knight, Arthur, *Saturday Review* (November 19, 1966).

NOTES TO CHAPTER 5

1. Prill, David, *Second Coming Attractions* (St. Martin's Press, 1998).

2. "Lord Chesterfield's Advice to His Son" (1748), http://personal.ashland.edu/~jmoser1/enlight/chesterfield.htm (accessed October 5, 2010).

3. White interview, op cit..

4. Garmanz, Robert, Family Films, interview by Manual Costa, Spring 1986, RURFA.

5. Marks, "Brief History of Church Films," op. cit., 2.

6. *Family Films Is 35 and Proud of It* (promotional guide, 1981), RURFA.

7. "Visual Aids for the Church" *CH* (October 1949), 42.

8. "Family Films Offer Moral Teaching Messages: Effective and Entertaining" *IJRE* (March 1950), 91.

9. Dorr, John, "Baptists and Film: A Historical Perspective" (MA thesis, Regent University, 1985), 6. In fact, *Bible on the Table* had been so popular for so many years that Family

Films and Broadman Films coproduced and released a modern color version in 1981. See also Waldrup, *Using Visual Aids in a Church*, op. cit.

10. Vernon, Walter, "For Church Showings: *As We Forgive*" *CA* (December 25, 1952), 1642. The director, Ken Kamkin, also dealt with a similar theme in the grittier *Seventy Times Seven* (ca. 1955), in which cross-country truckers learn to forgive.

11. This created an ecumenical tele-trilogy of the Way, the Answer, and the Life. Family Films also produced several motion pictures for the National Council of Churches.

12. Hockman, William, "AV in Religion: In Tribute" *ES & AV Guide* (April 1969), 31. Hockman wrote, "This Jewish-born businessman had great insight into things Christian and Protestant. He learned our words. He knew what they meant. He often smiled at our denominational differences and our semantic antics and evasions."

13. Hamilton, John, "An Historical Study of Bob Pierce and World Vision's Development of the Evangelical Social Action Film" (PhD diss., University of Southern California, 1980), 7–8.

14. Such groups as Bread for the World, the Franciscans, the American Friends Service Committee, and others associated with the Communication Commission of the National Council of Churches were more likely to take up social documentaries and appeals for peace, refugee relief, racial reconciliation, and related "justice" concerns. On television, one finds the works of the Paulist *Insight* (1960) and the Lutheran Hour's *This Is the Life* (1951) series. John Hamilton defined the "evangelical social action film" as a "humanitarian activist motion picture . . . about helping other people in some way . . . which has an underlying motivation or emphasis on Christian salvation." Ibid., 11.

15. See Fraser, Peter, *Images of the Passion: The Sacramental Mode in Film* (Praeger, 1998), 6–7.

16. Hamilton, op. cit., 38.

17. Ibid., 43.

18. See Hamilton's discussion of Pierce's film *The Least Ones* (1965), especially pp. 143–50.

19. Kinne, Matthew, "The Father of the Christian Film Industry" (Regent University Interviews, 1993), RURFA. As Kinne discovered, Anderson has been praised as the first great Christian film studio leader, a man marked by humility and gentleness, known for his piety as much as his perseverance.

20. Anderson, Doris, interview by Don Sears, May 7, 1981, transcript 1, RURFA.

21. Ibid., 1.

22. Sonneveltz, Jack, interview by Richard Nelson, August 2, 1989, RURFA.

23. *The Gospel through Motion Pictures for 30 Years, 1950–1980* (public relations brochure, Gospel Films, 1980), RURFA.

24. Wheaton College was one such place, in which the prodigal horror filmmaker Wes Craven was to incubate. Anderson worked with many of these conservative Christian colleges to produce films (e.g., Seattle Pacific College for *Prescription for Doc*, 1966; Taylor University for *Wandering Wheels*, 1971; Huntington College for *Don't Call Me, God: I'll Call You*, 1973; and Wheaton College for *Step over the Edge*, 1976).

25. Quoted in Biskind, Peter, *Easy Riders, Raging Bulls: How the Sex-Drugs-and-Rock-'n'-Roll Generation Saved Hollywood* (Simon & Schuster, 1998), 289.

26. Anderson, Dave, interview by Richard Nelson, August 2, 1989, RURFA.

27. Sonneveltz interview, op. cit.

28. "Free Films: Gospel Films" *CH* (October 1951), 73.

29. Anderson, Dave, interview, op. cit.

30. Anderson, Doris, interview, op. cit.

31. Zeoli's close connection to Republican politics would be satirized in the *Wittenburg Door*. See "Wanda Ritchie's Body Life" column, in which Zeoli cashes in on Vietnam war movies, using the "entire student body of Moody Bible Institute as the Viet Cong." *Wittenburg Door* (August/September 1979), 10.

32. Deford, Frank, "Reaching for the Stars" *Sports Illustrated* (May 3, 1976).

33. "The 21st Century Begins Now! Gospel Films 1984 Film and Video Guide" (Gospel Films, 1984), 28–29, RURFA.

34. Brice Fennig pointed out that New Year's Eve was another gold mine for film rentals, with the clergy's challenge to keep congregations awake through the midnight moment.

35. Mel White claims that he "ghost-wrote and directed the final version" of Schaeffer's *How Should We Then Live?* series. See White, Mel, *Stranger at the Gate: To Be Gay and Christian in America* (Simon & Schuster, 1994), 144.

36. Schaeffer, Franky, *Crazy for God: How I Grew Up as One of the Elect, Helped Found the Religious Right, and Lived to Take All (or Almost All) of It Back* (Da Capo Press, 2007).

37. "Entertainment, Humor, and Biting Satire in a $5,000/Minute 'Disaster' Movie" *Christian Film and Video Review* (January/February 1985), 1.

38. Schaeffer, op. cit., 276–77.

39. Seeking to be a maverick, Franky Schaeffer described himself as the "little shit from Switzerland" who would overturn the status quo. Schaeffer, op. cit.

40. Singer, David, "*Whatever Happened to the Human Race?* A Film Preview" *CT* (August 17, 1979), 28–29.

41. Mann, Judy, "No Matter How Moving, the Show Is Still Propaganda" *Washington Post* (January 2, 1981).

42. Schaeffer, op. cit., 283.

43. Whitehead, John W., "Refiner's Fire: A Challenge to Confront the World" *CT* (February 5, 1982), 44–45.

44. Schaeffer, Franky, *Addicted to Mediocrity: 20th-Century Christians and the Arts* (Crossway Books, 1981), 78: "How appalling [these categories are] when compared with the gutsy gist of the Bible itself."

45. Viscuso, Denise, "Franky Schaeffer: The Man behind the Anger" *CH* (April 1985), 20–24.

46. Desowitz, Bill, "New Production Entity Sets Feature Slate" *Hollywood Reporter* (November 21, 1985), 1. "Distribution is not a problem," McGuire continued. "The key is the quality of the distribution." See also Tusher, Will, "SB Prods. Plans Move from Dox to Feature Pix" *Hollywood Reporter* (September 5, 1985), 1; the ad for his film *Headhunter* in *Premier* (October 1989), 103; and Schaeffer, Franky, *Sham Pearls for Real Swine: Beyond the Cultural Dark Age—A Quest for Renaissance* (Wolgemuth & Hyatt, 1990). What is significant is that Franky realized his own personal renaissance of humility against what he saw as a dark age of pomposity characterizing the Christian community. See "The Return of Franky Schaeffer" *CT* (November 19, 1990), 37–38.

47. Personal correspondence from Paul McGuire, executive director, October 24, 1986, at RURFA.

48. Schaeffer, Franky, interview by Eric Karson, June 7, 1986, 2, RURFA. Schaeffer noted the influences of Fellini and the apocalyptic work of *Blade Runner* and *A Clockwork Orange* as significant in creating his own style. In fact, his vision for the film is aesthetically and intellectually superior to its actual production. Schaeffer, *Sham Pearls*, op. cit., 74.

49. Pierard, Richard, "The Unmaking of Francis Schaeffer: An Evangelical Tragedy" *Wittenburg Door* (April/May 1984), 30.

50. Senter, Mark, III, "Bringing Back Cinema Serials: Christian Style" *CT* (November 20, 1981), 37–38.

51. Franzen, Chris, "Dobson Brings the Family into Focus" *Christian Film and Video Review* (Spring 1987), 7.

52. The "Dobson effect" inaugurated the advent of blockbuster video sales, with teaching tapes bringing adult curricula into the home. Successful talking heads in the new boom included Richard Foster, Charles Colson, Leighton Ford, David and Karen Mains, Tony Campolo, Joyce Landorf, Josh McDowell, R. C. Sproul, and many others. The sudden popularity of these speech films, like the earlier Baptista works, emphasized "no characters, no plot, no drama. Just a speaker telling you what you need to know." Mark Tuttle pointed out that the format stripped away the facade of entertainment and directly addressed the troublesome issues of people's lives. Message usurped media. See "Christian Film and Video: Industry on the Move" *CT* (April 17, 1987), 55.

53. Flanagan, Edward, interview by Bill Harris, January 18, 1991, transcript 1, RURFA.

54. Tuttle, op. cit., 54.

55. Franzen, op. cit., 7.

56. Stevens, Mary, "Tapes Don't Preach, but Send a Message" *Chicago Tribune* (February 23, 1990), 71

57. Adventures in Odyssey Team, *Adventures in Odyssey: The Official Guide* (Focus on the Family, 2008), 1. Gospel distributed another series for children, *Buford and Friend*, once described as a church Muppets, about a stuffed hound dog with his friends (including a penguin, raccoon, koala bear, cow, and wolf) teaching basic biblical lessons on prayer and fellowship through skits, musical vignettes, Bible stories, and even a television quiz show format. Like *Sesame Street*, the PBS series that inspired it, the show regularly featured famous guests like Debbie Boone or Andraé Crouch.

58. The late 1970s and early 1980s saw a boom in such relational media products, all incorporating Christian principles, popular psychology, humor, sensitivity, and emotionally moving, personal "sharing." For example, see Joyce Landorf's engaging six-part series *His Stubborn Love* (ca. 1985).

59. "Christian Film Production: What's Happening Today" (interview with Billy Zeoli), *Christian Life* (March 1982), 42; see also Harvey Marks's remarks in "New Films Hit Grass Roots Issues" *Christian Life* (March 1981).

60. "Door Interview: Mel White" *Wittenburg Door* (October/November 1973), 8–14.

61. White, *Stranger at the Gate*, 92.

62. White interview, op. cit. White expressed his deep respect and liking for Zeoli, but sometimes, he said, "you had to hit him with a plank. He doesn't need any explanation of why you hit him over the head with a plank, but sometimes you needed to hit him with the plank even to get him to think the other way. And, I mean, he is totally

manipulative. I mean he manipulates everybody and everything. But, that's politics, that's show biz."

63. Ibid.

64. McFadden, Carol, "To Grapple with Pain" *CT* (July 4, 1975), 20.

65. McMath, Ann, "The Problem of Pain in Mel White's Films" (research paper, Regent University, November 1979), RURFA.

66. Lewis, C. S., *The Problem of Pain* (Fontana Books, 1940), 81; Price, Phil, "Mel White: Today's Christian Films" *Focus Magazine* (Spring 1981), 7.

67. Carpenter, Fred, "When Are You Going to Make *Real* Movies?" *Mediator* (Fall 1986), 1, 3.

68. Gospel Films catalog (1984), RURFA. The *Sunshine Factory* series of thirty-minute *Sesame Street*–like children's programs featured topics like honesty, with a Mr. Fix-It as a friend who guided children.

69. Zeoli, Billy, "Youth Films Report," CFVA Convention, 1989, RURFA.

70. Anderson, Dave, interview, op. cit..

71. Anderson, Doris, interview op. cit.

72. Anderson, Lane, interview by Matt Kinne, Spring 1993, RURFA.

73. Ibid..

74. Fussle, Heinz, interview by Mary Case, January 1991, RURFA.

75. McFadden, Carol, "Exorcising the Enemy" *CT* (April 11, 1975), 12

76. Anderson, Doris, interview, op. cit..

NOTES TO CHAPTER 6

1. See Vogler, Christopher, *The Writer's Journey: Mythic Structure for Writers* (Michael Wiese Productions, 1998); and McConnell, Frank, *Storytelling and Mythmaking: Images from Film and Literature* (Oxford UP, 1979).

2. Ferlita, Ernest and John May, *Film Odyssey: The Art of Film as Search for Meaning* (Paulist, 1976), 5. See also Ricoeur, Paul, *The Symbolism of Evil* (Beacon Press, 1969), 72–74.

3. C. S. Lewis compared the God-ward journey of the soul to the homeward journey of a child: "No amount of falls or detours will really undo us if we keep on picking ourselves up each time and heading home. We shall, of course, be very muddy and tattered children by the time we reach home. But the bathrooms are all ready, the towels put out, and the clean clothes in the airing cupboard. The only fatal thing is to lose one's temper or hope and give it up. It is when we notice the dirt that God is most present in us; it is the very sign of his presence." Lewis, C. S., *Collected Letters* (Harper, 2004), 2:507

4. In the late 1970s, cultural studies in media reassessed audiences as more active, constructing their own meanings from the media they encounter. George Gerbner suggested that repetitive programming was similar to popular ritualized religion. Larry Gross "Living with Television" *Television: The Critical View*, ed. Horace Newcomb (Oxford UP, 1979), 363–93. Victor Turner extended the idea of media as ritual to view it as a way of integrating change or transformation in personal and communal narratives. Turner's second stage in his rite of initiation was the transitional experience of "liminality," from the Latin *limen*, as in the threshold between two worlds. See Turner, *From Ritual to Theatre: The Human Seriousness of Play* (PAJ Publications, 1982).

5. Mr. Blackland, World Wide Pictures, interview by Jeri Rochester, 1981, Regent University, transcript, 2, RURFA.

6. Cryderman, Lyn, "The Taming of the VCR" *CT* (September 24, 1990), 65.

7. *Twenty Years under God: A Pictorial Review of the Billy Graham Ministries* (World Wide Pictures, 1970), 513.

8. Many records of the WWP are stored at the Archives of the Billy Graham Center on the campus of Wheaton College, in Wheaton, Illinois. The best-documented (and most successful) film in the collection is *The Hiding Place*, with the archive covering everything from strategies of fund-raising to personal testimonial responses.

9. Engstrom, Ken, interview, July 1992, Regent University, RURFA. Like Alfred Hitchcock, Graham would make cameos in all his films, usually at a crusade.

10. Brown, William, "Worlds Apart" *CT* (October 14, 1966), 57.

11. Engstrom interview, op. cit.

12. Henderson-Hart, Anne, "What Makes a Film Christian?" *Eternity* (June 1982), 19.

13. Blackland interview, op. cit.

14. Ibid.

15. Collier, James, interview by Steve Schaefer, 1981, Regent University, transcript 1, RURFA.

16. White, Mel, "Does Christian Film Work in the Neighborhood Theater?" *Christianity Today* (October 7, 1983), 14.

17. Coombes, David, "*Two a Penny*" *CT* (July 19, 1968), 49.

18. Ibid.

19. Forbes, Cheryl, "Film Evangelism: A Time to Change" *CT* (March 16, 1973), 17.

20. Ibid.

21. Collier believed that *The Hiding Place* would actually be nominated for several Academy Awards, especially the performances of Jeannette Clift and Julie Harris. Las Vegas gave both actresses odds for being nominated. But Hollywood continued to be uneasy with Christian films, as they were outside the "club," and the actresses were overlooked. Nevertheless, Jeannette Clift was nominated for Best Newcomer for the Golden Globes. White, "Does Christian Film Work?," op. cit., 14–20.

22. Blackland interview, op. cit.

23. Ibid..

24. Reed, Rex, "*The Hiding Place*" *Billboard* (February 15, 1986), 35.

25. Forbes, Cheryl, "The Refiner's Fire: *Hiding in Harmony*" *CT* (July 18, 1975), 14.

26. Thomas, Kevin, "Faith Triumphs in *Hiding Place*" *Los Angeles Times* (October 1, 1975), F1; Canby, Vincent "Screen: *Hiding Place*: Story of Dutch Family during Occupation" *New York Times* (November 6, 1975).

27. Collier interview, op. cit.

28. Lawing, John, "The Bad Guy Changes Hats" *CT* (December 1, 1978), 32–33.

29. "Before his conversion the Apostle Paul was an aggressive, dynamic, somewhat arrogant protector of the Jewish tradition. After his conversion he became the aggressive, dynamic, somewhat arrogant disseminator of the Christian faith." Ibid., 33.

30. Cheney, Harry, "*The Prodigal*" *CT* (October 7, 1983), 16.

31. White, "Does Christian Film Work?," op. cit., 14–20.

32. Ibid., 15. Ken Wales defined an "explicitly evangelistic film" as one that contained a crusade and showed how "people's lives are changed by a crusade and primarily by hearing the word of God through Billy's preaching."

33. Ibid., 18.

34. Wales pulled in the cinematographer Frank Stanley (*East of Eden*) and the production designer Bill Creber (*The Greatest Story Ever Told*) to help on *The Prodigal*. See White, "Does Christian Film Work?," op. cit., 18.

35. Cheney, Harry, "*The Prodigal*" *CT* (October 7, 1983), 16.

36. Nestingen, James *Martin Luther: A Life* (Augsburg Fortress, 2003), 111.

37. Werner, Barry, interview, July 13, 2001, ICVA Conference, Atlanta, RURFA.

38. Chattaway, Peter, "Billy Graham Goes to the Movies" *CT* (August 23, 2005).

39. The four spiritual laws from Campus Crusade for Christ are "First, God loves you and offers a wonderful plan for your life. Second, Man is sinful and separated from God. Therefore, he cannot know and experience God's love and plan for his life. Third, Jesus Christ is God's only provision for man's sin. Through Him you can know and experience God's love and plan for your life. Finally, we must individually receive Jesus Christ as Savior and Lord; then we can know and experience God's love and plan for our lives." "Four Spritiual Laws, English" *Campus Crusade for Christ*, http://www.campuscrusade.com/fourlawseng.htm (accessed February 6, 2011).

40. Werner interview, op. cit.

41. White, "Does Christian Film Work?," op. cit., 18. Collier remembered seeing *The Restless Ones* from a balcony in Bakersfield, California, and thinking, "If I knew they were going to show films in big barns like this, I'd only shoot in close-ups," since you couldn't see anything from up there.

42. Ibid., 18. Collier tells the story of an MGM studio executive who dropped into a preview showing and by the end of the film was crying; this executive later told Ken Wales that the film "opened up edges in me that I've kept covered for years" (20).

43. Ibid., 19.

44. "Film Evangelism Ideas" (publicity Sheet distributed in conjunction with the release of *Road to Redemption*, World Wide Pictures, 2001), RURFA.

45. Curtis went on to become a teaching assistant to Max Kerr at Gordon Conwell Seminary. Curtis, Ken, interview by Terry Lindvall, July 12, 2001, Christian Media Convention, Atlanta, RURFA.

46. Moss, Marquita, "Metamorphosis of a Rich Alcoholic" *CT* (October 22, 1971), 34–35.

47. Phillips, John McCandlish, "Baptists Are Taking to the Screen to Spread the Word" *New York Times* (June 7, 1972).

48. Curtis, Ken, interview by Richard White, 1987, Regent University, transcript 9, RURFA.

49. Phillips, op. cit.; Auletta, Ken, "The Man Who Disappeared" *New Yorker* (January 6, 1997).

50. Phillips, op. cit.

51. Thompson, Howard, "*The Cross and the Switchblade* (1970): Pat Boone Plays Preacher Hero in 'Cross and Switchblade'" *New York Times* (June 8, 1972).

52. See Evenson, John, "*The Cross and the Switchblade*" *CT* (June 19, 1970), 34.

53. Forbes, Cheryl, "Tom Harris: Seeking Celluloid Credibility" *CT* (January 19, 1973), 49.

54. Briggs, Joe Bob, "The Gospel according to Joe Bob" *Film Comment* (April 1987), 52, 54.

55. Evenson, op. cit., 34.

56. For Murray, here was a film that could "edify as well as entertain" in its presentation of "a Christ-centered conversion." Forbes, op. cit., 44.

57. Murray cited the example of an antagonistic LA critic who refused to review *The Cross and the Switchblade* because "my parents are Southern Baptist, devout church people—and I hate my parents and Christianity." Ibid., 49.

58. Forbes, Cheryl, "The Refiner's Fire: Gateway to Diversity" *CT* (February 28, 1975), 16.

59. Curtis, interview by Lindvall, op. cit.

60. Ibid.

61. Forbes, Cheryl, "Hazel's People" *CT* (February 28, 1975), 16.

62. Boeve, Ervina, "Ballad of Billie Blue" *CT* (March 3, 1972), 40–41; reviews from the *Banner* and *Insight* magazine are available in the personal archives of Ken Curtis (Worcester, Pennsylvania).

63. Forbes, "Refiner's Fire: Gateway to Diversity," op. cit., 16.

64. See Kracauer, Siegfried, *A Theory of Film: The Redemption of Physical Reality*, rev. ed. (Princeton UP, 1997).

65. Curtis, Ken and Bill Curtis, interview by Terry Lindvall, June 29, 2009, RURFA.

66. Review of *John Wesley, Preacher*, *Christian Film and Video Review* (November/December 1984), 6. That same year Gateway also released a feature on *John Wycliffe: The Morning Star* (1983). See the review in *Christian Film and Video* (November/December 1984), 5.

67. Grenville Films press release (1988), RURFA.

68. Curtis, interview by Lindvall, op. cit.

69. See Grant, Myrna, "C. S. Lewis through the Shadowlands" *CH* (October 1988), 32.

70. Curtis, interview by Lindvall, op. cit.

71. White, "Does Christian Film Work?," op. cit., 25.

NOTES TO CHAPTER 7

1. Rockett, Will, *Devouring Whirlwind: Terror and Transcendence in the Cinema of Cruelty* (Greenwood, 1988); Lieb, Michael, *Children of Ezekiel: Aliens, UFOS, the Crisis of Race, and the Advent of the End Time* (Duke UP, 1998).

2. See Ostwalt, Conrad, Jr., "Hollywood and Armageddon: Apocalyptic Themes in Recent Cinematic Presentation" *Screening the Sacred: Religion, Myth, and Ideology in Popular American Film*, ed. Joel Martin (Westview Press, 1995), 55–63.

3. Morgan, David, *Protestants and Pictures: Religion, Visual Culture, and the Age of American Mass Production* (Oxford UP, 1999), 159–88, 266.

4. Gough, Donna, "Heartland/Mark IV Interview w/Beverly Shelton" (Spring 1986), transcript 2, RURFA.

5. Thompson, Marge, interview by Richard Nelson, August 7, 1989, RURFA.

6. Thompson, Don, interview by David Kuder, Spring 1981, RURFA.

7. Ibid.

8. Ibid.

9. In *Cinéma, foi et morale* (Paris: Editions du Cerf, 1956), 46. Father René Ludmann cited a litany of cinematic elements unfavorable to faith (e.g., superficiality, uncritical adulation of celebrities, distraction, sentimentality, absence of God, etc.). But he concluded by pointing out the fertile possibilities of "the cinema as a means of evangelism." He based his defense of films on Jesus's speaking in parables, as well as the prophets' communication through symbolic actions and the sacramental use of "things" like bread and wine. Ludmann called on the church to recognize the revelations of divine intervention

that could occur through films; the seventh art could "translate God to men" in authentic and dramatic ways. Thus he campaigned for a cinema of parables. See also Ludmann, Rene, "Cinema as a Means of Evangelism" *Crosscurrents* (Spring 1958), 153–71.

10. Doughten, Russ, interview by Tom Jennings, Spring 1986, RURFA

11. Thompson, Don, interview, November 14, 2001, RURFA. Thompson and Doughten would eventually dissolve their arrangement due to disagreements about distribution. Their last film together was *The Shepherd* (1984), starring Dee Wallace of *E.T.* (1982) fame.

12. Cited in Hendershot, op. cit., 188.

13. Doughten, Russ and Don Thompson, interview by Andrew Quicke, July 2009, RURFA.

14. Frykholm, Amy Johnson, *Rapture Culture: Left Behind in Evangelical America* (Oxford UP, 2004), 5, 194.

15. Fraser, Benson, interview by Andrew Quicke, November 8, 2010, RURFA.

16. Doughten and Thompson interview, op. cit.

17. Thompson, interview by Kuder, op. cit.

18. Doughten, Tim, interview by Clay Greer, Spring 1987, transcript 13, RURFA.

19. Doughten, interview by Jennings, op. cit. Even films with a moral or generic biblical message were not "Christian" according to his definition.

20. Ibid..

21. McDonough, Jimmy, "Great Balls of Fire" *Film Comment* (March/April 1987), 46

22. Ibid., 46.

23. Ibid. The film would follow their classic *The Monster and the Stripper* (1968), shot at the Methodist Church's editing facility at TRAFCO in Nashville, becoming the raciest film ever shot under the purview of Methodists. See Duncan, David D. and Jim Ridley, "It Came from Nashville! The Saga of Music City's First Family of Film" *Nashville Scene* (April 18, 1996), http://www.nashvillescene.com/1996-04-18/news/it-came-from-nashville/ (accessed February 11, 2011).

24. McDonough, op. cit., 49.

25. Duncan and Ridley, op. cit.

26. Morgan, op. cit.

27. Boswell, James, *Life of Samuel Johnson, LL.D.* (University of Chicago Press, 1952), 351.

28. The best analysis of the apocalyptic genre is Brummett, Barry, "Premillennial Apocalyptic as a Rhetorical Genre" *Central States Speech Journal* 35 (1984), 84–93.

29. See Lindvall, Terry and Dennis Bounds, "Apocalyptic Imagination in Film" *Christianity and the Arts* (Winter 1999), 31–34; see also Robert Fuller, *Naming the Antichrist: The History of an American Obsession* (Oxford UP, 1995).

30. *Guidelines for New Producers* (Christian Film and Video Association, n.d.), RURFA. The pamphlet outlines various means of distribution for independent producers: (1) directly to local churches; (2) through an existing producer/distributor; or (3) by establishing one's own network through the Christian Film Libraries. If you choose the last option (and it is the optimal selection, according to the guidelines), you may choose to release your film through: (1) an outright sale; (2) a lifetime lease; (3) a fifty-fifty plan in which the producer and library share equally in the rental returns; or (4) a one-third–two-thirds plan in which the producer furnishes all promotional materials and mailing costs.

31. Bristow, Harry, interview by Robert Thompson, July 1980, RURFA.

32. Ibid.

33. Marks had learned to run a magic lantern stereopticon in high school and continued his interest through seminary, where his thesis was titled "The Use of Audio Visuals," in response to which his adviser told him that "everything had been written that could be said about audio visuals." Marks persevered in setting up a Religious Film Library in the Rocky Mountain area by 1945. See Froelich, Carl, "Long Since Overdue" *News of Reel People* (January 15, 1983), 2.

34. See the Harvey Marks Special Collections, box 308, at the Billy Graham Center in Wheaton College, Illinois. Marks also wrote the Christian film review columns for *Christian Life* magazine.

35. The CFDA's attempts to legitimize their films involved what David Freedberg called the process of "Consecration," a ceremony of anointing, blessing, and crowning images to "make them work." Freedberg, David, *The Power of Images: Studies in the History and Theory of Response* (University of Chicago Press, 1991), 83. As such, this annual event "elevated" the awards to a kind of "sacred ritual" recognizing those works that stood out as sacred vessels for evangelism or other good work.

36. Fete, Beverly Wilshire, "Religion in Media Awards Top Feature-Film Kudo to *Prodigal*" *Variety* (1987), clipping in RURFA.

37. *Expanding Our Horizons: Motion Picture and Video Producers Fellowship Conference Brochure* (Producers Council of CVMI, February 1990), RURFA.

38. Marks, Paul, interview by Andrew Quicke, December 2009, RURFA.

39. Brice Fennig observed wryly that finding a profitable film led, of course, to the inevitable sequels, *Sixteen* and *Going Steady*, both of which paled in comparison to the initial blockbuster. Personal interview, July 12, 2001, CVMI Conference, Atlanta, RURFA.

40. Randy Petersen, "What's Ahead for *Christian Film* and Video: Trend Watch for the 1990s" *Christian Film and Video Review* (March/April 1989).

41. "CFV: On the Move" special advertisement section, *CT* (April 17, 1987), 54.

42. Falwell quote from the jacket cover of the DVD release.

43. Gribben, Crawford, "Rapture Fiction and the Changing Evangelical Condition" *Literature and Theology* (March 2003), 59–75.

44. See Kate Davis and David Heilbroner's compelling, but somewhat reductionist, documentary on rapture-minded fundamentalists and Israel, *Waiting for Armageddon* (2009).

45. The Hollywood director Michael Tolkin's *The Rapture* (1991) and Richard Donner's *Omen* series surely deserve some credit in corrupting orthodox notions of eschatology, but also for inserting a desperate fatalism and pessimism into the Second Coming. See "Screening the End of the World" in Douglas Cowan's *Sacred Terror: Religion and Horror on the Silver Screen* (Baylor UP, 2008), 190–99.

NOTES TO CHAPTER 8

1. Settoon, Rick, *International Films: A Burden for Overseas Evangelism* (Virginia Beach: CBN University, 1986), 5.

2. *Films Afield* (promotional guide, 1989), 3, archive of the Conservative Baptist Foreign Mission Society, Denver.

3. Settoon, op. cit., 2.

4. Carpenter, Fred, "Class Interview" (Spring 1986), RURFA.

5. McDougal, Eddie, interview by Andrew Quicke, Spring 1994, RURFA.

6. Ibid., 22, 16, 17. In the 1990's International Films, by then located in Pasadena, California, became known as an excellent language- dubbing facility. Using video technology, the company took over the language versioning of *The Jesus Film* from Kensington Film Services in London, and was able to dub several of the more difficult dialects, such as Aztec (Mexico), Lingala (Zaire), Yoruba (Nigerian), and Twi (Ghana).

7. Mott, John R., *Addresses and Papers of John R. Mott* (Association Press, 1946–47).

8. Foer, Franklin, "Baptism by Celluloid: *The Passion*'s Precedent: Has 1979 Bible Film Become the Most-Watched Movie Ever?" *New York Times* (February 8, 2004).

9. Ibid.

10. Foer, op. cit.

11. Eshleman, Paul, "The 'Jesus Film': A Contribution to World Evangelism" *International Bulletin of Missionary Research* (April 2002), 68–70, 72.

12. Foer, op. cit.

13. Ibid.

14. Ibid.

15. Eshleman, op. cit.

16. Foer, ibid.

17. Eshleman, Paul, interview by Andrew Quicke, 1981, London, 1981, RURFA.

18. Quicke, Andrew, "My Life in Television—Worldwide" (July 29, 2009), http://www.andrewquicke.com/8.html.

19. Foer, op. cit.

20. Ibid.

21. See Jesus Film Project, http://www.jesusfilm.com/ (accessed July 29, 2009).

22. See Jesus Film Project, "Languages Completed and Official Statistics" (n.d.), http://jesusfilmproject.org/film-and-media/statistics (accessed July 29, 2009).

23. Ayotte, Melinda, "Beach Man Brings Christian Film to Indian Moviegoers" *Virginian-Pilot* (Norfolk, VA) (September 20, 1986), 20E; Adams-Lackey, Mary, "Movie Brings Christian Message to India" *Virginian-Pilot* (Norfolk, VA) (September 20, 1987), 23, 26

24. Gilman, John, "*Karunamayudu*" *Christian Life* (October 1984), 73.

25. Gilman, John, *A Report on Dayspring International's Ministry in India* (videotape, Dayspring International, 1985).

26. Gilman, "*Karunamayudu*" op. cit., 71.

27. Lancaster, Bill, "*Man of Mercy*" *Daily Press* (Newport News, VA) (January 12, 1984), C5.

28. Gilman, John, "Mission Statement: The Visual Gospel" *Freedom Cry: A Journey of Liberation* (Virginia Beach: Dayspring International Press, 2004), 25–30; see also Gilman, John, "On the Silver Screen" *They're Killing an Innocent Man: The Cry of Those Who Have Never Heard* (Virginia Beach: Dayspring International Press, 1991), 58–61.

29. Gilman, John, *An International Strategy to Reactivate the Great Commission* (promotional guide, Dayspring International, 1985).

30. Gilman, John, "Mission Statement" op. cit.

31. Ibid.

32. Ibid.

33. Sen, Dr. Gautam, "Religious Conversion and Interfaith Dialogue" *Conversion Agenda* (March 2009), http://conversionagenda.blogspot.com/2009/04/religious-conversion-and-interfaith.html (accessed July 29, 2009).

34. Ibid.

NOTES TO CHAPTER 9

1. Anderson, Dave and Terry Lindvall, executive producers, Ned Vankevich, producer, *We've Come a Long Way Baby: 40 Years of Christian Film* (CBN/Regent University, 1979).

2. Berckman, Edward, "The Changing Attitudes of Protestant Churches to Movies and Television" *Encounter* (1980), 293–306.

3. Robinson, Jim, "Class Interview; Business of Television and Film" (Spring 1986, Regent University, 1986), RURFA.

4. Carpenter, "Class Interview," op. cit.

5. Ibid.

6. Brown, William and Duane Meeks, "Experimenting with the Entertainment-Education Strategy in Film and Video" *Journal of Film and Video* (Winter 1997), 30–43; Brown, William and Arvind Singhal, "Ethical Considerations of Promoting Pro-social Messages through the Popular Media" *Journal of Popular Film and Television* (Fall 1994), 92–99; Beale, Lewis, "Apostles of Christian Film Making" *Los Angeles Times* (April 7, 1985); Beale, Lewis, "Can Christian Film Grads Find a Place in the Sun of Hedonistic Hollywood?" *Chicago Tribune* (April 1985); Mobley, Mark, "Divine Comedy" *Virginian Pilot* (August 25, 1987).

7. Georgakas, Dan, "Cinema as Soapbox: Social Issue Films, 1960–82" *Sightlines* (Spring 1982), 8–14.

8. See Briner, Bob, *Roaring Lambs: A Gentle Plan to Radically Change Your World* (Zondervan, 1993), 88–92.

9. The Harvard University religion professor Harvey Cox covered the Chaucerian style at Regent in "The Warring Visions of the Religious Right," *Atlantic Monthly* (November 1995).

10. The U.S. Air Force denied a film request from Regent students that showed the military executing Jesus Christ. Vartabedian, Ralph, "Films Give Image Boost to Military" *Los Angeles Times* (September 5, 1986), 1.

11. "The Taming of the VCR" *CT* (September 24, 1990), 61–68.

12. Reed, Ronald, personal correspondence with Terry Lindvall, March 18, 1986, RURFA.

13. "Christian Film and Video: Industry on the Move" *CT* (April 17, 1987), 56.

14. Ibid., 56.

15. Waugh, Evelyn, *Vile Bodies* (1930; Dell, 1960).

16. Ibid., 124, 125, 185.

17. Alexander, John, *Other Side* (February 1979), cited in Lindvall, Terrence, "Critical Steps to Maturity" *Christian Film and Video Review* (November/December, 1986), 7.

18. Ayfre, Amédée, "Neo-realism and Phenomenology" *Cahiers du Cinéma: The 1950s Neo-realism, Hollywood, New Wave*, ed. Jim Hillier (Harvard UP, 1985), 190.

19. Pascal, Blaise, *Pensées* (University of Chicago Press, 1952), 277.

20. Lindvall, Terrence, "Cinematic Dogma: the Evangelical Response to Hollywood" (paper presented at University Film and Video Association Conference, 1983), 10.

21. Wales quoted in Lindvall, "Critical Steps" op. cit., 7.

22. Coppenger, Mark, "A Christian Perspective on Film," *The Christian Imagination: Essays on Literature and the Arts*, ed. Leland Ryken (Baker, 1981), 302.

23. Cheney, Harry, review of *Chariots of Fire* in *CT* (October 1981), 18.

24. Lindvall, "Cinematic Dogma" op. cit., 10.

25. Schultze, Quentin, *Christianity and the Mass Media in America: Toward a Democratic Accommodation* (Michigan State UP, 2006).

26. Morris, Jeremy, *The Church in the Modern Age* (Tauris, 2007); see also Voskuil, Dennis, "Reaching Out: Mainline Protestantism and the Media" *Between the Times: The Travail of the Protestant Establishment in America, 1900-1960*, ed. William R. Hutchinson (Cambridge UP, 1989), 72–92.

27. McLuhan, Marshall and Quentin Fiore *The Medium Is the Massage: Inventory of Effects* (Bantam Books, 1967).

28. See Jacques Ellul's *The New Demons*, trans. C. Edward Hopkin (Seabury, 1975) and *The Humiliation of the Word*, trans. Joyce Main Hanks (Eerdmans, 1985).

Selected Bibliography

Anderson, Milton. *The Modern Goliath* (David Press, 1935).

Berckman, Edward. "The Changing Attitudes of Protestant Churches to Movies and Television" *Encounter* (Spring 1980), 293–306.

Biskind, Peter. *Easy Riders, Raging Bulls: How the Sex-Drugs-and-Rock-'n'-Roll Generation Saved Hollywood* (Simon & Schuster, 1998).

Black, Gregory. *The Catholic Crusade against the Movies, 1940–1975* (Cambridge UP, 1997).
———. *Hollywood Censored: Morality Codes, Catholics, and the Movies* (Cambridge UP, 1996).

Brady, Mary Beattie. "A New Era for the Church" *The Educational Screen* (December 1935), 289–290.

Briggs, Joe Bob. "The Gospel according to Joe Bob" *Film Comment* (April 1987), 52–54.

Briner, Bob. *Roaring Lambs: A Gentle Plan to Radically Change Your World* (Zondervan, 1993).

Brown, William and Duane Meeks. "Experimenting with the Entertainment-Education Strategy in Film and Video" *Journal of Film and Video* (Winter 1997), 30–43.

Brown, William and Arvind Singhal. "Ethical Considerations of Promoting Pro-social Messages through the Popular Media" *Journal of Popular Film and Television* (Fall 1994), 92–99.

Chesterton, G. K. *As I Was Saying* (Eerdmans, 1985).

Clements, Keith. *Friedrich Schleiermacher: Pioneer of Modern Theology* (Collins, 1987).

Comenius, John Amos. *The Great Didactic*, trans. M. W. Keatings (Black, 1896).

Coppenger, Mark. "A Christian Perspective on Film." *The Christian Imagination: Essays on Literature and the Arts*, ed. Leland Ryken (Baker, 1981), 285–302.

Couvares, Francis, ed. *Movie Censorship and American Culture* (Smithsonian Institute Press, 1996).

Cowan, Douglas. *Sacred Terror: Religion and Horror on the Silver Screen* (Baylor UP, 2008).

Cox, Harvey. "The Warring Visions of the Religious Right," *Atlantic Monthly* (November 1995), 59–69.

Crescenti, Peter. "Yabba-Dabba-David-and-Goliath" *Christianity Today* (October 3, 1986), 49.

DeMille, Cecil B. "The Screen as a Religious Teacher" *Theatre Magazine* (June 1927), 45–76.

"Door Interview: Mel White" *Wittenburg Door* (October/November 1973), 8–14.

Dorr, John. "Baptists and Film: A Historical Perspective" (MA thesis, Regent University, 1985).

Eastman, Fred. "The Menace of the Movies" *Christian Century* (January 15, 1930), 75–78.

———. "What Can We Do about the Movies?" *Parents' Magazine* (November 1931), 19, 52–54.

Ellul, Jacques. *The Humiliation of the Word*, trans. Joyce Main Hanks (Eerdmans, 1985).

———. *The New Demons*, trans. By C. Edward Hopkin (Seabury, 1975).

Evenson, John. "*The Cross and the Switchblade*" *Christianity Today* (June 19, 1970), 34.

Everest, Alton and Elva Everest. *Moody Films in Foreign Lands, 1963–1968* (Moody Institute of Science, 1994).

Fanning, Leah Irene. "A Study of the Use of Motion Pictures in the Program of Certain Protestant Churches" (MA thesis, University of Southern California, 1932).

Federal Council of Churches of Christ in America. *Public Relations of the Motion Picture Industry* (1931; Jerome Ozer, 1971).

Ferlita, Ernest and John May. *Film Odyssey: The Art of Film as Search for Meaning* (Paulist, 1976).

Flood, Robert and Jerry Jenkins. *Teaching the Word: Reaching the World: The Moody Bible Institute, the First 100 Years* (Moody Press, 1985).

Forbes, Cheryl. "The Refiner's Fire: Gateway to Diversity" *Christianity Today* (February 28, 1975), 16–17.

Friedrich, Elaine. "Biography of Jim Friedrich" (unpublished biography, 1975).

Friedrich, James. "Adventures in Film-making" *Christian Herald* (February 1948), 40–44.

———. "His Pulpit Is a Movie Screen" *Virginia Seminary Journal* (November 1988), 1–13.

Fuller, Robert. *Naming the Antichrist: The History of an American Obsession* (Oxford UP, 1995).

Georgakas, Dan. "Cinema as Soapbox: Social Issue Films, 1960–82." *Sightlines* (Spring 1982), 8–14.

Getz, Gene. *Audio-Visual Media in Christian Education* (Moody Press, 1958).

———. *MBI: The Story of the Moody Bible Institute* (Moody Press, 1969).

Gilbert, James. *Redeeming Culture: American Religion in an Age of Science* (University of Chicago Press, 1997).

Gilman, John. *Freedom Cry: A Journey of Liberation* (Dayspring International, 2004).

———. *They're Killing an Innocent Man* (Dayspring International, 1991).

The Gospel through Motion Pictures for 30 Years, 1950–1980 (public relations brochure, Gospel Films, 1980).

Hamilton, John. "An Historical Study of Bob Pierce and World Vision's Development of the Evangelical Social Action Film" (PhD diss., University of Southern California, 1980).

Haselden, Kyle. *Morality and the Mass Media* (Broadman Press, 1968).

Hellbeck, Robert. "The Film and Protestantism" *International Review of Educational Cinematography* (October 3, 1931), 923–25.

Hendershot, Heather. *Shaking the World for Jesus: Media and Conservative Evangelical Culture* (University of Chicago Press, 2004).

Hes, Jan. "Notes from the Diary of a Stepchild" *Media Development* (February 1980), 3.

Hormell, Sidney James. "The Presbyterian System: An Examination of the Formal Mass Communication System of the United Presbyterian Church, USA" (PhD diss., University of Illinois, 1966).

Hutchinson, William, ed. *Between the Times: The Travail of the Protestant Establishment in America, 1900–1960* (Cambridge UP, 1989).

Janes, H. Paul. *How to Stimulate Greater Activity in Your Church through Motion Pictures* (Religious Motion Picture Foundation, 1932).

Jones, William. *Sunday Night at the Movies* (John Knox Press, 1967).

Kahle, Roger and Robert Lee. *Popcorn and Parable: A New Look at the Movies* (Augsburg, 1971).

Konzelman, Robert. *Marquee Ministry: The Movie Theater as Church and Community Forum* (Harper and Row, 1972).

Kracauer, Siegfried. *A Theory of Film: The Redemption of Physical Reality*, rev. ed. (Princeton UP, 1997).

Krows, Arthur. "A Quarter-Century of Non-theatrical Films" *Educational Screen* (June 1936), 169–73.

———. "So the Pictures Went to Church" *Educational Screen* (October 1938), 252–53.

Lawing, John. "The Bad Guy Changes Hats" *Christianity Today* (December 1, 1978), 32–33.

LeSourd, Howard. "Church Use of Moving Pictures" *Christian Century* (March 19, 1930), 37.

Lieb, Michael. *Children of Ezekiel: Aliens, UFOS, the Crisis of Race, and the Advent of the End Time* (Duke UP, 1998).

Lindvall, Terry. *Sanctuary Cinema: Origins of the Christian Film Industry* (New York UP, 2007).

Lindvall, Terry and Dennis Bounds. "Apocalyptic Imagination in Film" *Christianity and the Arts* (Winter 1999), 31–34.

Ludmann, René. *Cinéma, foi et morale* (Editions du Cerf, 1956).

Maltby, Richard. "*The King of Kings* and the Czar of All the Rushes: The Propriety of the Christ Story" *Screen* (Summer 1990), 188–213.

Marks, Harvey. "A Brief History of Church Films" *Christian Film and Video Review* (January/February 1985), 1–8.

Marshall, Wendy. *William Beaudine: From Silents to Television* (Scarecrow, 2004).

Maus, Cynthia Pearl, ed. *The Church and the Fine Arts* (Harper and Bros., 1960).

McConnell, Frank. *Storytelling and Mythmaking: Images from Film and Literature* (Oxford UP, 1979).

McDonough, Jimmy. "Great Balls of Fire" *Film Comment* (March/April 1987), 38–50.

Morey, Anne. *Hollywood Outsiders: The Adaptation of the Film Industry, 1913–1934* (University of Minnesota Press, 2003).

Morgan, David. *Protestants and Pictures: Religion, Visual Culture, and the Age of American Mass Production* (Oxford UP, 1999).

Morris, Jeremy. *The Church in the Modern Age* (Tauris, 2007).

Mott, John R. *Cooperation and the World Mission* (Student Christian Movement Press, 1935).

"Movies in Church" *Newsweek* (February 11, 1946), 74.

Ostwalt, Conrad, Jr. "Hollywood and Armageddon: Apocalyptic Themes in Recent Cinematic Presentation" *Screening the Sacred: Religion, Myth, and Ideology in Popular American Film*, ed. Joel Martin (Westview Press, 1995), 55–63.

Parker, E. C., D. W. Barry, and D. W. Smythe. *Television-Radio Audience and Religion* (Harper Bros., 1955).

Phillips, John McCandlish. "Baptists Are Taking to the Screen to Spread the Word" *New York Times* (June 7, 1972).

Prelinger, Rick. *Field Guide to Sponsored Films* (National Film Preservation Foundation, 2006).

"A Producer Serves the Church" *Educational Screen* (December 1942), 389–390.

"Religious Classes in Film" *Newsweek* (December 23, 1940), 44.

Robins, Michela. "Films for the Church" *Hollywood Quarterly* (Winter 1947/48), 178–84.

Rockett, Will. *Devouring Whirlwind: Terror and Transcendence in the Cinema of Cruelty* (Greenwood, 1988).

Ross, Clyde. "A Presbyterian Elder, a Church Crusade, and the Period of 'Family Movies'" *Fides et Historia* (Fall 1993), 80–90.

Sayles, John. "The Big Picture" *American Film* (June 1985), 10.

Schaeffer, Franky. *Addicted to Mediocrity: 20th-Century Christians and the Arts* (Crossway Books, 1981).

———. *Crazy for God: How I Grew Up as One of the Elect, Helped Found the Religious Right, and Lived to Take All (or Almost All) of It Back* (Da Capo Press, 2008).

———. *Sham Pearls for Real Swine: Beyond the Cultural Dark Age—A Quest for Renaissance* (Wolgemuth & Hyatt, 1990).

Schillaci, Anthony. *Movies and Morals* (Fides, 1968).

Schleiermacher, Friedrich. *On Religion: Addresses in Response to Its Cultured Critics*, trans. Terrence Tice (John Knox Press, 1969).

———. *On Religion: Speeches to the Cultured Despisers*, trans. John Oman (John Knox Press, 1994).

Schulze, Quentin. *Christianity and the Mass Media in America* (Michigan State UP, 2003).

Sermons from Science: A Story of God at Work (Moody Institute of Science, 1976).

Skinner, James. *The Cross and the Cinema: The Legion of Decency and the National Catholic Office for Motion Pictures, 1933–1970* (Praeger, 1993).

Stout, Harry. *The New England Soul: Preaching and Religious Culture in Colonial New England* (Oxford UP, 1986).

Sumner, Robert. *Hollywood Cesspool: A Startling Survey of Movieland Lives and Morals* (Sword of the Lord Publishers, 1955).

Thorp, Margaret. *America at the Movies* (Yale UP, 1939).

Turner, Victor. *From Ritual to Theatre: The Human Seriousness of Play* (PAJ Publications, 1982).

Twenty Years under God: A Pictorial Review of the Billy Graham Ministries (World Wide Pictures, 1970).

Vogler, Christopher. *The Writer's Journey: Mythic Structure for Writers* (Michael Wiese Productions, 1998).

Waldrup, Earl. *Using Visual Aids in a Church* (Broadman Press, 1949).

Wall, James. *Church and Cinema* (Eerdmans, 1971).

Waugh, Evelyn. *Vile Bodies* (1930; Dell, 1960).

White, Mel. "Does Christian Film Work in the Neighborhood Theater?" *Christianity Today* (October 7, 1983), 14–20.

———. *Stranger at the Gate: To Be Gay and Christian in America* (Simon & Schuster, 1994).

Wolff, Rich. "*Davey and Goliath*: The Response of a Church-Produced Children's Television Program to Emerging Social Issues" *Journal of Popular Film and Television* (Fall 1990), 112–21.

Index

About the Authors

TERRY LINDVALL is C. S. Lewis Professor of Communication and Christian Thought at Virginia Wesleyan College. He is the author of *Sanctuary Cinema: Origins of the Christian Film Industry* (NYU Press, 2007); *The Mother of All Laughter: Sarah and the Genesis of Comedy*; and *The Silents of God: Selected Issues and Documents in Silent American Film and Religion, 1908–1926*, among other works.

ANDREW QUICKE is Professor in the School of Communication and the Arts at Regent University and the author of several books, most recently (with Andrew Laszlo) *Every Frame a Rembrandt: The Art and Practice of Cinematography.*